Decolonization and Conflict

Decolonization and Conflict

Colonial Comparisons and Legacies

Edited by
Martin Thomas and Gareth Curless

BLOOMSBURY ACADEMIC
LONDON • NEW YORK • OXFORD • NEW DELHI • SYDNEY

BLOOMSBURY ACADEMIC
Bloomsbury Publishing Plc
50 Bedford Square, London, WC1B 3DP, UK
1385 Broadway, New York, NY 10018, USA

BLOOMSBURY, BLOOMSBURY ACADEMIC and the Diana logo are
trademarks of Bloomsbury Publishing Plc

First published in Great Britain 2017
Paperback edition published 2018

A catalogue record for this book is available from the British Library.

ISBN: HB: 978-1-4742-5038-2
PB: 978-1-4742-5037-5
ePDF: 978-1-4742-5040-5
eBook: 978-1-4742-5039-9

Library of Congress Cataloging-in-Publication Data
Names: Thomas, Martin, 1964- editor. | Curless, Gareth, editor.
Title: Decolonization and conflict : colonial comparisons and legacies /
edited by Martin Thomas and Gareth Curless.
Description: London ; New York, NY, USA : Bloomsbury Academic, an imprint of
Bloomsbury Publishing, Plc, [2017] | Includes bibliographical references
and index.
Identifiers: LCCN 2016051240| ISBN 9781474250382 (hb) |ISBN 9781474250399
(epub) | ISBN 9781474250405 (epdf)
Subjects: LCSH: Decolonization–History–20th century–Case studies. |
Autonomy and independence movements–History–20th century–Case studies.
| Political violence–History–20th century–Case studies. |
Counterinsurgency–History–20th century–Case studies.
Classification: LCC JV151 .D357 2017 | DDC 325/.309–dc23LC record available at
https://lccn.loc.gov/2016051240

Typeset by Deanta Global Publishing Services, Chennai, India

To find out more about our authors and books visit
www.bloomsbury.com and sign up for our newsletters.

Contents

Notes on Contributors

Huw Bennett is Reader in International Relations at Cardiff University. He specializes in British defence and security since 1945, and co-edits the journal *Critical Military Studies*. He is currently writing a book, *The British Army's War in Northern Ireland, 1966-1979*, for Cambridge University Press, with support from the Leverhulme Trust.

Emmanuel Blanchard is Senior Lecturer in Political Science at the University of Versailles Saint-Quentin-en-Yvelines and Sciences Po Saint-Germain-en-Laye. He is also a researcher at the Center for Sociological Research on Law and Criminal Justice Institutions (CESDIP, UMR 8183, CNRS and French Ministry of Justice). His research interests include the history of immigration and colonial policing, especially in the France-North Africa area. He is the author of *La police parisienne et les Algériens, 1944-1962* (2011), and the editor of two special issues on colonial policing (*Crime, History and Societies*, vol. 15, no. 2 (2011); *Genèses. Histoire & Sciences sociales*, no. 86 (2012)).

Katherine Bruce-Lockhart is a PhD candidate in history at the University of Cambridge. Her dissertation is a social history of the Uganda Prisons Service, focusing in particular on the period between Uganda's independence in 1962 and the fall of Idi Amin in 1979. Katherine's previous research on the detention of women during the Mau Mau Rebellion has been published in the *Journal of Eastern African Studies* and the *Journal of World History*. Prior to coming to Cambridge, she did an MSc in African Studies at the University of Oxford and a BA in History and African Studies at the University of Toronto.

Gareth Curless is a lecturer in history at the University of Exeter. He is currently writing up the results of an ESRC-funded project (2013–16) on the relationship between labour unrest and decolonization in the British Empire. From 2016 he will be coordinating a Leverhulme Trust research network, Understanding Insurgencies: Resonances from the Colonial Past, with Professor Martin Thomas.

Brian Drohan is an active duty US Army officer. He has led an armoured platoon in Iraq with the 1st Infantry Division, worked at the US Embassy to Sri Lanka and the Maldives and taught history at the US Military Academy – West Point. He holds a PhD from the University of North Carolina at Chapel Hill as well as a BA and an MA from the University of Pennsylvania.

Moritz Feichtinger is Postdoctoral Research Assistant at the University of Berne. He has published on decolonization, counter-insurgency, population removal and developmentalism. He received his PhD in 2016 for his dissertation entitled

"'Villagization" A Peole's History of Strategic Resettlement and Violent Transformation. Kenya & Algeria 1952-1962'. Recent publications include '"A Great Reformatory": Social Planning and Strategic Resettlement in Late Colonial Kenya and Algeria, 1952–63', in *Journal of Contemporary History* (online only); 'Transformative Invasions: Western Post-9/11 Counterinsurgency and the Lessons of colonialism', in *Humanity. International Journal of Human Rights, Humanitarianism and Development* 3, no. 1 (2012): 35–63 (with Stephan Malinowski).

Roel Frakking completed his PhD at the European University Institute, Florence, Italy. His thesis, '"Collaboration is a Very Delicate Concept": Alliance-formation and the Wars of Independence in Indonesia and Malaysia, 1945-1957', is a case study in the interface of late European empires and colonized societies. Specifically, it investigates how the Dutch and British empires tried to recruit local forces in Indonesia and Malaysia, respectively, to protect their economic assets, and how local communities and power brokers negotiated decolonization to their own ends. Frakking's research takes empires as a single analytical unit, and as spaces of multidirectional causes and effects. His most recent publication (*International History Review*, 2016) analyses how during the war for Indonesian independence (1945-9) the Sundanese of West Java pursued an alternative path to independence and how they, in the process, clashed with both the Dutch colonial authorities and their opponents in the Republik Indonesia.

Karl Hack is Senior Lecturer in History and Head of the School of History, Religious Studies, Sociology, Social Policy and Criminology (HRSSC) at The Open University. He was previously Associate Professor of History at the Nanyang Technological University, Singapore. Related publications include *Dialogues with Chin Peng: New Light on the Malayan Emergency* (2004), and *War Memory and the Making of Modern Malaysia and Singapore* (2012). He is currently working on a major book on the Malayan Emergency of 1948–60.

Miguel Bandeira Jerónimo (PhD, King's College London, 2008) is a research fellow at the Centre for Social Studies, University of Coimbra, Portugal. He was a visiting assistant professor at Brown University (2011 and 2012). Recently, he has been working on the historical intersections between internationalism(s) and imperialism, namely in the interwar period, and on the entanglements of idioms and repertoires of development and of societal control and coercion in late European colonial empires. He recently authored *The 'Civilizing Mission' of Portuguese Colonialism (c.1870-1930)* (2015) and co-edited *The Ends of European Colonial Empires: Cases and Comparisons* and *Os passados do presente: Internacionalismo, imperialismo e a construção do mundo contemporâneo* (2015). He is also co-editor of the book series 'História&Sociedade' at Edições 70 (Portugal) and 'The Portuguese Speaking World: Its History, Politics and Culture' at Sussex Academic.

Jeremy Kuzmarov teaches at the University of Tulsa and is the author of *Modernizing Repression: Police Training and Nation Building in the American Century* (2012) and *The Myth of the Addicted Army: Vietnam and the Modern War on Drugs* (2009). He is currently working on a history of American technowar since the Second World War. He is a blogger for the *Huffington Post* and writes for other online media.

Neil MacMaster, Honorary Reader at the University of East Anglia (Norwich, UK), researches in twentieth-century French and British colonial history. His publications include *Colonial Migrants and Racism. Algerians in France, 1900-62* (1997), *Racism in Europe* (2001), with Dr Jim House, *Paris 1961: Algerians, State Terror, and Memory* (2006) and *Burning the Veil: The Algerian war and the 'emancipation' of Muslim women, 1954-62* (2009). He is currently writing a study of Algerian peasant society and counter-insurgency in the Dahra and Ouarsenis mountains, c.1945–58.

Martin Thomas is Professor of Imperial History and Director of the Centre for the Study of War, State and Society at the University of Exeter. A specialist in the politics of contested decolonization, his most recent publications are *Violence and Colonial Order: Police, Workers and Protest in the European Colonial Empires, 1918-1940* (2012) and *Fight or Flight: Britain, France, and their Roads from Empire* (2014). With Gareth Curless he is currently coordinating a Leverhulme Trust research network, Understanding Insurgencies: Resonances from the Colonial Past.

Mathilde von Bülow is a lecturer in history at the University of Glasgow, where she also directs the Scottish Centre for War Studies. Since completing her PhD at the University of Cambridge in 2007 she has authored several articles and chapters, exploring the international and intelligence dimensions of decolonization in French Algeria. She is the recipient of the Christopher Andrew-Michael Handel prize for best article published in *Intelligence & National Security* in 2013. Her first monograph, *West Germany, Cold War Europe and the Algeria War*, was published by Cambridge University Press in 2016. She is now preparing a monograph titled *International Labour, the Global Cold War and the End of Empire in French North Africa*.

Kim A. Wagner is Senior Lecturer in British Imperial History at Queen Mary, University of London. He received a PhD from the University of Cambridge in 2003, supervised by the late professor Sir C. A. Bayly. Wagner's research is situated at the cusp of Imperial and Global history, focusing on knowledge and resistance in British India, and on colonial violence and warfare in the nineteenth and early twentieth century in a more general sense. Providing a novel reading of the colonial encounter, and informed by a genuinely interdisciplinary and global approach, his work engages with broader debates on the forms and functions of violence and cultural (mis-)understanding between the Western and the non-Western worlds. Wagner's publications include *Thuggee: Banditry and the British in Early Nineteenth-century India* (2007); *The Great Fear of 1857: Rumours, Conspiracies and the Making of the Indian Uprising* (2010); '"Treading Upon Fires": The "Mutiny"-Motif and Colonial Anxieties in British India', *Past & Present* (2013); and '"Calculated to Strike Terror": The Amritsar Massacre and the Spectacle of Colonial Violence', *Past & Present* (2016). https://qmul.academia.edu/KimAWagner.

Introduction: Decolonization, Conflict and Counter-insurgency

Martin Thomas and Gareth Curless

This is a book about the surge in anti-colonial violence before and after 1945, about the contested end of empires that reshaped the political world of the mid- to late twentieth century. Wars of decolonization and associated political violence against white minority rule triggered massive geopolitical change in the global South. Empires were for centuries a predominant organizational form in global politics, but they faced unprecedented, existential challenges politically, ethically and militarily in the central decades of the twentieth century, spanning the 1920s to the 1970s.[1] Such seismic changes defy simple explanation. Certain commonalities may be identified even so. For one thing, violent decolonization, its non-violent equivalent and the extraneous pressures, first of World War and then of Cold War competition, were interconnected. Some of these connections were strongest within empires, others between them. One aim of this book is to illustrate how these connections played out. But the principal focus of the chapters to follow is on the violence of decolonization itself – its origins, its expression and, above all, its repression.

Most of this violence was linked to contestation between imperial authorities and their local opponents over the reimposition, the continuation or, paradoxically, the termination of colonial rule. Arguments at the macro-level were, though, matched by multiple claims, grievances and rivalries at the local, or micro, level of communities – from city districts to village settlements, village settlements and resettlement camps. Where sustained collective violence resulted, it usually took the form of covertly organized guerrilla warfare, or insurgency.[2] The declared aim of most anti-colonial insurgencies was to overthrow the incumbent colonial authority or, at minimum, to force imperial powers to concede fundamental reforms, whether self-government, enhanced majority (or, in some cases, minority) rights or, in the case of the rebellion in British-ruled Cyprus, full political union with another country: Greece.[3]

Insurgencies, then, originated as rebellions against constituted authority. Often they began with small groups of activists linked to a particular political group. Their turn to violence was usually catalysed by some trigger event. This might be the legal proscription of the parent organization and a heightened threat of incarceration for its members. It might be divisions over a policy choice within the group itself. Or it might be the perceived inadequacy of a promised reform.[4] Sometimes the trigger was more calamitous: famine, epidemic, war or loss. Such trigger events were underlain by deeper causal factors: on the political-economic side, land shortage, underemployment and hunger; on the sociocultural side, constraints on the articulation of identity or the injustice of racially configured colonial societies. Phrased differently, the trigger might explain the precise timing of a violent outbreak, but cannot account for the underlying sociopolitical grievances that made colonial societies so tense. Small clusters of armed activists were the kernel of guerrilla movements, many of which recruited on the basis of ethnic attachment, confessional belief and ideological affiliation. Other determinants – age, gender, occupation and educational background – as well as matters of geography and physical proximity to conflict rendered individuals more or less likely to become insurgents or insurgent supporters. But, just as it is ahistorical to pinpoint a generic colonial 'counter-insurgency', so it is inaccurate to suggest a definitive anti-colonial 'insurgent' rolling off some sort of causal conveyor belt. Taking these short-term triggers and longer-term causes into account makes it harder to codify precisely when anti-colonial insurgencies and consequent colonial counter-insurgencies began and ended. Other factors complicate the process even more. For one thing, insurgent movements, especially those that eventually seized power at independence, tended to conflate their long-standing political campaigns with shorter periods of armed insurrection and war. For another thing, colonial authorities, as we shall see, were reluctant to acknowledge the existence of nationwide rebellion, still less of a state of 'war' within their colonial territories. To do so carried significant political, military and juridical consequences. It meant conceding the scale of anti-colonial opposition. It suggested that fundamental political choices and substantial military commitments would have to be faced. And it conferred legitimacy and legal rights on rebel forces, which could justifiably claim the status of an alternative government backed by recognized combatants.

The matter of legitimacy was critical. Insurgent groups insisted that their resort to violence was a justifiable response to colonial exclusion even though their actions were often highly coercive in practice. For their part, the imperial authorities orchestrating counter-insurgency campaigns did their utmost to discredit insurgents as unrepresentative, predatory and illegitimate. These clashing claims were more than rhetorical; they had real juridical consequences. Put differently, colonial insurgencies and counter-insurgencies were fought in a liminal space, their violence conducted beyond the conventions and restrictions of conventional 'war'. This duality between insurgent pressure for recognized status as political combatants motivated by genuine grievance and counter-insurgent determination to deny their opponents' legitimacy was integral to the forms of violence conducted, and is a central concern of this book.

Regular 'soldiers' in recognized wars enjoyed legal protections as fighting forces and as captives, or prisoners of war.[5] 'Rebels' did not.[6] Insurgents operated in a legal limbo, likely to face rigorous punishment under martial law, but also subject to criminal penalties as 'bandits', 'seditionists', 'terrorists' or plain killers.[7] Such criminalization offered imperial governments a means to deny insurgents political validation, and it enabled colonial authorities to evade the strictures of international law regarding the treatment of enemy personnel. Economically, too, admitting the existence of a decolonization war, as opposed to more limited 'troubles', might be disastrous, sapping the confidence of domestic publics, colonial settlers, corporations, insurers and investors that imperial supremacy would be restored. It was, for instance, sadly predictable that Dutch military offensives against Indonesian Republican forces in July 1947 and December 1948 were described as *politionele acties*, or 'police actions'.[8] British policymakers applied the same combination of political understatement and legal obfuscation in conflicts such as Aden, Cyprus, Kenya and Malaya, which were all defined as 'emergencies'.[9]

The nomenclature of counter-insurgency was thus highly politicized, and it remains so. To describe insurgencies as campaigns of low-intensity violence is both misleading and indelicate. Some insurgencies were punctuated by campaigns of targeted assassination and resource destruction rather than large-scale military confrontations and widespread environmental spoliation. Outwardly, the 'normal' civilian and commercial life of a colonial territory might continue, albeit alongside the introduction of 'emergency powers' or more limited legal restrictions on rights of movement, speech and association. Elsewhere, though, the impact of insurgency and, even more so, counter-insurgency cut deeper. Decolonization conflicts in the Dutch East Indies, French Vietnam, French Algeria and Portuguese Angola witnessed levels of direct military confrontation, of environmental destruction and of mass killing sufficient to register in lasting demographic change. And that is to say nothing of the psychological scars left on those caught up in these conflicts whose mental worlds were forever changed. As several contributors make plain, perhaps the most uncomfortable truth about contested decolonization was the violent coercion of local communities intrinsic to it. Viewed from the perspective of village settlements, urban *quartiers* or isolated resettlement camps, the political claims and counterclaims of the warring parties were belied by the everyday violence civilians encountered. The point bears amplification, particularly when assessing the validity of insurgent demands or security force doctrines of 'minimum force': everywhere, civilian victims predominated. Indeed, the very concept of a civilian population to be protected from a predatory group of insurgent combatants rarely held much traction in colonial counter-insurgency. Imperial security forces, often operating with minimal information about the surrounding population, might treat entire communities as actively hostile or potentially disloyal. Insurgents were themselves treated both in practice and under variants of martial law as illicit, as rebels, making distinctions between civilian and fighter difficult to sustain. In short, many of the issues of civilian status and appropriate targeting associated with contemporary counter-terrorist-operations were prefigured in the colonial counter-insurgencies examined here.[10]

Even in those cases, where overall numbers of deaths through violence were low by comparison with interstate wars, thousands of families were directly affected by killings or injury while their local communities faced competing pressures and abiding suspicions directly attributable to the outbreak of violence. Cyprus is again illustrative. The most recent scholarly assessment suggests that between 1955 and 1959 the armed insurgents of the National Organization of Cypriot Fighters (Ethniki Organosis Kyprion Agoniston – EOKA) numbered less than 500 mainly young, predominantly male fighters at any one time.[11] Their shootings, bombings and ambushes of security force personnel on Cyprus failed to dent British military capacity on the island. But EOKA also targeted its local opponents and, especially, those identified as Greek Cypriot 'traitors'. Its intimidation of the Greek Cypriot community presented the greatest obstacle to British schemes to end the 'Cyprus Emergency'.[12] Cyprus, then, was an island living in a climate of fear. EOKA attacks and community coercion are only part of the explanation. To understand the visceral imminence of this anxiety and the politics underlying it in Cyprus or elsewhere, we need to explore the inverse of insurgency; in other words, the violent security force responses of colonial powers. To sum up, counter-insurgency is a term fraught with paradox. Justified by its practitioners as an essential means to restore peace and security, it usually generated higher numbers of deaths and, on occasion, increased insecurity among local populations than the 'rebellions' it sought to defeat.

Many of these conflicts were rooted in rural grievances, such as land alienation by white settlers in Kenya, the iniquities of rice and rubber cultivation in Vietnam, or the eviction of Chinese squatters from Malaya's jungle fringes.[13] The subsistence needs of day labourers and peasant cultivators, always prone to the ecological vagaries of climate and harvest, were acutely susceptible to fluctuations in the availability of basic staples. Contested access to land, unaffordable foodstuffs and consequent hunger were already widespread colonial phenomena during the global economic crisis of the 1930s, and they returned with a vengeance during the Second World War. Wartime famine left millions dead in British-ruled Bengal and claimed hundreds of thousands more in Northern Vietnam. Devastating outbreaks of epidemic illness, often exacerbated by malnourishment, stalked numerous colonies from Japanese-occupied Indonesia to French-ruled Algeria. Allied 'war efforts' were unilaterally imposed on African and Indian populations, who were denied any say in the matter, even though imperial governments justified their exacting demands for manpower and materials with a rhetoric of common sacrifice in defence of democracy. Imperial governments sometimes accompanied their heightened wartime impositions with assurances of political and material rewards once the war was won, only to backtrack as victory came into view. When push came to shove, erstwhile demands for empire-wide equality of sacrifice were not matched by a lasting commitment to equality of rights. As a result, by 1945 numerous colonial societies stood on the brink of revolution.

Nowhere was this more apparent than in South East Asia, where Japanese occupation of the region's British, Dutch and French colonial territories provoked widespread population displacement, chronic social and economic distress, and sharper inter-communal conflict.[14] For those groups who had either resisted the Japanese or filled the political vacuum in the absence of the European colonial administrators, any reimposition of European colonial rule at war's end without the introduction of fundamental reforms was intolerable. In the wake of the Japanese surrender febrile coalitions of nationalists and leftists in French Indochina and the Dutch East Indies announced the creation of independent republics. Very much a race against time, their assertions of statehood were intended as a fait accompli – a unilateral seizure of power before the old colonial masters could return.

Post-1945 insurgency, however, was not simply a last-resort response of revolutionaries who found their preemptive seizures of power frustrated by the greater military strength of their imperialist opponents. On the one hand, the after-effects of wartime dislocation lingered, and were felt in everything from sluggish demobilization to shortages of foods and fuel. On the other hand, the immediate post–Second World War years were also a time of reform. Expectations of better futures were evident throughout the colonial world. Ideas of self-determination and inalienable human rights, while in some ways ill-defined and open to contestation, were at least firmly established in the vocabulary of international diplomacy and the workings of the United Nations (UN) and its affiliate agencies.[15] Other appeals to transnational, regional or interethnic solidarity, whether clothed as pan-Africanism and pan-Arabism or as leftist internationalism, shared a commitment to anti-colonialism.[16] Perhaps most importantly, colonial peoples increasingly articulated demands for political inclusion, better working conditions and improved living standards in terms of a basic equalization of rights. These reforms might apply inside a particular territory or between that territory and its governing 'mother country' or 'metropole'.[17] Militant anti-colonialism, present in many places, nascent in others, meanwhile served as a looming spectre, something likely to gather momentum if the pace of colonial reform lagged too far behind people's hopes of a better life.

Rising pressure for enhanced rights and improved living standards was thus a product of local crises and ideational change, of the growing recognition in the mid-twentieth century that systems of governance founded on supposed hierarchies of racial difference were unacceptable.[18] There is a parallel here with modern humanitarianism, which, as Keith Watenpaugh argues, 'often functioned in the absence of, or in the face of, the collapse of the state and its institutions, as a consequence of either war or natural disaster'. Just as modern humanitarianism presumptively occupies a high moral ground, supposedly beyond political partisanship and sectional interest, so anti-colonialism claimed a universal appeal, a generic equivalence with claims to statehood and the assertion of basic rights to freedom.[19]

Empires, it was now clear, were prone to serious internal challenge. They also faced corrosion externally as colonialism was more widely judged to be ethically indefensible. The point should not be overstressed. For one thing, counter-insurgency strategies after 1945 were often inseparable from development projects intended to raise living standards and welfare provision, thereby disarming anti-colonialist critics locally and globally. Portugal's Salazarist dictatorship, which laid claim to a unique imperial integrationism, went so far as to claim that anti-colonialism in Lusophone Africa amounted to a 'black racism', a blind hatred of European intervention that refused to acknowledge the essential contribution made by white settlers to societal modernization.[20] Even so, in the decade after the Second World War changes in international alignment and outlook nourished the argument that the old imperial order would be swept away by the fast-moving currents of anti-colonial nationalism. Furthermore, the so-called 'first wave' of late 1940s decolonization in South Asia and the Middle East suggested that imperial authorities might simply be overtaken by events. The tide of history, it seemed, was on the side of the insurgents, not their opponents.[21] This was a view that was lent credibility by the emergence of the Soviet Union as a global superpower, by the communist victory in China and by India's co-sponsorship of the Non-Aligned Movement. The sense of inexorability grew stronger from the late 1950s. British and French withdrawals from black Africa followed one after the other between 1957 and 1963. The Sino-Soviet split and the Cuban Revolution of 1959 meanwhile heralded the rise of a 'Third Worldism', proclaimed by certain communist bloc nations and newly independent states, which identified decolonization as their rallying cry.[22] For anti-colonial activists these critical shifts in the non-Western world lent a global resonance to their local struggles. And for many of their leaders, state socialism appeared to offer a solution to the inequities of colonialism and an alternative path to modernity.[23]

Economic imperatives also strengthened imperial governments' determination to retain valuable colonial territories, particularly in a post-war climate in which rising commodity prices helped satisfy Western European demand for dollar earnings. Even in cases such as the war in French Indochina where a lengthy decolonization conflict drained the domestic treasury, the geopolitics of Cold War intervened. By 1953 the United States was bankrolling over 70 per cent of the French war effort in Vietnam.[24] Nearby British Malaya, with its extensive rubber and tin reserves, was critical to the British Empire's dollar-earning capacity. Malaya's economy, however, was under increasing threat from the Malayan Communist Party (MCP). By 1948 the colonial government, facing mounting pressure from British commercial interests to end Malaya's industrial unrest, had turned to repressive policing, including the use of lethal force, the imposition of restrictive trade union legislation and the deportation of union officials.[25] Although the interests of private capital were clearly a critical factor in British prosecution of counter-insurgency in Malaya from 1948 onwards, Nicholas White has argued that the relationship between British business and the colonial government was often discordant. Throughout the Emergency planters' representatives complained about the unwillingness of the military to provide troops for the protection of economic infrastructure. Other commercial leaders resented the heavy financial burden imposed upon business as a result of the Emergency.[26]

Disagreements between private industry and colonial governments are indicative of a broader point, namely, that an exclusive focus on the relationship between imperialist and anti-colonial violence can obscure the complexities and ambiguities of contested decolonization. Anti-colonial groups, although united in their opposition to imperial rule, were often in bitter competition. Arguments covered a wide spectrum of issues ranging from the use of violence to the status of different sections of the local community, including women, ethnic minorities or those of different faith. In the Indonesian Republic the armed groups fighting the Dutch were ideologically diverse and differently organized. The coexistence of Republican troops, bands of *pemuda* (irregulars), and Islamic and communist militias was fraught with rivalry. These groups had discreet visions for the political orientation and cultural construction of a postcolonial Indonesia, and were willing to fight each other to realize their objectives.[27] As the Indonesian example suggests, cohesion within and between insurgent groups could prove near impossible to maintain. The task was made harder still because breaking the social connections between insurgent groups was something on which counter-insurgent security forces fixated. As Paul Staniland puts it in the context of Sri Lanka's civil war and other recent South Asian insurgencies, 'Insurgents try to build and protect these social ties in order to expand their organizational power, while counterinsurgents try to disrupt them and induce collapse. This struggle is the core battle of guerrilla warfare.'[28]

Divisions were also apparent when it came to the civilian population. Peasant cultivators constituted the majority in a large number of colonial societies. They were economically marginalized within the prevailing structures of export-oriented colonial agronomy. Yet rural loyalty to anti-colonial insurgents was by no means axiomatic. As Neil MacMaster indicates in the context of French Algeria, support for nationalist insurgency was never unconditional. It had to be won or extracted, and it required constant reinforcement.[29] Volunteering support for rebellion was intrinsically dangerous. Colonial security forces targeted precisely such networks of civilian helpers in an effort to deny insurgents their principal source of essential refuge and supply.

The degree to which insurgents were willingly aided is also questionable. Families and communities strove to avoid taking sides for fear of becoming targets. Avoiding open commitment, or *attentisme*, became harder to sustain as both insurgents and counter-insurgents used intimidation and punishment to compel popular compliance.[30] Such was the situation in much of Peninsula Malaya where the rural population found itself caught between the competing demands of the security forces and the Min Yuen – the civilian wing of the MCP. Support for the MCP, such as hiding insurgents or providing them with supplies, could result in the imposition of curfews, the withholding of rations, forced relocation, detention, and even deportation. Failure to support the insurgents, however, could have equally disastrous consequences, including the execution of suspected 'collaborators' or the collective punishment of recalcitrant villages.[31]

Rural women perhaps felt such conflicting pressures most intensely. They were often held to exacting standards of purity and were, at the same time, singled out by the warring parties, whether as living embodiments of the nation or as the key constituency for primary healthcare and welfare initiatives meant to consolidate support for the incumbent regime. That is to say nothing of the threat and actuality of sexual violence.[32] Abuses tended to increase, either at moments of mass population displacement, as during India's violent partition, or in tandem with the greater intensity of counter-insurgency campaigns, as in Kenya during Operation Anvil in 1954 or the Battle of Algiers in 1957.[33] As a result, for many colonial subjects, the decision to support an insurgency derived less from abstract loyalty to an ideology or cause than from the immediate security context and its implications for survival.

Any notion of a unified national liberation struggle further disintegrates when one considers the role played by so-called 'loyalist' forces – a subject discussed in several of the succeeding chapters. Colonial governments, unable to deploy sufficient numbers of European army and police personnel, relied on locally recruited paramilitaries, such as the Home Guard in Kenya. A dependence on indigenous auxiliaries had always been a feature of colonial rule, but levels of recruitment to locally raised units after 1945 were unprecedented. During the course of the emergency in Malaya the Home Guard expanded to include 250,000 recruits. In Algeria some 200,000 Algerian soldiers and auxiliaries fought alongside the French.[34] Numerous regular colonial regiments boasted long histories, from the King's African Rifles (of British East Africa) to the Tirailleurs sénégalais (of French West Africa) and the Dutch colonial army, or KNIL, in Indonesia.[35] After 1945, though, regular colonial army units were outnumbered by those serving in paramilitary militias. Often these paramilitaries were lightly armed and 'irregular' in the sense that they were never formally incorporated into imperial security forces or made wholly subject to military discipline. (Their exemption from military rules of engagement and punishment helps explain why irregular forces were disproportionately implicated in the maltreatment of detainees, although local rivalries and score-settling perhaps played the larger role.) Sometimes these militias worked alongside police or specialist military units. More often they served as 'self-defence units': static forces supposed to protect their home community from insurgent infiltration. Although these militias performed a variety of roles during counter-insurgency operations, historians are increasingly focusing on their involvement in campaigns of counter-terror directed against the civilian population.[36]

In Kenya the predominantly Kikuyu Home Guard was responsible for much of the violence inflicted upon the Mau Mau insurgents and the civilian population, including fellow Kikuyu who backed the insurgency. As part of this campaign of counter-terror, the Home Guard perpetrated numerous violations, including theft and destruction of property, the abduction of civilians, and even murder.[37] Initially these actions increased support for the insurgency but, by mid-1954, Mau Mau fighters could no longer protect civilians from the predations of the Home Guard. Consequently, as the social and economic costs of supporting the rebellion became unsustainable for the civilian population, increasing numbers of Kikuyu concluded that their interests were better served by supporting the 'loyalist' cause.[38]

As the Kenyan example indicates, the term 'loyalist' is a misnomer. For the most part loyalist militias were motivated, not by any sense of imperial allegiance but by local factors, including the opportunity for social and economic advancement, political opposition to the insurgent movement or the prevailing insecurity of their home district. Put differently, the decentralization of violence had the effect of introducing private agendas into the conflicts as individuals and groups reacted to political instability by pursuing discreet objectives or resolving personal grievances that had little or no relationship to the conflict's declared military aims. The expediency of the relationship between local auxiliaries and imperial authorities meant that alliances were contingent and temporary. In Algeria some locally raised militias alternated between support for the French security forces and the Front de Libération Nationale (FLN).[39] And the retribution meted out to 'traitorous' former *harkis* after Algerian independence in 1962 concealed the multiplicity of factors that had persuaded so many to take up arms alongside French security forces.[40] Matters were comparable in Palestine, where, during the Arab Revolt of the late 1930s, the loyalty of Palestinian militias proved malleable.[41] The high degree of militia autonomy underlines the extent to which imperial policymakers were unable to control the dynamics of the violence waged, reminding us that a straightforward binary division between insurgents and counter-insurgents misses the multiple layers of the colonial conflicts examined here.

For the civilian populations who were subject to militias' escalating demands and constant raiding, it became increasingly difficult to distinguish between pro-government forces and anti-colonial insurgents.[42] Rural insecurity was exacerbated by the fact that both the imperial authorities and the insurgents recruited informants in an effort to exert tighter social control over local communities. In areas of high FLN activity in the Algerian interior for instance, individuals, unsure of who could be trusted, denounced others for fear of being accused. Others incriminated local rivals in order to settle disputes relating to land, livestock, marriage alliances, insults and honour.[43] The interplay between personal and political objectives was also apparent in Malaya, where feuding families with competing allegiances to the MCP and the

Kuomintang would settle scores by accusing each other of being communist or pro-government informants.[44] In Cyprus, too, denunciations were crucial to security force arrests and EOKA reprisals.[45]

Such examples point to the intimate nature of insurgent and counter-insurgent violence. Where insecurity prevailed personal disputes became caught up in the wider dynamics of conflict. Decisions about taking sides or remaining silent depended as much on matters of purely local concern as on macro-questions of ideological affiliation.[46] It is therefore misleading to describe the resultant violence as 'structural' or, in some way, uniquely colonial. More analytically rewarding is to follow the model developed by researchers into colonial counter-insurgency in the Dutch East Indies. They suggest that conflicts of this type were characterized by 'excessive violence' in which a lack of discrimination between combatants and non-combatants and reciprocal cycles of demonstrative killing by security forces and insurgents became the norm.[47]

Extensive recruitment of local allies and highly visible or 'performative' violence confirm something else as well: counter-insurgency campaigns built on earlier practices of imperial repression. Typical in this regard was the widespread resort by colonial security forces to collective punishment. Such punishments had been a feature of wars of colonial conquest and, as Martin Thomas's chapter describes, they remained integral to imperial policing methods after the First World War. Ironically, while wars of decolonization were often more violent in absolute numerical terms than the repression that preceded them, post-1945 campaigns were distinguished from the earlier period of 'pacification' by a begrudging acceptance among imperial policymakers that European military personnel were likely to face international censure for egregious acts of violence.[48] Hostile foreign scrutiny and the longer reach of international law help explain why, in 1947, the Netherlands government, under pressure from the United Nations, stepped back from complete reconquest in Indonesia, much to the frustration of Dutch military commanders on the ground. Anti-colonial insurgents were understandably keen – and commensurately quick – to exploit increased international sensitivity to colonial state violence and its attendant human rights abuses.[49] Algeria's FLN never achieved military victory, but the movement's overseas political leadership won stronger support within global forums including the UN General Assembly, the Non-Aligned Movement and the Arab League. All condemned French military actions, further eroding the legitimacy of colonial rule in North Africa.[50] France did not stand alone in the court of international opinion at the United Nations. Imperial governments, anxious to disarm such criticism, used a combination of juridical argument and counter-propaganda in response. Their central argument was that wars of decolonization remained wholly internal problems beyond the purview of international law. Security operations were portrayed as essential policing, guided by precepts of 'minimum force' or proportionate military response, and meant to restore calm, often as the prelude to reform.[51]

Some features of 'emergency' regulations remained hard to reconcile with this image of restorative policing. The creation of free-fire zones, the right to detain without trial, and the suspension of civil liberties, such as the imposition of curfews, underlined the coercion intrinsic to counter-insurgency. The shifting legal context as security regulations proliferated also rendered abuses by military and police forces more likely, particularly during the early phases of counter-insurgency operations when inadequate command and control structures and limited intelligence capacity left units scrabbling for information and thus more inclined to shoot first. Among the most infamous examples in the British case was the Batang Kali massacre in Malaya, when a company of the 2nd Scots Guards killed twenty-four unarmed villagers.[52] Summary killings of civilians became commonplace in wars of decolonization, so much so that soldiers sometimes developed a macabre *patois* of seemingly innocuous phrases to describe the practice. During a search of the West Javanese village of Rawagede, for example, Dutch troops rounded up and executed a large proportion of the male population, with reports indicating that between 150 and 431 men may have been killed.[53]

Interpreting dreadful events of this type is difficult. Describing these events as unusual, as hot-blooded excesses, risks ignoring the permissive political environments, the judicial powers and military cultures that rendered mass killing more likely in the first place. The other extreme would be to suggest that slaughter of civilians or maltreatment of detainees was merely typical of a 'state of exception' – a facet, in other words, of regimes of absolutist military control in which colonial subjects could be killed with impunity.[54] Such characterizations overstate their case. Nor can they be applied generically. Massacres of the type described above were systemic in some conflicts but not in others. The state of exception argument also invests too much power in imperial security forces. Their resort to extreme violence was as likely to be in reaction to insecurity as it was an expression of overwhelming military might. What may be said is that colonial counter-insurgencies as forms of asymmetric warfare were marked by corresponding asymmetries of violence. Village massacres or the mass killing of detainees were the logical culmination of a pervasive culture of coercion.

In Malaya, as Karl Hack's chapter documents, historians have argued that the initial phase of counter-terror represented a deliberate strategy to instil fear and intimidate the ethnic Chinese communities that provided most support to the MCP. The evidence adduced includes competitive kill tallies, the use of hunting metaphors to describe military operations, the summary execution of prisoners and the mutilation of corpses, including one instance where British Royal Marine Commandoes posed with heads as trophies.[55] Colonial governments tended to close ranks in reaction to alleged misdeeds. Their administrators, military commanders and politicians sometimes colluded to stifle investigations or whitewash their findings. This was unfortunate. With regard to Kenya, David Anderson argues that the colonial administration's tolerance of extreme violence during the early phases of the Mau Mau insurgency contributed to the institutionalization of torture in its later stages, particularly in Kenya's detention camps of the sort described in Katherine Bruce-Lockhart's chapter, where inmates were subject to routine physical and psychological abuse.[56]

It is too soon to suggest that the governmental impulse to cover up the dark side of colonial counter-insurgency has passed into history. Only in the last decade or so have historians have begun to challenge conventional national myths regarding decolonization and its implications for the legacy of empire in post-imperial Britain. Most notably historians, such as David Anderson, Huw Bennett and David French, have repudiated the idea that the doctrine of minimum force governed the actions of British security personnel. It is becoming clear that even well-intentioned 'hearts and minds' tactics could be as violently coercive as traditional military methods.[57]

As this collection of essays confirms, similar revisionism is now well established among historians of French, Dutch and Portuguese decolonization.[58] In France the war in Algeria remained difficult to research in the years following the conflict. It was not until the late 1980s that historians could revisit the violence perpetrated by the French military although bureaucratic obstacles to archival access persisted until the early 2000s.[59] Outstanding examples of this revisionist literature include the work of Raphaëlle Branche, Sylvie Thénault and Emmanuel Blanchard, who have demonstrated how torture, rape and judicial bias became intrinsic to the conflict's prosecution.[60]

If cases of civilian maltreatment may be found among all contested decolonization, why has it taken so long for historians to destabilize and challenge orthodox histories? Atrocities, such as the Batang Kali and Rawagede massacres, were public knowledge but their exact circumstances were subject to cover-ups, denials and official silences.[61] In other cases, it was argued that violent atrocities were exceptional and, therefore, were not necessarily indicative of a culture of impunity among European security personnel. When whistle-blowers, such as Eileen Fletcher, came forward to argue that human rights abuses were, in fact, intrinsic to colonial counter-insurgency campaigns, the authorities sought to discredit them. In Fletcher's case, the former rehabilitation officer, who had witnessed first-hand the scale of maltreatment within Kenya's detention camps, was patronizingly dismissed as a hysterical troublemaker.[62]

In the British case accusations of state-led cover-ups have gained greater traction as a result of the 'discovery' of the so-called migrated archives at Hanslope Park. During a legal case brought against the UK government by five former Kenyan detainees, the Foreign and Commonwealth Office (FCO) was forced to admit, in spite of previous denials, that it held 1,500 unreleased files on Kenya.[63] This admission was followed by the announcement that the 'secret archive' contained more than one million Foreign Office files, some of which date back to the nineteenth century.[64] The FCO has maintained that the failure to disclose the existence of these records was the result of administrative oversight, a claim to which historians have reacted with scepticism.[65] It had long been suspected by historians of decolonization that material had been destroyed in the colonies prior to independence or had been secretly transferred back to the UK, only to be kept out of the public domain. The discovery and subsequent analysis of the migrated archives has confirmed historians' suspicions. In the case of Malaya, Edward Hampshire has documented the process by which officials selected files for transfer or destruction.[66] In this sense, the fate of the archive mirrors that of the violence it describes. The 'migration' of this administrative record was less the product of bureaucratic confusion than a fundamental aspect of the decolonization process as colonial governments sought to retain censored control over records that were either of strategic value to the British government or had the potential to cause embarrassment to public officials.

Britain's migrated archives and the court case arising from their disposition have prompted heightened scrutiny of Britain's conduct during decolonization conflicts, with major implications for the reputation and liability of the post-imperial state. Similar processes are in train in the Netherlands, whose victims of colonial state violence, it appears, are far more widespread than once assumed.[67] Unsurprisingly, these claims have prompted angry reactions from imperial apologists, resentful at what they see as attempts to put empire on trial, inflicting reputational damage on former colonial officials and service personnel.[68]

The risk, of course, is that measured analysis is drowned out by the opposing polemics of condemnation and imperial apologia. Ann Stoler gets to the heart of things here. When it comes to public discussion, few have yet found the appropriate frame of analysis to relate violent decolonization to wider national narratives.[69] Separation between national and imperial histories is still too readily made.[70] Relevant to us here is Stoler's suggestion that this occlusion of imperial history from national history is reinforced by a focus on colonial atrocities and consequent arguments over whether present-day governments should issue formal apologies. The risk, Stoler contends, is that such misdeeds are treated in isolation as rogue actions, rather than as embedded in practices of colonial counter-insurgency.[71]

One way in which historians can move beyond the focus on colonial atrocities – what Matthew Hughes terms the 'ethnography of nastiness' – is to consider the social dynamics of late colonial conflicts and, in particular, the gendered dimensions of the violence involved.[72] As Katherine Bruce-Lockhart explains in her chapter, only recently have historians investigated the experiences of women during colonial insurgencies and there is certainly more work to be done on women's and girls' experiences of violent decolonization from the perspective of both the colonizer and the colonized. From the emerging research it is abundantly that, far from being passive victims or bystanders, women played a pivotal role during anti-colonial insurgencies.[73] Many were motivated to take up arms against the colonial state for much the same reasons as men.[74] In Malaya Mahani Musa notes that women joined the MCP thanks to a combination of factors, including anti-colonial nationalism and socio-economic deprivation. Female MCP members were also motivated by gender-specific factors, such as the global growth in feminist activism, the desire to escape patriarchal structures, and the party's support for equal pay and the abolition of polygamy.[75]

Another crucial determinant of women's support for an insurgency were their experiences of violence, not least because, as discussed earlier, in numerous conflicts such violence was highly gendered.[76] In Algeria the French claimed to 'liberate' Algerian Muslim women through forced 'un-veiling' ceremonies. These supposedly emancipatory initiatives were accompanied by enhanced provision of health and education services, which placed particular emphasis on the European model of domesticity.[77] The assumption underpinning this modernizing agenda was that Algerian women could be reshaped in the image of their metropolitan counterparts and thereby dissuaded from supporting the nationalist cause.[78] The coercion implicit in these largely urban initiatives was writ larger in the countryside where, quite apart from forcibly removing their veils, army units compelled Algerian women to accept the services provided by specialist medical and social teams.[79] Put simply, the reliance on force to implement these allegedly emancipatory reforms underscores their bankruptcy.

The hypocrisy of the modernizing agenda was also evident in the resettlement schemes pursued by European imperial powers during wars of decolonization from the New Villages in Malaya to the Agrovilles in Vietnam, and the Aldamentos in Angola to the Centres de Regroupement in Algeria.[80] (For the latter pairing, see the chapters by Moritz Feichtinger and Miguel Bandeira Jerónimo in this book.) The very depiction of forcible population removal as resettlement reminds us that such programmes came packaged in a distinct rhetoric of development. It was argued that, not only would the residents of the new settlements be protected from the insurgents, but the provision of education, health and economic infrastructure would raise welfare standards and promote rural development. Such claims were belied by conditions in the settlements. In Algeria civilians were forcibly relocated to new sites ill-suited to the basic needs of their inhabitants. Many were forced to live in tents because permanent accommodation was unavailable. New sites were often far removed from the residents' homes, making sharp declines in agricultural production and consequent dietary health almost inevitable. This gave rise to increased rates of malnutrition, disease and morbidity, with women and children the worst affected.[81] Matters were comparable in Malaya, where the resettlement programme separated, not just communities, but individual families. Once settled in the New Villages, residents often lacked adequate access to medical and sanitary facilities. Reports of widespread corruption and profiteering among resettlement officers proliferated, while women were subject to sexual assault during routine screening operations.[82] The social and economic dislocation of resettlement highlights the fact that 'non-violent' methods of counter-insurgency could be as punitive as traditional military tactics.

Land alienation and social dislocation were not issues easily resolved with the attainment of independence. This was equally true of the social divisions resulting from the imperial authorities' use of local allies. By the end of the conflict in Algeria, there were more Algerians fighting for the French than for the ALN.[83] As the demobilization of *harki* units gathered momentum in late 1961, it quickly became apparent that the French state would offer little or no formal protection to its Algerian auxiliaries. The profound social divisions wrought by the war's brutal conduct left the *harkis* exposed to immediate and violent retribution.

The opposite applied in Kenya, where, as Daniel Branch has shown, the British government's 'loyalist' Kikuyu supporters exploited their erstwhile alliance with the colonial state to further their political and economic interests.[84] Elite loyalists eventually monopolized positions within Kenya's provincial administration and civil service, providing job security, well-paid salaries and social standing, which enabled them to act as 'conduits of power' between the state and local communities.[85] Loyalists were, therefore, well positioned to distribute land and other resources to their supporters while, in the process, marginalizing the former insurgents. The resultant divisions marred Kenyan politics during the 1960s and beyond.[86] As Branch argues, 'The fault lines between individuals, ideologies and identities that surfaced ... [during the Emergency] remained visible throughout subsequent decades.' The long-term consequences were devastating: the emergence of an authoritarian-bureaucratic state, the politicization of ethnicity and periodic bouts of political violence as groups have competed for access to state resources.[87] Put simply, as a number of chapters in this book indicate, the violence of decolonization had consequences that lasted far beyond the formal withdrawal of European control.

All of the chapters in this collection touch upon one or more of the issues discussed in this introduction. The collection starts with Kim Wagner's chapter on the politicization of the Amritsar Massacre and its contested legacy for historians of colonial violence. Wagner challenges those historians who argue that the doctrine of minimum force had a restraining influence on the actions of British military personnel. Instead Wagner emphasizes the importance of reading colonial records against the archival grain, arguing that historians should pay close attention to the 'prose of counter-insurgency'. For Wagner, British references to unruly and hysterical mobs served to legitimize the use of disproportionate lethal force. This highly politicized language, Wagner argues, was symptomatic of colonial anxieties regarding the fragility of imperial rule in South Asia, where British officials relied on performative violence in order to uphold the limited authority of the colonial state.

In the French Empire, too, the years immediately following the First World War witnessed a spillover of the preceding violence of interstate conflict into the repressive strategies adopted to suppress local opposition to the consolidation of French imperial power. As in the British case, a self-consciously modernist rhetoric of pacification clashed with the overwhelming firepower used by French commanders to suppress insurgencies in Morocco's Riffian highlands and the Syrian Mandate. The justifications advanced for such methods are explored in Martin Thomas's chapter. It reveals the extent to which counter-insurgency tactics commonly identified with late colonial conflicts of contested decolonization were prefigured in the violent extension of European imperial power in the aftermath of the Great War. As Thomas indicates, while the 'conflict structure' in 1920s Morocco and Syria was shaped by their forcible incorporation into France's empire, the patterns of insurgent and counter-insurgent violence anticipated those of societies in the grip of decolonization.

If Wagner's chapter supports recent efforts to challenge the myth of a 'British way' of counter-insurgency and Thomas questions the neat periodization of 'late colonial' counter-insurgency, Karl Hack's contribution complicates the picture still further. Focusing on the Malayan case, Hack contends that it is too simplistic to argue that counter-insurgency campaigns were shaped by one dominant strategy. Instead Hack makes the case for a 'phased' understanding of counter-insurgency, arguing that the Malayan Emergency can be divided into distinct phases that were characterized by a combination specific tactics. While a particular phase of a counter-insurgency campaign may have been characterized by the preponderance of a particular method, such as counterterror or collective punishment, Hack argues that tactics persisted across different phases of a conflict with differing levels of intensity. Acknowledgement of this is critical to understanding how and why counter-insurgency campaigns evolve.

As with Wagner's contribution, the chapter by Neil MacMaster and Emmanuel Blanchard also sets out to challenge contemporary myths regarding colonial counter-insurgency. David Galula, who served in the French military in Algeria between 1956 and 1958, has attracted increasing attention in recent years as a colonial counter-insurgent strategist. MacMaster and Blanchard argue that while Galula achieved some notable successes in Algeria, his influence was more limited than the recent attention implies. Focusing on Galula's arrival in Paris in 1958, MacMaster and Blanchard argue that his influence was marginal when compared with that of Maurice Papon, who was in the process of consolidating his control over France's strategy for combating the FLN in the metropole.

A recurring theme in this collection is the hypocrisy of the imperial authorities' modernizing rhetoric. This is particularly evident in the chapters by Moritz Feichtinger and Miguel Bandeira Jerónimo on forced resettlement. Both Feichtinger and Jerónimo demonstrate that while resettlement was conceived of in modernizing terms, for those populations affected by such schemes the consequences were catastrophic, with resettlement contributing to increased rates of disease, malnutrition and morbidity. The failure of the post-1945 modernizing agenda is also explored by Gareth Curless in his chapter on colonial policing. Using British Guiana and Singapore as case studies, Curless explores the parallels between the policing of civil unrest and the conduct of colonial counter-insurgencies. Echoing Wagner's chapter on Amritsar, Curless argues that colonial governments regarded civil unrest as signalling the possible collapse of the colonial state, and, as such, responded to strikes and riots with maximum, not minimum, force.

The increased focus on issues such as resettlement is part of a broader 'social turn' in the history of counter-insurgency. In her chapter on Kenya, Katherine Bruce-Lockhart argues for a gendered approach to late colonial conflict. In doing so, she highlights the role of Kenyan women as active participants of the Mau Mau movement, as well as the gendered nature of British counter-insurgency strategy in Kenya. Specifically, Bruce-Lockhart documents how the authorities' efforts to transform 'deviant' female subjects into 'loyal' citizens were informed by British gender ideals, particularly with regard to ideas of female domesticity.

Bruce-Lockhart's emphasis on the role of women in the Mau Mau highlights the agency of colonial subjects, which is a theme that is also explored in Brian Drohan's chapter on Cyprus. Drohan argues that colonial legal regimes, although weighted in favour of the colonial power, were spaces of contestation. In the case of Cyprus Drohan demonstrates that the presence of a Greek Cypriot legal elite inhibited British efforts to prosecute EOKA members and their supporters, with the result that the ratio of judicial executions in Cyprus was much lower than in other conflicts.

Another emerging trend in the historiography of colonial violence is the focus on paramilitary units. In his chapter on the Phoenix Program in Vietnam, Jeremy Kuzmarov argues that the formation of the Provincial Recruitment Units, which were financed through illegal means, allowed the CIA to conduct a campaign of counter-terror through locally recruited allies. As with the 'loyalist' militias during the wars of decolonization, Kuzmarov argues that these clandestine police operations offered the United States a degree of plausible deniability and were regarded by policymakers as a way of waging covert counter-insurgency on the cheap.

While Kuzmarov's chapter highlights the continuities between the wars of decolonization and later conflicts, Huw Bennett's contribution problematizes this relationship. Focusing on the British Army in Northern Ireland during the late 1960s and early 1970s, Bennett argues that while the colonial experience of counter-insurgency did influence strategy, British military elites were not unthinking automatons. According to Bennett the situation in Northern Ireland was regarded as civil unrest, not outright rebellion. As such, the army recognized that traditional 'colonial' methods for dealing with insurgency were not appropriate for Northern Ireland. Bennett argues, therefore, that while British strategy may have felt 'colonial' at time, historians should not assume that the military uncritically transferred strategy from one conflict to another.

The resonance of colonial conflicts for contemporary insecurity is also apparent in the conflicts that currently criss-cross the Middle East and serves to underscore the point that insurgencies are rarely contained by national borders. Such trends were also evident during the wars of decolonization, particularly in South East Asia where insurgents in both Malaya and Indochina developed logistical networks across territorial boundaries. The inter-territorial nature of colonial conflicts is explored in the chapter by Mathilde von Bülow, who argues that the development of 'external sanctuaries' were critical to the FLN's campaign against the French, with Algerian militants using West Germany as a logistical platform to extend the war of independence to mainland Europe. Her stress on the depth of connection between colonial counter-insurgency and illicit security force practices within Western Europe reminds us that the study of contested decolonization is intrinsically transnational and often most revealing when viewed comparatively.

Taken together, these chapters confirm the extent to which the historiography of violent decolonization has moved away from its traditional focus on the military dimensions of colonial counter-insurgency campaigns. Historians are now broadening their focus to examine a greater range of issues, ranging from the diplomatic campaigns waged by insurgent movements to the role of gender in shaping counter-insurgency strategy. They are revisiting the meaning of key terms, such as 'loyalist' and 'anti-colonial nationalist', recognizing that such labels reveal little about the motivations of the actors to which they refer. This collection, we hope, contributes to this more nuanced understanding of the causes of violent decolonization, one that pays greater attention to the interdependent relationship between macro-level factors, such as the changes in global geopolitics, and micro-level factors linked to ethno-religious divisions and community-based grievances. One advantage of this more holistic approach to the study of decolonization is that the consequences of conflict for those societies affected by it are now integral to the analysis. Much remains to be researched and said. This collection of essays, then, offers contributions to what is sure to be a crucial and long-running debate.

Notes

1   On empire and imperialism as norms in global politics and history's *longue durée*, see Jane Burbank and Frederick Cooper, *Empires in World History: Power and the Politics of Difference* (Princeton, NJ: Princeton University Press, 2010); John Darwin, *After Tamerlane: The Global History of Empire* (London: Allen Lane, 2007).
2   Richard Jackson and Helen Dexter, 'The Social Construction of Organized Political Violence: An Analytical Framework,' *Civil Wars* 16, no. 1 (2014): 8–18.
3   David French, *Fighting EOKA: The British Counter-Insurgency Campaign on Cyprus, 1955-1959* (Oxford: Oxford University Press, 2015).
4   Jeff Goodwin, *No Other Way Out. States and Revolutionary Movements, 1945-1991* (Cambridge: Cambridge University Press, 2001); Kathleen Gallagher Cunningham, *Inside the Politics of Self-Determination* (New York: Oxford University Press, 2014). On the timing of nationalist insurgent outbreaks, see Adria Lawrence, 'Triggering Nationalist Violence: Competition and Conflict in Uprisings against Colonial Rule,' *International Security* 35, no. 2 (2010): 90–104.
5   Raphaëlle Branche, *Prisonniers du FLN* (Paris: Payot & Rivages, 2014).

6   Sibyelle Scheipers, *Unlawful Combatants: A Genealogy of the Irregular Fighter* (Oxford: Oxford University Press, 2015), 171.

7   Philip Deery, 'The Terminology of Terrorism: Malaya, 1948-52,' *Journal of Southeast Asian Studies* 34, no. 2 (2003): 231–47.

8   Dirk A. Moses and Bart Luttikhuis (eds), *Colonial Counter-insurgency and Mass Violence: The Dutch Empire in Indonesia* (Abingdon: Routledge, 2014), 260.

9   David French, *The British Way in Counter-insurgency, 1945-1967* (Oxford: Oxford University Press, 2011), 74–104.

10 For illuminating contemporary parallels, see Helen Kinsella, *The Image before the Weapon: A Critical History of the Distinction between Combatant and Civilian* (Ithaca, NY: Cornell University Press, 2011); Adam Roberts, 'Counter-Terrorism, Armed Force, and the Laws of War,' *Survival* 44, no. 1 (2002): 7–32; Roland Paris, 'The "Responsibility to Protect" and the Structural Problems of Preventive Humanitarian Intervention,' *International Peacekeeping* 21, no. 5 (2014): 569–603.

11 French, *Fighting EOKA*, 54–5, 64–6, 108. Colonial security forces deployed to Cyprus numbered some 25,000 by the spring of 1956.

12 French, *Fighting EOKA*, 158–70. According to David French, figures compiled from the Greek Cypriot press suggest that EOKA killed 148 fellow Greek Cypriots and injured a further 69. Security force reports and English-language press sources on the island suggest figures of 187 killed and 181 injured.

13 John Lonsdale, 'The Moral Economy of Mau Mau: Wealth, Poverty, and Civic Virtue in Kikuyu Political Thought', in *Unhappy Valley: Conflict in Kenya and Africa*, II, ed. Bruce Berman and John Lonsdale (London: James Currey, 1992), Chapter 12; Tabitha Kanogo, *Squatters and the Roots of Mau Mau, 1905-1963* (London: James Currey, 1987); Ngô Vĩnh Long, *Before the Revolution: From Peasant Insurrection to Total War, 1959-1968* (New York: Columbia University Press, 1991); Tim N. Harper, *The End of Empire and the Making of Malaya* (Cambridge: Cambridge University Press, 1999), 96–114.

14 Harper, *End of Empire*, pp. 35–45; Cheah Boon Kheng, *Red Star Over Malaya: Resistance and Social Conflict During and After the Japanese Occupation of Malaya, 1941-1946* (Singapore: Singapore University Press 1983).

15 Roland Burke, *Decolonization and the Evolution of International Human Rights* (Philadelphia, PA: University of Pennsylvania Press, 2010), introduction; Brad Simpson, 'The Curious History of Self-Determination,' *Diplomatic History* 36, no. 4 (2012): 676–81. Simpson, however, makes plain the depth of American and other great power opposition to a wholehearted embrace of self-determination as a guiding principle of Western international politics after 1945.

16 The literature on anti-colonial nationalism is extensive. Standout examples include Elizabeth Schmidt, *Mobilizing the Masses: Gender, Ethnicity, and Class in the Nationalist Movements in Guinea, 1939-1956* (Portsmouth, NH: Heinemann, 2005); Adria K. Lawrence, *Imperial Rule and the Politics of Nationalism: Anti-Colonial Protest in the French Empire* (Cambridge: Cambridge University Press, 2013); Heather Sharkey, *Living with Colonialism: Nationalism and Culture in the Anglo-Egyptian Sudan* (Berkeley: University of California Press, 2003).

17 Frederick Cooper, *Citizenship between Empire and Nation: Remaking France and French Africa, 1945-1960* (Ithaca, NY: Cornell University Press, 2014), 4–8.

18 A. G. Hopkins, 'Rethinking Decolonization,' *Past and Present* 200 (2008): 216.

19 Keith David Watenpaugh, *Bread from Stones: The Middle East and the Making of Modern Humanitarianism* (Berkeley, CA: University of California Press, 2015),

10. Instructive here are the Algerian FLN's humanitarian efforts, particularly in the field of healthcare, see Jennifer Johnson, *The Battle for Algeria: Sovereignty, Health Care, and Humanitarianism* (Philadelphia, PA: University of Pennsylvania Press, 2015).

20   Caio Simões de Araújo and Iolande Vasile, 'The world the Portuguese developed: racial politics, luso-tropicalism and development discourse in late Portuguese colonialism,' in Joseph M. Hodge, Gerald Hödl and Martins Kopf (eds), *Developing Africa: Concepts and Practices in Twentieth-Century Colonialism* (Manchester: Manchester University Press, 2014), 310.

21   Todd Shepard, *The Invention of Decolonization: The Algerian War and the Remaking of France* (Ithaca, NY: Cornell University Press, 2006), 97–100, 114–15.

22   See Seng Tan and Amitov Acharya (eds), *Bandung Revisited: The Legacy of the 1955 Asian-African Conference for International Order* (Singapore: National University Press, 2008); Christopher J. Lee (ed.), *Making a World After Empire: The Bandung Moment and its Political Afterlives* (Athens: Ohio University Press, 2010).

23   The long history and distinctive course of populist anti-colonialism in urban Tanzania is instructive here, see James R. Brennan, 'Youth, the TANU Youth League, and Managed Vigilantism in Dar es Salaam, Tanzania 1925-1973,' *Africa* 76, no. 2 (2006): 221–46. See also Jeffrey James Byrne, 'Our Own Special Brand of Socialism: Algerian and the Conquest of Modernities in the 1960s,' *Diplomatic History* 33, no. 3 (2009): 427–47.

24   Hugues Tertrais, 'Le poids financier de la guerre d'Indochine,' in *L'armée française dans la guerre d'Indochine*, ed. Maurice Vaïsse (Bruxelles, Editions Complexe, 2000), 33–51; Hugues Tertrais, 'L'économie indochinoise dans la guerre (1945-1954),' *Outre-Mers: Revue d'histoire* 88, no. 330 (2001) : 113–29.

25   Michael Stenson, *Repression and Revolt: The Origins of the Communist Insurrection in Malaya and Singapore* (Athens, OH: Ohio University Press, 1969).

26   Nicholas J. White, 'Capitalism and Counter-insurgency? Business and Government in the Malayan Emergency, 1948-57,' *Modern Asian Studies* 32, no. 1 (1998): 149–77.

27   Luttikhuis and Moses, *Mass Violence*, 66.

28   Paul Staniland, *Networks of Rebellion: Explaining Insurgent Cohesion and Collapse* (Ithaca, NY: Cornell University Press, 2014), chapter 1: 'Organizing Insurgency'.

29   Neil MacMaster, *Burning the Veil: The Algerian War and the 'Emancipation' of Muslim Women, 1954-62* (Manchester: Manchester University Press, 2009), 87.

30   Neil MacMaster, 'The "Silent Native": *attentisme*, being Compromised, and Banal Terror During the Algerian War of Independence, 1954-62,' in *The French Colonial Mind: Violence, Military Encounters, and Colonialism*, ed. Martin Thomas (Lincoln, NE: University of Nebraska Press, 2012), 283–303.

31   Karl Hack, 'Malaya – Between Two Terrors: People's History and the Malayan Emergency,' in *Hearts and Minds: A People's History of Counter-insurgency*, ed. Hannah Gurman (New York: The New Press, 2013), 37–8; MacMaster, *Burning the Veil*, 230.

32   Raphaëlle Branche, 'Sexual Violence in the Algerian War,' in *Brutality and Desire: War and Sexuality in Europe's Twentieth Century*, ed. Dagmar Herzog (London: Palgrave Macmillan, 2009), 247–60.

33   Panikos Panaye and Pippa Virdee (eds), *Refugees and the End of Empire*; Caroline Elkins, *Britain's Gulag: The Brutal End of Empire in Kenya* (London: Jonathan Cape, 2005); Marnia Lazreg, *Torture and the Twilight of Empire: From Algiers to Baghdad* (Princeton, NJ: Princeton University Press, 2008), 154–64.

34   Karl Hack, 'The Origins of the Asian Cold War: Malaya 1948,' *Journal of Southeast Asian Studies* 40, no. 3 (2009): 472.

35 We are not, therefore, suggesting that colonial recruitment of either regular or militia forces was a late-twentieth-century phenomenon or one confined to the British, French or Dutch Empires. For other illustrative examples, see Douglas Wheeler, 'African elements in Portugal's armies in Africa (1961-1974),' *Armed Forces and Society* 2, no. 2 (1976): 233–50; Miles Larmer, 'Of Local Identities and Transnational Conflict: The Katangese Gendarmes and Central-Southern Africa's Forty Years War, 1960-99,' in *Transnational Soldiers: Foreign Military Enlistment in the Modern Era*, ed. Nir Arielli and Bruce Collins (Basingstoke: Palgrave Macmillan, 2012), 160–80; Nir Arielli, 'Colonial Soldiers in Italian Counter-Insurgency Operations in Libya, 1922-33,' *British Journal of Military History* 1, no. 2 (2015): 47–66.

36 David M. Anderson and Daniel Branch, 'Allies at the End of Empire—Loyalists, Nationalists and the Cold War, 1945–76,' *The International History Review* 39, no. 1 (2017): pp. 1–13.

37 Daniel Branch, *Defeating Mau Mau*: Creating Kenya (Cambridge: Cambridge University Press, 2010), 72–9.

38 Daniel Branch, 'Footprints in the Sand: British Counter-insurgency and the War in Iraq,' *Politics and Society* 38, no. 1 (2010): 15–34.

39 MacMaster, *Burning the Veil*, 230–2.

40 Martin Evans, 'Reprisal Violence and the Harkis in French Algeria, 1962,' *International History Review* 39, no. 1 (2017): 89–106.

41 Matthew Hughes, 'Palestinian Collaboration with the British: The Peace Bands and the Arab Revolt in Palestine, 1936-9,' *Journal of Contemporary History* (2015): 2–24.

42 MacMaster, *Burning the Veil*, 231.

43 Ibid.

44 Hack, 'Malaya – Between Two Terrors,' 46.

45 French, *Fighting EOKA*, 158–68.

46 This admixture of micro and macro factors is not intrinsically colonial, being symptomatic of civil wars and insurgencies in authoritarian states, see Stathis Kalyvas, *The Logic of Violence in Civil War* (Cambridge: Cambridge University Press, 2006), 174–82, 195–207; Elisabeth Wood, *Insurgent Collective Action and Civil War in El Salvador* (Cambridge: Cambridge University Press, 2003), 2–13.

47 The 'excessive violence' model is being studied by researchers at KITVL, the Royal Netherlands Institute of Southeast Asian and Caribbean Studies, in Leiden.

48 Scheipers, *Unlawful Combatants*, 171.

49 Luttikhuis and Moses, *Mass Violence*, 272.

50 Matthew Connelly, *A Diplomatic Revolution: Algeria's Fight for Independence and the Origins of the Post-Cold War Era* (New York: Oxford University Press, 2002).

51 Fabian Klose, 'The Colonial Testing Ground: The International Committee of the Red Cross and the Violent End of Empire,' *Humanity: An International Journal of Human Rights, Humanitarianism, and Development* 2, no. 1 (2011): 107–26; Wm. Roger Louis, 'Public Enemy Number One: the British Empire in the Dock at the United Nations, 1957–71,' in *The British Empire in the 1950s: Retreat or Revival?*, ed. Martin Lynn (Basingstoke: Palgrave Macmillan, 2006), 187–95.

52 Christopher Bayly and Tim Harper, *Forgotten Wars: The End of Britain's Asian Empire* (London: Penguin, 2008), 445–56.

53 Luttikhuis and Moses, *Mass Violence*, 257.

54 Building on German jurist Carl Schmitt's coining of the term in 1922, Italian philosopher Giorgio Agamben revisited the 'state of exception' concept in the context of civil war and the so-called post-9/11 'war on terror,' see Giorgio Agamben, *State of Exception*, English translation (Chicago, IL: University of Chicago Press, 2005), 1–31.

55 Bayly and Harper, *Forgotten Wars*, 445–56; Huw Bennett, "'A Very Salutary Effect": The Counter-Terror Strategy in the Early Malayan Emergency, June 1948 to December 1949,' *Journal of Strategic Studies* 32, no. 3 (2009): 415–44.

56 David M. Anderson, 'British Abuse and Torture in Kenya's Counter-Insurgency, 1952–1960,' *Small Wars & Insurgencies* 23, nos. 4–5 (2012): 700–19.

57 David Anderson, *Histories of the Hanged: Britain's Dirty War in Kenya and the End of Empire* (London: Weidenfeld and Nicolson, 2004); Huw Bennett, *Fighting the Mau Mau: the British Army and Counter-Insurgency in the Kenya Emergency* (Cambridge: Cambridge University Press, 2013); Caroline Elkins, *Britain's Gulag: The Brutal End of Empire in Kenya* (London: Jonathan Cape, 2005); David French, *The British Way in Counter-Insurgency, 1945-1967* (Oxford: Oxford University Press). These works followed in the wake of the revisionist study by John Newsinger, *British Counter-insurgency: From Palestine to Northern Ireland* (Basingstoke: Palgrave Macmillan, 2002).

58 Todd Shepard, *The Invention of Decolonization: the Algerian War and the Remaking of France* (Ithaca and New York: Cornell University Press, 2006); Luttikhuis and Moses, *Mass Violence*.

59 On the historiography of the Algerian conflict see Martin S. Alexander, Martin Evans, J. F. V. Keiger, 'The "War without a Name," the French Army and the Algerians: Recovering Experiences, Images and Testimonies,' in *Algerian War and the French army, 1954-62: Experiences, Images, Testimonies*, ed. Martin S. Alexander, Martin Evans and J. F. V. Keiger (Basingstoke: Palgrave Macmillan, 2002), 1–42.

60 Raphaëlle Branche, *La Torture et l'armée pendant la guerre d'Algérie, 1954–1962* (Paris: Gallimard, 2001); Sylvie Thénault, *Une Drôle de justice. Les magistrats dans la guerre d'Algérie* (Paris: La Découverte, 2001). See also Neil MacMaster, 'The Torture Controversy (1998-2002): Towards a "New History" of the Algerian War?' *Modern and Contemporary France* 10, no. 4 (2002): 449–59.

61 Bayly and Harper, *Forgotten Wars*, 449–56; Stef Scagliola, 'Cleo's "Unfinished Business": Coming to Terms with Dutch War Crimes in Indonesia's War of Independence,' *Journal of Genocide Research* 14, nos. 3–4 (2012): 419–39. Ian Ward and Norma Miraflor, *Slaughter and Deception at Batang Kali* (Singapore: Media Masters, 2009).

62 Elkins, *Britain's Gulag*, 287–9.

63 The process by which the Kenyan migrated archives came be discovered is the subject of a recent article by David Anderson, 'Guilty Secrets: Deceit, Denial, and the Discovery of Kenya's "Migrated Archive,"' *History Workshop Journal* 80, no. 1 (2015): 142–60.

64 Ian Cobain, 'Foreign Office Hoarding 1m Historic Files In Secret Archive,' *The Guardian*, 18 October 2013.

65 Richard Drayton, 'Britain's Secret Archive of Decolonisation,' *History Workshop Online*, 19 April 2012, [Online], available at: Http://Www.Historyworkshop.Org.Uk/Britains-Secret-Archive-Of-Decolonisation/ (accessed 16 November 2015).

66 Edward Hampshire, "'Apply the Flame More Searingly": The Destruction and Migration of the Archives of British Colonial Administration: A Southeast Asia Case Study,' *Journal of Imperial and Commonwealth History* 41, no. 2 (2013): 334–52; Mandy Banton, 'Destroy? "Migrate"? Conceal? British Strategies for the Disposal of Sensitive Records of Colonial Administrations at Independence,' *Journal of Imperial and Commonwealth History* 40, no. 2 (2012): 321–35.

67 Leonard Doyle, 'Colonial Atrocities Explode Myth of Dutch Tolerance,' *The Independent*, 23 October 2011.

68 Tim Stanley, 'The British Must Not Rewrite the History of the Mau Mau Revolt,' *The Daily Telegraph*, 6 June 2013.

69   Ann Laura Stoler, 'Colonial Aphasia: Race and Disabled Histories in France', *Public Culture* 23, no. 1 (2011): 121–56.

70   Paul Bijl, 'Colonial Memory and Forgetting in the Netherlands and Indonesia', *Journal of Genocide Research* 14, nos. 3–4 (2012): 441–61.

71   Stoler, 'Colonial Aphasia', 155.

72   Matthew Hughes, 'Introduction: British Ways of Counter-insurgency', *Small Wars and Insurgencies* 23, nos. 4–5 (2012): 585.

73   See, for example, Natalya Vince, *Our Fighting Sisters: Nation, Memory and Gender in Algeria, 1954-2012* (Manchester: Manchester University Press, 2015), especially chapters 1 and 2.

74   Katherine Bruce-Lockhart, '"Unsound" Minds and Broken Bodies: The Detention of "hardcore" Mau Mau Women at Kamiti and Gitamayu Detention Camps, 1954-1960', *Journal of Eastern African Studies* 8, no. 4 (2014): 590–608; Tabitha Kanogo, 'Kikuyu Women and the Politics of Protest: Mau Mau', in *Images of Women in Peace & War: Cross-Cultural and Historical Perspectives*, ed. Sharon MacDonald, Pat Holden and Shirley Ardener (Basingstoke: Macmillan Education, 1987), 78–99; Cora Ann Presley, *Kikuyu Women, The Mau Mau Rebellion, and Social Change in Kenya* (Boulder, CO: Westview Press, 1992).

75   Mahani Musa, 'Women in the Malayan Communist Party, 1942-89', *Journal of Southeast Asian Studies* 44, no. 2 (2013): 226–49. Also see the collection of oral history interviews collected in Agnes Khoo, *Life as the River Flows: Women in the Malayan Anti-Colonial Struggle* (Monmouth: Merlin Press, 2007).

76   MacMaster, *Burning the Veil*, 209–244, quote at 219.

77   Jennifer Johnson, *The Battle for Algeria: Sovereignty, Health Care, and Humanitarianism* (Philadelphia: University of Pennsylvania Press, 2016), 4–7, 53–6.

78   MacMaster, *Burning the Veil*. See also Ryme Seferdjeli, 'The French Army and Muslim Women during the Algerian War (1954–62)', *Hawwa* 3, no. 1 (2005): 40–79.

79   MacMaster, *Burning the Veil*.

80   Christian Gerlach, *Extremely Violent Societies: Mass Violence in the Twentieth-Century World* (Cambridge: Cambridge University Press, 2010), chapter five; Teng-Phee Tan, '"Like a Concentration Camp, lah": Chinese Grassroots Experience of the Emergency and New Villages in British Colonial Malaya', *Chinese Southern Diaspora Studies* 3 (2009): 216–28.

81   MacMaster, *Burning the Veil*, 227–8.

82   Tan, '"Like a Concentration Camp, lah," 216–28; Harper, *The End of Empire*, 176–96.

83   The following is based on Martin Evans, 'The Harkis: The Experience and Memory of France's Muslim Auxiliaries', in *The Algerian War and the French Army, 1952-1962*, ed. Martin S. Alexander, Martin Evans and J. F. V. Keiger (Basingstoke: Palgrave Macmillan, 2002), 117–36.

84   Daniel Branch, *Defeating Mau Mau, Creating Kenya: Counter-insurgency, Civil War, and Decolonization* (Cambridge: Cambridge University Press, 2009).

85   Ibid., 149.

86   Ibid., see chapters 5 and 6.

87   Ibid., 177. See also Daniel Branch and Nicholas Cheeseman, 'The Politics of Control in Kenya: Understanding the Bureaucratic-Executive State, 1952-78', *Review of African Political Economy* 33, no. 107 (2006): 11–31; Daniel Branch and Nicholas Cheeseman, 'Democratization, Sequencing, and State Failure in Africa: Lessons from Kenya', *African Affairs* 108, no. 430 (2008): 1–26; Daniel Branch, *Kenya: Between Hope and Despair: 1963-2012* (New Haven, CT: Yale University Press, 2013).

1

Seeing Like a Soldier: The Amritsar Massacre and the Politics of Military History[1]

Kim A. Wagner

While ethicists and pundits may moralize about the past, historians should not. They must take the past on its own terms. This means reconstructing events, interpreting them within the context of their own era, and then considering how they fit into broader patterns of change over time. The historian of British counter-insurgency must, therefore, evaluate the behaviour of soldiers and police in past campaigns not according to our standards but by those of their own day.

Thomas R. Mockaitis[2]

The massacre was a deeply sad and tragic event, ending the lives of hundreds of Indians, but it was also unique; not an example of premeditated imperial murder, but rather the result of a series of unfortunate and unexpected events that came together one afternoon with devastating results. Dyer did not enter the Jallianwala Bagh with a plan already hatched in his mind, but walked up the narrow entrance, alone and alert, unsure of what would confront him. It was only when he saw that vast space and the huge crowd that had gathered inside did he understand what had happened; it was only then, in those few precious seconds, that he allowed fear to grip him. There were thousands of them. There was no time for anything else. He had to open fire.

Nick Lloyd[3]

Within the last few decades, and especially following the wars triggered by the 9/11 attacks, there has been an increasing focus within military history on counter-insurgency and the lessons to be gleaned from colonial warfare.[4] For military historians, the Amritsar Massacre of 1919 assumes a particularly important position as its lessons supposedly underwrote the formal doctrine of minimum force, according to which the British army should apply the least amount of force required when involved in the suppression of riots or counter-insurgency operations.[5] The 1919 unrest in Punjab thus famously made up one of the case studies in Charles Gwynn's classic work, *Imperial Policing* from 1934, and has since been the subject of numerous articles and dissertations on operational history and the origins of the minimum force doctrine.[6] The emphasis on minimum force as a principle of restraint has led some military historians to argue that the violence and brutality of decolonization after 1945 were isolated cases and in no way reflected British military practice, which emphatically did not rely on coercion.[7] Rod Thornton in particular has argued that the British Army invariably acted according to Victorian values of gentlemanliness and fair play, and that 'British colonies were, overall, created and controlled by the Army with a general appreciation for the need to avoid bloodshed.'[8] This rather rose-tinted view has been met with considerable criticism from scholars working on the Malayan Emergency and the campaign against the Mau Mau; Huw Bennett, for instance, has demonstrated that minimum force did not entail restraint and that British counter-insurgency campaigns were in fact characterized by the extensive use of brute force as part of official policy.[9] The debates on colonial counter-insurgency within military history thus evolve around issues of legitimation and legality, and are very much shaped by contemporary political concerns – not least in light of the ongoing British involvement in various conflicts and the recent lawsuit by former Mau Mau detainees.[10]

The Amritsar Massacre has for generations been synonymous with colonial brutality and constitutes for many an indisputable blemish in the history and legacy of the British Empire.[11] On 13 April 1919, General Reginald Dyer ordered his colonial troops to fire on an illegal gathering of thousands of Indian civilians in the enclosure known as the Jallianwala Bagh in the city of Amritsar in British Punjab; at least 379 were killed and more than a thousand wounded.[12] In India itself, the massacre has long been mythologized and assumes a central position in nationalist narratives of Gandhi and the struggle for independence.[13] As indicated by the quotes above, however, an altogether different analysis exists, according to which the massacre was merely a tragic accident that furthermore should be examined purely 'on its own terms'. In a recent book, military historian Nick Lloyd thus suggests that it was Indian nationalists who were the real perpetrators of violence, while the British response to anti-colonial unrest was 'proportionate' and 'reasonable'.[14] This argument has been generally well received and its findings have been incorporated into a number of recent works on British counter-insurgency.[15] It is in point of fact not just the product of a few authors' idiosyncrasies but reflects the more general approach to the study of colonial violence within certain quarters of military history. A closer reading of these narratives accordingly has wider implications for the manner in which we might assess attempts at rehabilitating colonial violence and the contemporary defence of Empire.

'Military history' is of course a broad and generic label that covers a wide range of different, and at times incompatible, ways of studying conflict and warfare, in varying institutional, cultural and societal contexts. This chapter considers more specifically the approach and politics of what I describe as 'parochial military history' or 'weaponized history': the scholarship that overwhelmingly adopts the practitioners' perspective and that often emerges from institutions with close military affiliations, which in the United States has been described as the 'military-academic complex'.[16]

Weaponizing history

There is of course no reason why a thematic focus on military doctrine, leadership or tactics and armament in counter-insurgency and imperial policing could not make a real contribution to historiography and provide new insights on events like the Amritsar Massacre. There is, however, something deeply problematic in studying military history as if it constituted a discipline of its own which, crucially, is not based on the same theoretical and methodological rigour as other historical subjects. Right from its inception, military history has followed a separate trajectory, operating with aims, priorities and methodologies quite its own. In Michael Howard's foundational article from 1961, 'The Use and Abuse of Military History', he outlined a future path for the field:

> The historian of peace can only chronicle and analyse *change*. But the military historian knows what is victory and what defeat, what is success and what failure. When activities do thus constantly recur, and their success can be assessed by a straightforward standard, it does not seem over-optimistic to assume that we make judgements about them and draw conclusions which will have abiding value.[17]

Central to the military historian's craft, which is here presented as eclipsing that of 'historians of peace', is accordingly the *objective measure of success* and the *making of judgements*. The abiding value of this endeavour, Howard concludes, is to 'directly improve the officer's competence in his profession'.[18] Whereas military historians working on war and society, for instance, have long since moved beyond the confines of operational history, parochial military history remains essentially weaponized history: the instrumentalization of the past as a tool to be deployed in the present; hence the exclusive focus on victories and defeats – the former to be emulated and the latter to be avoided, or what is sometimes referred to as 'good general, bad general'.[19] Parochial military historians may tell themselves that their approach is every bit as comprehensive and sophisticated as that of other historical schools, yet one need only to cast a cursory glance at their theoretical and methodological engagement to recognize the hollowness of such claims. When it was suggested that Nick Lloyd might have benefited from reading Ranajit Guha's article 'The Prose of counter-insurgency', in order to engage more critically with the British sources relating to the Amritsar Massacre, he responded as follows:

> The reason why I did not reference Guha was very simple. Nothing that Guha has written has been of any use in addressing the questions my book seeks to answer: how and why crowds formed in 1919; how the British responded; and in what ways the Government restored control. No amount of post-colonial theory can answer these questions, only extensive research in the archival record.[20]

Theory and methodology, in other words, are regarded as separate issues from archival research – as somehow irrelevant to the historian's real task. This is by no means a unique view, as evidenced by Robert Johnson's recent attempt at addressing postcolonial theory in his book *The Afghan Way of War*:

> Some more recent post-colonial scholars are so concerned to remove the 'taint of colonialism' in their analyses that they have suggested that a bricolage of myth and memory should take the place of 'empiricism' as *the* history of those peoples as they see it. ... Historians, with their preference for the empirical, have still been circumspect. Myths are not a substitute for what Leopold von Ranke called the past *'wie es eigentlich gewesen'* (essentially as it happened); they may augment our understanding of the cultural world view of those who confronted the Europeans, but they do not give us the rendering of strategy or tactical decision-making that would satisfy a rigorous analysis. [Italics in original][21]

While an uncritical investment in the ideals of positivist objectivity may not have been quite so anachronistic in the 1960s, when Howard wrote his article, the enduring empiricism and obeisance to a Rankean view of history exhibited by parochial military historians today seems almost wilfully naïve. Obviously there are such things as historical facts – some things are more likely to have happened than others, and some explanations are more plausible than others. Yet, the belief that it is possible for historians to know the past *as it actually was* will find few advocates within any serious academic discipline today. One need not, of course, subscribe to postmodern relativism or indulge in deliberately obtuse theory, and there is no requirement that all scholars working on non-Western subjects or imperialism must endorse the writings of, say, Edward Said – far from it.[22] Parochial military historians, however, cannot claim to be engaged in the same endeavour as other scholars within the historical field, broadly defined, when they so consistently ignore the key theoretical and methodological developments of the past forty years or more. Many are still wedded to the notion of an absolute truth that can somehow be unearthed like gold nuggets wrestled from the soil through sufficient research in the archives.

It is in that context noteworthy that such military historians often feel persecuted by scholars in other fields who query the overly instrumental and political approach taken to the study of conflicts in the past (and present). In a recent article, Thomas Mockaitis puts the critique of military history down to 'contemporary sensibilities' and the onward march of 'political correctness':

> At their most simplistic, revisionist interpretations condemn counter-insurgency merely because it was a tool of imperialism. Once considered a quaint American reluctance to call a spade a bloody shovel, political correctness appears to have swum the pond to infect British scholarship once deemed immune to such notions. Military historians are suspected of being apologists for the armed forces, and anyone who fails to kick the corpse of the British Empire with sufficient vigour and enthusiasm risks being called a closet imperialist.[23]

Parochial military history, however, is not criticized or ignored because of some prevailing hegemony of leftist or liberal political correctness, as is often alleged. Nor is it silenced because it dares to speak the truth when other historians merely contend themselves with discourse theory and postmodernist jargon. The fact is that it is militarized historians who most often fail to engage with the broader debates within the discipline and the isolation felt by some is thus, to a certain extent, self-imposed. Parochial military history operates as completely distinct from other historical approaches because it concerns itself mainly with questions relevant only to politicians and practitioners, and suitable mainly for the classrooms of military institutions.

Amritsar reimagined

Studies of colonial conflicts and violence offer particularly strong examples of the particular manner in which parochial military historians engage with the past. In the context of the Amritsar Massacre, Nick Lloyd's approach consists mainly in citing and confirming the veracity of British accounts and as such the discussion of the unrest in 1919 is permeated by historical verdicts and pronouncements: The arrest of nationalist leaders 'were not necessarily un-justified', and during riots at Delhi 'the authorities were justified in firing when they did', while two officers who fired on a crowd 'were justified in doing so because anti-European violence had already taken place'.[24] None of this is the language, or indeed conclusions, of a balanced and nuanced historical analysis. On the contrary, it is an account that insists on adopting the perspective of its historical interlocutors. And so Lloyd continues: 'Like many at Amritsar, Dyer was convinced – with some justification – that he was faced with a dangerous rebellion', and 'because he had so few troops he had no option but to keep firing'.[25] The overall effect of British threat-assessments consistently being echoed is ultimately that Dyer is rehabilitated and colonial violence justified. At no point do we divert from the worm's-eye perspective of British officials and achieve anything resembling a critical distance to the historical events or the primary evidence. This analysis amounts to little more than a form of historical ventriloquism, making it difficult to determine where Dyer ends and Lloyd begins.

Any discussion based on the premise that the British Empire was a force for good, and which relies almost exclusively and uncritically on British accounts, will invariably, struggle to make sense of anti-colonial nationalist movements as anything other than the work of agitators misleading a gullible population. In Lloyd's analysis, anti-British sentiments among the local population had nothing to do with British colonial rule but were caused by the irresponsibility of Indian nationalist leaders and the virulence of the native press.[26] It was, Lloyd argues, Gandhi's Satyagraha movement that was at the heart of the unrest and 'that caused crowds to gather and protest against the Rowlatt Bills, although knowing very little about what they actually did'.[27] The implication appears to be that if only Indians had appreciated the exact nature of British legislation, rather than being misled by the likes of Gandhi, they would have realized that they were just and necessary measures, introduced for their own benefit, and they would accordingly not have been protesting against them. The possibility that a colonized population might hold genuine grievances against its rulers, without the need for agitators to rile them up, is never given serious consideration.

A propensity for replicating colonial stereotypes is also revealed in Lloyd's description of the Indian crowds that were involved in the disturbances of 1919.

According to Lloyd, 'Many British witnesses even recorded similar adjectives of the attitude and demeanour of the crowds. … At least three British witnesses all recorded that the crowds were "howling."'[28] 'Howling', however, is not merely a neutral term to describe a rowdy or noisy crowd – it is a highly emotive term that serves to represent Indians as unhuman, irrational and thus devoid of legitimate grievances. The very consistency of the terminology, which Lloyd regards as evidence of its basic veracity, is in fact indicatory of a particular colonial mindset harking back to the 1857 'Mutiny'.[29] Labelling rioters as a 'mob', or rebels as 'terrorists', are not objective and neutral descriptors but deeply political interventions.[30] Since Callwell's *Small Wars* or Gwynn's *Imperial Policing*, the analytical advances made in terms of how to make sense of the motivations and actions of those opposing Western imperialism thus appear to be negligible. A non-Western 'enemy' is constructed by militarized historians as inherently irrational and incapable of engaging in 'proper' politics, much as it was during the heyday of the Empire.[31] While most scholars working on imperialism or global history strive not to replicate colonial stereotypes, those working within the military–academic complex simply adopt the cultural assumptions handed down from their colonial predecessors – hence the enduring popularity and uncritical use of concepts such as 'fanaticism', 'the Arab mind' or indeed the 'Afghan way of war'.[32]

It is in that regard perhaps not so surprising that cultural stereotypes or racial hierarchies should play such little role in the revisionist examination of colonial violence during the unrest in Punjab in 1919. Apart from the widespread use of collective punishment and public flogging, the most infamous reprisal during the aftermath of the disturbances was undoubtedly the so-called 'crawling order' passed by Dyer: in the alley where a female missionary had been assaulted, locals were forced to crawl on all fours. Dyer himself explained the reasoning behind this particular form of humiliation: 'My object was not merely to impress the inhabitants, but to appeal to their moral sense in a way which I knew they would understand.'[33] This was in other words a form of punishment specifically aimed at the cultural sensibilities of Indians and like most of the measures introduced during martial law, it served to emphasize and remind them of what Partha Chatterjee has described as the 'rule of colonial difference'.[34] But in citing Dyer's dismissal of the crawling order as a 'trivial accident' and a 'minor incident', Lloyd similarly concludes that 'what is striking about the incident, is its insignificance'.[35] Lloyd actually argues that 'by denouncing racial humiliation', it was the secretary of state for India, Sir Henry Montagu, who did 'immense damage to the British cause in India' – not the crawling order, which Lloyd considers to be 'understandable, if overzealous'.[36]

The ease with which acts of racial humiliation can be dismissed as 'insignificant' speaks to a particular framework of moral relativism deployed by parochial military historians and is clearly expressed by Mockaitis in the quote at the beginning of this chapter: 'The historian of British counter-insurgency must … evaluate the behaviour of soldiers and police in past campaigns not according to our standards but by those of their own day.'[37] Referring to Huw Bennett's work on British atrocities during the Malayan Emergency, Mockaitis for instance mentions that there were 'only' seventy-seven cases of suspects being shot while trying to escape: 'He [Bennett] is probably correct in concluding that the casualty figures are incomplete, but it is also probable that at least some of those trying to escape were communist insurgents.'[38] If some of those shot 'while trying to escape' (which is simply a euphemism for not taking any prisoners) were in fact communist insurgents, Mockaitis seems to imply, then the actions of the British troops were perhaps not so reprehensible after all and certainly did not amount to 'terrible results'.[39] Historians should not 'moralize' about the past, Mockaitis argues, and few would disagree with this. To refrain from moralizing, however, hardly suggests that one should instead seek to relativize and thus effectively legitimize historical violence, which is essentially what happens when British imperialism is compared to that of the French or Belgians. Some historians appear to operate within a barely concealed military paradigm where collateral damage is inevitable and therefore fully acceptable. Since their history consists exclusively of judging the past 'on its own terms', they end up having to justify violence regardless of the circumstances.[40]

One of the key points of criticism raised against Dyer, then and now, is the fact that he kept up the firing for ten full minutes on a crowd of thousands unable to escape. In Lloyd's account, however, the death toll was not so much the result of Dyer's decision to open fire but rather an unfortunate accident – and one that was moreover fully in compliance with the minimum force doctrine:

> Dyer continued to fire for one simple reason: *there were still people in the Jallianwala Bagh and it was his duty to disperse them.* ... Admittedly, it took a considerable amount of time for the thousands of people to disperse because there were only several small exits out of the Bagh, but Dyer would not have known this. Therefore, from a purely legal perspective, Dyer *did* fire until the crowd dispersed. Unfortunately, it took ten minutes for this to occur. Had there been more exits, Dyer's men would not have had to fire for so long. [italics in original][41]

Readers can make of such an argument what they want, but the claim that Dyer was simply trying to disperse the crowd is entirely unsustainable and does not correspond with the established facts. At no point did the crowd actually turn against the troops, which means that all the casualties were incurred as people were running away from the firing, that is, dispersing, and in some instances, being shot as they were trying to scale the walls to escape. Lloyd also implies that Dyer could not order the firing to stop sooner because he could not make himself heard above the noise – yet he had no problem directing his troops to fire towards the very exits that he allegedly sought to disperse the crowd through.[42] To suggest that the massacre was carried out in accordance to the minimum force doctrine is self-evidently nonsensical and begs the question of what maximum force would have looked like.

In the context of Amritsar, military historians and practitioners have for almost a century focused on the technical justification and legal framework for the deployment of force rather than questioning the assumptions concerning the perceived necessity and supposed efficacy of such violence. The lessons that Gwynn in 1934 drew from the circumstances surrounding the Amritsar Massacre was that the exact legal framework and relationship between civil and military authorities must be clarified prior to deployment, that warning shots should be fired and the wounded cared for. If we look at the findings of the Hunter Inquiry, and the lessons identified by Gwynn, it is thus difficult not to conclude that if only Dyer had fired warning shots and provided care for the wounded he would not have been censured for massacring the crowd gathered at the Jallianwala Bagh. Yet if the Amritsar Massacre is to provide any lessons, or to put it in less instrumental terms, offer any historical insights, it would surely be that colonial authorities often misread the nature of local unrest and furthermore drew on inappropriate historical precedents to inform their threat assessment and guide their response. Gwynn himself touched on these very points stating that 'when rioting results from an organised movement, the Mutiny becomes present to all European minds'; crucially he also added that 'the traditions of the Indian Mutiny, for example, would hardly be a safe guide for officers called on to deal with a modern revolutionary outbreak'.[43] The 'traditions of the Mutiny', however, aptly sums up the very rationale that informed the British threat assessment and Dyer's actions at Amritsar:

> It is sufficient to say that I know that the final crisis had come, and that the assembly was primarily of the same mobs which had murdered and looted and burnt three days previously, and showed their truculence and contempt of the troops during the intervening days, that it was a deliberate challenge to the Government forces, and that if it were not dispersed effectively, with sufficient impression upon the designs and arrogance of the rebels and their followers we should be overwhelmed during the night or the next day by a combination of the city gangs and of the still more formidable multitude from the villages.[44]

The people gathered in the Jallianwala Bagh on 13 April, however, were almost certainly not the same ones who had participated in the riots of the 10th – these had consisted mainly of Kashmiri Muslims and low-caste Hindus, neither of whom figure extensively on the list later compiled of the victims of the massacre.[45] Amritsar had moreover been quiet ever since the 10th and when Dyer entered the Jallianwala Bagh there were neither 'rebels' nor 'multitudes from the villages' ready to invade the British lines. The anti-colonial violence of 1919 was brutal and explosive, but it was not the result of a conspiracy, nor can it appropriately be characterized as a 'rebellion'. The British misreading of the unrest can in fact only be described as a catastrophic instance of what the late C. A. Bayly termed 'information panic'.[46]

What Lloyd and others fail to grasp is that there is a crucial distinction between a critical study of imperialism and a critique of imperialism. A critical reading of a primary source need not amount to a moral condemnation of the long-dead author, nor entail an implicit assumption that he or she ought to have acted differently – most scholars have moved beyond the teleological judgement of the past as the main occupation of the historical inquiry. The question of whether or not Dyer was justified in shooting on the crowd at the Jallianwala Bagh is in fact analytically meaningless and cannot form the basis of a serious academic inquiry. Most military historians nevertheless seem beholden to legal authority and invoke British military law as the ultimate arbiter in the question of justification.[47] The Amritsar Massacre may have been an unfortunate incident, so the argument goes, but since the gathered Indians were clearly breaking the law and the firing was carried out in accordance to the doctrine of minimum force, Dyer's actions were ultimately defensible. When Lloyd writes that Dyer 'had to open fire' he is making a historical judgement – one that he moreover let stand as the final words of the final chapter of his book. One does not have to imagine the same remark being used in a study of, say, Barbi Yar, the Katyn Massacre or the shooting of a prisoner by Nguyễn Ngọc Loan during the Vietnam War to realize just how problematic it is for historians to see like a soldier and identify so completely with their historical interlocutors. If the verdict of nationalist historiography is one of 'premeditated murder', Lloyd's is unequivocally one of 'involuntary manslaughter'. Neither is analytically satisfactory nor academically astute.

Conclusion

In a recent radio interview explicitly celebrating the close relationship between the British army and military historians, Antony Beevor highlighted what he perceived to be the 'wrong' way of studying conflicts and the military:

> One of the problems certainly with history recently is war is being a very controversial aspect and it's attracted sociologists, cultural historians, and they have tried to impose an ideological grid on an organization they don't fully understand.[48]

Proper military history, we are given to understand, is accordingly one that requires the historian to write from within the institution of the army and, it follows, in sympathy with the army and in recognition of the basic necessity of conflict. While parochial military historians perceive their own approach to be rigorously objective, it is in fact weaponized history, as this chapter has suggested, and invariably yoked to one agenda or another.[49] Ultimately, Nick Lloyd is no more unique to British parochial military history than Dyer was to British rule in India, and he evidently took inspiration from Andrew Roberts' particular brand of Empire nostalgia touted in the 2006 book *A History of the English-Speaking Peoples Since 1900*. Roberts' final remarks about the Amritsar Massacre reflect the general thrust of the argument:

> If the Amritsar district, Punjab region or northern India generally had carried on in revolt, many more than 379 people would have lost their lives. (As a postscript, it is worth recording that, on 6 June 1984, the Government of India sent tanks against Sikh extremists who were inside the Golden Temple in Amritsar, massacring over 250 people. The orders were given by Indira Gandhi, who largely escaped global criticism since she was not a British imperialist like Reginald Dyer.)[50]

In Robert's reassessment, then, the Amritsar Massacre was implicitly justified and, furthermore, as the postscript reminds us, criticism of Dyer is misplaced as violence in independent India has not been denounced in the same manner.[51] Lloyd obligingly picked up from where Roberts left off and wrote an entire book about the Amritsar Massacre, replete with an epilogue in which the violence of 1919 was compared with the attack on the Golden Temple in 1984. Historical comparisons are, of course, perfectly valid modes of analysis, but in Lloyd's teleological account the brutality of the government of independent India retrospectively exonerates that of the British colonial state and supposedly 'gives lie to the accusation that the British ruled Punjab with anything approaching the "iron fist" of legend'.[52] Lloyd's conclusion is indeed that Indians were far better off under the British:

> Even if one considers the British response to have been disproportionate or overly brutal, the number of dead and wounded from the disorders remains tiny when compared with the vast numbers who became victims of the struggles in the 1980s. The Indian National Congress began the decade on a crusade to win the Hindu vote and in the Punjab it could only do so by increasing communal tensions. This was the reality of democracy in India, a far more volatile and unstable type of rule than the British imposed.[53]

The resurgence of Raj nostalgia among military historians thus appears to have a clear, and wistful, message: if only 'we' had stayed on, had remained firm in the face of adversity and not given in to anti-colonial nationalism or the self-hatred of liberals, the violence of partition or later conflicts would never have happened.[54] The fact that Lloyd believes that the Amritsar Massacre and the assault on the Golden Temple in 1984 are comparable events speaks for itself. One was a massacre of an unarmed gathering, while the other was a military assault on a heavily fortified position held by armed militants. The British incurred no casualties at Jallianwala Bagh, because it was a one-sided massacre and not a battle. During Operation Blue Star, Indian forces suffered 83 killed and 220 wounded during the two-day encounter, which left more than 500 militants and civilians dead.[55] These are indisputable facts, not 'post-colonial' spin. The only thing that the two events have in common is the fact that they both occurred at Amritsar; the people involved were different, the politics were different and the circumstances were different. The tragic irony of an Englishman proclaiming that British rule was preferable to Indian independence, however, seems to be lost on Lloyd.

Parochial military historians are today rewriting the history of Britain in a manner that allows the Empire to retain its respectability and afterglow of global status.[56] It turns the slaughter of the battlefields of the First World War into a 'just war' and the massacres of decolonization into unfortunate 'excesses', which leaves the prestige and honour of Britannia untarnished.[57] The primary function of this scholarship is thus to reassure Britons of the twenty-first century that they have nothing to be ashamed about, that what we thought of as defeats and disasters were really nothing of the sort.[58] The general tenor of these accounts reflects an unabashed nostalgia for the Empire and are indeed characterized by a sense of sentimentality and loss – clearly reflected in Lloyd's article for the *Telegraph* entitled 'Amritsar massacre: how Britain lost the will to rule'.[59] Like the famous Victorian battle-paintings that turned military catastrophes into moments of national heroism and pride, Lloyd's account thus turns the unrest in Punjab into a story of the brave officers on the spot, betrayed by incompetent politicians, yet doing their very best under difficult circumstances.[60] This is a recurring trope in parochial military histories, especially of the British Empire. In a recent study of the British political agents on the North-West Frontier, for example, Christian Tripodi argues that 'there are grounds for genuine admiration and reflection on a job well done in the main'.[61] This is not history as much as eulogy, and by insisting that the Amritsar Massacre was a unique event, and that Dyer's actions were isolated, much as Churchill did in 1920, violence can further be marginalized within the grander narrative of British imperialism.[62] This sentiment was expressed in no uncertain terms by the popular historian Lawrence James when he responded to the discovery of yet more evidence of British brutality in Kenya during the 1950s: 'Yes, mistakes were made, but we must never stop being proud of the Empire.'[63]

It is of course possible to describe, analyse and make sense of historical occurrences of violence without having to either condone or condemn them. In fact, such blatant partisanship effectively precludes a deeper understanding of complex events. If one aspires towards a fair and balanced view, to use Lloyd's terms, it is incumbent to maintain a critical distance to the primary material regardless of its provenance. History is indisputably relevant in the present, but it cannot be written for the explicit purpose of being weaponized in today's politics and conflicts. It may be the case that parochial military historians are perfectly happy to carry on the way they have: enjoying solid sales and a huge readership in addition to an enviable 'impact factor' in terms of military engagement. But if they wish to engage with the broader field of history, on equal terms, they will have to make a choice – one cannot serve both Clio and Mars and do both well.

Notes

1   This chapter has benefited from the comments and suggestions of Mark Condos, Dan Todman, Gajendra Singh, Huw Bennett, Jonathan Boff and Gavin Rand. Needless to say, the views expressed are entirely my own. I am indebted for the generous support of the British Academy and the Leverhulme Trust.
2   Thomas R. Mockaitis, 'The Minimum Force Debate: Contemporary Sensibilities Meet Imperial Practice', *Small Wars & Insurgencies* 23, nos. 4–5 (October to December 2012): 762–80, 766.
3   Nick Lloyd, *The Amritsar Massacre: The Untold Story of One Fateful Day* (London: I. B. Tauris, 2011), 203.
4   For an overview of this literature see Ian Beckett, 'British Counter-Insurgency: A Historiographical Reflection', *Small Wars & Insurgencies* 23, nos. 4–5 (2012): 781–98.
5   See Charles Townshend, *Britain's Civil Wars: Counterinsurgency in the Twentieth Century* (London: Faber and Faber, 1986), 134–9; and Hew Strachan, *The Politics of the British Army* (Oxford: Clarendon Press, 1997), 166–9.
6   Major General Sir Charles W. Gwynn, *Imperial Policing* (London: Macmillan, 1934). See also Simeon Shoul, *Soldiers, Riot Control, and Aid to the Civil Power in India, Egypt, and Palestine, 1919-1939* (unpublished PhD thesis, University College London, 2006); and Bell R. Irish, *The Amritsar Massacre: The Origins of the British Approach of Minimal Force on Public Order Operations* (Fort Leavenworth, KS: School of Advanced Military Studies, 2009).
7   See for instance Thomas R. Mockaitis, *British Counterinsurgency: 1919-1960* (London: Macmillan in association with King's College, 1990); and John A. Nagl, *Learning to Eat Soup with a Knife: Counterinsurgency Lessons from Malaya and Vietnam* (Chicago: University of Chicago Press, 2005).
8   Rod Thornton, 'The British Army and the Origins of its Minimum Force Philosophy', *Small Wars & Insurgencies* 15, no. 1 (2004): 83–106, 86. Following Thornton's line of reasoning, it seems the Amritsar Massacre would never have happened if only Dyer had gone to public school and read more Henty.

9 Huw Bennett, *Fighting the Mau Mau: The British Army and Counter-insurgency in the Kenya Emergency* (Cambridge: Cambridge University Press, 2013). See also Matthew Hughes, 'The Banality of Brutality: British Armed Forces and the Repression of the Arab Revolt in Palestine, 1936–39', *English Historical Review* CXXIV, no. 507 (2009): 313–54; Bruno Reis, 'The Myth of British Minimum Force in Counterinsurgency Campaigns During Decolonization', *The Journal of Strategic Studies* 34, no. 2 (2011): 253–79; David French, 'Nasty not Nice: British Counter-insurgency Doctrine and Practice, 1945-1967', *Small Wars & Insurgencies* 23, nos. 4–5 (2012): 744–61. Rod Thornton and Huw Bennett's debate in the pages of *Small Wars & Insurgencies* is particularly instructive in this regard: Bennett, 'The Other Side of the COIN: Minimum and Exemplary Force in British Counterinsurgency in Kenya', *Small Wars & Insurgencies* 18, no. 4 (2007): 638–64; Thornton, '"Minimum Force": A Reply to Huw Bennett', *Small Wars & Insurgencies* 20, no. 1 (2009): 215–26; Bennett, 'Minimum Force in British Counterinsurgency', *Small Wars & Insurgencies* 21, no. 3 (2010): 459–75.

10 Huw Bennett, 'Soldiers in the Court Room: The British Army's Part in the Kenya Emergency under the Legal Spotlight', *The Journal of Imperial and Commonwealth History* 39, no. 5 (2011): 717–30.

11 See Derek Sayer, 'British Reactions to the Amritsar Massacre 1919-1920', *Past & Present* 131, no. 1 (1991): 130–64; and Nigel Collett, *The Butcher of Amritsar: General Reginald Dyer* (London, 2005). The most recent scholarship touching on the subject includes Taylor Sherman, *State Violence and Punishment in India, 1919-1956* (London: Hambledon and London, 2010); Erez Manela, *The Wilsonian Moment: Self-determination and the International Origins of Anticolonial Nationalism* (Oxford and New York: Oxford University Press, 2007); Susan Kingsley Kent, *Aftershocks: Politics and Trauma in Britain, 1918-1931* (Basingstoke: Palgrave, 2009); and Robert McLain, *Gender and Violence: The Road to Amritsar, 1914-1919* (Basingstoke: Palgrave, 2014).

12 These are the official numbers and contemporary Indian estimates are considerably higher, see *Correspondence between the Government of India and the Secretary of State for India on the Report of Lord Hunter's Committee* (London, 1920), and *Report of the Commissioners appointed by the Punjab Sub-Committee of the Indian National Congress, vol. I* (Lahore, 1920).

13 K. L. Tuteja, 'Jallianwala Bagh: A Critical Juncture in the Indian National Movement', *Social Scientist* 25, nos. 1/2 (January to February, 1997): 25–61.

14 Lloyd, *The Amritsar Massacre*, xxx. For a more blunt reiteration of his argument, see Lloyd's response to my review of his book: http://www.history.ac.uk/reviews/review/1224, 'Author's response'.

15 See reviews in *BBC History Magazine* (27 January 2012), *Mars & Clio: The Newsletter of the British Commission for Military History* (Autumn 2011), and *Contemporary Review* (September 2012). The review by Nigel Collett, it might be noted, is highly critical, see *Asian Review of Books* (17 July 2012). See also Mockaitis 'The Minimum Force Debate', 763–4; and Daniel Whittingham, '"Savage Warfare": C.E. Callwell, the Roots of Counter-insurgency, and the Nineteenth Century Context', *Small Wars & Insurgencies* 23, nos. 4–5 (October to December 2012): 591–607, 604.

16 See Henry A. Giroux, *The University in Chains: Confronting the Military-Industrial-Academic Complex* (Boulder, CO and London: Paradigm Publishers, 2007). The Defence Studies Department, affiliated with King's College London, is an obvious, though by no means a singular, example and it is indeed noteworthy how many academics are today employed by institutions catering to the requirements of

the military – in Britain and elsewhere. Other examples include intelligence and terrorism studies, which have similarly experienced an explosive growth since 2001.

17 Michael Howard, 'The Use and Abuse of Military History', *Royal United Services Institution Journal* 107, no. 625 (1962): 4–10, 7.

18 Ibid., 10.

19 See Mark Moyar, 'The Current State of Military History', *The Historical Journal* 50 (2007): 225–40. See also: http://warhistorian.blogspot.co.uk/. Niall Ferguson and Graham Allison's recent call for a 'council of historians' to advise American politicians reflects a similar view of the instrumental utility of the past in the present, see *The Atlantic*, September 2016.

20 Lloyd, 'Author's response'. The article in question is Ranajit Guha, 'The Prose of Counter-Insurgency', in *Selected Subaltern Studies*, ed. Ranajit Guha and Gayatri Chakravorty Spivak (Oxford: Oxford University Press, 1988), 45–88.

21 Rob Johnson, *The Afghan Way of War* (London: Hurst, 2011), 31. Some might say that Johnson's reading of Subaltern Studies and Said is less than comprehensive.

22 My own work, it might be added, is by no means uncritical of scholarship in the Saidian vein; see Ricardo Roque and Kim A. Wagner (eds), *Engaging Colonial Knowledge: Reading European Archives in World History* (Cambridge Imperial and Post-Colonial Studies Series, Basingstoke: Palgrave, 2011).

23 Mockaitis, 'The Minimum Force Debate', 764.

24 Lloyd, *The Amritsar Massacre*, 75 and 100.

25 Ibid., 178 and 198.

26 Ibid., 36, 64–6.

27 Ibid., 127, see also 31–41, and 197.

28 Ibid., 74.

29 Historians should obviously cite their sources, yet they cannot uncritically adopt the language of these sources, and it is indeed noteworthy that Lloyd himself describes a 'baying' crowd of natives without quotation marks; ibid., 79.

30 The same obviously applies to positive labels used in nationalist accounts, including 'martyrs' or 'freedom fighters'.

31 Recognizing a broader range of motivation behind anti-colonial protests does not, it might be added, amount to a justification of anti-colonial violence, nor reify anti-colonial nationalist claims to legitimacy.

32 See Priya Satia, *Spies in Arabia: The Great War and the Cultural Foundations of Britain's Covert Empire in the Middle East* (New York: Oxford University Press, 2008). Patrick Porter's work constitutes a rare exception within military history, see his *Military Orientalism: Eastern War Through Western Eyes* (London: C. Hurst & Co, 2009).

33 'Statement by Brig.-General R.E.H. Dyer, C.B.' (3 July 1920), Disturbances in the Punjab (London, 1920), 17.

34 Partha Chatterjee, *The Nation and its Fragments: Colonial and Postcolonial Histories* (Delhi, 1994), 10 and 19. As a point of comparison, it might be worth recalling that even during the 'Troubles' in Ireland, when the British pursued a brutal campaign of reprisals, there was still nothing comparable to the racialized forms of punishment meted out to Indians in Punjab in 1919, see for instance D. M. Leeson, *The Black and Tans: British Police and Auxiliaries in the Irish War of Independence* (Oxford: Oxford University Press, 2011).

35 Lloyd, *The Amritsar Massacre*, 136. Lloyd cites an instance when four Europeans were fined by the authorities in Punjab for not letting their vehicles be impounded for official use to argue that martial law was 'not always enforced on a solely racial basis'; ibid., 138.

36 Ibid., 136 and 202.
37 Mockaitis, 'The Minimum Force Debate', 766.
38 Ibid., 768.
39 Ibid.
40 It may be noted that Mockaitis describes the American campaigns in the Philippines at the beginning of the twentieth century – which saw the introduction of the 'water-cure' (the predecessor to waterboarding), widespread burning of villages and indiscriminate killing of locals – as a 'highly effective approach to counter-insurgency', the success of which 'depended on more than brute force'; ibid., 774. For a less uncritical perception of American colonial warfare, see Brian McAllister Linn, *The Philippine War, 1899-1902* (Lawrence, KS: University Press of Kansas, 2000); and Russell Roth, *Muddy Glory: America's 'Indian Wars' in the Philippines 1899-1935* (W. Hanover, MA: Christopher Publishing House, 1981).
41 Lloyd, *The Amritsar Massacre*, 179.
42 'Statement by Dyer' (3 July 1920), 8; and report of Capt. F. C. Briggs; ibid., Appendix A, 25.
43 Gwynn, *Imperial Policing*, 6 and 37. See also Kim A. Wagner, '"Treading Upon Fires": The "Mutiny"-Motif and Colonial Anxieties in British India', *Past & Present* 218, no. 1 (February 2013): 159–97.
44 'Statement by Dyer' (3 July 1920), 7.
45 See testimony of Mr Miles Irving and Lt. Colonel Henry Smith before the Hunter Committee, *Disorders Inquiry (Hunter) Committee 1919-1920: Evidence vol III: Amritsar* (Calcutta, 1920), 9 and 52; and *Report of the Commissioners appointed by the Punjab Sub-Committee of the Indian National Congress, vol. I-II* (Lahore, 1920).
46 C. A. Bayly, *Empire and Information: Intelligence Gathering and Social Communication in India, 1780-1870* (Cambridge: Cambridge University Press, 1996), 143, 149, 171–4 and 316. For a more detailed discussion of 'information panic', or what in military jargon would be described as 'intelligence failure', see Wagner, 'Treading upon Fires'.
47 Within the colonial context, the adherence to the rule of law was always contingent on practical requirements, and in reality it left much room for both confusion and discretionary powers, see Nasser Hussain, *The Jurisprudence of Emergency: Colonialism and the Rule of Law* (Ann Arbor, 2003); and R. W. Kostal, *A Jurisprudence of Power: Victorian Empire and the Rule of Law* (Oxford: Oxford University Press, 2008).
48 World at One, BBC Radio 4, 25 June 2015: http://www.bbc.co.uk/programmes/p02vkgp5.
49 It goes without saying that this is also the case with anti-colonial nationalist historiography – to mention but one example.
50 Andrew Roberts, *A History of the English-Speaking Peoples since 1900* (London: Weidenfeld & Nicolson, 2006), 153.
51 It may be noted that Roberts' assumption is incorrect: the Amritsar Massacre did not put a stop to the unrest, as even Lloyd acknowledges; some of the most extensive violence occurred on 14 April at Gujranwala and only gradually abated over the following days. To suggest that the unrest would spread throughout northern India and that more people would have died had Dyer not opened fire at Jallianwala Bagh is in any case pure speculation – or, it might be noted, exactly what the British claimed at the time.
52 Lloyd, *The Amritsar Massacre*, 208.
53 Ibid., 209.

54   And, it might be added, we could still have our feet manicured by attentive native servants while reading the newspaper on the veranda of our bungalows.

55   See Mark Tully and Satish Jacob, *Amritsar: Mrs Gandhi's Last Battle* (London: Cape, 1985).

56   The outpouring of jingoistic sentiments before and after the EU referendum of June 2016, colloquially known as 'Brexit', would seem to bear out this point.

57   Lloyd goes so far as to argue that Indian nationalists 'were wholly responsible for the bloodshed that followed, not the British', and claims that it was the latter who were the real victims of the Amritsar disturbances in 1919; Lloyd, 'Author's response'.

58   I am not suggesting that Britons should be ashamed of their past, only that the celebration of one's history tends to be based largely on politicized mythology rather than a comprehensive understanding of the complexities of the past.

59   *The Telegraph*, 3 January 2014.

60   The liberal politician Edwin Montagu comes a close second after Gandhi as the arch villain in Lloyd's narrative, and we are repeatedly reminded of how disastrous his handling of the affair was: 'This was not the way to run an empire.' Lloyd, *The Amritsar Massacre*, 161.

61   Christian Tripodi, *Edge of Empire: The British Political Officer and Tribal Administration on the North-West Frontier, 1877-1947* (Farnham: Ashgate, 2011), 228.

62   This furthermore explains the readiness with which the British prime minister David Cameron cited Churchill when visiting the Jallianwala Bagh memorial in 2013. See also Purnima Bose, *Organizing Empire: Individualism, Collective Agency, and India* (Durham: Duke University Press, 2003).

63   *Daily Mail*, 18 April 2012.

2

Confronting Revolt in France's Interwar Empire: Counter-insurgency in 1920s Morocco and Syria

Martin Thomas

How should we read the near simultaneous outbreak of major rebellions against French imperial authority in Morocco and Syria during 1925? Efforts by the Riffian Berbers of northern Morocco to carve out an autonomous zone in the highlands separating the French Moroccan Protectorate from its smaller Spanish neighbour escalated into war between 1920 and 1926. The French authorities in Rabat, having stood back from Spanish campaigning in the Rif in the early 1920s, went to war against several of the region's Berber clans in April 1925. The Syrian Mandate exploded into rebellion meanwhile after a local revolt centred in the southern Jabal Druze region in mid-1925 quickly spread to other provincial centres. Violence reached Damascus and its hinterland within weeks.

Should these uprisings, the largest, most sustained revolts within the French empire of the early twentieth century, be placed within the broader analytical field of contested decolonization? Or are they better understood, not as 'late colonial' phenomena, but as reactions to early colonial implantation? Much would suggest that the latter makes more sense. France's immersion in the Rif War was bound up with the northerly consolidation of its Moroccan Protectorate in the teeth of virulent local opposition. Equally, Syria's Great Revolt originated in the political enactment of a League of Nations type A Mandate about which Syria's people had been denied any say. It was surely no coincidence that each uprising flared in interior spaces where French dominion had been, until very recently, more nominal than real. Indeed, each was catalysed by basic administrative changes that threatened customary ways of life, from agricultural production and the payment of taxes to the application of civil law and the selection of local representatives to uphold it. Focusing on the grievances that triggered rebellious acts does not imply that French policy choices were of secondary importance; far from it: the two are inseparable. It follows that a sequential view of Moroccan or Syrian reaction to prior French action is an analytical dead end. A more promising way forward is to treat the contributory factors to French colonial insurgencies and violent 'counter' responses to them holistically; their local and 'micro' dynamics meshed with their imperial and 'macro' determinants.[1]

At the micro level Morocco's Rif War and Syria's Great Revolt shared certain attributes. Each presented a major, even an existential, challenge to imperial state-building efforts still in their infancy. The French Protectorate in Morocco, formally announced by the Treaty of Fez in 1912, had been prefigured in a decade of creeping frontier infringements and informal political influence.[2] Slowed by the First World War, the extension of French governance was still contested throughout much of the Moroccan interior during the governorship of the Protectorate's foundational figure, Marshal Louis-Hubert Lyautey.[3] Such was the intensity of local hostility to the nature and pace of French administrative change in Syria by 1925 that it is worth recalling that France's titular primacy as holder of the League of Nations Mandate was only internationally ratified two years earlier. A functioning Syrian Arab Republic had, by that point, been violently overthrown, a partition between Syria and Lebanon arbitrarily imposed, and contentious reorganizations of federal and provincial government pursued.[4] For all that, in Mandate Syria, even more than in Protectorate Morocco, these waves of administrative experimentation only underlined the depth and diversity of opposition to any French presence. In Morocco and Syria, powerful communal allegiances and simmering anger about loss of land and status, fostered regional and transnational networks of cooperation among those disadvantaged by the abrogation of customary rights and the consequent deepening of French regulation.[5] Yawning gaps remained between what imperial officials sought and what could be made to work.

Pulling back to the macro level, the broader issue of decolonization hoves into view. If neither Morocco nor Syria could be accommodated within the French 'imperial nation state', it is perhaps misleading to identify any cleavage between their initial conquest and their ultimate escape from empire.[6] Take the basic methods of rule adopted. Throughout French-ruled North Africa and the new Middle East Mandates similar administrative practices devolved limited powers to conservative, often Europeanized Muslim elites. These arrangements, however expedient in the short term, bore the seeds of their own destruction. During the interwar period, one propaganda victory common to anti-colonial movements in the Maghreb, Syria and Lebanon was to convince domestic audiences (and some international observers of the League of Nations' Permanent Mandates Commission – PMC) that local authority figures who served imperial government were irredeemably compromised by it.[7] Popular support for integral nationalism grew and, since anti-colonial groups and cultural associations were repeatedly outlawed, backing for more extreme, even violent, political dissent increased as well.[8]

Turning to the repression enacted when dissent turned violent, again it is continuity, not cleavage, that emerges. French counter-insurgency practices employed against Riffian Berbers and Syrian oppositionists in the 1920s were part of a longer process of organizational learning, refined during decades of military government in the colonies in the late 1800s and set to continue until empire's dissolution in the latter twentieth century. Evolving French repressive techniques of social control evinced the same basic preoccupations throughout. Those to be studied here include administrative pluralism (the persistence, in other words, of local legal regimes and governmental structures alongside colonial ones), restricting access to resources, and abiding concern with what were thought to be key constituencies among the colonial civilian population, including women and waged workers. Counter-insurgency in 1920s Morocco and Syria, in other words, not only anticipated the practices and techniques of France's later and larger decolonization conflicts, it was in many respects identical to them.

The colonial context

Before analyzing France's 1920s counter-insurgency efforts in more detail, we need to consider the broader imperial context that informed them. Styles of colonial governance in French Africa, the Indochina federation and, in adapted form, the Levant Mandates emerged from colonial officials' understanding of community hierarchies, religious affiliations and the political economy of peasant societies. As foodstuff and other commodity prices rose sharply in the 1920s these agricultural societies were compelled to adjust to the demands of colonial economic policies that valued export production above all. Colonial officials invested greater effort into calculating the productive capacity of the lands and peoples under their sway and, more pertinent to us here, the ability of local communities to withstand heightened colonial exactions. Data of all kinds was sought and accumulated. In practice, the construction of this knowledge bank rested heavily on anthropological and ethnographic surveys of rural and urban communities as well as information about political geography and agronomics.[9] In epistemological terms, the information acquired was lent particular constructions both by those who gathered the material and those who exploited it. This work of compiling social inventories of community cultures was also undertaken enthusiastically by numerous soldier-administrators in Morocco and Syria. These were usually 'native affairs officers', regional officials who saw themselves as pioneers of imperial implantation.[10] In Foucaultian terms, their role was to instrumentalize colonial governmentality, to codify colonial subjects, to monitor them as groups and individuals, and thus to make orderly regulation tangible. These were methods intrinsic to French policing, which was imbued with Republican concepts that linked the preservation of public order and close surveillance of the economically marginalized to efficient governance and the avoidance of revolutionary upheaval.[11]

Internal security forces in the French empire drew heavily on the accumulated administrative 'knowledge' of the dependent population and echoed the concern with data collection and profiling of potential subversives that characterized policing in the Third Republic. Policing in the colonies was further politicized by the fact that the maintenance of 'law and order' entailed the imposition of distinct hierarchies – of race and gender, of culture and belief. In this layered conception of society, crimes against the person as well as thefts or destruction of property were easily conflated with overtly political violence because they were frequently viewed as lesser manifestations – or portents – of a breakdown of colonial control. Marieke Bloembergen captures this schizoid quality of colonial police forces perfectly in her description of the Dutch East Indies example:

> The modern police in the Dutch East Indies ... was meant to be the answer to a typical colonial problem: the struggle of a colonial state that wanted to be civilized, but witnessed its legitimacy crumbling. Compelled to use force to impose its authority, the state nonetheless sought to govern by consent. ... Since the colonial

police was the instrument used to pursue these diverse goals, it became a two-headed beast: in trying to safeguard the state's authority, it provoked resistance, while in reaching out to fulfill society's need for security, it required and sought the cooperation of the local population.[12]

Whereas colonial security forces typically maintained that their efforts to maintain public order benefited rulers and ruled alike, the fact that their day-to-day operations overwhelmingly targeted dependent populations suggested otherwise.[13] For instance, the nature of colonial control made for remarkably similarly policing systems across territories. Centralized command structures, a strong paramilitary component and the creation of secret police units to monitor oppositional activity were, for instance, common to French, British and Portuguese colonial police forces.[14] These structural similarities reflected the fact that colonial governance provoked generic security problems.

Broadly comparable trends towards heightened economic extraction, increased tax collection, and closer identification of security forces with state efforts to divide communities were evident in the two regions of the French empire in which insurgencies took root in the 1920s: Morocco and Syria.[15] Annual collection of taxes was frequently conducted under the aegis of police or military intelligence personnel, especially in rural districts. This was important work. In Mandate Syria and Lebanon, tax burdens followed political rights and access to education in favouring non-Muslim and non-Sunni minorities.[16] At the same time, taxes of peasant cultivators predicated on crop yield and livestock counts undermined traditional, communally based agricultural practices in favour of fiscally regulated sharecropping. In French North Africa taxation policy was also bound up with broader issues of property rights, agricultural tenancy and European expropriation of the best cultivable land. One factor remained constant across all of these territories: Muslim peasant smallholders provided more revenue than any other sector in the indigenous economy, making taxation of land and livestock contentious and politically explosive.[17] Military recruitment was another bone of contention. Differing army practice between territories was increasingly determined by local security needs and fear of communal dissent. In Morocco, where the demands of internal pacification operations were greatest, locally raised Armée d'Afrique regiments were entirely composed of long-service professionals. In Algeria, a mixture of long-service enrolment and short-service conscription was employed, the assumption being that most tirailleur algérien regiments would serve in metropolitan France, leaving internal security in the hands of Foreign Legion and West African tirailleur sénégalais units. By contrast, in Tunisia, there were no professional Armée d'Afrique regiments, and short-service conscription was the norm.

Differing French recruitment practices revealed something deeper about Republican ideas of citizens' obligations to the nation, especially in times of crisis. Subjecting oneself to the discipline of a military organization was highly gendered and racially coded. Men were required to substitute their traditional masculine role as head of household for a military masculinity that, in some ways, negated ethnic particularity while, in others reaffirming it as soldiers became the martial embodiment of the nation.[18] People in the colonies enjoyed neither equal citizenship nor nationhood whereas, of course, their French overseers did. What is more, the French people had – famously – engaged in revolutionary violence to achieve citizenship, and France had only recently fought a war of national survival. As anti-colonialists such as the young Nguyễn Ái Quốc (the future Ho Chi Minh) were asking, why weren't colonial peoples entitled to do the same?[19] As historian John Horne notes, by the start of the twentieth-century liberal states had accepted the principle that democratic revolution and wars of national liberation could be legitimate responses to unjust government – at least within Europe. Civilian participation in national defence was revalidated as intrinsic to the obligations of citizenship.[20] In the aftermath of the First World War, a conflict in which tens of thousands of colonial subjects had fought and died assisting these liberal states, the hypocrisy of citizenship denied to colonial peoples became harder to conceal. Nowhere more so than in the francophone world. The supposedly universal, colour-blind values of French republicanism, in other words, clashed with the stark reality of racial differentiation in the empire.[21]

Targeted repression?

The fact remained that any equation between Republican citizenship and defence of the nation was difficult to invoke colonially where rights of citizenship and putative nationhood were substantially withheld. Admittedly, by the early 1920s French imperial authorities were conceding additional individual rights to a favoured few. But there were few signs that the choice of targets in repressive operations would be similarly selective. French military and police commanders in the empire instead justified their extensive powers of detention and punishment in preventive terms, maintaining that swift repressive measures either averted social disorder or contained it. Dedicated paramilitary gendarmeries, garrison troops and, with growing frequency, military airplanes were the cutting edge of consequent anti-insurgency tactics. All three were deployed against the insurgencies in the Rif highlands and in Syria's cities and countryside.

Once again, it is tempting to consider the First World War as pivotal here. Empire-wide, wartime rural uprisings, urban riots, workplace protests and other forms of civil disobedience precipitated clashes with police and troops – what, in Charles Tilly's terms, would be described as 'contentious action'.[22] Among French colonies badly affected, Algeria and much of French West Africa stood out. Reactions there were sharpest to the recruitment drives of 1915 to 1917. At the height of the West African disturbances from December 1915 to July 1916 French soldiers and police destroyed over 200 villages along the Niger River valley in punishment for dissent, sadly, already a commonplace of colonial counter-insurgency.[23] Empire unrest was quickly followed during 1918–19 by a spate of race riots in French industrial cities, which targeted colonial immigrant labourers.[24] The subsequent repatriation (some might say 'expulsion') of thousands of these workers nourished the connection in security force thinking between orderliness and tighter restrictions over colonial population movement.[25]

The example of immigrant war workers in France reminds us that the rapid expansion of colonial security service activity mirrored surveillance practices developed behind the frontlines during wartime. A preoccupation with leftist sedition and incipient anti-colonial nationalist organization, plus a willingness to impose severe restrictions on freedom of movement, would become staples of French imperial counter-insurgency thereafter. While French security services' obsession with organized communist violence seems in hindsight overblown, their preoccupation with – some might say their provocation of – colonial nationalist opposition bore closer correlation with actual episodes of protracted disorder.[26]

Another distinct challenge for French colonial security agencies nervous of violent dissent was to secure information regarding the activities and outlook of local women. Concern was greatest in Muslim societies within which varying degrees of segregation by gender operated in the public sphere. Women's use of the veil in public was simultaneously portrayed in official reports, popular literature and colonial imagery as affirmation of the impermeability of Muslim society. For anti-colonialists veiling and unveiling on their own terms symbolized women's resistance to French intrusion.[27] The distinct public and private spheres inhabited by Muslim women compounded the French tendency to stereotype them as mysterious, potentially seditious and generally opposed to colonial modernism. In the male-dominated world of policing and counter-insurgency, women's meeting places and the interiors of Muslim homes, with few, if any, external windows and courtyards deliberately closed off from public gaze, ranked among the most difficult urban spaces to monitor.[28]

In Syria male hostility to non-deferential or non-Islamic behaviour by women persisted throughout the Mandate, making it easier for Mandate officials to excuse gender discrimination in their territories as part of the fabric of indigenous society.[29] French feminist criticisms of the treatment of women in the empire meanwhile focused on insufficient state efforts to curtail notorious local practices such as female circumcision and child labour. In other words, even feminist critics conceded that colonial administration could be a positive force for change as far as women's rights were concerned. Whatever the ideological arguments made about them by colonial outsiders, women in the territories most affected by insurgency were increasingly treated as a discrete constituency to be monitored, regulated and policed. They also bore the brunt of French counter-insurgency, sometimes as combatants, but more often as civilian casualties, displaced populations and victims of sexual violence.

The social dislocation occasioned by rebellion and counter-insurgency restrictions inevitably changed women's lives. In rural areas especially, the wives and families of rebel fighters had to take on the jobs traditionally performed by their menfolk. In the Moroccan Rif many used their relative anonymity and public inviolability to serve as agents, arms providers and covert suppliers of insurgents. Whether smuggling ammunition and food to their menfolk or reporting on the deployments of imperial forces, women were essential auxiliaries to insurrectionists. In the process, they registered an impact in nationalist politics and extended their own spheres of sociopolitical activity.[30]

Separation of the sexes within Muslim societies, in public life, religious observance, jobs performed, and even recreation, limited women's ability to break into male-dominated political activity. At the same time, it preserved distinct female systems of power. Muslim households, women's bathhouses, communal washhouses as well as tribal villages where clusters of women shared child-rearing, household and village welfare tasks were among the most impenetrable and resilient elements of indigenous society.[31] During the interwar period the French authorities in North Africa and the Levant, while dimly aware of this, were generally unsure of how to respond.[32] Extreme violence sometimes resulted. Moroccan tribeswomen's role in resisting French pacification reinforced the image of Muslim women as unknowable and potentially subversive. It also placed women more squarely in the firing line. At the Battle of Bou Gafer from 18 to 28 February 1933, in one of the French Army's last major military engagements in southern Morocco, French forces killed at least 117 women of the Ait Atta tribe.[33]

Counter-insurgency and asymmetry

The example of maltreatment of women provides a route into broader discussion of counter-insurgency practices. Part of a longer continuum certainly, these methods took a particularly violent turn in the French empire between the wars. What had typically been a combination of demonstrative punishments and deterrence, the 'repressive consensus' about the use of counter-insurgent violence often collapsed into acrimony between French politicians, military commanders and other interested parties between the wars. Dramatic instances of bitter civil–military recrimination were apparent in the two cases of rebellion outlined earlier. Faced with the French Communist Party's uncompromising opposition to the prosecution of an 'imperialist war' in Morocco, on 2 July 1925 Premier Paul Painlevé told his fellow French senators that counter-insurgency in the Rif was something different: 'a vast police operation'.[34] An early example of official distinction between warfare and the suppression of colonial rebellion, and a rhetorical strategy familiar to scholars of late twentieth-century decolonization conflicts, Painlevé's words were carefully chosen. Invoking the idea of a police action was meant to convey several messages at once: that counter-insurgency punished criminal behaviour, that its conduct occurred within the normative spectrum of colonial security operations, and that the burdens it imposed did not require special parliamentary approval. This last point was probably the most important for Painlevé. Nervous lest details of the casualties and financial costs incurred in Morocco sap the unity of his governing coalition, the premier was quick to remind senators that the 400 colonial troops killed during the first three months of Rif campaigning only represented a 25 per cent increase on the average losses incurred during routine 'pacification' of the Moroccan Protectorate. Evidently, the French Senate agreed, passing a unanimous vote of confidence in the government's military action.[35]

Closer to the harsh reality of the Rif War, decision makers in Rabat were less easily persuaded. Confrontation between the French Moroccan Residency and France's centre-left 'Cartel' coalition over the level of military repression needed to pacify the Rif drove French Morocco's defining governor (or 'Resident-General') Marshal Lyautey to resign – a case of jumping before being pushed. His high-profile replacement, Philippe Pétain, abandoned Lyautey's efforts to split the Riffian clan coalition through targeted violence and covert negotiation. Armed with instructions from Prime Minister Painlevé to end the insurgency quickly by whatever means necessary, Pétain abandoned Lyautey's more limited use of force. Riffian resistance would be crushed through military saturation and overwhelming firepower – an indicator of the asymmetric warfare practices increasingly pursued by colonial commanders under political orders to achieve rapid results. Infantry assaults, heavy artillery and aerial bombardments supplanted the more sporadic attacks on insurgent villages favoured by Lyautey's colonially trained field officers. The outcome was unsurprising. The Rif rebellion was stifled, but, as Lyautey's staff predicted, local resentments burnt on long after Riffian leader Abdel Krim el-Khattabi was dispatched into exile on the island of Réunion in 1926.[36]

The same two tendencies – noisy French political demands for decisive victory and a consequent shift from limited military commitment to unrestrained violence – were evident in French Syria during 1925–6. The political pressure registered first in an administrative shake-up within the Levant High Commission and the Syrian military intelligence service, the Service de Renseignements (SR), which furnished a significant proportion of provincial administrators in the Mandate's nascent governmental apparatus.[37] In Paris political circles, the over-assertion of SR staff in the Jabal Druze was widely blamed for the Great Revolt's outbreak. SR officers determined to integrate Syrian local government within the Mandate's newly delineated federal structure encountered powerful opposition within communities to whom it appeared that customary power structures were about to be dismantled. Well-intentioned modernizers to their defenders, the SR's regional governors were depicted as blundering autocrats by their critics. While there was some truth in this, the readiness to scapegoat the SR conveniently overlooked the economic pressures and community grievances that fed support for rebellion, not just within Druze lands but beyond them as well.[38]

As in Morocco, changes in the Syrian Mandate's civil–military command heralded a dramatic upturn in state violence. Again, following Moroccan precedent, collective punishment of entire village populations in areas of high rebel activity became the norm. State of siege regulations, already in place before the Syrian Revolt, provided the juridical basis for martial law. On 1 December 1925 the Levant army command issued detailed instructions about the conduct of counter-insurgency in Syria. At first glance, these orders, modelled on the desert policing of Syria's Bedouin communities, were a model of minimum force restraint. Civilian populations were to be respected, property was not to be wantonly destroyed, and religious sites were to be scrupulously protected. Collective fines were reserved for situations where there was insufficient local intelligence available to allow hostage taking from the families of known rebels – the preferred method of communal coercion.[39] Each of these injunctions was ignored in practice. And even the new orders permitted 'exemplary executions' if villagers refused to surrender suspected insurgents.

By February 1926 local commanders were excusing their resort to harsher, arbitrary repression by claiming that the entire country remained 'closed' to French political influence.[40] Those earlier efforts to codify the country's political economy and to read the intentions of its men and women had brought little reward, leaving the door ajar to unconstrained repression Across wide expanses of Syria's rural interior exemplary punishment was making the writ of French authority tangible for the first time. Henceforth, military tribunals issued death sentences *en bloc* to those accused of insurgent activity without right of appeal. During 1926 the largest such tribunal, in Damascus, condemned 355 Syrians to hang. Families of those found guilty of rebellion could expect their homes to be destroyed and their farmland seized.[41] Absolute military jurisdiction, strict censorship regulations, and the consequent lack of political or press scrutiny of rural counter-insurgency widened the scope for abuses in encounters between security forces and civilians. Rapes, summary executions, the display of corpses, livestock killing and other acts of demonstrative violence became commonplace as greater reliance was placed on irregular units, Circassian cavalry and Armenian refugee auxiliaries prominent among them. Their military sweeps through the Syrian countryside were devastating.[42]

In the major towns, meanwhile, General Maurice Sarrail and his deputy Colonel Charles Andréa, a ruthless former Bedouin control officer, used colonial infantry assaults and, more infamously, artillery shelling to crush resistance in Hama and, above all, Damascus. By early October 1925 some of the capital's most-densely populated *quartiers* were identified by the SR as nests of insurgent activity, harbouring rebel fighters and raising funds for weapons. In truth, Druze fighters came and went, occasionally infiltrating the capital and gathering supplies, but rarely staying long. The depth of alleged Damascene 'support' for their incursions was questionable at best. Indeed, it was less any firm evidence of complicity between the city's population and the insurgents than a spectacular act of incendiarism – the burning of the 'Azm Palace', home to the Mandate's central bureaucracy – that provoked the sternest collective punishment of all. Between 18 and 20 October the city's southern districts through which the fighters had made their entry and escape were pounded with artillery and bombed from the air.[43] No concession was made to the fact that the insurgents were long gone. The urban destruction was colossal; the civilian death toll, appallingly high, ran to several hundred.[44]

Nor was this an end to such asymmetric tactics. A frontal military assault in the Revolt's original southern heartland in the Jabal Hawran secured its eventual reoccupation in April–May 1926. Violence also persisted in village settlements in the Ghouta region surrounding the capital. From there rebel fighters periodically infiltrated back into Damascus, particularly its Maydan quarter, a crucial trading hub that had already witnessed repeated punitive operations and house burnings. Matters came to a head on 7 May 1926 when Andréa ordered a twenty-two-hour shelling of the district. This second Damascus bombardment, like the first, punished a civilian population for alleged complicity with a small number of insurgents. With incendiary shells fired at timber-framed homes and water supplies cut off, fire took hold. Predictably, indeed deliberately, the Maydan was laid to waste More than a thousand died and at least sixty thousand were left homeless.[45]

So overwhelming was the evidence of disproportionality in Syria and so numerous were anti-colonial petitions and other international complaints about it to the League of Nations' PMC that the League felt bound to investigate. In the event, the PMC accepted the French Foreign Ministry's insistence that the Mandates Commission should inquire solely into allegations of maltreatment, pillage and collective punishments. A wider investigation of the war in Syria or the number of civilian victims was ruled out. Most importantly, the PMC accepted Foreign Minister Aristide Briand's claims that the evidence of military violence laid before it was intrinsic to the conflict. France, as Mandate holder, was entitled to use all means at its disposal to suppress an internal rebellion and this had been done. Briand was equally dismissive of allegations of a high civilian death toll; mere exaggeration, he claimed.[46]

The League of Nations' specialist observers may have been duped in 1926, but should we read into the Rif War and the Syrian Revolt a departure from the more judicious and politically astute use of counter-insurgent violence favoured by French colonial officers schooled in the methods of Lyautey and his forebear, Joseph Gallieni? Their successors, Pétain in Morocco, Maurice Sarrail and Maurice Gamelin in Syria, each of them renowned as metropolitan army commanders, might be taken to personify the new tendency to use asymmetric force – to use division-sized formations and heavy weapons – to stamp out insurgency.[47] But this would be to miss important strands of continuity. For one thing, recourse to punitive columns and collective punishments of local communities was a long-established French colonial practice. Much as it was redolent of late-nineteenth-century conquests in West Africa, Algeria and Indochina, its use in 1920s Morocco and Syria was less exceptional than might be imagined.[48] During the first years of the Moroccan Protectorate established in 1912, for instance, French administrative and fiscal demands were widely resisted or ignored. In response, military intelligence service officers turned to locally recruited auxiliary forces to coerce highland populations in the Rif, the Atlas and Anti-Atlas mountains, the Casablanca hinterland and the pre-Saharan South-East.[49] Native affairs officers, lacking the military means to do otherwise, fomented inter-clan violence to sow division between communities. Punitive raiding was encouraged, and land and livestock were redistributed among loyalist irregulars.[50]

Lyautey, then, was no stranger to the repressive population control characteristic of counter-insurgency. Quite the reverse: he was one of its innovators.[51] By late 1925 his objections to the strategic changes enacted by Pétain focused on the political utility of unrestrained warfare, not on the ethics of collective punishment and its unspoken corollary – the deliberate targeting of civilians.[52] Punishment columns of the interwar variety, often comprising Foreign Legion armoured car units as deployed in Damascus, and five years later against peasant supporters of the Nghe–TInh soviet movement in central Vietnam, were variants of the original Legionnaire columns that had raided Algerian rural settlements in the mid-nineteenth century.[53] And the underlying practice of sweeping through territory, intimidating the resident population, sometimes displacing it, and thus denying rebels the material resources needed to sustain themselves within their communities, would remain a grimly familiar feature of wars of decolonization. Coming full circle, such methods reached their apogee in French Algeria where, as Moritiz Feichtinger's chapter demonstrates, millions of rural dwellers endured forcible eviction and life in camps.

Micro and macro factors

For all that, it is tempting to trace an ascending arc of French empire insurgencies in the 1920s as the French protectorates in Morocco and its Syrian Mandate were coercively constructed. Yet, certain factors should perhaps give us pause. Quite different narratives could be invoked to explain the oft-cited revolts above. Lyautey's protectorate regime in Morocco was dragged into the Rif War by two primordial concerns: the adventurism of a Spanish colonial army defying political constraint from Madrid and the inexorable logic of Lyautey's determination to harness the agricultural output of the Riffian highlands to the commercial development of a fertile agricultural zone: the Ouergha River valley.[54] The first factor was extraneous, contingent and, until Lyautey's Protectorate government resolved to intervene, beyond French control. The second factor was the exact reverse: a matter of deliberate intention to use violence to consolidate French Morocco as an economic unit.[55]

The decision to fortify the Ouergha Valley resulted from discussion among the SR's native affairs officers embedded among the region's Berber clans. They were striving to undermine the clan affiliations that wove together the main tribal confederations along the Rif frontier. Auxiliary forces, often small, mobile cavalry units, were crucial to the tactics employed. They worked with colonial army troops in raiding dissentient villages and pastoralists' encampments, confiscating farm animals and driving people from their land until they acknowledged the writ of French authority. The Protectorate government's native affairs bureau followed the progress of this rural coercion programme carefully, advising field units on who and where to strike next.[56] The intention was clear: gradually the famous 'oil stain' of imperial administrative control – a metaphor coined by General Joseph Gallieni, its arch practitioner in nineteenth-century Vietnam and Madagascar – would radiate outwards, blotting out remaining pockets of resistance.[57]

As this military pressure intensified over the winter of 1924–5, incoming native affairs reports suggested that the Berber confederation was cracking. Lyautey's staff dared to hope that they could establish a secure northern Moroccan frontier without resorting to all-out war as the Spanish had done.[58] The ruthlessness of this low-intensity violence also carried an obvious risk. The pressure on Berber community food supplies was explosive. Consequent shortages and chronic price inflation were as likely to stir resistance as to quell it. For the Rif's Berber communities the Ouergha Valley was an essential wheat basket, the principal source of their staple foodstuff. It was unsurprising, then, that the string of army blockhouses constructed along the valley would be targeted in the initial Riffian assault on French frontier defences in April 1925. The blockhouses were not just obvious military targets along this French-delineated front line, they were the hated symbols of an imperial strategy of resource denial. Meanwhile, the native affairs bureau's failure to understand the tenets of community allegiance was made manifest in the fact that several warring Berber clans were armed with First World War surplus weapons previously supplied by SR officers as recompense for their submission to French authority.[59]

The causes of revolt in Syria were also multivalent. Political leaders and former officials of the country's short-lived independent Republic, some of them former officers in the Ottoman army, raged at the regime's violent overthrow and the eclipse of their experiment in liberal constitutionalism.[60] These opponents of the Mandate were not about to disappear. Their informal networks and civil society connections remained substantially intact despite their exclusion from government. Other political, communal and confessional links would be rewelded as support for the revolt against French rule grew.[61]

A basic question to ask is why Syria's mid-1920s rebellion, before it escalated into nationwide revolt, initially cohered around discrete communities that perceived themselves to be under threat. Conflict in colonial societies often erupted at the point where imperialists' ideas and schemes became real to local people trying to limit the impact of unmediated changes to their lives and cultures. These sites of contestation were partly ideational and abstract, a matter of clashing outlooks and objectives. But they were also materially tangible in acts of protest and violence. Each confronted those in positions of administrative authority with their most fundamental dilemma: how to govern imperially without arousing overwhelming opposition. It was here that the Mandate's military-administrative elite of army intelligence officers – the SR – erred most dramatically. Their mistakes were amplified because overturning traditional hierarchies of power was easily portrayed by regime opponents, not as the precursor to necessary modernization but as colonially motivated and socially devastating.[62]

Local defiance was fuelled by Syria's administrative partition and French claims to economic modernization that cut across preexisting Ottoman and Syrian Republican administrative apparatus.[63] The chronic price inflation, famine devastation and population displacements characteristic of the First World War years in Ottoman-ruled Syria were echoed in abiding food shortages, the continuing fragility of the agricultural sector and inflationary pressure on a Syrian currency now unrealistically pegged to the French franc.[64] The heady concoction of bureaucratic overhaul, ill-judged economic interventionism and cultural insensitivity confirmed the overbearing influence of leading SR officers who were appointed, one after the other, as regional governors between 1921 and 1925.[65] An ill-thought-out and invasive reorganization of everything from the apparatus of local government to infrastructural development and the reordering of public space in the Jabal Hawran's regional capital of Suwayda undermined the clientelist networks and cultural integrity of the Druze community. Little wonder that they were the first to take up arms in the summer of 1925.[66]

Dwelling of the specificities of insurgent outbreaks is worthwhile because it disaggregates the individual causes of political violence, complicating the empire-wide picture of French imperial rule in crisis. For one thing, a microhistorical approach of this sort raises fundamental questions about the nature and consequences of the clashes involved. What forms did this political violence take and what levels did it reach? It seems, for instance, that we might usefully superimpose the moral economies of collective dissent – the cultural attachments to particular ways of life – onto political economies of colonial extraction, including coercive labour regimes, land shortages and heightened tax burdens. For another thing, we need to address the composition and institutional practices of the security forces engaged. Who were they, what were they called upon to do and why? Clearly, SR officers in Syria, many of them trained in Protectorate Morocco, were pivotal to the explosive contact points with communities resentful of their disregard for local networks of power and established patterns of economic activity.[67]

Conclusion

Violence, social theorists agree, both constructs difference between people and entrenches it.[68] To use the language of political psychology, levels of political violence are likely to reflect patterns of socialization in a particular community as well as the form and extent of centralized state control over that community. Its form and frequency is also conditioned by the 'conflict structure' that pertains in the society in question; in other words, violence is substantially contingent on the extent of social division, economic iniquity and perceived cultural difference between the parties involved.[69] It follows that colonial violence practised in sharply unequal societies should reveal extreme examples of such difference. But does that set the collective violence of colonial insurgencies and counter-insurgencies apart as a discrete phenomenon? Framing the problem in a twentieth-century context, if colonial violence has identifiably unique qualities, then surely those qualities are intrinsically linked to imperial powers' recurrent experiences of conflict, occupation, rights' abuses, military and paramilitary violence.[70]

This chapter's episodes of French counter-insurgency in the 1920s suggest that we should tread warily. Identifying local – and colonial – causes of insurgent violence and security force counter-violence is essential. But so, too, is the need to make connections between the ways in which such violence was thought about, justified and enacted and prevailing imperial attitudes to social control and the value of empire. Repression of the rebellions discussed here also makes plain that any presumptive link between the violence of counter-insurgency and the imminence of colonial collapse stretches back into the early twentieth century, possibly much further. Much as the conflict structures evident in interwar Morocco and Syria were recognizably colonial, they were also those of societies in the grip of contested decolonization.

Notes

1   This approach, of course, owes much to two landmark analyses, one in the realm of colonial history, the other in the study of civil war violence. Respectively, these are, first: Frederick Cooper and Ann Laura Stoler, 'Between Metropole and Colony: Rethinking a Research Agenda,' in their edited collection, *Tensions of Empire: Colonial Cultures in a Bourgeois World* (Berkeley, CA: University of California Press, 1997). Their work's relationship to French colonial history scholarship is further discussed in Ann Laura Stoler, 'Colonial Aphasia: Race and Disabled Histories in France,' *Public Culture* 23, no. 1 (2011): 121–56. Secondly: Stathis Kalyvas, *The Logic of Violence in Civil Wars* (Cambridge: Cambridge University Press, 2006).

2   Ministère des Affaires Etrangères (MAE), La Courneuve, 179CPCOM238/Dossier: EMA 2ᵉ Bureau, 'Notice sur le Maroc: géographie, armée, politique intérieure, intérêts internationaux,' n.d. December 1900, pp. 1–13; 179CPCOM185, EMA 2ᵉ Bureau report, 'Le Maroc en 1904,' pp. 6–7, 13–16; 179CPCOM425, no. 496-9/II, EMA Section d'Afrique, to Direction des affaires politiques et commerciales, 'A.S. du livre jaune sur les affaires du Maroc,' 31 January 1912.

3   Daniel Rivet, *Lyautey et l'institution du protectorat français au Maroc, 1912-1925* (Paris L'Harmattan, 1988), vol. I; idem, *Le Maghreb à l'épreuve de la colonisation* (Paris Hachette, 2002); William A. Hoisington Jnr., *Lyautey and the French Conquest of Morocco* (Basingstoke: Macmillan, 1995), chapters 2–5; Jonathan C. Katz, *Murder in Marrakesh: Émile Mauchamp and the French Colonial Adventure* (Bloomington, IN: Indiana University Press, 2006), 9–14, 62–3.

4   Vital here are James L. Gelvin, *Divided Loyalties. Nationalism and Mass Politics in Syria at the Close of Empire* (Berkeley, CA: University of California Press, 1998), and Daniel Neep, *Occupying Syria under the French Mandate: Insurgency, Space And State Formation* (Cambridge: Cambridge University Press, 2014), especially chapters 2–4.

5   For background, see two classic studies: Edmund Burke III, *Prelude to Protectorate in Morocco: Precolonial Protest and Resistance, 1860-1912* (Chicago: University of Chicago Press, 1976); Philip S. Khoury, *Syria and the French Mandate. The Politics of Arab Nationalism, 1920-1945* (London: I. B. Taurus, 1987). Also essential is Moshe Gershovich, *French Military Rule in Morocco. Colonialism and its Consequences* (London: Frank Cass, 2000), 128–41.

6   The term and the concept derive from Gary Wilder, *The French Imperial Nation-State. Negritude and Colonial Humanism between the Two World Wars* (Chicago: University of Chicago Press, 2005).

7   Susan Pedersen, *The Guardians: The League of Nations and the Crisis of Empire* (Oxford: Oxford University Press, 2015), 147–58. The characterization of local notables and other locally recruited public servants as venal was, of course, crassly oversimplistic. The social backgrounds of these local authority figures and the broad political and juridical powers they conserved are thoughtfully examined in David Lambert, *Notables des colonies. Une élite de circonstance en Tunisie et au Maroc (1881-1939)* (Rennes: Presses Universitaires de Rennes, 2009), especially 182–219; see also Mary Dewhurst Lewis, *Divided Rule: Sovereignty and Empire in French Tunisia* (Berkeley, CA: University of California Press, 2013).

8   Michael Goebel, *Anti-Imperial Metropolis: Interwar Paris and the Seeds of Third World Nationalism* (New York: Cambridge University Press, 2015), 153, 158–62, 174–5.

9   Indispensable here are Edmund Burke III, *The Ethnographic State: France and the Invention of Moroccan Islam* (Berkeley, CA: University of California Press, 2014), especially part II; Alice L. Conklin's *In the Museum of Man: Race, Anthropology, and Empire in France, 1850-1950* (Ithaca, NY: Cornell University Press, 2013), especially chapters 5–6.

10 French Morocco's Berber highlands were a favoured locale here; see Burke III, *The Ethnographic State*, 128–45; Henri Simon, 'Les études berbères au Maroc et leur applications en matière de politique et administration,' *Archives Berbères* 1915-1916, 9; also cited in Lahsen Jennin, 'Le Moyen Atlas et let Français Évolution des connaissances et du savoir sur l'espace et sur la société rurale,' in *Présences et Images Franco-Marocaines au Temps du Protectorat*, ed. Jean-Claude Allain (Paris: l'Harmattan, 2003), 59. See also: *Le Commandant en tournée*.

11 Robert Tombs, 'Crime and the Security of the State: The "Dangerous Classes" and Insurrection in Nineteenth-century Paris,' in *Crime and the Law. The Social History of Crime in Western Europe since 1500*, ed. V. A. C. Gatrell, Bruce Lenman and Geoffrey Parker (London: Europa, 1980), 214–18.

12 Marieke Bloembergen, 'The Perfect Policeman: Colonial Policing, Modernity, and Conscience on Sumatra's West Coast in the Early 1930s,' *Indonesia* 91 (April 2011): 165–91, at 169.

13 Alice Hills, 'Towards a Critique of Policing and National Development in Africa,' *Journal of Modern African Studies* 34, no. 2 (1996): 279.

14 Hills, 'Towards a Critique of Policing,' 279–84; David Killingray, 'The Maintenance of Law and Order in British Colonial Africa,' *African Affairs* 85, no. 340 (1986): 426; Martin Thomas, *Violence and Colonial Order: Police, Workers, and Protest in the European Colonial Empires, 1918-1940* (Cambridge: Cambridge University Press, 2012), chapters 2–3.

15 Martin Thomas, *Empires of Intelligence: Security Services and Colonial Disorder after 1914* (Berkeley, CA: University of California Press, 2008), 148–50, 157–60.

16 This was in stark contrast to the Syrian Arab Congress constitution promulgated during the short-lived Syrian Republic in 1920, which was notable for its secular and inclusive character; see Elizabeth F. Thompson, 'Rachid Rida and the 1920 Syrian-Arab Constitution,' in *The Routledge Handbook of the History of the Middle East Mandates*, ed. Cyrus Schayegh and Andrew Arsan (Abingdon: Routledge, 2015), 244–55.

17 Centre des Archives Diplomatiques, Nantes (CADN), Fonds Beyrouth, Cabinet Politique, vol. 986, no. 326/SP/3, report to SR Damascus, 29 April 1924; vol. 986, DR25, SR *Contrôle bédouin*, 'Etat de la transhumance au 15 juillet 1925.'

18 Robert A. Nye, 'Western Masculinities in War and Peace,' *American Historical Review* 112, no. 2 (April 2007): 417–18, 421; see also Glenda Sluga, 'Masculinities, Nations, and the New World Order: Peacemaking and Nationality in Britain, France, and the United States after the First World War,' in *Masculinities in Politics and War: Gendering Modern History*, ed. Stefan Dudink, Karen Hagemann and John Tosh (Manchester: Manchester University Press, 2004), 240.

19 Goebel, *Anti-Imperial Metropolis*, 5–6, 155–6.

20 John Horne, 'Defining the Enemy: War, Law, and the *levée en masse* from 1870 to 1945,' in *The People in Arms. Military Myth and National Mobilization since the French Revolution*, ed. Daniel Moran and Arthur Waldron (Cambridge: Cambridge University Press, 2003), 114.

21 Discussion of the antagonism between French left and right over issues of demobilization, the length of conscription, and retention of a large professional army could be profitably expanded to consider the military's role as an agent of colonial control: Richard S. Fogarty and David Killingray, 'Demobilization in British and French Africa at the End of the First World War,' *Journal of Contemporary History* 50, no. 1 (2015) : 100–23; Elizabeth Kier, 'Culture and Military Doctrine: France between the Wars,' *International Security* 19, no. 4 (Spring 1995): 72–7.

22 Michael Hanagan, 'Charles Tilly and Violent France,' *French Historical Studies* 33, no. 2 (2010): 283–5.

23 Service Historique de la Défense-Département de l'Armée de Terre (SHD-DAT), 5H6/D2, Philippe Pétain report, 'Troubles et soulèvements intérieurs en AOF pendant la guerre 1914–1918,' 26 March 1925.

24 The prevalence of racial violence in Europe and North America amid the demobilization of the immediate post-war period is thoughtfully analysed in Mark Edele and Robert Gerwarth, 'The Limits of Demobilization: Global Perspectives on the Aftermath of the Great War,' *Journal of Contemporary History* 50, no. 1 (2015): 3–14. For other instances, see the essays in Robert Gerwarth and John Horne (eds), *War in Peace: Paramilitary Violence in Europe after the Great War* (Oxford: Oxford University Press, 2013); David F. Krugler, *1919, the Year of Racial Violence: How African Americans Fought Back* (Cambridge: Cambridge University Press, 2015).

25 Tyler Stovall, 'The Color line Behind the Lines: Racial Violence in France during the First World War,' *American Historical Review* 103, no. 3 (1998): 739–69; Clifford Rosenberg, *Policing Paris: The Origins of Modern Immigration Control between the Wars* (Ithaca, NY: Cornell University Press, 2006).

26 Georges Vidal, 'Violence et politique dans la France des années 1930: le cas de l'autodéfense communiste,' *Revue Historique* CCCVIII, no. 4 (2008): 901–22.

27 Frantz Fanon, 'L'Algérie se dévoile,' in *Sociologie d'une Revolution* (Paris: Maspero, 1968), 17–24.

28 Janet R. Horne, 'In Pursuit of Greater France: Visions of Empire among Musée Social Reformers, 1894-1931,' in *Domesticating the Empire. Race, Gender, and Family Life in French and Dutch Colonialism*, ed. Julia Clancy-Smith and Frances Gouda (Charlottesville, VA: University of Virginia Press, 1998), 38–9.

29 The most authoritative source is Elizabeth Thompson's *Colonial Citizens: Republican Rights, Paternal Privilege, and Gender in French Syria and Lebanon* (New York: Columbia University Press, 2000), particularly Part III; MAE, Fonds Beyrouth, Cabinet Politique, vol. 843/D1, no. 551/CP, High Commissioner de Martel to Foreign Ministry, 3 August 1934.

30 C. R. Pennell, 'Women and Resistance to Colonialism in Morocco: The Rif, 1916-1926,' *Journal of African History* 28 (1987): 112–15; see also N. R. Keddie, 'Problems in the Study of Middle Eastern Women,' *International Journal of Middle East Studies* (1979): 225–40.

31 Pennell, 'Women and Resistance,' 107–8.

32 SHD-DAT, Archives de Moscou, C323/D122, SEA (Algiers), Commandant Delor to SR (Paris), 'Note sur les conditions psychologiques d'une mobilisation générale en Algérie,' 22 May 1935; C464/D174, Rapport de Commandant Schlesser, annex I: 'L'interpénétration des renseignements en Afrique du Nord,' n.d. May 1938.

33 Assia Benadada, 'Les femmes dans le mouvement nationaliste marocain,' *CLIO, Histoire, Femmes et Sociétés* 9 (1999): 69; Moshe Gershovich, *French Military Rule in Morocco. Colonialism and its Consequences* (London: Frank Cass, 2000), 157–8. It is doubtful that these women fought in the battle, but they clearly suffered its outcome. Total Ait 'Atta casualties were estimated at between 1,300 and over 2,000, most of whom were non-combatants.

34 TNA, FO 371/11078, W6433/39/28 & W5092/186/28, Marquess of Crewe (Paris) to FO, 2 June & 6 July 1925.

35 TNA, FO 371/11078, W6433/39/28, Marquess of Crewe to FO, 6 July 1925; M'Barka Hamed-Touati, *Immigration maghrébine et activités politiques en France de la première guerre mondiale à la veille du front populaire* (Tunis: Université de Tunis, 1994), 155–6.

36 Hoisington, *Lyautey*, 204.

37 Jean-David Mizrahi, *Genèse de l'État mandataire. Service de renseignements et bandes armées en Syrie et au Liban dans les années 1920* (Paris: Publications de la Sorbonne, 2003), 88–96; TNA, AIR 23/89, BS/S/10, record of British liaison officer meeting with Colonel Andrea, 22 December 1925.

38 Michael Provence, *The Great Syrian Revolt and the Rise of Arab Nationalism* (Austin, TX: University of Texas Press, 2005); idem, 'An Investigation into the Local Origins of the Great Revolt,' in *France, Syrie et Liban 1918-1946. Les ambiguities et les dynamiques de la relation mandataire*, ed. Nadine Méouchy (Damascus: IFEAD, 2002), 378–93.

39 MAE, série E, 1922–29, vol. 196, 'Note pour le chef d'état-major de l'armée française du Levant,' 1 December 1925.

40 SHD-DAT, 7N4181/D1, no. 393/1G, Gamelin to War Ministry/EMA-1, 10 February 1926.

41 Michael Provence, 'French Mandate Counterinsurgency and the Repression of the Great Syrian Revolt,' in *The Routledge Handbook of the History of the Middle East Mandates*, ed. Schayegh and Arsan, 140–3.

42 CADN, Fonds Beyrouth, vol. 840/D2, no. 4537/K3, 'Directives sur l'action du SR pendant la phase de consolidation politique,' 14 September 1926.

43 MAE, série E, Levant, vol. 194, tel. 600/KD, Sarrail to Foreign Ministry Direction Levant, 25 October 1925.

44 Significantly, international protest against the bombardment focused on the lack of warning given to the city's European residents, particularly British consular staff, see TNA, FO 371/10852, E7250/357/89, Consul W.A. Smart to Austen Chamberlain, 10 November 1925.

45 Provence, 'French Mandate Counterinsurgency', 147.

46 Pedersen, *The Guardians*, 159–60.

47 SHD-DAT, 4H67/D2, no. 936/2, Gamelin, Commandant supérieur des troupes du Levant, to Cabinet du Ministre (Guerre), 1 July 1926.

48 For details of the military methods in these earlier conquests, see A. S. Kanya-Forstner, *The Conquest of Western Sudan: A Study in French Military Imperialism* reprint (Cambridge: Cambridge University Press, 2009), 174–214; Benjamin Claude Brower, *A Desert Named Peace: The Violence of France's Empire in the Algerian Sahara, 1844-1902* (New York: Columbia University Press, 2009), parts I & II; Michel Bodin, *Les Français au Tonkin 1870-1902: Une conquête difficile* (Paris: SOTECA, 2012).

49 Daniel Rivet, *Lyautey et l'institution du protectorat français au Maroc* (Paris: l'Harmattan, 1988), vol. 2, 62–5, 82–4.

50 SHD-DAT, 3H107, no. 6487/DR/I, Lyautey to EMA Section d'Afrique: 'Emploi des partisans en Maroc', 18 November 1922.

51 Hoisington, *Lyautey*, 14–17, 24–30.

52 Lyautey letter to Aristide Briand, 10 October 1925, in Pierre Lyautey (ed.), *Lyautey l'Africain, 1912-1925: Textes et lettres du maréchal Lyautey* vol. 4 (Paris Plon, 1957), 577–8; also cited in Hoisington, *Lyautey*, 204.

53 Brower, *A Desert Named Peace*, 17, 259, n. 1; William Gallois, *A History of Violence the Early Algerian Colony* (New York: Palgrave Macmillan, 2013), chapters 2–3; Archives Départementales de l'Aude, Albert Sarraut papers, 12J301, Annam Resident-Superior Le Fol to Pierre Pasquier, 'A.S. des incidents de Vinh et Ha Tinh, Septembre 1930'.

54 Sebastian Balfour, *Deadly Embrace. Morocco and the Road to the Spanish Civil War* (Oxford: Oxford University Press, 2002), 52–121 *passim*; SHD-DAT, 3H107/EMA, Ministère de Guerre, 'Note au sujet des origines de l'agression Rifiane', n.d. 1926.

55 Both the French Socialist Party Congress and the Second International, which, in 1925, convened in Marseilles, called upon the French authorities to acknowledge Rif Berber rights to political and economic autonomy. Lyautey, meanwhile, claimed that occupation of the lucrative Ouergha River valley was essential to protect the city of Fez from Riffian attack, see Archives Nationales (AN), Paris, Lyautey Papers, 475AP/86, no. 227 Lyautey report, 'Bulletin périodique de renseignements: Situation sur le front de l'Ouergha,' 4 July 1924; Claude Liauzu, *Histoire de l'anti-colonialisme en France. Du XVIe siècle à nos jours* (Paris: Armand Colin, 2007), 143.

56 SHD-DAT, 3H107/Notes et travaux divers, no. 6487/DR/I, Direction des affaires indigènes et du SR memo. to EMA Section d'Afrique, 18 November 1922.

57 Patrice Morlat, *Les Affaires politiques de l'Indochine (1895-1923). Les grands commis du savoir au pouvoir* (Paris: l'Harmattan, 1995), 251–4.

58 This theme can be traced in native affairs service monthly intelligence reports. See Service Historique de l'Armé de l'Air, Vincennes, 2C35/D3, Direction des affaires indigènes 'Rapport mensuel d'ensemble du protectorat,' February 1921; SHD-DAT, 3H101/EMA Section d'Afrique, Direction des affaires indigènes situation reports, 1925.

59   SHD-DAT, 2N243/D2, General Serrigny inspection tour report, 4 June 1925; Gershovich, *French Military Rule*, 130–32.

60   As Elizabeth Thompson has shown, support for accountable, constitutional government was a generic phenomenon in the Middle East: see her *Justice Interrupted: The Struggle for Constitutional Government in the Middle East* (Cambridge, MA: Harvard University Press, 2013), especially chapter 4.

61   Michael Provence, 'A Nationalist Rebellion without Nationalists? Popular Mobilizations in Mandatory Syria, 1925-1926,' in *The British and French Mandates in Comparative Perspectives*, ed. Nadine Méouchy and Peter Sluglett (Leiden: Brill, 2004), 673–91.

62   Philip S. Khoury, 'The Syrian Independence Movement and the Growth of Economic Nationalism in Damascus,' *British Society for Middle Eastern Studies Bulletin* 14, no. 1 (1988): 25–37.

63   Jan-Karl Tanenbaum, *General Maurice Sarrail 1856-1929. The French Army and Left-Wing Politics* (Chapel Hill: University of North Carolina Press, 1974), 191–206.

64   Useful examinations of the impact and legacies of Syria's wartime famine are Linda Schatkowski-Schilcher, 'The Famine of 1915-1918 in Greater Syria,' in *Problems of the Modern Middle East in Historical Perspective*, ed. J. P. Spagnolo (Reading: Ithaca Press, 1996), 229–58; Najwa al-Qattan, 'When Mothers ate their Children: Wartme Memory and the Language of Food in Syria and Lebanon,' *International Journal of Middle East Studies* 46, no. 4 (2014): 719–36; Simon Jackson, 'Compassion and Connections: Feeding Beirut and assembling Mandate rule in 1919,' in *The Routledge Handbook of the History of the Middle East Mandates*, ed. Schayegh and Arsan, 62–75; Najwa al-Qattan, 'Historicising hunger: the famine in wartime Syria and Lebanon,' in *The First World War and its Aftermath: The Shaping of the Modern Middle East*, ed. T.G. Fraser (London: Gingko Library, 2015), 111–26.

65   Mizrahi, *Genèse de l'État mandataire*, 76–7, 186–98.

66   AN, Paul Painlevé Papers, 313AP/248, Captain Carbillet report to Painlevé, 'La situation actuelle en Syrie,' n. d. 1925.

67   CADN, Fonds Beyrouth, Cabinet politique, vol. 840/D2, SR Service Central note, 'A/S action politique des commandants de colonnes,' 6 January 1926, vol. 840/D1, 'Service de Renseignements organisation et directives,' n. d. 1930.

68   M. Ross, 'Cross-Cultural Theory of Political Conflict & Violence,' *Political Psychology* 7 (1986): 427–69. As social theorist Charles Tilly has warned us, while it is rash to claim that collective violence conforms to generic laws or theories, discrete 'repertoires' may be discerned nonetheless. Tilly, 'Repression, Mobilization, and Explanation,' in *Repression and Mobilization*, ed. C. Davenport, H. Johnston and C. Mueller (Minneapolis, MN: University of Minnesota Press, 2005), 211–14.

69   Roberta Senechal de la Roche, 'Collective Violence as Social Control,' *Sociological Forum* 11, no. 1 (1996): 105–16.

70   Robert Gerwarth and Erez Manela, 'The Great War as a Global War: Imperial Conflict and the Reconfiguration of World Order, 1911-1923,' *Diplomatic History* 38, no. 4 (2014): 786–800.

3

The Plantation as Counter-insurgency Tool: Indonesia 1900–50

Roel Frakking

When the payment of the individual labourers is done, a roll call is held for the men and women, who have spent the day in the gardens weeding and cutting, the full-time workers, who are paid once a week. Ten by ten squatted in perfect order, with in front the [indigenous managers], the European employee calls their name and notes them in his ledger. … Such, then, is the contact between employer and employee present … to at least prevent muddling and intrigue. Because behind those ostensibly unmoved faces[,] behind all that calm activity, hides the full life of the dessa, where sexuality, as much as in our big cities, plays such an important role.[1]

This quote, from a serialized 1930s exposé on life on 'allotment Soekamadé', a relatively new plantation some four and a half kilometres from Java's south coast, described a process that was emblematic for plantations in the Netherlands East Indies.[2] In fact; this tableau captured colonial Indonesia at large. The indigenous manager, or *mandoer*, acted as the European managers' eyes and ears; with this unassailable hierarchy in place, they ruled over the workers living in the plantation's *kampongs* and surrounding *desas*. The 'ten by ten' squatting reflected the way the plantation system had promoted the colonial infiltration of indigenous space: it engendered order and control. Obviously, the colonial state and its planter agents feared what lay beyond those controlled spaces, as exemplified by the apprehension kindled by supposedly unbridled indigenous 'sexuality'.[3] As it threatened to seep unto the plantation itself, these uncontrolled areas were to be subjugated, too.

If the plantation's 'shadow was cast everywhere you turned', the ignominious 1942 defeat of the Dutch at the hands of Japan and the chaotic, violent circumstances following the sudden Japanese surrender of 1945 dispelled all such shadows.[4] With Japanese troops withdrawing to their barracks prior to evacuation and no oppressive colonial administration in situ to hold them back, politicized Indonesian youths took to the streets. Meanwhile, Ir. Sukarno and Dr Hatta, as president and vice president respectively, proclaimed the Republik Indonesia on 17 August 1945. Albeit gradually at first, Indonesia's anti-colonial revolution largely coalesced around the Republic.[5] This was the starting point of a bloody yet relatively short four-year (guerrilla) war as the Dutch authorities had a hard time relinquishing their overseas empire in the East. The Dutch needed no fewer than four rounds of negotiations and agreements – at the Hoge Veluwe (1946), Linggadjati (1947), Renville (1948) and Rooijen-Van Rum (1949) – and two military actions (1947 and 1948–9) to finally give up Indonesia through a fifth agreement, the Round Table Conference of 1949. During these years, the Republican Army, supported by a massive number of irregulars, was able to fight the Dutch army to a standstill.

Before such time, the returning Dutch civil and military authorities and large privately owned land-owning corporations needed the plantations, regardless of whether Indonesians hailed them as liberators – as many Dutch expected – or as enemies to be driven off. Yet, the central role of the plantation system and the continued focus of military and civil authorities it garnered throughout Indonesia's war of independence have been overlooked historically. Recent research instead focuses on the violence of decolonization, the nature of the Dutch approach to it and the ultimate failure of Dutch counter-insurgency in Indonesia.[6] The plantations are scarcely mentioned as distinct sites of conflict.

It is this chapter's contention that the plantations were critically important both to the Dutch and to the anti-colonial resistance. It argues that the plantations in the Netherlands East Indies represented a primary nexus where colonial and anti-colonial discourses and practices met. This had been the case before 1942 and would again be so at the end of the Japanese interlude. After 1945, the Dutch introduced practices to the plantations, which, taken together, were deemed instrumental to winning an increasingly violent guerrilla war. First, the plantations constituted the physical expression of a renewed colonial project the Dutch sought to pursue after 1945. Making plantations operable once more would prove to local communities that the Dutch were back in power. Re-establishing large-scale production, furthermore, would spark the failing Dutch and indigenous economies back to life, confirming the benefits of lasting Dutch rule. Lastly, the plantations would be, in the course of the war, transformed into garrisoned centres from which colonial security forces would make their presence known. In other words, plantations were used as counter-insurgency tools. Controlling plantations and the areas around and between them would allow authorities the opportunity to separate communities from the Indonesian freedom fighters. For the latter, the opposite held true. Combating the Dutch presence on the plantations and resisting their pernicious attempts to cut them off from the population were central to insurgent action.

Ignoring the plantations leaves key aspects of this violent episode in Southeast Asian decolonization hidden. For one thing, much research continues to zoom in on the transfer of sovereignty, including the various negotiation rounds, the role of the United Nations and the two 'Police Actions' in 1947 and 1948 that preceded the final colonial dénouement of December 1949.[7] Dutch measures seeking to reshape colonial spaces and to determine 'loyal' versus disruptive behaviour remain unexplained. Researchers often proclaim that the Dutch held narrow, military perspectives and little was done to garner local support. This chapter challenges this latter notion, highlighting that, alongside violent recolonization, less aggressive means were deployed, albeit rather minimally. What is more, local troops were heavily utilized in the defence of plantations. Their presence, as well as the concentration of thousands of Indonesians in one place, combined with Commander-in-Chief General Simon Spoor's insistence that the estates figured centrally in his 1949 anti-guerrilla plans, provoked specific kinds of subversion – which remain concealed when counter-insurgency in Indonesia is studied from a Dutch command-and-control perspective that devotes less attention to grass-roots violence.[8] If the Dutch lost the initiative to the guerrillas, a likely place this happened was on the plantations.

Equally important is the fact that once plantations and estates come into view, we see that aspects from the Indonesian war of independence hitherto hidden from sight come to the fore. The people targeted – either by Dutch or Indonesian forces – were not supportive of either side; they tried to remain neutral as much as possible. The quest for neutrality in the face of danger may seem a moot point to make as it is common to most conflicts, but in the case of Indonesia, this obvious point has hardly been made.[9] Still, with a Dutch 'Department of Intelligence & Loyalty Inquiries' in operation during at least part of the war, perceived loyalties were no trifling matter.[10] The battle for the plantations was also a struggle for labour. Some thirty years ago, two researchers commented on the absence of the planters as historical nodes of analysis; they averred that they almost passively suffered their violent fates.[11] And yet, as this chapter will show, planters were pivotal to harsher, more punitive measures, playing a much larger role in counter-insurgency than is generally acknowledged. Broadly speaking, with the plantations as a departure point for analysis, this chapter seeks to deepen understanding of the Indonesian war for independence.

The Indonesian plantation system as colonial space

To understand why the plantations loomed large in Dutch operational planning, it is instructive to consider their significance in the Netherlands East Indies from a broader perspective, especially as the Indonesian war for independence is under-represented in English-language discourses on decolonization. Unsurprisingly, what follows applies to most plantation economies, colonial or otherwise. A number of studies on colonial plantation economies, have been disposed to merely debate the conceptual nature of such economies and determine whether they are feudal, (proto) capitalist or an admixture of both systems.[12] Worse still, a minority of commentators outright dismissed the asymmetrical, coercive relations that flow from 'unfree labour', claiming labourers entered into contracts cognizant of the consequences.[13] More insightful analyses – the majority – did not gloss over the plantation economy's coercive nature, its 'eliminating [of] the ability of owners of the commodity labour-power to exchange it as they choose' and its inherent class and 'race-making'.[14] This chapter falls in the latter category, yet it seeks to bring out the practical consequences of what others have more euphemistically called 'coercion'. However, contrary to Breman but similar to Stoler (both focused on the plantation system's inherent violent streak), the current analysis seeks to add another layer to the coercive characteristics of the specifically Indonesian plantation system: its use as a counter-insurgency tool during unrestricted guerrilla warfare.[15] In doing so, the analysis will veer away from ground covered by more traditional plantation economy narratives.

As the opening quote suggested, plantations across Indonesia served another function aside from fuelling an extractive economy: plantations became the site where visions of colonial modernity were wedded to far-reaching social control. This had been an outgrowth of a shift in thinking in the closing decades of the nineteenth century. New ideas culminated in an 'Ethical Policy' inaugurated in 1901. Its proponents claimed that administrators would improve the lives of the indigenous population, thereby making amends for the exploitative economy the Ethical Policy replaced.[16] It was not to be. Instead, the new policy provided unprecedented opportunities to make deeper inroads into everyday Indonesian life. The positions of the Europeans, within both the plantation economy and colonial governmental structures, were strengthened.[17] The plantation system which expanded massively from 1870 onwards became the stage upon which the colonial government and the planter community performed the Ethical Policy.[18] They reshaped Indonesians into controllable, docile subjects and subjected communities to the trappings of the colonial police state.[19]

The creation of colonially defined spaces on Netherlands East Indies plantations asserted control through delineations of the permissible. Colonial space-production sought to alter indigenous behavioural repertoires, the plantation system imposing a 'homogeneous, clearly demarcated space complete with horizon and a vanishing point'; or at least, that was the objective.[20] The colonial enclosure had simultaneously to capture and deconstruct social relationships in order to reassemble them into the behavioural patterns demanded.[21] The Dutch colonial state thus established particular boundaries ranging from the geographical and material to the mental and discursive. The plantation system was politicized and imbued with highly symbolic content. Everything, including the use of various languages that established social hierarchies, reinforced colonial power.[22] Timetables determined when a person should be where; when sick, it was the planter who decided whether a labourer would visit the plantation's infirmary. Power was projected onto the body.[23] Indigenous intermediaries and racial segregation, violently enforced, were to insulate the European planters from supposedly debasing themselves.[24] Planters bore responsibility for 'hygienic circumstances'; they accrued 'police rights' to apprehend deserting workers.[25] So-called 'lazy' Indonesians, in short, were subjected to a regime that combined surveillance and the threat of force with education in agricultural techniques and personal hygiene.[26]

Other forms of spacial domination were more tangible and physical, but equally symbolic, making Lefebvre's 'logic of visualization [of power]' strongly applicable.[27] The plantation's central emplacement was the site where all roads and rail roads leading into the gardens and factories converged.[28] More often than not, the workers' day began and ended there, receiving instructions and payment. The elevated nature of many plantations reflected how power trickled down: 'Great height [has] ever been the spatial expression of potentiality violent power.'[29] The overseeing European manager lived in a sprawling villa at the top of the plantation, surveying his properties.[30] In a semicircle below lay the villas of the lesser European administrative personnel. Lower, on the various smaller emplacements, lived the European planters. Still further down, in the gardens, but close to the indigenous overseers, lived the workforce.

Indigenous villages were rebuilt. Identical houses stood in neat rows complete with small gardens.[31] Plantation interest groups disseminated instructions on constructing the gardens, stipulating how and where workers' dwellings were to be erected, down to the dimensions of every house.[32] After all, warned the Commission for Village Amelioration in 1939, 'In a population, that has to live in messy and dirty [villages], the tendency for social dissatisfaction and unruliness is enhanced.'[33]

The return to the plantations

These vestiges of Dutch colonial power, whose executive instruments were combined in the police forces and the Royal Netherlands Indisch Army (KNIL), were thoroughly destroyed by the Japanese. In 1945 the first step towards restoration saw Dutch policymakers rebuild the police forces and the KNIL at a furious pace while ever more troops were shipped in from the Netherlands and prisoner of war camps across Southeast Asia – totalling almost 80,000 front line troops in 1948 alone.[34] The reintroduction of the Inland Administration was the other step. Following close on the heels of the advancing military, administrators tried to connect with local Indonesians willing to cooperate, typically selected from influential families that had traditionally governed. The Inland Administration's attempts to rebuild these patron–client networks were generally unsuccessful. In parts of Indonesia, such as East Sumatra, youths (*pemuda*) inflamed with revolutionary fervour had 'wreaked vengeance on the [indigenous] aristocratic sector of the colonial establishment' killing 'sultans and rajas and their families'.[35] Across the archipelago locals – both former administrators and those inexperienced in the art of governing – proved reluctant to cooperate as Republican reprisals were rife.[36] Broadly speaking, the less a locality was contested, the more prospective administrators stepped forward. Still, the Dutch needed Republican supporters to serve the Dutch government who, given the chance, continued to report to the Republic. They assisted in the formation of 'shadow administrations' that slowly formed to vie for influence with local, Dutch-installed village committees.[37] This created a basic dilemma for Dutch administrators involved: a de facto reliance on, aside from less-trustworthy people, other individuals who lacked any prior administrative or police experience, such as 'teachers, ... railway officials, Dutch soldiers and, in one case, a pharmacist'.[38] To ameliorate the situation, military officials demanded to take up the slack. The subsequent military primacy opened the door to more violence. Instead of cooperating with local interests the military demanded obeisance. Where this was not forthcoming, violence quickly followed. Furthermore, the military was not above suppressing regional autonomous initiatives (part of the federative reconstruction of Indonesia) and was given responsibility for 'special courts-martial' tasked with swiftly convicting anyone connected to anti-Dutch behaviour. Not surprisingly, the military made ample yet violent use of its ever-growing mandate.[39]

It is no exaggeration to state that the deployment of Dutch civil administrators throughout Indonesia was largely a function of the economic opening up of Indonesia to international trade. Under Article Fourteen of the Linggadjati Agreement, ratified in March 1947, Dutch entrepreneurs secured the right to return to their plantations, even in those territories on Java, Sumatra and Madura officially conceded to the Indonesian Republic.[40] Article Fourteen provided much-needed breathing space: the Indische and Dutch economies stood on the brink of complete collapse, experts thought.[41] With hundreds of millions to be earned through export trade, plantations became focal points of restoration. Due to the Dutch economy's open (and relatively small) nature and '75 percent of national income' (in the 1920s) deriving from foreign trade and overseas economic enterprise, the prospect of Indonesian independence caused economic consternation.[42] The Dutch economy, however, had never been truly dependent upon Indonesian trade for its growth and maintenance.[43] After 1949, Indonesian and Dutch economic relations were maintained and 'even the disruption of these contacts after 1957 [the *Indonesianisasi* of the Indonesian economy] failed to depress the Dutch economy'. The 60,000 returning Dutch eventually contributed to the domestic economy and foreign trade was directed elsewhere.[44] During the war for independence such realities were drowned out by a swelling chorus claiming that without Indonesia, the Netherlands would sink to the 'rank of a country like Denmark'.[45] Tellingly, the first 'Politionele Actie' in the summer of 1947 was called 'Operation Product' – a reference to the rubber, tea, palm oil and other export goods to be captured.

After the Police Action – a euphemism for a military operation that was supposedly to 'liberate' the people from the Republic – Dutch forces reoccupied two thirds of Java and large parts of Sumatra. Much of Central Java, specifically Yogyakarta where the Republican government resided, was not attacked, but the majority of plantations and production centres were brought under control. What is little known is the extent to which planters manoeuvred the Dutch governments in The Hague and Jakarta towards military aggression. Citing Republican intent to evade Linggadjati's stipulations, they railed against the Republic's demands, which had been accepted by Governor General Hubertus Van Mook, and which required planters to pay handsomely for access to product cultivated during their absence from what was now Republican territory.[46] On 8 May 1947, less than two months before the Police Action, planter representatives invited General Spoor to lunch, sounding him out about smashing the Republic.[47] Two days later a large planter delegation representing oil companies and various trading houses lobbied governmental envoys from The Hague. They vehemently defended the necessity of military action, making plain their readiness to break with the 'Palace' and the Department of Economic Affairs unless a show of strength was agreed upon. They dangled the tidy sum of 500 million guilders in front of the Dutch representatives – a figure they anticipated would be earned through extraction unhampered by Republican meddling. Lastly, planters helped draw up the economic clauses within the eventual Dutch ultimatum to the Republic.[48]

Now that Article Fourteen had been forcefully swept off the table by Dutch forces compressing Republican authority towards Yogyakarta, the much-vaunted restoration of 'peace and order' could start in earnest. In rural locations the attempt to rebuild colonial administration radiated outwards from the plantations, factories and estates that often lay hidden, isolated within the vast territories of Java and Sumatra. In fact, the returning planters faced a daunting task. 'The extremists had applied some kind of scorched earth-policy,' said one of their numbers, 'and when we, protected by soldiers … could take a cautious look', they found that the entire 'factory, as well as … all houses … including those of the labourers, had been totally destroyed'. Reconstruction was the order of the day: 'Everyone was full of confidence in the future and in good spirits.'[49]

The plantation as counter-insurgency tool

Optimism would soon succumb to frustration and fear. The Tentara Nasional Indonesia, the Republican National Army, and the *laskar*, local paramilitary groups (loosely) connected to it, had simply let the Dutch road-dependent military convoys pass while they remained hidden in the jungles and mountainous areas. Soon after the Police Action resistance fighters resumed their activities, killing planters and their staff. Anyone collaborating with the Dutch or connected to the plantations faced the threat of death. Planters conceded in December 1947 that a well-led insurgency was gathering momentum, leaving them caught in the middle.[50] From this point onwards, the already tentative connection between Dutch administrators and local government began to break down. Police constables attempted taking on a neutral stance, now also working for Republican forces to safeguard their lives. More and more villages severed ties with Dutch officials during the course of 1949 under the pressure of anti-Dutch resistance and the shadow administrations.[51]

Despite the rising threat planters had a specific task to perform, assigned to them by Van Mook before they journeyed back into the interior.[52] Conditions conducive to social unrest had to be normalized as much as possible. This was a pressing matter as thousands of labourers were being rounded up by Dutch troops and brought back to the plantations.[53] A functioning economy, therefore, was deemed to be of great importance to the population, its restoration to be pursued despite planters' complaints of 'political insecurity and lack of safety'.[54]

As they had been before the Police Action, planters became agents for the distribution of 'inducement goods' such as rice and clothing to the destitute who had flocked to the plantations.[55] Medical staff were sent to the emplacements to provide health services, although Indonesian doctors proved reluctant to work for the government, preferring to open more lucrative private practices.[56] A General Instruction dictated that wherever planters and officials of the Department of Economic Affairs encountered organizations engaged in economic activities – 'distribution, managing plantations or companies, trade unions' – these organizations should be maintained 'in so far as they are prepared to co-operate'.[57] Whether this included the Republican National Army or the various irregulars is doubtful, although these authorities did control many plantations.[58] The Kantor Besar Perkebunan, the Plantation Head Office in Sumatra, managed fourteen plantations, whereas other local fighters organized workers into defence groups known as *laskar buruh* (worker irregulars) in case of Dutch attacks.[59] The General Instruction admonished planters to counteract vandalism, to distribute 'as much food as possible' and to 'prevent disorder and general displeasure between personnel and labourers'. Plantations were to become the centres from which structured colonial social order would be rebuilt.[60] This matter was so important that plantation administrators were demobilized from the KNIL despite its acute manpower shortages. In all, planters became the guardians of 'social order'.[61] Surplus labourers were to be retained with exactly this in mind.

It would be stretching classic counter-insurgency theory and reality too far to claim that Dutch civil administrators, the military and the planters had been busy practising population-centred warfare. Whereas the military opened a school or two in some areas with the Inland Administration in attendance, large-scale projects identifiable with an integrated 'hearts-and-minds' programme do not seem to have taken place.[62] Attempts were made to broker trust between the authorities and the population, however. With military and police forces closely connected to the plantations – although this connection diminished sharply when more and more territory had to be protected – security personnel did deploy activities geared towards winning over local communities. Not by coincidence, local *laskar* gangs did exactly the same in Republican territory.[63] Plantations could only grow into food hubs in 'military centres', that is, where the military was present in some strength and in a semi-permanent capacity. Soldiers were also allowed to hire workers and pay them, which would have established a modicum of rapport – for better or worse.[64]

More importantly, police and the military assisted planters in trying to transform the plantations into a functioning system, and this might be viewed as an attempted structural solution designed to separate the population from the insurgents – a key premise of counter-insurgency. With this separation in place, security forces would stand a chance of securing the population, which would ideally lead to its cooperation with the government in engaging the insurgents more effectively. Clear and hold operations could then ensue. The insurgents, denied food, shelter and intelligence, would eventually surrender or be captured or killed by forces of the incumbent government.[65] The Dutch Indonesian authorities certainly tried population control measures. Labourers, for example, could buy discounted food only with a registered licence using Netherlands Indisch Civil Authority (NICA) money. This currency, issued by the NICA, was the only valid money; the Republic of Indonesia currency then in circulation would be rejected.[66] The contents of their wallet was thus taken as an indicator of where an individual's sympathies lay.

Larger-scale population control measures revolved around plantation and estates as well. One commander in the Banjar area of West Java pushed his military posts further into the interior to 'enlarge the circle of security around various plantations in such a way that rehabilitation could ensue'. His death at the hands of the resistance during a military engagement came as a shock to the local planter community.[67] Many plantations were fortified to raise physical barriers between those who could be trusted on the plantation grounds and those outside. The Rayon Representative of the General Agrarian Syndicate of Buitenzorg (Bogor) wrote an extensive list of preparations to be followed. Telephone lines should be kept operable. Sirens needed to be installed, as well as powerful night lights covering areas remote from protected buildings. Sandbags would be placed strategically to control road access and the entrances to living quarters and factories. Watchdogs, barbed wire and gun pits would complete the fortifications.[68]

Arguably, these fortifications were devised to protect the work force, but labourers themselves were hitched to the counter-insurgency effort as well. Following the return of the planters an irregular security force was created in response to mounting guerrilla resistance. This 'Plantation Guard' – rather similar to the Home Guard and the Special Constabulary during the Malayan Emergency (1948–57) – patrolled the plantations, factories and emplacements. An indigenous force, sometimes led by former army personnel, the Plantation Guard gave the labourers a stake in their own protection. Ultimately, more than 18,000 guards, mostly armed and uniformed, tried to secure the plantations they worked on. Planters' influence on military and governmental circles grew further based on their control of such a large number of men.[69] Their first-hand knowledge of anti-colonial resistance cemented their central role. 'By virtue of their knowledge of Country and People' they were called upon to function as 'a source of trustworthy intelligence' to enhance cooperation between army and police in protecting lives and property.[70] Planters would once again spy on their workforce to keep them in line. High-ranking military and police officers and local civil administrators all frequented planter meetings to listen to their security needs.[71] Dutch ministers of parliament made sure to respond to critiques planters aired publicly.[72] At the end of 1947, it had been planters' continued stream of complaints that had sent authorities scrambling to aid them – with more automatic weapons, for instance – and to accuse each other of failing to act resolutely. The acting director of the Inland Administration actually wondered whether more had been done than strictly responsible.[73]

By December 1948 the Dutch authorities were convinced that the dallying Republican leaders had to be removed once and for all. With the old Republic gone a more malleable government could take its place, its members willing to cooperate within a federation of Indonesian states – the United States of Indonesia – irrevocably connected to the Dutch Crown. In the early hours of 19 December the second Police Action commenced. Spoor warned his men to be 'resolute' yet 'humane'. The Police Action, after all, was to bring 'justice and security to a population, that had been crushed by terror and suppression for too long'.[74] As during the first assault, Republican resistance soon crumbled. Republican forces could not stop the Dutch from parachuting into Yogyakarta's airport, while other troops converged on the city to take the Republican government prisoner. Military victory soon turned into political defeat. In a very definite way the second Police Action spelled the end to the Dutch empire in Indonesia. International pressure forced the Dutch to release the Republican leadership and to negotiate a final date for the transfer of sovereignty to the Republic by the end of that year.[75]

In the interim, General Spoor launched one last plan to save the situation following the second Police Action. Its inception flowed directly from Spoor's notion that since Indonesian–Dutch negotiations had begun, 'unrest among the population had increased, the activities of the gangs had become more insolent and subversive propaganda, led by the same intellectuals, who sit at the conference table, had taken on a more intensive character'. Spoor concluded that under such circumstances, 'Army command could give no guarantee [of success], nor carry responsibility' for developments pursuant to the restoration of the Republic.[76] The resultant plan was cumbersomely called the 'System of Security in Unruly Areas on Java and Sumatra'; it was designed to counter the effects of the Police Action's direct drive for Yogyakarta.

While the attack had 'like a knife cut through the crust of resistance', it had not dealt conclusively with the actual resistance itself.[77]

Even in the Netherlands, several news outlets now expressed grave doubts about the military's ability to weather the guerrilla storm. *The Flame*, originally a resistance newspaper founded under German occupation, printed an eyewitness account of the Police Action. It recounted a gruelling episode in which Dutch soldiers had shot some twenty Indonesians at a checkpoint east of Yogyakarta, throwing the bodies off the bridge into the river below. Van Mook, who had at this point been relieved from his duties as governor general, openly criticized the military leadership for the way it had chosen to pursue the war.[78] Planter interest groups panicked and called for action citing increased levels of violence directed at (indigenous and European) personnel, the inability of police and Plantation Guards to function without proper military support, and the presence of shadowy revolutionary councils everywhere.[79] Worse still was that police and military forces could not work together. Even before Spoor refused responsibility for the consequences of Sukarno and Hatta being released, the Inland Administration and its police forces had already in 1947 denied any blame for the deluge of violence. 'No police-organization in the world', officials complained, could face such widespread resistance vigorously animated with a 'political-religious and revolutionary' spirit – this was the army's task.[80]

Doggedly, Spoor plotted on. In terms of the counter-insurgency the general wanted his security forces to wage, his 'System of Security' constituted a last-ditch effort to bring the police, the military, the planters and all paramilitary forces together. It has to be noted, however, that this was not the first attempt of its kind to ensure effective command structures. Recent research has suggested that issues relating to 'civil-military co-operation' had only been discussed in first months of 1948 when the Renville Agreement, signed in January, provided a much-needed pause in the fighting.[81] This assertion is not completely accurate, although Dutch civil–military relations undoubtedly soured after 'Renville'. Rather, the attempts at coordination made in 1948 were themselves an outgrowth of earlier unsuccessful endeavours to improve security force cooperation. With hindsight it might appear that these 1948 arrangements to establish a concerted civil–military approach resembled the British war-by-committee in Malaya *avant la lettre*. If Spoor pursued a war-by-committee, its origins lay in July 1947 when he brought military and civilian policymakers together to establish the Directorate of Inland Security. Led by KNIL Colonel Santoso, but supervised by Van Mook, it was to control the police forces, the Plantation Guard and the Chinese Security Corps, or the Pao An Tui (PAT). Other bodies concerned with security, such as the Inspection-Plantation Guard, liaised with the directorate, while yet another inspectorate – for Police and Safety Battalions – coordinated the various needs and interests of the police, military, the Chinese and the planters. The latter group selected one prominent member to promote smoother relations with the police.[82]

The 'System of Security' of 1949, then, constituted Spoor's final attempt in the vein of his earlier coordinatory projects. He finally came to grips with the fact that his strategy to capture 'key positions as soon as possible' was not conducive to clear and hold operations. Spoor began by acknowledging that he had too few troops – supported by too few police – to protect too many 'key positions and vital objects'. Determined to pursue the resistance nonetheless, he devised a complex of circles, each surrounding several vital positions, most of which were plantations and estates. Within each circle all security forces would adhere to a single plan, with the police in a central role supported by rapid reaction military forces held in reserve. The PAT and the Plantation Guard were important pillars of the system; they would fight off an initial attack until the army's mobile units were called in. If the system proved successful, Spoor argued, the fragmentation of his forces could be reversed, and the circles expanded to secure ever more territory.[83] If anything, the system approached French General Joseph Gallieni's much-vaunted *tache d'huile* strategy – or, to a lesser degree, the system of New Villages that, as part of General Harold Briggs's plan along with labour line restructuring, rather effectively separated Chinese communities from their co-nationals in the Malayan Communist Party. Unlike the Briggs plan, however, Spoor's system aimed for restoration. It was never intended to forcefully relocate hundreds of thousands of people into new locations, with all the concomitant social destruction and upheaval – although the reconstructionist elements of both plans bear striking similarities.[84] In this sense Spoor's plan was indeed attractive as 'Long-lasting control spawns robust informational' policies. The territorial control theoretically created would give the Dutch civil–military apparatus ample time to 'socialize populations' to the merits of its presence.[85] The plan was not necessarily universally practicable, however. In East Java the Territorial Commander sent out a flurry of orders in an effort to bring the circles system into practice. Commanders in Sumatra, conversely, reported that the system could never be implemented. 'The "liberation war"' had become a 'war of occupation', one reported. The second Police Action had opened his eyes to the fact that the population did not want to be liberated; with this second military operation the Dutch had sacrificed the last remnants of the population's support.[86]

Revolutionary violence against the plantations

When the planters first heard of Spoor's system they were underwhelmed, dismissing it as wildly over-optimistic. Nor did they take to the idea that certain valuable assets would fall outside the circles – specifically because mere soldiers would determine which plantations would thus be denuded of support.[87] These criticisms notwithstanding, Spoor's plan clearly echoed the plantations' pre-war functions of social control. The new system once more served to distinguish loyal subjects from disloyal ones, albeit even more violently than before.

The plantation system was never fully insulated. Even before the war, at the height of colonial control, communities and individuals resisted regulation. Scattered uprisings that sprung up during the 1920s, which the colonial government feared were communist- or nationalist-inspired, led it to endorse greater repression. Planters made good use of this reflex. Violence directed at the plantations before 1942, however, never escalated into high-intensity, anti-colonial rebellion, nor was the resistance particularly well-coordinated. In hindsight, even the war in Aceh that continued to flare up well into the twentieth century, but was brutally suppressed by the Dutch, never presented a true existential threat to the colonial state. Where plantation labourers attacked indigenous or European overseers, their motivations were – judging from reports and newspapers – connected to personal, often work-related, grievances.[88] Yearly criminal statistical data reveal that social unrest, such as strikes, was of a small scale.[89] Where suspected communist plots were discovered on plantations, it seems they were written off as having been caused by travelling agitators.[90]

The one feature that anti-plantation resistance shared was its violent repression. Where labourers resorted to arson to express labour-related grievances, a tactic they employed prolifically, planters directly involved themselves with rural policing.[91] Police forces unapologetically fired on demonstrators. Prison sentences were high; death sentences were common and usually carried out.[92] The estates, then, became synonymous with 'order and peace', to use that catch-all euphemistic term. Ultimately, workers had only limited means to act out violent resistance. The colonial state and its colonial agents – including a great many Indonesians – controlled indigenous populations sufficiently, and, when needed, it created additional instruments of surveillance, control and coercion.

The inherently violent scope of colonial enforcement in the name of economic extraction was enlarged during the war of independence. Security personnel behaviour never mirrored Spoor's call for humane behaviour during the dirty guerrilla war – but neither did the Republican freedom fighters' actions. This final section focuses on the nature of the guerrilla conflict and Dutch military reactions to it. Once again, it discusses the kinds of violence that existed on the plantations. Arguably, such anti-colonial aggression possessed of two interrelated components: violence *specifically* targeted at plantations and the labour disputes connected with it. Both have been neglected, despite their manifest importance – and the effect they had on the form that (anti-)colonial violence took.

Military and planters' archives reveal how centrally plantations figured in revolutionary violence. In May 1949, a 200-strong, 'well-armed and organized gang' aided by some 500 inhabitants of a nearby *kampong* burnt the Padang Halaban plantation to cinders. Most European planters had been out drinking with the commander responsible for the plantation's protection. When they finally arrived at the scene, the gang had become – aided by the late hour – indistinguishable from the plantation's inhabitants. Although two people were shot and wounded, the Plantation Guard was heavily outnumbered.[93] This event was by no means unusual – except insofar as no one was killed. By the end of 1948, similar incidents were being reported almost daily. They detailed guard desertions, plantation shoot-outs, the ambushing of goods and vehicles, arson, and the shooting of European staff. Indonesian foremen and village heads, but also Chinese persons, were kidnapped or brutally murdered.[94]

Aside from being definitely anti-colonial in nature, the violence of these incidents had a particular dimension: it was plantation specific. The aggression signified a direct reaction to what the plantations had always stood for: the physical representation of the coercive colonial drive to reconstruct the indigenous socially and economically. With the complete breakdown of colonial order at hand, the resistance vented its animus against colonialism through the destruction of the plantations. In fact, the

Republic's military commander of Java, A. H. Nasution, ordered the attack on these isolated targets, recognizing that the plantations were the foundation upon which Dutch economic power rested. For the guerrillas the presence of the Plantation Guard offered a further temptation. They, the planters and Nasution all rightly recognized that the Plantation Guards' weapons – tens of thousands of them – comprised a most accessible arsenal for the resistance.[95] Unable to stem the tide of resistance violence, the Guards themselves bent to its will.

If the Plantation Guard proved a catalyst, planters willingly compounded the problem by demanding more extreme military action, creating another spiral of violence with a specific meaning distinct from the wider conflict. Spoor was relentlessly pushed for 'extra efforts locally'.[96] He promised something 'spectacular' and had the Special Troops Corps, led by Raymond Westerling and infamous for executing scores of suspected guerrillas in South-Celebes (Sulawesi), set an example. They hanged thirty terrorists at the side of the road near Purwakarta.[97] This hugely disproportionate reaction fits the image of Dutch counter-insurgency – as counterterrorism – that is slowly emerging.[98] During separate patrols in Malang, for example, sixteen prisoners were shot on patrol in March 1949, supposedly while trying to flee from the Dutch and Indonesian soldiers who had removed them from prison to identify their fellow fighters. When the first thirteen did not return, those asking questions were told not to worry: they had been released.[99] One high-placed military commander intimated to the chairman of the General Agrarian Syndicate that he would happily cause a second 'Celebes-Affair'.[100]

Anti-plantation violence hid another aggressive streak that was linked to old plantation disputes: a battle for labour. The struggle for independence afforded Indonesians the opportunity to renegotiate established labour ordinances. Sometimes attempts happened peacefully: shortly after his proclamation in 1945, sugar farmers from Jombang in East Java wrote to Sukarno to tell him personally that Dutch contracts had to be abrogated now that Indonesia was independent.[101] Likewise, a Railway Workers congress in Bandung demanded that certain penalties considered detrimental to the workers and their dependants should be removed.[102] In their dealings with Republican officials, planters came face to face with these demands for new-style labour relations. The Republican Plantation Workers' Union, a branch of the anti-Dutch Indonesian Central Organization of All Labourers, 'went far' in demanding a forty-hour working week, the retreat of Dutch troops, more Indonesians on managerial positions and 'the abolition of private lands'.[103] For their part, Indonesian rebels targeted those plantations where old asymmetrical power relations were still upheld and European planters refused to acknowledge the changing times.[104]

The violence that ensued was calibrated to make these changes seem inevitable. The Plantation Workers Union ordered members to apply scorched earth tactics.[105] As the resistance gained traction, *laskar* groups and emboldened labourers drew closer in their shared attempts to oppose the Dutch and their indigenous allies, despite the *laskars'* preying on the labourers.[106] At great personal risk, fighters dressed as workers in order to assassinate European planters and their escorts up close. News of such cases often persuaded other European employees to quit.[107] Plantation Guards became compromised and were frequently forced to work with the resistance if they wanted to live.[108] Labourers themselves were constantly threatened with death for their betrayal of the revolution; incessant 'whispering campaigns' reinforced the threat. Naturally, the Republic's Ministry of Information was quick to publicize Dutch atrocities, further scaring the population. As a neutral stance became elusive, for many the best option to escape Republican and Dutch violence was to abscond. As with desertion rates, labourers fled so frequently that their flight became a staple of planter reportage.[109]

Conclusion

With 1949 drawing to a close and the transfer of sovereignty near, General Spoor's security system remained incomplete. Miscommunication between police and the military persisted – harmonious cooperation between them rendered impossible by an all-consuming guerrilla war that heightened the army's primacy over the police against a backcloth of international condemnation.[110] Meanwhile, the Plantation Guard had been fatally hollowed out by the resistance, despite last-ditch efforts to shore up Guard units with additional police support.[111] Labour relations also remained highly contested, with planters having to concede ground to 'covertly political, communist-oriented organisations' that encouraged workers to demand land and improved working conditions.[112] By highlighting its longevity, this chapter has analysed how the plantation system in the Netherlands East Indies, from its inception to its violent demise in 1949, functioned as the space in which indigenous populations were classified, deconstructed and rearranged according to the needs of an extractive economy backed by the threat of violence. Whereas in the decades before the Japanese occupation the system functioned well enough to keep sporadic violence in check, the Republic and its fighters, aided by the international opprobrium caused by Dutch military aggression, took less than five years to destroy the plantation system for good.

The chapter has touched upon several often-neglected issues that, like the plantation system itself, are likewise characterized by a high degree of continuity. The first is that the plantations were a critical site of colonial counter-insurgency, bringing the activities of planters and security forces together. Immediately after 1945, counter-insurgency measures on Indonesia's plantations – initially non-violent in intent at least – tried to offer incentives to those ravaged by the developing decolonization conflict. Even Republican leaders, among them Nasution, acceded that the Dutch 'could win at least the passive acceptance of their rule' in some areas.[113] We should not, however, ascribe too much importance to soft measures because this chapter has also demonstrated the extent to which the colonial state turned to greater violence as the resistance became more powerful. Ultimately, this precluded the continuation of more conciliatory efforts to separate perpetrators from those wishing to remain neutral. While it cannot be ignored that the Republic was partly responsible for this coercive turn, disproportionate Dutch-sponsored violence exacerbated an already volatile situation. The inability of colonial civil and military authorities to work together to counter the rebellion complicated matters further.

A final objective of the chapter has been to show that other, specific kinds of violence, connected to distinct characteristics of the plantations, were integral to the forms of aggression evident during the war of independence. Republican forces made the plantation system a high-priority target precisely because it symbolized the return of Dutch colonialism. The planters responded in kind, fuelling the flames as brokers in violence, a role which historians have overlooked so far.[114] Taken together, both parties created a vortex of brutality that centred on the plantation system. Perhaps at the risk of collapsing categories, where 'rampok' – an almost derogatory, orientalist term connoting supposedly apolitical raiding activities under circumstances of lawlessness – has been conflated with politically motivated violence, I have further shown that labour disputes, as part of plantation-specific violence, became bound up with the wider conflict – together constituting two sides of the same anti-colonial coin. It cannot be denied that both Republican Army commanders and labour organizations wanted to steer the resistance – and with it the *rampok* gangs – towards the plantations. The TNI itself sought to control plantations for financial gain in territory unoccupied by Dutch troops, and it was not for nothing that the oddly named irregulars of the Tentara Putera Negara Nehru declared their intention to 'destroy the domination of capitalism *and* imperialism in Asia in general and in Indonesia in particular'.[115]

Notes

1   'Plantersleven, Zorgen en Doening. II', *Soerabaiasch Handelsblad*, 6 February 1930.
2   'Plantersleven, Zorgen en Doening. II', *Soerabaiasch Handelsblad*, 1 July 1930.
3   'Plantersleven, Zorgen en Doening. II', *Soerabaiasch Handelsblad*, 6 February 1930. Mandoer Saidja had fallen in love with rubber tapper Adinda, who unfortunately loved another 'Apollo'; he therefore proposed to fine her.
4   The quote is from Ann Laura Stoler; Interview by E. Valentine Daniel, *Public Culture. An Interdisciplinary Journal of Transnational Cultural Studies* (2012), 24, 3.
5   The Republic never truly controlled the many paramilitary organizations that sprouted everywhere; when Hatta tried to 'rationalise' the great many official and unofficial troops in 1948, many (officers) resisted. Colonel A. H. Nasution, commander of the Siliwangi Division in West Java, continued to devote time to disarming unruly *laskar*; George McTurnan Kahin, *Nationalism and Revolution in Indonesia* (Ithaca: Cornell University Press, 1952), 262–4 and H. W. van den Doel, *Afscheid van Indië. De Val van het Nederlandse Imperium in Azië* (Amsterdam: Prometheus, 2001), 285.
6   David French, 'Nasty Not Nice: British Counterinsurgency Doctrine and Practice, 1946–1967', *Small Wars & Insurgencies* 23, nos. 4–5 (2012): 744–61; Rémy Limpach, 'Business as Usual: Dutch Mass Violence in the Indonesian War of Independence, 1945-49', in *Colonial Counterinsurgency and Mass Violence. The Dutch Empire in Indonesia*, eds. Bart Luttikhuis and A. Dirk Moses (London: Routledge), 64–90; Gert Oostindie with Ireen Hoogenboom and Jonathan Verwey, *Soldaat in Indonesië, 1945-1950 Getuigenissen van een Oorlog aan de Verkeerde Kant van de Geschiedenis* (Amsterdam: Prometheus-Bert Bakker, 2015); Thijs Brocades Zaalberg, 'The Use and Abuse of the "Dutch Approach" to Counter-Insurgency', *Journal of Strategic Studies* 36, no. 6 (2013): 867–87; Joseph Soeters, 'Do Distinct (National) Operational Styles of Conflict Resolution Exist?', *Journal of Strategic Studies* 36, no. 6 (2013): 898–906.

7   See, for example, van den Doel, *Afscheid van Indië*; A. M. Taylor, *Indonesian Independence and the United Nations* (London: Stevens & Sons, 1960); this focus on the political side of the conflict has a rich pedigree: Kahin, *Nationalism and Revolution in Indonesia*; F. G. Gerretson, *Indië onder Dictatuur: de Ondergang van het Koninkrijk uit de Beginselen Verklaard* (Amsterdam: Elsevier, 1946).

8   For such an approach, including the missing planters, see Thijs Brocades Zaalberg, 'The Civil and Military Dimensions of Dutch Counterinsurgency on Java, 1947-49', *British Journal for Military History* 1, no. 2 (2015): 67–83.

9   For a non-colonial, more recent example of the search for neutrality in the face of danger, see D. Stoll, *Between Two Armies in the Ixil Towns of Guatemala* (New York: Columbia University Press, 1993), 95.

10 Recomba West-Java, Afdeling Intelligence & Loyaliteitsonderzoek, N. 453, 13 January 1948, Ministerie van Defensie: Strijdkrachten in Nederlands-Indië, The National Archives, The Hague [hereafter NL-HaNA, Strijdkrachten Ned.-Indië] 2.13.132/417.

11 J. A. A. van Doorn and W. J. Hendrix, 'De Planters Belegerd. De Positie van de Europese Planters Tussen Nederlandse Steun en Indonesisch Verzet', in *De Politionele Acties*, eds. G. Teitler and P. M. H. Groen (Amsterdam: De Bataafsche Leeuw, 1987), 44–72.

12 D. Tomich, 'Rethinking the Plantation: Concepts and Histories', *Review (Fernand Braudel Centre)* 34, 1–2 *Rethinking the Plantation: Histories, Anthropologies, and Archaeologies* (2011), 15–39; A. Graves and P. Richardson, 'Plantations in the Political Economy of Colonial Sugar Production: Natal and Queensland, 1860-1914', *Journal of Southern African Studies* 6, no. 2 (1980): 214–29; J. R. Mandle, 'The Plantation Economy: An Essay in Definition', *Science & Society* 36, no. 1 (1972): 46–62; R. C. Young, 'The Plantation Economy and Industrial Development in Latin America', *Economic Development and Cultural Change* 18, no. 3 (1970): 342.

13 For a discussion on such revisionist claims, see T. Brass and H. Bernstein, 'Introduction: Proletarianisation and Deproletarianisation on the Colonial Plantation', in *Plantations, Proletarians and Peasants in Colonial Asia*, eds. E. Valentine Daniel, H. Bernstein and T. Brass (London: Frank Cass, 1992), 12–13. Graves and Richardson speak of planters' 'hegemony of social and economic life' but fail to mention the social consequences of the plantation economy; Graves and Richardson, 'Plantations in the Political Economy of Colonial Sugar Production', 222.

14 Tomich, 'Rethinking the Plantation', 15; Brass and Bernstein, 'Introduction', 7; Koentjaraningrat, *Anthropology in Indonesia: A Biographical Review* ('s-Gravenhage: Nijhoff, 1975), 58; R. C. Young, 'The Plantation Economy and Industrial Development in Latin America', *Economic Development and Cultural Change* 18, no. 3 (1970): 354; E. Wolf, 'Specific Aspects of Plantations Systems in the New World: Community Sub-cultures and Social Classes', in *Plantation Systems of the New World*, ed. V. Rubin (Washington, DC: Pan American Union, 1959), 136.

15 J. Breman, *Taming the Coolie Beast. Plantation Society and the Colonial Order in Southeast Asia* (Delhi: Oxford University Press, 1989); A. L. Stoler, 'Working the Revolution: Plantation Laborers and the People's Militia in North Sumatra', *Journal of Asian Studies* 47, no. 2 (1988): 227–47; A. L. Stoler, *Capitalism and Confrontation in Sumatra's Plantation Belt, 1870-1979* (New Haven: Yale University Press, 1985).

16 H. A. Idema, *Parlementaire Geschiedenis van Nederlands-Indië 1891-1918* ('s-Gravenhage: M. Nijhoff, 1924), 137; Herman Burgers, *De Garoeda en de Ooievaar. Indonesië van Kolonie tot Nationale Staat* (Leiden: KITLV Uitgeverij, 2012), 114–16.

17 Burgers, *De Garoeda en de Ooievaar*, 115, 117.

18 Ibid., 100–3.

19 Marieke Bloembergen, 'Koloniale Staat, Politiestaat? Politieke Politie en het Rode Fantoom in Nederlands-Indië, 1919-1927', *Leidschrift* 21, no. 2 (2006): 69–90; John Darwin, 'What was the Colonial State?' *Itinerario. European Journal of Overseas History* 23, nos. 2–3 (1999): 73–82.

20 Henri Lefebvre, *The Production of Space*, trans. Donald Nicholson-Smith (Oxford: Basil Blackwell Ltd., 1991), 79.

21 Lefebvre, *The Production*, 79, 99, 101.

22 On languages used, see J. Plomp, *De Theeonderneming. Schets van Werk en Leven van een Theeplanter in Indië/Indonesië* (Breda: Warung Bambu, 1992), 47.

23 David Arnold, *Colonizing the Body: State Medicine and Epidemic Disease in Nineteenth-Century India* (Berkeley: University of California, 1993), 8.

24 Breman, *Taming the Coolie Beast*, 174.

25 'De Koelie-Ordonnantie', Handboekje voor den Deli-Planter, Aflevering 1, 1 January 1917 (Medan: Typ Varekamp & Co., 1917), 28–9; 'De Hygienische Toestanden op de Particuliere Landbouwondernemingen op Java', *Tijdschrift voor het Binnenlands Bestuur*, 48e Deel, Jaargang 1 (Batavia: G. Kolff & Co., 1915), 391–9.

26 C. J. Hasselman, 'Onthouden van Bestuursbemoeienis in Landbouwaangelegenheden', *Tijdschrift voor het Binnenlands Bestuur*, 25e Deel, 1–6 (Batavia: G. Kolff & Co., 1903), 244–55. In 1930, for example, 'coolies' in Sumatra's east coast filed some 357 *klapzaken* or 'slap cases' alone; *Indisch Verslag. II. Statistisch Jaaroverzicht van Nederlands-Indië over het Jaar 1931* (Batavia: Landsdrukkerij, 1932), 187.

27 Lefebvre, *The Production*, 98, 141, 164.

28 Stoler, *Capitalism and Confrontation*, 2.

29 Lefebvre, *The Production*, 98.

30 'Gouvernements Kina-onderneming Tjinjiroean in de Preanger Regentschappen', ca. 1925, image code 4432, Universiteit Leiden, Collections KITLV, Digital Image Library.

31 Stoler, *Capitalism and Confrontation*, 2.

32 See, for example, N. L. Swart and A. A. L. Rutgers (eds), *Handboek voor de Rubbercultuur in Nederlandsch-Indië* (Amsterdam: J. H. de Bussy, 1921), 34.

33 Commissie W. H. van Helsdingen, *Eerste Verslag van de Kampongverbeteringscommissie, ingesteld bij het Gouvernementsbesluit van 25 Mei 1938* (Batavia: Landsdrukkerij, 1939), 35.

34 H. Th. Bussemaker, *Bersiap! Opstand in het Paradijs. De Bersiap-periode op Java en Sumatra 1945-1946* (Zutphen: Walburg Pers, 2005), 66–71; P. M. H. Groen, *Marsroutes en Dwaalsporen: Het Nederlands Militair-strategisch Beleid in Indonesië, 1945–1950* (The Hague: SDU, 1991), 117, 119–20, 141.

35 Michel van Langenberg, 'East Sumatra: Accommodating an Indonesian Nation Within a Sumatran Residency', in *Regional Dynamics of the Indonesian Revolution. Unity from Diversity*, ed. A. R. Kahin (Honolulu: University of Hawaii Press, 1985), 124–5.

36 G. C. Zijlmans, *Eindstrijd en Ondergang van de Indische Bestuursdienst. Het Corps Binnenlands Bestuur op Java, 1945–1950* (Amsterdam: de Bataafsche Leeuw, 1985), 64, 66–8.

37 Zijlmans, *Eindstrijd en Ondergang*, 57–60, 65–8.

38 C. Otte and G. C. Zijlmans, 'Wederopbouw en Ondergang van de Indische Bestuursdienst. Het Corps Binnenlands Bestuur op Java 1945-1950', *Zuiver Wetenschappelijk Onderzoek Jaarboek* (1980): 182–4.

39   J. A. A. van Doorn and W. J. Hendrix, *Ontsporing van Geweld. Over het Nederlands/Indisch/Indonesisch Conflict* (Rotterdam: University Press Rotterdam, 1970), 88–94; Limpach, 'Business as Usual', 64–90; R. Frakking, '"Gathered on the Point of a Bayonet"; The Negara Pasundan and the Colonial Defence of Indonesia, 1946-50', *International History Review* 39, no. 1 (2017): 38.

40   Van den Doel, *Afscheid van Indië*, 185–6; J. Bank, *Katholieken en de Indonesische Revolutie* (Baarn: Amboboeken, 1983), 216–31; J. de Kadt, *De Indonesische Tragedie: Het Treurspel van Gemiste Kansen* (Amsterdam: G. A. van Oorschot, 1989), 116–17.

41   Aantekening van Posthuma (Toegevoegd aan de Commissie-generaal) voor de Commissie-generaal, 8 febr. 1948, in *Officiële Bescheiden betreffende de Nederlands–Indonesische Betrekkingen 1945–1950*, eds S. L. van der Wal, P. J. Drooglever and M. J. B. Schouten ('s-Gravenhage: Instituut voor Nederlandse Geschiedenis, 1971) [hereafter *NIB*] 7, 369–70.

42   Pierre van der Eng, 'Economic Benefits from Colonial Assets: The Case of the Netherlands and Indonesia 1870-1958', Research Memorandum Groningen Growth and Development Centre (1998), 2–3, 23, 27. Income from Indonesia constituted circa 14 per cent of the Dutch national income, 'probably the highest ratio of any country in the world'; Friend, *The Blue-eyed Enemy: Japan Against the West in Java and Luzon, 1942-1945* (Princeton: Princeton University Press, 1988), 17.

43   That the Netherlands would survive economically without Indonesia was already known in 1945; see J. B. D. Derksen and J. Tinbergen, 'Berekeningen over de Economische Beteekenis van Nederlandsch-Indië voor Nederland', *Maandschrift van het Centraal Bureau voor de Statistiek* (1945): 210–23.

44   Van der Eng, 'Economic Benefits from Colonial Assets', 27.

45   H. Baudet, 'Nederland en de Rang van Denemarken', *BMGB- Low Countries Historical Review* 90, no. 3 (1975): 431.

46   Jhr. Mr. W. J. de Jonge to the Federation van Vereenigingen van Nederlands-Indische Bergcultuurondernemingen te Amsterdam, No. 22, 1 May 1947, in 'Correspondentie van Jhr. Mr. W. J. de Jonge, Voorzitter van de Federatie van Vereenigingen van Nederlands-Indische Bergcultuurondernemingen te Amsterdam, Gedurende diens Verblijf te Batavia van 24 Februari tot 5 Mei 1947 Gericht aan de Federatie Voornoemd', Nederlandsche Handels-Maatschappij, The National Archives, The Hague [hereafter NL-HaNA, NHM] 2.20.01/8911; Beknopt Verslag van eene Bespreking ten Paleize Koningsplein Noord, 29 April 1947, Federatie van Verenigingen van Bergcultuurondernemingen in Indonesië (FEDERABO), 1913–81, The National Archives, The Hague [hereafter NL-HaNA, Federabo] 2.20.50/68.

47   Mr J.G. van't Oever to P.A. Verhulst, No. V.V.O. 90, 7 May 1947, NL-HaNA, Federabo 2.20.50/68.

48   Verslag van de Besprekingen gevoerd door Hirschfeld en Albarda (Financieel Adviseurs van de Minister-President (Beel) en de Minister van Overzeese Gebiedsdelen (Jonkman)), 8 May 1947, *NIB* 8, 588–9; Verslag van de Mededeelingen-Vergadering van den Indischen Ondernemersbond, 6 June 1947, Ondernemersraad voor Indonesië te 's-Gravenhage, The National Archives, The Hague [hereafter NL-HaNA, Ondernemersraad Indonesië] 2.20.02.01/107.

49   Plomp, *De Theeonderneming*, 60–1.

50   R. Frakking, '"Who Wants to Cover Everything": The Organization of Indigenous Security Forces in Indonesia, 1945-50', *Journal of Genocide Research* 14, nos. 3–4 (2012): 340–1.

51   Zijlmands, *Eindstrijd en Ondergang*, 88–93.

52 Kort Verslag van de 191e Vergadering van het Algemeen Bestuur van de
    Ondernemersraad voor Nederlandsch-Indië, 2 October 1947, NL-HaNA,
    Ondernemersraad Indonesië 2.20.02.01/21.
53 Verslag van de Regeringscommissaris voor Bestuursaangelegenheden Noord-Sumatra
    (Gerritsen) 'betreffende de Politieke- en Economische Toestand van het Bezette
    Gebied van de Oostkust van Sumatra' over de Maand October 1947, *NIB* 11, 475.
54 Kort Verslag van de 191e Vergadering van het Algemeen Bestuur van de
    Ondernemersraad voor Nederlandsch-Indië, 2 October 1947, NL-HaNA,
    Ondernemersraad Indonesië 2.20.02.01/21.
55 Verslag van een Conferentie ten Paleize Koningsplein, 3 March 1947, NL-HaNA,
    Ondernemersraad Indonesië 2.20.02.01/6; L. A. Verwey, 'Het Nederlands-Indische
    Rubberfonds en het Herstel der Rubbercultuur in Indonesië', *Economisch Weekblad
    voor Indonesië*, 14e jaargang, 17 January 1948; J. M. Gast to A. Poutsma, 12 August
    1946, NL-HaNA, Federabo, 2.20.50/60.
56 Verslag van Regeringscommissaris voor Bestuursaangelegenheden Noord-Sumarta
    (Gerritsen), *NIB* 11, 475–76.
57 Herziene Instructie Inzake Economische Beleid. Algemene Instructie II, NL-HaNA,
    Federabo 2.20.50/57.
58 Mostly before the arrival of the Dutch; see Stoler, 'Working the Revolution', 234–5.
59 Politiek Verslag Sumatra van Regeringsadviseur voor Politieke Zaken (Van de Velde)
    over June 1947, *NIB* 9, 556.
60 Herziene Instructie Inzake Economische Beleid.
61 Instructie voor Ondernemingen en Bedrijven, NL-HaNA, Federabo 2.20.50/57;
    Verslag van de Mededelingen-vergadering van de Indische Ondernemersbond, 7
    November 1947, NL-HaNA, Ondernemersraad Indonesië 2.20.02.01/107.
62 See, for example, Dagverslag Det.Poeraseda aan Hoofd I.V.D.3 Regt.Prinses Irene,
    29 May 1948, NL-HaNA, Strijdkrachten Ned.-Indië 2.13.132/3428.
63 Stoler, 'Working the Revolution', 235–6.
64 Herziene Instructie Inzake Economische Beleid.
65 See Robert Thompson, *Defeating Communist Insurgency: The Lessons of Malaya
    and Vietnam* (St. Petersburg: Hailer Publishing, 2005); Richard Clutterbuck, *The
    Long, Long War: The Emergency in Malaya, 1948–1960* (Singapore: Cultured
    Lotus, 2003); Richard Stubbs, *Hearts and Minds in Guerrilla Warfare: The Malayan
    Emergency, 1948–1960* (Singapore: Oxford University Press, 1993) or David Galula,
    Counterinsurgency Warfare: Theory and Practice (New York: Praeger, 1964).
66 Herziene Instructie Inzake Economische Beleid; Verslag over de Maand November
    1948, 10 December 1948, NL-HaNA, Federabo 2.20.50/60.
67 Verslag over de Maand November 1948, 10 December 1948, NL-HaNA, Federabo
    2.20.50/60.
68 Richtlijnen en Aanbevelingen i.v.m. Ondernemingswachten, het Contact met Militair
    en Burgerlijk Gezag en de Beveiliging van de Ondernemingen in het Algemeen,
    H. J. van Holst Pellekaan to the Commander of the Ist Infanterie Brigade Buitenzorg,
    NL-HaNA, Strijdkrachten Ned.-Indië 2.13.132/3937; A. van Hoboken to the
    Federation, 3 January 1948, Fed. 221, quoted in Van Doorn and Hendrix, 'De Planters
    Belegerd', 44.
69 Prof Dr V. J. Koningsberger, Sinninghe Damsté, Van 't Oever to the Kwartiermeester
    Generaal, Voorziening in Wapenbehoefte Ondernemingen en Bedrijven op Java en
    Sumatra, no. Pr. 3603, 20 March 1949, NL-HaNA, Defensie/Strijdkrachten Ned.-Indië
    2.13.132/654; Aanwijzingen voor het Vormen van Ondernemingswachten, Opgesteld
    door het Departement van Economische Zaken, in Overleg met de Dienstleiding

van de Algemene Politie, 7 November 1947, NL-HaNA, Defensie/Strijdkrachten Ned.-Indië 2.13.132/303; on the interest for ex-military personnel, see Uit Resumé Nr. 4, 28 January 1948, Bespreking DB Syndicaten en Onder-Voorzitters Bonden, NL-HaNA, Federabo 2.20.50/67.

70 W. A. C. Bijvoet to Directies, Vertegenwoordigers en Administrateurs van de bij de (Prae-) Rehabilitatie-organisatie van het Algemeen Landbouw Syndicaat aangesloten Ondernemingen, 10 August 1948, Algemene Secretarie van de Nederlands-Indische Regering en de Daarbij Gedeponeerde Archieven, The National Archives, The Hague [hereafter NL-HaNA, Alg. Secretarie Ned.-Ind Regering] 2.10.14/3458.

71 'Vergadering Kring Garoet', *De Bergcultures. Orgaan van het Algemeen Landbouw Syndicaat, het Zuid- West-Sumatra Syndicaat, de Centrale Vereniging tot Beheer van Proefstations voor de Overjarige Cultures in Indonesië en de Algemene Vereniging van Rubberplanters ter Oostkust van Sumatra* 18, no. 16 (1949): 335.

72 W. J. de Jonge and P. A. Verhulst to E. M. E. A. Sassen, Minister van Overzeese Gebiedsdelen, 'De Onveiligheid in Java', *De Bergcultures* 17, no. 5 (1948): 84–5; 'Een Antwoord van den Minister', *De Bergcultures* 17, no. 7 (1948): 121–2.

73 De wnd. Directeur van Binnenlands Bestuur to Van Mook, No. Pol. 1911, 30 December 1947, NL-HaNA, Strijdkrachten Ned.-Indië 2.13.132/1396.

74 Dagorder, 18 December 1948, Collectie 216 S. H. Spoor, 1946–9, The National Archives, The Hague [hereafter NL-HaNA Spoor] 2.21.03.01/84.

75 Taylor, *Indonesian Independence and the United Nations*, 174–5; Beknopt Verslag van de Vergadering van de Commissie van de Verenigde Naties voor Indonesië met de Nederlandse en Republikeinse Onderhandelingsdelegaties op 7 May 1949, *NIB* 18, 596–7; Van den Doel, *Afscheid van Indië*, 345, 350–1.

76 Memorandum, Terugkeer Republikeinse Regering naar Djokja, No.: Kab./2088a, 26 April 1949, NL-HaNA Spoor 2.21.03.01/45.

77 Systeem van Beveiliging in Onrustige Gebieden op Java en Sumatra, No.: Kab./237, 31 January 1949, NL-HaNA, Strijdkrachten Ned.-Indië 2.13.132/1300.

78 J. W. E. Riemens (ed.), *Wat gebeurt in Indonesië* (Amsterdam: Comité voor Vrede in Indonesië, 1949), 4, 9.

79 Toenemende Onveiligheid in Oud-bezet Gebied, Prof Dr V. J. Koningsberger to Kolonel A. A. J. J. Thomson, S. 225/K., 14 January 1949, NL-HaNA, Alg. Secretarie Ned.-Ind Regering 2.10.14/3458.

80 D. A. Scheerboom to the governor general, No. Pol. 1745, 17 December 1947, NL-HaNA, Strijdkrachten Ned.-Indië 2.13.132/1396.

81 Brocades Zaalberg, 'The Civil and Military Dimensions', 76–8.

82 Notulen van de Bespreking gehouden ten Huize van den Legercommandant op Vrijdag 19 September 1947 te 10.00 uur, NL-HaNA, Defence/Armed Forces 2.13.132; De Tien Pijlers van de Gendarmerie-organisatie, 11 July 1947, no. Kab/878, NL-HaNA, Spoor 2.21.036.01/63; Lt. Gouverneur-Generaal (Van Mook) aan Minister van Overzeese Gebiedsdelen (Jonkman), 22 February 1948, *NIB* 13, 16; Instructie Kolonel de Vries, Nr. 2034 DCO 520, 14 January 1948, NL-HaNA, Defensie/ Strijdkrachten Ned.-Indië 2.13.132/415; Uit Notulen Ledenvergadering A.L.S. en Z.W.S.S. dd. 17 July 1948, NL-HaNA, Federabo 2.20.50/67.

83 Systeem van Beveiliging in Onrustige Gebieden op Java en Sumatra.

84 'A Note in the Handwriting of the Late Sir Henry Gurney Recently Found amongst His Papers and Known to Have Been Written Two Days Before his Death', 19 November 1951, The National Archives, Kew, Colonial Office 1022/148; Laleh Khalili, *Time in the Shadows: Confinement in Counterinsurgency* (Stanford, CA: Stanford University Press, 2013), 178–9; Indian Affairs. Note of a Meeting, 16 May 1952, The

Indian Community and the Emergency, Arkib Negara Malaysia, Kuala Lumpur, Confidential D.O.K.P. 136/1952.

85 S. N. Kalyvas, *The Logic of Violence in Civil War* (Cambridge: Cambridge University Press, 2006), 125.

86 See the annexes to Generaal-Majoor der Generale Staf, W. J. K. Baaij to (among others) Spoor, No. 140/O/OPN/12, 30 April 1949; Systeem van Beveiliging van Onrustige Gebieden, Kolonel F. Mollinger to Spoor, 1 March 1949; Beschouwing Over het 'Systeem van Beveiliging in Onrustige Gebieden op Java en Sumatra', annex to No. 03/08/Zeer geheim/Adj., Kolonel J. C. C. van Erp, 18 March 1949, all in NL-HaNA, Defensie/Strijdkrachten Ned.-Indië 2.13.132/1300.

87 Jhr Mr W. J. de Jonge to Mr J.G. van't Oever, Nr. 420/VV.13, 22 February 1949, NL-HaNA, NHM 2.20.01/8909.

88 'Ongevallen en Misdrijven', *Limburgsch Dagblad*, 25 February 1929; *Indisch Verslag 1932. II. Statistisch Jaaroverzicht van Nederlands-Indië over het Jaar 1931* (Batavia: Landsdrukkerij, 1932), 216; 'Bloedig Gevecht in Soenggai', *De Sumatra Post*, 26 September 1931.

89 *Indisch Verslag 1932*, 118, 145–6, 216; *Indisch Verslag 1938 II. Statistisch Jaaroverzicht van Nederlands-Indië over het Jaar 1937* (Batavia: Landsdrukkerij, 1938), 173; *Indisch Verslag 1939 I. Tekst van het Verslag van Bestuur en Staat van Nederlandsch-Indië over het Jaar 1938* ('s-Gravenhage: Landsdrukkerij, 1939/1940), 431.

90 'Jarenlange Cursussen in Opruiing', *De Indische Courant*, 15 August 1939; 'Geletterde Koelies', *Nieuwe Rotterdamse Courant*, 17 March 1929; 'Kleine Kroniek. En Toch ...', *De Tribune: Sociaal-Democratisch Weekblad*, 20 August 1928.

91 Marieke Bloembergen, *De Geschiedenis van de Politie in Nederlands-Indië. Uit Zorg en Angst* (Amsterdam: Boom, 2009), ch. 3.

92 'Nederlandsche Kolonien. Koelie-row', *Algemeen Handelsblad*, 18 November 1896; 'De Moord op Van Vessem', *Nieuwe Rotterdamsche Courant*, 15 June 1928.

93 J. A. van Hasselt to the Board of Directors of the Sumatra Caoutchouc Maatschappij, Sumcama No. 38/5/1948, 16 May 1949, NL-HaNA, Federabo 2.20.50/59.

94 Maandverslag Rayon Sukabumi over October 1948, Rayon-Vertegenwoordiger A.L.S. C. E. Wenckebach; Maandverslag Rayon Sukabumi over November 1948, Rayon-Vertegenwoordiger A.L.S. C. E. Wenckebach; Maandverslag Ressort Poerwakarta over de Maand October, 3 November 1948, C. M. Frijlinck, all in NL-HaNA, Federabo 2.20.50/59.

95 Frakking, '"Who Wants to Cover Everything"', 341; Mr J. G. van't Oever to Jhr Mr W. J. de Jonge, V.V./No. 63, 25 June 1949, NL-HaNA, NHM 2.20.01/8910.

96 Mr J. S. Sinninghe Damsté to W. J. de Jonge, V.V./No. 61, 30 July 1948, NL-HaNA, NHM 2.20.01/8910.

97 Dpp Atjeh to SIM Jogjakarta, No. 635, 4 December 1948, Arsip Nasional Republik Indonesia Kejeksaan Agung-Kejaksaan Agung Tentara 137; Mr J. G. van't Oever to Jhr Mr W. J. de Jonge, V.V./No. 62, 2 Augustus 1948; Mr J. G. van't Oever to Jhr Mr W. J. de Jonge, V.V./No. 73, 12 September 1948, NL-HaNA, NHM, 2.20.01/8910.

98 Rémy Limpach, *De Brandende Kampongs van Generaal Spoor* (Amsterdam: Boom, 2016); Joeri Boom, 'De Excessennota Moet Opnieuw', *De Groene Amsterdammer* 5 December 2008.

99 Proces-verbaal van Jan Huisman, 12 April 1949, Onderzoek Inzake het Neerschieten van 13 I.V.G. Arrestanten, die ter Verstrekking van Aanwijzingen in de Nacht van 2/3 Maart 1949 waren Medegegeven met Patrouilles van Infanterie IV in de Omgeving van Malang, No: Mlg. 365/'49, NL-HaNA, Strijdkrachten Ned.-Indië 2.13.132/1334; the entire case is contained in this file.

100 Van 't Oever to De Jonge, V.V./No. 72, 16 July 1949, NL-HaNA, NHM 2.20.01/8910.
101 Barisan Tani Djombang Pemimpin Oemoem Partai to Presiden Repoebliek Indonesia Djakarta, No. 287, undated, Jakarta, Arsip Nasional Republik Indonesia, Sekretariat Negara Republik Indonesia [hereafter ANRI, Sek.Neg.RI.] 999.
102 Resolusi-resolusi Kongres Persatuan Buruh Api, 3–5 December 1949, ANRI, Sek. Neg.RI. 1017.
103 'Het Standpunt der Sobsi', *De Locomotief*, 8 December 1948; Jhr Mr W. J. de Jonge to the Federation van Vereenigingen van Nederlands-Indische Bergcultuurondernemingen te Amsterdam, No. 16, 16 April 1947, in 'Correspondentie', NL-HaNA, NHM 2.20.01/8911.
104 Aantekening naar Aanleiding van het Bezoek van den Heer Wisaksono, Secretaris van Staat van het Departement van Landbouw en Visscherij aan de Rubber-stichting en de Voorzitter van den Ondernemersraad, 27 September 1948, annex to Nr. F.2318/V.V.81, 30 September 1948, NL-HaNA, NHM 2.20.01/8909.
105 'Sarboepri en Brandstichting', *Het Dagblad*, 20 February 1948.
106 Stoler, 'Working the Revolution', 241–4, 231.
107 Onveiligheid in Indië, Nederlandsch Indische Landbouw Maatschappij to de Federabo, No 0/63, 18 December 1948, NL-HaNA, Federabo 2.20.50/58.
108 Correspondence with F. Dijkstra, May–April 2009; Dijkstra was a sergeant in the 3–9 Regiment Infantry.
109 Peristiwa di Probolinggo tg. 31/I-1948, Djawatan Peneranan Kr. Malang, Pemimpin Sapari, No.: 550/AIII, 21-2-1948, Arsip Nasional Republik Nasional, Kementerian Penerangan 93; Maandverslag Rayon Sukabumi over October 1948; Van 't Oever to De Jonge, V.V./No. 52, 24 May 1948, NL-HaNA, NHM 2.20.01/8910; Maandverslag over October 1948 Rayon Noord-Midden-Java, J. W. Werkman, 8 November 1948, NL-HaNA, Federabo 2.20.50/60.
110 On the tensions between police and the military, see Nota Kolonel De Vries, 28 April 1948, NL-HaNA, Strijdkrachten Ned.-Indië 2.13.132/1395.
111 Verslag van de Commissie ter Bestudering van de Veiligheid op de Ondernemingen in het Algemeen n.a.v. de Aanval op de Og. Goalpara op 20 July j.l., Kolonel De Vries, 22 October 1948, NL-HaNA, Alg. Secretarie Ned.-Ind Regering 2.10.14/3463.
112 Enkele Passages uit Résumé Nr. 7, van de Vergadering van de Dagelijke Besturens ALS, ZWSS en CPV met de Ondervoorzitters der Bonden, 9 May 1950, NL-HaNA, NHM 2.20.01/8911.
113 R. Cribb, 'Military Strategy in the Indonesian Revolution: Nasution's Concept of "Total People's War" in Theory and Practice', *War & Society* 19, no. 2 (2001): 151–2, note 15.
114 R. Frakking, 'Het Middel erger dan de Kwaal? De Opkomst en het Failliet van het Instituut derOndernemingswachten in Nederlands-Indië, 1946–1948' (MA thesis, Utrecht University, 2011).
115 Politiek Verslag Sumatra van Regeringsadviseur voor Politieke Zaken Sumatra (Van de Velde) over June 1947, *NIB* 9, 556, my emphasis.

4

The Sten Gun is Mightier than the Pen: The Failure of Colonial Police Reform after 1945

Gareth Curless

The Accra riots of 1948, when several African ex-servicemen were shot and killed by the Gold Coast police force, prompted a great deal introspection among officials in the Colonial Office regarding the nature and purpose of colonial policing.[1] Up to this point colonial police forces had been 'more black-and-tan than boys in blue'.[2] Sequestered from the local population in military-style barracks, colonial police forces were paramilitary gendarmeries, more concerned with the suppression of internal dissent, parade drills and weapons training than community service.[3] Even when colonial police forces did trouble themselves with the detection and prevention of crime, it was usually to combat activities that the colonial state regarded as a threat to colonial authority and the established social order. Of course, the criminalization of these activities, whether it was street hawking, beer brewing or prostitution, only served to penalize the most vulnerable within colonial society.[4] In the wake of the Accra riots, however, the Colonial Office, aware that colonial governments could no longer use violent repression to quash civil unrest without attracting domestic and international criticism, introduced a series of reforms that aimed to demilitarize colonial police forces and promote civil forms of policing based on the metropolitan model.[5]

These reform initiatives, however, soon came up against the realities of policing during the era of decolonization, with the political instability resulting from rising anti-colonial nationalism and Cold War security imperatives undermining the reformist agenda.[6] From the perspective of colonial police commissioners, many of whom resented metropolitan interference in local affairs, their primary duty remained the internal defence of a colony, and the upsurge in political unrest in many colonies after 1948 necessitated the continuation of the colonial police's traditional paramilitary role.[7] In fact, far from precipitating a shift from a military to a civil style of policing, the political turmoil of 1948 and beyond actually strengthened the paramilitary tendencies of many colonial police forces.[8] In Kenya and Malaya, for example, the police played an important role in support of the military during counter-insurgency operations.[9] When it came to episodes of urban unrest, the colonial police developed new paramilitary strategies to deal with civil disorder, such as mobile riot control units, whose members were often just as heavily armed as ordinary soldiers.[10] These riot control units were frequently called upon during the 1950s and 1960s, and while the police sought to use 'non-lethal' methods to disperse crowds, including baton charges and tear gas, there remained a tendency among colonial police forces to rely on firearms.[11] In other words, while the use of lethal force was an increasing source of embarrassment for the Colonial Office and successive British governments during the period of decolonization, efforts to initiate police reforms were hampered by not only the conservatism and military traditions of the colonial police but also the rapidly changing political circumstances in many colonies, where under-resourced and understrength colonial police forces continued to tread a 'fine line between soldiering and policing', believing that violent coercion remained the only viable means of maintaining control and suppressing internal dissent amid the rapid growth of anti-colonial nationalism.[12]

Using the policing of labour disputes in British Guiana and Singapore as case studies, the aim of this chapter is to examine the tension between the modernizing agenda emanating from London and the countervailing forces in the colonies that contributed to the increased militarization of the colonial police during decolonization. Since the colonial state was often the principal employer of waged labour in a colony and was dependent upon the tax revenues derived from the production of primary commodities, colonial police practice was closely related to a colony's economic structure – as the work of Martin Thomas has demonstrated.[13] The clearest example of this was during the interwar years when colonial police forces were regularly called upon to suppress labour protests. The police also played a more routine role in the daily functioning of the colonial economy, which included the guarding of strategic economic infrastructure, such as mining compounds and railways, and maintaining labour discipline and imposing workplace regulations in colonial industries. The role of the colonial police as the enforcers of the colonial state and European employers meant that they were unpopular with colonial workers and this contributed to the cycle of worker protest and violent state repression that occurred with increasing frequency in many colonies from the interwar period onwards – which is the focus of the first part of this chapter.[14]

After 1945 it was the policing of industrial disputes that 'first exposed' colonial police forces to the 'political dimensions of reorganizing policing in the midst of emergent nationalism'.[15] The policing of labour unrest was particularly fraught. Not only were the Colonial Office and the new Labour government wary about the use of violence to contain industrial disputes, but Clement Atlee's administration, regarded the emergence of trade unions as an integral part of its efforts to cultivate metropolitan-style civic organizations in the colonies.[16] In this context colonial governments were encouraged to regard labour disputes as an inevitable consequence of capitalist relations and that where possible such disputes should be resolved through peaceful arbitration, not violent suppression.[17] However, the merging of labour disputes with nationalist politics, to the extent that the boundary between industrial protest and popular civil unrest became increasingly blurred, meant that colonial administrators regarded labour militancy not as the product of legitimate work-related grievances but as the prelude to communist insurrection and the possible collapse of the colonial state.[18] Such fears were then used by colonial governments to justify the use of repressive measures, including the use of emergency legislation to limit trade union freedoms, the mobilization of the intelligence services to monitor the activities of labour leaders and the deployment of colonial state violence in response to industrial strikes, labour riots and civil disorder. The point is that while the policing of civil disorder was never as violent as the suppression of insurgencies, colonial policing methods after 1945 remained distinctly 'colonial' in the sense that colonial governments continued to draw a distinction between the deployment of force on the streets of colonial cities and what was considered permissible in metropolitan Britain.[19]

Colonial policing during the interwar years

Prior to the island becoming a separate crown colony in 1946, the Singapore police force was part of the Straits Settlements police. This was a federal police force, with the departmental and territorial divisions of Malacca, Penang and Singapore each reporting to their respective chief police officers, who, in turn, answered to an inspector general based in Singapore.[20] Initially its rank and file were predominantly Sikh recruits, but as the twentieth century progressed, they were gradually replaced with locally recruited Malays, to the exclusion of the island's majority Chinese population.[21] It was a comparable situation in British Guiana, where the police force was established in 1839. Although the early police recruits were black constables drawn from elsewhere in the Caribbean, by the early twentieth century the majority of the rank and file were locally recruited Afro-Guianese.[22] This did not, however, make the police any more representative of the local population since the colony's Indo-Guianese community was grossly under-represented within the force. In 1925, for example, of the 708 Guianese constables only thirty-one were locally born Indians.[23]

In both British Guiana and Singapore the recruitment strategy was informed by the prejudices of British officials, who were of the opinion that certain ethnic groups were innately suited to the rigours of colonial policing.[24] In Singapore Sikhs were favoured because their perceived 'martial' qualities and, as such, were deployed primarily for guard and escort duties.[25] During the interwar period Sikhs also provided the manpower for Singapore's riot squad. This unit was organized along military lines, with recruits housed in separate barracks on Pearl Hill, where the emphasis was on developing regimental discipline through military-style training.[26] The paramilitary nature of Singapore's riot squad was indicative of the strong military ethos that pervaded all colonial police forces. In British Guiana the police started out as a civil force but was remodelled as a military force along the lines of the Royal Irish Constabulary following the withdrawal of British troops in 1891.[27] Isolated from reinforcements elsewhere in the Caribbean, the paramilitary nature of the police was regarded as a necessity by the authorities, for whom violent police intervention was the most appropriate response for dealing with labour unrest, as was the case during riots in 1905 and 1924.[28]

Neither British Guiana nor Singapore experienced significant episodes of labour protest during the depths of Depression.[29] It was not until economic conditions improved in the mid-1930s that both colonies were affected by a series of strikes and workplace stoppages. The unrest in British Guiana peaked between June and October 1938, with thirty-two separate strikes involving some 12,000 workers.[30] It was a similar situation in Singapore, where there were repeated MCP-led strikes in the period 1936–40.[31] Colonial officials and employers were dismissive of the unrest, arguing in the case of British Guiana that the protests spread 'like an infectious disease' and that the epidemic was sparked, not by legitimate grievances, but irrational mob violence.[32] In practice, of course, the strikes were not without valid cause. Between 1933 and 1936 rubber prices increased in Singapore by 250 per cent, which contributed to an overall increase in the cost of living. Employers, however, attempted to withhold wage increases from workers and did little to address the abuses associated with the contract labour system.[33] Likewise, in British Guiana, wages were in decline for much of the 1930s, while arbitrary discipline and corruption among overseers remained endemic features of the plantation system.[34] In other words, as economic conditions improved, workers struck in response to employers' violation of the 'moral economy', provoked not only by immediate economic grievances but also by a desire to redress perceived inequalities, change discriminatory working practices and gain improved labour rights.

This was reflected in the actions of the protestors. Workers' anger manifested itself in instances of industrial sabotage, including cane burning and damage to company property, as well as assaults against management representatives.[35] In one incident in Singapore striking workers threw sand in machinery, burnt account books and shot and killed an unpopular factory foreman.[36] Such acts had symbolic value. In British Guiana it was reported that during one strike two overseers were forced to carry red flags and march with the striking workers, thereby subverting the strict hierarchy of the plantation.[37] David Arnold has recorded similar incidents among workers in India, arguing that acts such as sabotage, which had benefit of anonymity and did not depend on the solidarity of others, were indicative of 'an underlying hostility to the industrial environment' and its working practices that in the absence of formal mechanisms for the resolution of disputes could only find expression in periodic bouts of violence.[38]

This is not to imply, however, that colonial workers were innately predisposed to violence. As Rajnarayan Chandavarkar argued in relation to India, colonial discourses of violence were central to elite constructions of the working class. Colonial workers were regarded by employers and colonial officials as being ill-suited to the demands of industrial discipline and, as such, strike action, rioting and anti-colonial violence were regarded as an ever-present threat.[39] Such fears were evident in British Guiana and Singapore, where the industrial strife provoked considerable unease among the authorities in both colonies. In British Guiana the memory of previous episodes of unrest loomed large in the minds of officials. During one strike in 1935 the inspector general of police commented on the similarities between the present protests and the riots of 1924, noting that on both occasions Indo-Guianese and Afro-Guianese workers overcame the racial divisions that were so critical to the maintenance of colonial rule in order to protest against their mistreatment by employers.[40] Officials' fears were heightened by concerns regarding interracial violence directed against the minority white population. Following the 1924 riots, the governor, Sir Graeme Thomson, referred to rumours of 'anti-white talk' among rioters, and he expressed the belief that without the intervention of the police the unrest would have 'given over to wholesale rioting accompanied ... by general attacks on Europeans, pillage, and ... incendiarism'.[41] The concern among colonial officials was that even the smallest of incidents could spark a much larger revolt, the assumption being that labour unrest could develop political overtones where the ultimate objective was not just violence against the white minority but the overthrow of colonial rule.[42] Ann Laura Stoler has documented comparable concerns among Dutch planters in Sumatra, where acts of individual or private violence, such as assaults on overseers by labourers, developed political overtones amid growing concerns about the rise of anti-colonial nationalism and communist insurrection during the interwar period.[43]

Anxieties concerning the vulnerability of colonial rule were then used by the authorities to justify the use of lethal force. Writing to Malcolm Macdonald, the secretary of state for the colonies (1938–40), Sir Wilfred Jackson, the governor of British Guiana (1937–41), stated:

All police dispatched on strike duty ... are armed with long batons as well as firearms, and instructions are issued to officers laying stress on the use of batons where this likely to be sufficient and effective. ... The most satisfactory methods of quelling disturbances is to concentrate an overwhelming force police at the required moment when violent disorder threatens.[44]

The statement implies that the use of violence was carefully coordinated, but, as the governor also acknowledged in his note, the decision to deploy lethal force was typically 'left to the discretion of the officer in command'. As reports from the period indicate, colonial police forces frequently resorted to firearms 'more often out of panic than as part of a planned escalation of coercive force'.[45] To take one example from British Guiana, during a protest at the Leonora plantation in February 1938 a police contingent of thirty-two men quickly found themselves separated from each other as they sought to protect vulnerable points within the plantation.[46] Fearing that the police were about to be overwhelmed by a crowd of several hundred protestors, the commanding officer, without reading the Riot Act, gave the order to open fire, resulting in the death of four workers.[47] The commission of inquiry into the incident concluded that use of firearms was justified, commending the police for their 'discretion, presence of mind and self-control'.[48] At the same time, however, the commission reported that 'there is not sufficient evidence from which we can conclude that any of the persons who were killed or injured by rifle fire were actually engaged at that moment in acts of violence'.[49] In fact, from the narrative of events presented in the commission's report, the use of violence by the police, which started with baton charges, followed by the arrest of alleged 'ringleaders' and concluded with the use of firearms, not only betrays the inability of the colonial security forces to control the course of the protest but suggests that use of violent coercion only served to provoke the crowd.[50] Put simply, the use of what Jackson described as 'overwhelming force' by the colonial police was often the 'crucial escalatory factor' during protests.[51]

Linked to this, while police violence could restore order in the short term, the use of lethal force often became the catalyst for more organized forms of political opposition. In 1927 the killing of seven demonstrators during a march to commemorate the second anniversary of the death of Kuomintang founder, Sun Yat

Sen, resulted in the boycott of the British-owned Singapore Traction Company.[52] Colonial officials and the pro-British press blamed the Kreta Ayer incident and the subsequent boycott on professional agitators, arguing that the Chinese population of Singapore was being intimidated into supporting the protest and that it would collapse within days.[53] Such claims, however, were undermined by the conduct of the boycott, which remained effective for over a month and was accompanied by a number of parallel demonstrations, with the result that the riot squad and even the military had to be deployed to maintain order.[54] This was what made the boycott so threatening as Singapore's various Chinese communities coalesced around a campaign that challenged the economic and political status quo.

Although colonial police forces regularly intervened on behalf of European employers to maintain order in colonial workplaces, relations between the colonial state and private capital were not always harmonious.[55] The Sugar Producers' Association (SPA), the representative body for the sugar companies in British Guiana, was critical of the colonial government and, in particular, what it regarded the police's inadequate response to the labour unrest of the late 1930s.[56] Company directors wrote to senior officials in both London and British Guiana, complaining about the perceived bias of the Labour Bureau during the arbitration of industrial disputes, which, they argued, was siding too readily with the plantation workers. SPA representatives also demanded that the police provide European personnel with individual protection, that the police increase their efforts to search workers for weapons and that the administration recruit additional police, including a 'military man' with experience of serving either in India or Palestine.[57] Such criticism were echoed in the press in Singapore, where during the trolleybus boycott the *Straits Times* called for the authorities to forcibly intervene and end the protest, asking 'is British authority going to make itself felt or is a handful of half-baked Bolsheviks to be allowed to have its own way?'[58]

In an attempt to exert pressure on the colonial administration, the SPA threatened to withdraw its recognition of the principal trade union, the Man-Power Citizens' Association.[59] The SPA also denied government labour inspectors access to its members' plantations and instructed the Labour Bureau not to intervene in disputes concerning the eviction of workers from company housing since these were 'purely domestic matters between the Management and the employees'.[60] The demands of the SPA were met with a sense of incredulity within official circles. Sir Wilfred Jackson wrote that it was 'gross overstatement to suggest that the situation … [had] got out of hand', while a Colonial Office official noted that 'present situation' was 'due to deep rooted social and economic causes, for which the companies themselves cannot escape responsibility'.[61] Officials also sought to exculpate the police, pointing out that police numbers had been increased since the outbreak of unrest in 1935, including the recruitment of hundred additional policemen in 1938.[62] It was argued that even with the increase in police manpower, the force simply did not have the resources to provide individual armed protection to European personnel or permanently station a contingent of police on every plantation.[63] Instead colonial officials accused the estate management of being too quick to call in the police following the outbreak of an industrial dispute and that arbitration was the solution, not 'premature interference' by the security forces.[64]

From military to civil policing?

The disagreement between the SPA and colonial administration in British Guiana was symptomatic, in part, of the lack of imperial consensus concerning the degree of force to be used by colonial police when confronted with civil unrest.[65] As a result, when confronted with the rising tide of anti-colonial protest after 1945, the Colonial Office sought to systematize the procedures for dealing with industrial strikes and civil unrest.[66] In June 1948 Arthur Creech Jones, the colonial secretary (1946–50), issued a memorandum to all colonial governments advising them that since 'the use of firearms against civilians tends to arouse and perpetuate' 'bitter feelings', colonial police forces should develop more 'effective and humane weapons' to disperse 'rioting crowds', such as tear gas.[67]

Increased guidance from the metropolitan centre was supplemented by the revision of local riot control procedures in the colonies. In British Guiana new riot drill manuals were issued in 1944 and 1945, which outlined the circumstances in which force should be deployed, as well as describing in great detail the various formations and techniques that police riot squads should adopt when confronted with unruly crowds.[68] In practice, however, the policing of labour protests and civil unrest continued to be a haphazard and violent affair that rarely followed the proscribed guidelines in the manuals or adhered to the principles of civil policing. In Singapore the MCP defied the authorities by staging an 'illegal' rally on 15 February 1946 to commemorate the anniversary of the fall of Singapore. When the crowd of approximately 250 protestors refused to obey the police's instructions to disperse, the demonstration followed the usual pattern: a police baton squad was met with resistance and, believing that the crowd was about to rush the police, the commanding officer issued instructions to open fire, resulting in the death of one demonstrator.[69] It was also reported that the Malay constables had used their batons to beat the predominantly Chinese protestors as they lay on the ground.[70]

A more serious incident occurred in British Guiana during a long-running strike by plantation workers led by the Guiana Industrial Workers' Union. On 16 June 1948 five workers were killed and fourteen others wounded by police during a demonstration at Plantation Enmore. Although it ruled the shootings to be legal, a commission of inquiry reported that the available evidence indicated that a number of the protestors had been shot in the back as they turned to flee.[71] Police actions in the aftermath of the shooting only served to enflame the situation. Police were dispatched to all sugar estates, certain areas were designated as 'Proclaimed Districts', which gave the police considerable legal powers to arrest suspected persons, and when the funeral march of the deceased sugar workers took place in Georgetown, the police cordoned off the city.[72] The overzealous reaction of the police meant that the Enmore strike became a watershed moment in the anti-colonial struggle in British Guiana, contributing to the politicization of labour and the emergence of leaders, including the future prime minister, Cheddi Jagan, who repeatedly singled out the police for criticism in the Legislative Council.[73] Jagan later claimed that the police had developed a 'storm trooper attitude' and that they were abusing ill-defined legal powers to harass the public and disrupt meetings.[74]

The police response to the Enmore strike and the MCP protest is indicative of a broader point that Taylor Sherman has made concerning the rule of law and colonial violence. Sherman argues that the use of spontaneous or illegal violence by state actors – such as the shooting of demonstrators as they fled or the beating of protestors as they lay on the ground – should not be regarded as a violation of an 'otherwise just' legal order.[75] Unofficial and extrajudicial violence were part of what Jonathan Saha has described as the 'repertoire of state punishments' in a legal context, where, as historians of colonial counter-insurgency have demonstrated, the security forces had considerable freedom to act with impunity.[76]

In the aftermath of the protests in British Guiana and Singapore, it was acknowledged privately by British officials that the use of force by the police had been excessive.[77] Far from precipitating a shift to a more civil style of policing, however, the police forces in British Guiana and Singapore became increasingly militarized. In British Guiana there continued to be an emphasis on military-style training for new recruits.[78] The paramilitary culture of the police was reflected in the composition and function of the Emergency Force, which was equipped with Bren and Sten guns and performed its duties in paratrooper-style uniforms.[79] In Singapore the catalyst for the increased militarization of the police was the declaration of the Emergency in 1948, which had been preceded by an increasing number of violent strikes throughout the Malayan peninsular, involving attacks on European personnel and repressive police action.[80] Following the start of the Emergency, police stations in Singapore were reinforced with barbed wire so that no one could approach without being observed.[81] This measure enabled stations to be defended with the minimum number of men, thus releasing extra police for the counterattack in the event of an assault on a station. A system of identity registration was also established, and with the introduction of the Emergency Regulations, the police acquired considerable legal scope to detain suspected persons without trial.[82]

Although the militarization of the Singapore police helped to ensure its success in limiting the influence of the MCP, it remained ill-suited for the demands of policing civil unrest. This was most apparent, as the work of Khairudin Aljunied has demonstrated, during the Maria Hertogh controversy of December 1950, when riots broke out following a British court's decision to return a Dutch-Muslim girl to her European parents.[83] The subsequent commission of inquiry into the riots attributed police failings to a number of factors, including poor leadership among senior police officers, the failure to deploy the Ghurka reserve at the appropriate moment, and the predominance of Malay constables who had been reluctant to enforce order because the majority of the protestors were also Malay.[84] Such criticisms echoed earlier findings by Johnson, who criticized the force's paramilitary culture, including its reliance on mobile rather than foot patrols.[85] Johnson's report had provoked considerable resistance from senior police officers in Singapore, who complained that not only was the force under-resourced but that metropolitan methods were largely irrelevant to a situation where the police were dealing with an insurgency, with one officer noting that it was 'ridiculous to expect police to deal with armed, well trained and ruthless criminals armed with note books and pencils or perhaps truncheons'.[86]

In the wake of the Maria Hertogh riots limited reforms were initiated. To improve police morale, working hours were reduced, salaries increased and a Police Muslim Benevolent Association was established in 1953.[87] More foot patrols were also introduced, stations were kept open at night, and the police budget was increased. To further boost public confidence in the police, new riot control equipment was purchased and a riot unit modelled along the line of the Shanghai Riot Squad was established in September 1951, which was an example of the 'cross-fertilisation' of policing practices within the Empire.[88] The police also held joint anti-riot drills with the military, known as 'Operation Popper'. In a visible display of force, riot squads cordoned off areas of the city and practiced baton and bayonet charges. In effect, new civil reforms coexisted alongside traditional paramilitary practices, which were informed by the belief that the authority of the colonial state could only be upheld with a symbolic demonstration of its coercive capacity.

Policing the colonial endgame

Anxieties regarding the internal security situation in many colonies were compounded by the process of constitutional development. In 1955 David Marshall was elected as Singapore's chief minister following the success of his Labour Front party in the Legislative Assembly elections. Marshall's government was soon confronted with a rising tide of industrial unrest, as trade unions affiliated to the People's Action Party (PAP) exploited the lifting of the Emergency Regulations. The most serious incident occurred in late April when members of the Singapore Bus Workers' Union (SBWU) clashed with police following a dispute with the Hock Lee Bus Company. The British authorities advised Marshall to reintroduce the Emergency Regulations and deploy troops to quash the unrest, but the chief minister refused, opting to seek a peaceful resolution instead. When further clashes occurred on 10 and 11 May, resulting in four deaths, Marshall was forced to concede to British pressure: troops from Malaya were deployed to restore order, the Emergency Regulations were reintroduced, and four Chinese schools, whose students had struck in sympathy with the SBWU, were closed.[89]

The liberalization of politics provoked similar concerns among officials in British Guiana. In April 1953 the People's Progressive Party (PPP), led by Cheddi Jagan, an Indo-Guianese dentist, triumphed in the first elections to be held under universal suffrage. The PPP was a leftist, multiracial and pro-independence party, which was regarded by the British authorities as sufficient evidence to suspect Jagan and his fellow ministers of being communist sympathizers.[90] In September 1953 Jagan's government openly supported the Guyana Agricultural Workers' Union (GAWU) strike action for recognition as the representative body of the sugar workers. The PPP also sought to raise the rent on the lands that the sugar companies leased from the Crown, and it attempted to increase the tax on profits made by companies involved in bauxite production.[91]

The mixing of industrial relations and politics, combined with the PPP's attempts to address long-standing social and economic inequalities, was too much for the British authorities. On 9 October 1953, the governor, Sir Alfred Savage, suspended the constitution, called in British troops, and had the leaders of the PPP arrested and imprisoned.[92] A White Paper explained the official reasons for the removal of Jagan's government, including the accusation that the PPP intended to provoke civil disorder – although no substantive evidence was provided to support this claim.[93]

Following the suspension of the constitution, the governor ruled by emergency decree until 1956, during which time the police were deployed to harass the PPP: public meetings and demonstrations had been prohibited, travel bans imposed and party members subjected to constant surveillance.[94] Far from transitioning to a 'politically neutral body', which was one of the key objectives of the post-war reform agenda, British Guiana's police, as was the case with other colonial police forces throughout the Empire, 'remained unequivocally the agent ... of the colonial state'.[95]

In Singapore, Marshall's refusal to forcibly suppress the Hock Lee Bus strike led British officials to question his ability to maintain a firm grip on the security situation. As a result, when Marshall insisted upon full control over internal security and a timetable for complete independence, his demands were rejected by the British and he was forced to resign.[96] Marshall was succeeded by his minister of labour, Lim Yew Hock, who did not hesitate to curb the power of the trade union movement or the emerging civil society and cultural organizations that had flourished following the repeal of the Emergency Regulations. Using the Preservation of Public Security Ordinance (PPSO), which had replaced the Emergency Regulations in October 1955, Lim ordered the dissolution of the Singapore Women's Federation, the Chinese Gong Musical Society, and the Chinese Middle School Students' Union, as well as issuing banishment orders against seven persons.[97]

The prohibition of the civil society organizations and the banishment orders provoked a sit-in protest by Chinese Middle School students, which began on 9 September 1956 and escalated into a city-wide riot on 26 October. It was at this point that the police requested military assistance, and troops were deployed to protect key infrastructure, patrol the streets and man road blocks, thus freeing up the police for anti-riot duties. Over the course of the next two days, the police and protestors engaged in a series of running street battles, which resulted in thirteen deaths, twelve of which were inflicted by the security forces.[98] As a result of the riots, over 2,000 persons were arrested, including Lim Chin Siong, the general secretary of the SFSWU.[99] Senior British officials congratulated themselves on the success of the operation, but the joint civil–military operation exposed the limits of the police reform initiatives.[100] For all the talk of introducing metropolitan standards, the response to the 1956 riots demonstrated that policing in Singapore remained distinctly 'colonial', where the deployment of soldiers on the streets, the imposition of curfews, mass detentions, the prohibition of civil society organizations and the even the shooting of civilians remained, in the eyes of the authorities at least, a legitimate response to the outbreak of civil unrest.

This was reflected in the rhetoric of the British authorities and the pro-government press, which characterized the riots as both the product of an organized communist plot and irrational mob violence. Neither charge had foundation. Correspondence relating to a Special Branch raid on the SFSWU's headquarters stated that seized documents referred not to a campaign of destabilization but instead emphasized the importance of protecting civil liberties.[101] In terms of the violence itself, far from being irrational or random, it was primarily directed against symbols of oppression and inequality. English-language schools and the police and state buildings, not ordinary civilians and private property, were the principal focus of protestors' anger.[102] In other words, during a protest against the curbing of civil liberties it was unsurprising that the police became the target, given that the force had played such a prominent role in the enforcement of the Emergency Regulations, whether this was subjecting civilians to ignominy of routine identity checks or the violent suppression of industrial and civil protest.[103]

The 1956 riots were the last major episode of civil unrest in Singapore prior to the attainment of independence through merger with Malaysia in 1963. British Guiana, in contrast, continued to endure frequent strikes and riots, effectively descending into a state of racial conflict by the early 1960s. Following the end of the Emergency in 1956, new elections were held in 1957, which the PPP won. In the interim period, however, the PPP had split along racial lines between Jagan's largely Indo-Guianese faction and an Afro-Guianese faction, led by Forbes Burnham, a lawyer and leader of the People's National Congress (PNC).[104] The deepening political tension contributed to the outbreak of anti-government riots in Georgetown in February 1962. Since the protestors were largely drawn from the city's black population, the predominantly Afro-Guianese police refused to intervene, and the governor, Sir Ralph Grey, rejected Prime Minister Jagan's request for British troops to restore order.[105] The riots spread throughout the city and, although the military were eventually deployed, the unrest resulted in the widespread destruction of property and the death of four rioters.[106] The riots of 1962 were followed by an eighty-day general strike in 1963, which was characterized by further episodes of rioting, arson, bombings and murder.[107]

The instability culminated in a wave of racial violence during 1964. When the GAWU called a strike demanding recognition for workers at Plantation Leonara, the company responded by recruiting Afro-Guianese labour to replace the largely Indo-Guianese strikers, which sparked a cycle of retributive violence.[108] Interracial tensions were exacerbated by inter-union rivalries. Reports from the period indicate that members of the Progressive Youth Organisation, the PPP's youth wing, sought to intimidate fellow Indo-Guianese, who were suspected of supporting the MPCA.[109] It was alleged that MPCA members were beaten and their houses stoned. In response the MPCA formed 'vigilance committees', which were responsible for protecting union members and burning the houses of known PPP supporters.[110] The combination of inter-racial and intra-racial violence during the strike corroborates the point made in the Introduction to this book that violence during times of conflict was determined as much by the immediate security context as it was by abstract loyalties.

The worst incident of this period occurred at Wismar when some 1,800 Indo-Guianese were driven from their homes and businesses and subjected to rape, assault and murder by their Afro-Guianese neighbours.[111] What was striking about this violence was its intimate nature. From the evidence supplied to the commission of inquiry into the atrocity, it was clear that the Afro-Guianese attackers knew their victims by name and that the violence was not random but was directed at specific members of the Indo-Guianese community as part of a coordinated campaign of terror.[112] The police were heavily criticized by the subsequent commission of inquiry. The police who were present at Wismar were locally recruited Afro-Guianese and in their evidence to the commission they claimed not to have witnessed any incidents of arson, assault or looting. However, other witnesses claimed to have seen police and looters collaborating, including incidents of police constables supplying looters with gasoline. The commission also condemned the commissioner of police, P. G. Owen, for failing to deploy sufficient numbers of police to Wismar and for the delay in requesting military assistance.[113] The inadequacy of the police response to the violence at Wismar was symptomatic of wider police failings during this period, when Special Branch investigations into the violence were suppressed and where the police did intervene it was to target the striking Indo-Guianese workers, not the PNC and its Afro-Guianese supporters.

The police's failure to treat supporters of the PNC and the PPP equally has parallels with other colonial situations, such as in Cyprus, Kenya and Malaya, where the impartiality of the police was compromised by ethnic patterns of recruitment.[114] In the case of British Guiana, in spite of a recruitment drive to address the ethnic imbalance during the early 1960s, by 1965 the Indo-Guianese accounted for only 18 per cent of the police's rank-and-file members. This imbalance meant that the force was ill-equipped for the demands of political policing at a time when the colony's politics was becoming increasingly fractured along racial lines. The result was that while the police adopted what Joan Mars describes as 'soft tolerance' approach to the policing of PNC-inspired violence, striking Indo-Guianese workers were subjected to the same coercive methods that had characterized the policing of earlier industrial disputes, including the use of tear gas, baton charges and lethal force.[115] This was further evidence of the failure of the post-war civil reforms, underscoring the point that as the pace of decolonization quickened the British authorities did not have the time, resources or political appetite to remodel colonial police forces so that they reflected the communities they were supposed to represent.

Conclusion

Writing about the culture of political violence in post-independence East Africa, David Anderson and Øystein Rolandsen have argued that one of the contributing factors has been the legacy of colonial policing methods, with the failure to introduce more comprehensive civil reforms after 1945 enabling political elites to continue deploying the police in an overtly political role to quash internal dissent.[116] Such practices have not been limited to Africa. In Guyana Forbes Burnham, who assumed power in 1964, used the police to consolidate his authoritarian rule, while in Singapore the PAP used the Internal Security Act, which replaced the PPSO, to detain opposition figures without trial, most infamously during the period of 1963 to 1965 when members of the principal opposition party, Barisan Sosialis, were subject to considerable harassment by state security forces. Such eventualities were not unforeseen by British colonial officials. In the early 1950s the Colonial Office, without any sense of irony, expressed concern regarding the possibility of the police being used as an 'instrument of tyranny' following the withdrawal of British imperial power.[117] To this end, the Colonial Office encouraged colonial governments to establish political and constitutional safeguards to protect the independence and impartiality of the police. The problem, as this chapter has demonstrated, was that 'the attempt to transform the colonial police into a politically neutral body that would be a loyal and impartial servant of the successor state had a poor base from which to build'.[118]

Although after 1945 the Colonial Office and successive British governments recognized the need to modernize colonial police forces, the realization of this objective was hampered by the political realities of decolonization. Rising nationalism, which manifested itself in the form of civil unrest and in some cases full-scale insurgencies, slowed the process of reform as colonial police forces fell back on traditional military methods for dealing with anti-colonial protest. Concerns regarding the internal security situation in many colonies were compounded by Cold War security imperatives, resulting in the use of the police to monitor and suppress the activities of suspected communists, such as trade union and political leaders, thus moving colonial police forces further still from the civil ideal. The result was that on the eve of independence in many colonies the police force was poorly equipped to deal with the task it had been set. In many cases the police retained their paramilitary equipment and outlook, few forces were genuinely representative of the wider community they policed, and the institutional and legal apparatus governing the administration of the police was susceptible to abuse by political elites. In short, like so much of the modernizing agenda that accompanied Britain's withdrawal from Empire, whether this was economic development, social welfare provision or constitutional advancement, colonial police reform was corrupted by strategic objectives, financial constraints and insufficient political will to implement the necessary changes.

Notes

1 Josiah Brownell, "'Bloody Coxcombs, But No Bodies'": The Policy and Practice of Crowd Control in Post-War British Africa, 1948–1959', *Journal of Colonialism and Colonial History* 13, no. 2 (2012), https://muse.jhu.edu/journals/journal_of_colonialism_and_colonial_history/v013/13.2.brownell.html (accessed 21 January 2016).
2 Martin Thomas, 'Policing the Colonial Crowd: Patterns of Policing in the European Empires During the Depression Years', in *Writing Imperial Histories*, ed. Andrew S. Thompson (Manchester: Manchester University Press, 2013), 145.
3 David M. Anderson and David Killingray, 'Consent, Coercion and Colonial Control: Policing the Empire, 1830-1940', in *Policing the Empire: Government, Authority, and Control, 1830-1940*, ed. David M. Anderson and David Killingray (Manchester: Manchester University Press, 1991), 1–15; David Arnold, *Police Power and Colonial Rule, Madras 1859-1947* (New Delhi: Oxford University Press, 1986); Anthony Clayton and David Killingray, *Khaki and Blue: Military and Police in British Africa* (Athens, OH: Ohio University Centre for International Studies, 1989); Georgina Sinclair, *At the End of the Line: Colonial Policing and the Imperial Endgame, 1945-80* (Manchester: Manchester University Press, 2006); Martin Thomas, *Violence and Colonial Order: Police, Workers, and Protest in the European Colonial Empires, 1918-1940* (Cambridge: Cambridge University Press, 2012).
4 David French, *The British Way in Counter-Insurgency, 1945-1967* (Oxford: Oxford University Press, 2011), 16. On the policing of the informal economy in a colonial context see Justin Willis, 'Thieves, Drunkards and Vagrants: Defining Crime in Colonial Mombasa, 1902-1930', in *Policing the Empire: Government, Authority, and Control, 1830-1940*, ed. David M. Anderson and David Killingray (Manchester: Manchester University Press, 1991), 219–35.

5   The Colonial Office's attempt to introduce metropolitan-style civil policing during the era of decolonization is the subject of Sinclair's *At the End of the Line*.
6   Ibid., 63–4.
7   Ibid., 63.
8   On the growth of paramilitary style policing in British Africa after 1945, see Brownell, "'Bloody Coxcombs, But No Bodies'".
9   On the role of the police in the Emergencies in Kenya and Malaya see Huw Bennett and Andrew Mumford, 'Policing in Kenya During the Mau Mau Emergency, 1952-60', in *Policing Insurgencies: Cops as Counterinsurgency*, ed. C. Christine Fair and Samit Ganguly (New Delhi: Oxford University Press, 2014), 83–106; Kumar Ramakrishna, 'The Police Must be Part of the People and the People Part of the Police: Policing in the Malayan Emergency, 1948-60', in *Policing Insurgencies*, 46–82.
10 Sinclair, *At the End of the Line*, 152–4.
11 Brownell, "'Bloody Coxcombs, But No Bodies'".
12 Sinclair, *At the End of the Line*, 104.
13 Thomas, *Violence and Colonial Order*. This point is also made by David Killingray and David M. Anderson, 'An Orderly Retreat? Policing the End of Empire', in *Policing and Decolonisation Politics, Nationalism, and the Police, 1917-1965*, ed. David M. Anderson and David Killingray (Manchester: Manchester University Press, 1992): 10–11.
14 David Arnold, 'Industrial Violence in Colonial India', *Comparative Studies in Society and History* 22, no. 2 (1980): 248.
15 Killingray and Anderson, 'An Orderly Retreat? Policing the End of Empire', 10.
16 Ronald Hyam, 'Africa and the Labour Government, 1945-1951', *Journal of Imperial and Commonwealth History* 16, no. 3 (1988): 148–72; Paul Keleman, 'Modernising Colonialism: The British Labour Movement and Africa', *Journal of Imperial and Commonwealth History* 34, no. 2 (2006): 223–44.
17 On trade union policy during this period, see Frederick Cooper, *Decolonization and African Society: The Labor Question in French and British Africa* (Cambridge: Cambridge University Press, 1996), 202–16.
18 Writing about the future course of colonial insurgencies, Sir Henry Gurney, drawing on his experience in Palestine and Malaya, argued that insurgents would seek to dominate the trade union movement and instigate strike action prior to launching a full-scale insurgency. TNA, CO 537/5068, Sir Henry Gurney to Colonial Secretary, 30 May 1949.
19 For example, the 1949 War Office manual, *Imperial Policing and Duties in Aid of the Civil Power*, drew a distinction between the policing of industrial policing in Britain and the Empire: 'The degree of force necessary and the methods of applying at will obviously differ very greatly as between the United Kingdom and places overseas. In the United Kingdom the use of the armed forces during the industrial disputes, except in the form of military assistance … becomes more and more unlikely with the development of organizations designed to bridge the gap between management and labour; and the need for armed forces to quell a riot and insurrection, directed against the government of the country, is a still less likely commitment. Overseas, however, this may well not be the case.' TNA, WO 279/391, *Imperial Policing and Duties in Aid of the Civil Power 1949*, War Office, 15 June 1949.
20 Thomas, *Violence and Colonial Order*, 197–8. See also Kah Choon Ban, *Absent History: The Untold Story of Special Branch Operations in Singapore, 1915-1942* (Singapore: Raffles, 2001).

21 Thomas, *Violence and Colonial Order*, 197; René Onraet, *Singapore: A Police Background* (London: Dorothy Crisp, 1946), 17.

22 For a history of the police see Joan R. Mars, *Deadly Force, Colonialism, and the Rule of Law: Police Violence in Guyana* (Westport: Greenwood Press, 2002), 74–6; Sinclair, *At the End of the Line*, 89–95.

23 W. A. Orrett, *The History of the British Guiana Police* (Georgetown: The Daily Chronicle, 1951), 42. Rajnarayan Chandavarkar cautioned against a view that characterized the colonial police as being completely isolated from the communities they policed, arguing that in British India colonial police forces often became intimately involved in local political networks. De Barros has recorded similar findings in British Guiana where the authorities expressed anxieties about links between the police and the urban poor of Georgetown. Rajnarayan Chandavarkar, *Imperial Power and Popular Politics: Class, Resistance and the State in India, c. 1850-1950* (Cambridge: Cambridge University Press, 1998), 180–233.

24 On the recruitment strategy in British Guiana and the colonial government's preference for Afro-Guianese recruits, see Mars, *Deadly Force*, 63–88.

25 The National Archives (TNA), CO 273/551/15, Sir Hugh Clifford, Governor of the Straits Settlements, to Leo Amery, 28 April 1928. On Sikh police recruits in Malaya and the Straits Settlements, see Arunajeet Kaur, *Sikhs in the policing of British Malaya and Straits Settlements: (1874-1957)* (Saarbrücken: VDM Verlag Dr Müller, 2010). On 'martial races' more generally see Heather Streets, *Martial Races: The Military, Race and Masculinity in British Imperial Culture, 1857-1914* (Manchester: Manchester University Press, 2004).

26 The riot squad was profiled in various articles in the *Straits Times*; see 'Singapore's Huskiest Policemen', *Straits Times*, 23 October 1938, 17; 'Every Member of Unit Specially Selected', *Straits Times*, 23 October 1938, 17; 'Recruiting Police in Northern India', *Straits Times*, 2 November 1939, 10.

27 Sinclair, *At the End of the Line*, 89.

28 On the 1905 and 1924 riots see Walter Rodney, *A History of the Guyanese Working People, 1881-1905* (Baltimore: John Hopkins University Press, 1981), 190–9; de Barros, *Order and Place in a Colonial City*, 138–67.

29 On socio-economic conditions in Singapore during the Depression, see Loh Kah Seng, 'Beyond Rubber Prices: Negotiating the Great Depression in Singapore', *South East Asia Research* 14, no. 1 (2006): 5–31.

30 On the strikes in British Guiana during this period, see Thomas, *Violence and Colonial Order*, 220–1; Nigel Bolland, *The Politics of Labour in the British Caribbean: The Social Origins of Authoritarianism and Democracy in the Labour Movement* (Kingston: Ian Randle Publishers, 2001), 340–56.

31 On the strikes in Singapore during this period, see Michael Stenson, *Industrial Conflict in Malaya* (London: Oxford University Press, 1970), 11–37; Yeo Kim Wah, 'The Communist Challenge in the Malayan Labour Scene, September 1936–March 1937', *Journal of the Malaysian Branch of the Royal Asiatic Society* 49, no. 2 (1976): 36–79.

32 TNA, CO 111/726/4, Butterworth to Beckett, 18 October 1935; Officer Administering the Governor to Sir Phillip Cunliffe-Lister, 24 January 1936; Chairman, Booker Brothers, McConnell and Co. Ltd to Under Secretary of State for the Colonies, 2 January 1940. TNA CO 111/770/6, Copy of a Letter from the Sugar Producers' Association of British Guiana to the Colonial Secretary, 2 January 1940.

33 Stenson, *Industrial Conflict*, 15–17.

34 Bolland, *The Politics of Labour*, 338–43.
35 TNA, CO 111/726/4, Copy of a Report from the Inspector-General of Police to the Honourable the Colonial Secretary, 15 November 1935.
36 TNA, CO 273/630/7, Straits Settlements Police, Special Branch Report for the Year 1936, Supplement No. 1 of 1937, 2.
37 Ibid.
38 Arnold, 'Industrial Violence', 234–55, quote at 242.
39 Chandavarkar, *Imperial Power and Popular Politics*, 143–79.
40 TNA, CO 111/726/4, Copy of a Report from the Inspector-General of Police to the Honourable the Colonial Secretary, 15 November 1935. This is reminiscent of Kim Wagner's point regarding 'information panic' in British India, where fears and anxieties in the decades after the 'Mutiny' of 1857 served to inform colonial policy, often hampering 'the ability of the authorities to respond in a measured manner to threats (real or imagined)'. Kim Wagner, '"Treading Upon Fires": The "Mutiny"-Motif and Colonial Anxieties in British India,' *Past and Present* 218 (2013): 159–97, quote at 161.
41 TNA, CO 111/652, Graeme Thomson, Governor of British Guiana, to J. H. Thomas, M.P., 13 April 1924.
42 Thomas, *Violence and Colonial Order*, 206.
43 Ann Laura Stoler, 'Perceptions of Protest: Defining the Dangerous in Colonial Sumatra', *American Ethnologist* 12, no. 4 (1985): 642–58.
44 TNA, CO 111/770/6, Sir Wilfred Jackson, Governor British Guiana, to Malcolm Macdonald, Secretary of State for the Colonies, 12 February 1940.
45 Thomas, *Policing the Colonial Crowd*, 158.
46 *Report of the Leonora Enquiry Commission* (Georgetown: The Argosy Company, 1939), 10–11.
47 Ibid., 14.
48 Ibid., 22.
49 Ibid.
50 Ibid., 6–15.
51 Thomas, *Violence and Colonial Order*, 212.
52 On the Kreta Ayer incident and its aftermath see C. F. Yong and R. B. Mckenna, *The Kuomintang Movement in British Malaysia, 1912-49* (Singapore: Singapore University Press, 1991); Thomas, *Violence and Colonial Oder*, 77–8; Kah, *Absent History*, 98–106.
53 TNA, CO 273/538/2, Report on the Kreta Ayer Incident in Enclosure No. 1 to Straits Dispatch No. 493, 27 August 1927. 'Boycott in Singapore', *Straits Times*, 26 March 1927, 8; 'Traction Company Boycott', *Straits Times*, 8 April 1927, 8; 'The Boycott', *Straits Times*, 29 March 1927, 8.
54 'Disturbances at People's Park', *Singapore Free Press*, 28 March 1927, 16; 'Trolley Bus Boycott: Government View of the Trouble', *Straits Times*, 31 March 1927, 8.
55 Thomas, *Violence and Colonial Order*, 27.
56 TNA, CO 111/770/6, Alfred Sherlock, McConnel and Co., 29 November 1940; Parker to Lord Lloyd of Dolobran, Principal Secretary of State for the Colonies, 25 October 1940; Minute by Colonial Office Official, 8 January 1940.
57 TNA, CO 111/770/6, Copy of a Letter from the Sugar Producers' Association of British Guiana to the Colonial Secretary, 2 January 1940; Minute by Colonial Office Official, 1 February 1940; TNA, CO 111/770/6, Minute by J. Griffiths, 28 November 1940.
58 'The Boycott', *Straits Times*, 12 April 1927, 8.

59 TNA, CO 111/770/6 Summary of Report from the Governor of British Guiana, History of Disputes.

60 TNA, CO 111/770/6, Sir Wilfred Jackson to H. Beckett, Colonial Office, 5 March 1940; British Guiana Sugar Producers Association to Labour Welfare Department, 15 February 1940.

61 TNA, CO 111/770/6, Sir Wilfred Jackson to Malcolm Macdonald, 24 January 1940; Minute by Colonial Office Official, 1 March 1940.

62 TNA, CO 111/770/6, Sir Wilfred Jackson to Malcolm Macdonald, 20 January 1940.

63 TNA, CO 111/770/6, Copy of a Minute by Commissioner of Police to the Honourable Colonial Secretary, 17 January 1940.

64 TNA, CO 111/726/4, Officer Administering the Governor to Sir Phillip Cunliffe-Lister, 24 January 1936.

65 Thomas, *Violence and Colonial Order*, 64–86.

66 French, *The British Way*, 200–18; Brownell, "'Bloody Coxcombs, But No Bodies'".

67 The National Archives, London (TNA), CO 537/2712, Arthur Creech Jones, Methods of Dealing with Civil Disturbances, 24 June 1948. This memorandum is discussed in Brownell, "'Bloody Coxcombs, But No Bodies'".

68 TNA CO 111/796/6, *British Guiana Police Force Drill Manual 1945* (Port of Spain: Guardian Commercial Printer, 1945); *Riot Manual* (Georgetown: Argosy, 1944).

69 TNA, FCO 141/14380, Comments by Deputy Chief Civil Affairs Officer (DCCAO), Singapore [N.D.] enclosed in DCCAO to Secretary to the Supreme Allied Commander, 1 March 1946. See also 'Police Raids', *Straits Times*, 15 February 1946, 1; 'Police and Demonstrators Clash: One Chinese Killed', *Straits Times*, 16 February 1946, 3.

70 TNA, FCO 141/14380, Comments by Deputy Chief Civil Affairs Officer (DCCAO), Singapore [N.D.] enclosed in DCCAO to Secretary to the Supreme Allied Commander, 1 March 1946

71 TNA, CO 111/796/5, Note by Colonial Office Official 5 October 1948; Report of the Enmore Enquiry Commission, (Georgetown, 1948). The strike and the shooting at Enmore is discussed at length in Bolland, *The Politics of Labour*, 604–8.

72 'Penalties for Assembling Disorderly in a Proclaimed Area', *Daily Chronicle*, 17 June 1948, 4; 'City Proclaimed as Strikers March Down from Estate', *Daily Chronicle*, Friday 18 June 1948, 1; 'Public Await Naming of Enquiry Commission', *Sunday Chronicle*, 20 June 1948, 1. The Enmore funeral procession was an example of what Charley Tilly termed a 'repertoire of contention'. As Juanita de Barros has documented, funeral processions were often used by communities in British Guiana to shame the authorities in the wake of violent clashes between the colonial state and protestors. For a definition of a 'repertoire of contention' see Charles Tilly, *Contentious Performances* (Cambridge: Cambridge University Press, 2008), 8–27; de Barros, *Order and Place in a Colonial City*.

73 Clem Seecharan, *Sweetening Bitter Sugar: Jock Campbell, The Booker Reformer in British Guiana, 1934-1966* (Kingston: Ian Randle, 2005), 132–51; Cheddi Jagan, *The West on Trial: My Fight For Guyana's Freedom* (St John's, Antigua: Hansib, 1997), 97–8.

74 'Police Accused of Using "Storm Trooper Tactics"', *Daily Chronicle*, 9 March 1951, 4.

75 Taylor Sherman, *State Violence and Punishment in India* (London and New York: Routledge, 2010), 174 cited in Saha, 'Histories of Everyday Violence', 849.

76 Ibid. See also David Anderson, *Histories of the Hanged: The Dirty War in Kenya* (New York: Norton, 2005); Huw Bennett, *Fighting the Mau Mau: The British Army*

and Counterinsurgency in the Kenya Emergency (Cambridge: Cambridge University Press, 2012).

77 TNA, CO 111/796/5, Note by Colonial Office Official 5 October 1948; TNA, FCO 141/14380, Comments by Deputy Chief Civil Affairs Officer (DCCAO), Singapore [N.D.] enclosed in DCCAO to Secretary to the Supreme Allied Commander, 1 March 1946.

78 'Training Police Recruits', *Sunday Chronicle*, 3 April 1949, 9.

79 *Annual Report of the Commissioner of Police for the Year 1954* (Georgetown: The Daily Chronicle, 1956), 13 and 29.

80 The unrest of this period is discussed at length in Stenson, *Industrial Conflict in Malaya*, 81–197.

81 TNA, FCO 141/16744, *The Emergency in Singapore*, Report of the Commissioner of Police (Singapore: Government Printer, 1949).

82 *Colony of Singapore Annual Report for the Year 1948* (Singapore: Government Printer, 1949), 112–13.

83 Syed Muhd Khairudin Aljunied, *Colonialism, Violence and Muslims in Southeast Asia: The Maria Hertogh Controversy and its Aftermath* (London and New York: Routledge, 2009).

84 TNA, CO 717/194/12, *Report of the Singapore Riots Inquiry Commission 1951* (Singapore: Government Printing Office, 1951). The politics of the inquiry and its impact on the findings are discussed by Aljunied, *Colonialism, Violence Muslims*, 69–75.

85 TNA, CO 5374748, William C. Johnson, Colonial Office Police Adviser to His Excellency the Governor of Singapore, October 1949.

86 TNA, FCO 141/14424, Comments on Report on Colonial Police Service, enclosed in R. E. Foulger 18 November 1950.

87 Aljunied, *Colonialism, Violence Muslims*, 106–14.

88 TNA, CO 717/194/12, J. P. Pennefather-Evans, Commissioner for Police, Report for the Month of August 1951, 28 September 1951; Georgina Sinclair and Chris A. Williams, '"Home and Away": The Cross-Fertilisation between "Colonial" and "British" Policing, 1921–85', *The Journal of Imperial and Commonwealth History* 35, no. 2 (2007): 221–38.

89 James Low, 'Kept in Position: The Labour Front Alliance Government of Chief Minister David Marshall in Singapore, April 1955-June-1956', *Journal of Southeast Asian Studies* 35, no. 1 (2004): 45–50.

90 Bolland, *The Politics of Labour*, 610–14.

91 Richard Drayton, 'Anglo-American "Liberal" Imperialism, British Guiana, 1953–64, and the World Since September 11', in *Yet More Adventures with Britannia: Personalities, Politics, and Culture in Britain* ed. William Roger Louis (London: I. B. Tauris, 2005), 327–8.

92 Bolland, *The Politics of Labour*, 620.

93 TNA, CO 968/223, British Guiana, Suspension of the Constitution, Presented by the Secretary of State for the Colonies to Parliament by Command of Her Majesty (London: Her Majesty's Stationary Office, 1953).

94 Joan Mars, 'Colonialism, Political Policing, and the Jagan Years', in *Caribbean Labor Politics: Legacies of Cheddi Jagan and Michael Manley*, ed. Perry Mars and Alma H. Young (Detroit: Wayne State University Press, 2004), 75. The PPP's publication, *Thunder*, carried numerous articles detailing harassment by the police. See, for example, 'Operation Terror', *Thunder*, Vol. 5, No. 19, 7 August 1954, p. 1; 'A Civil

Right Strangled', Vol. 5, No. 16, 17 July 1954, p. 1; 'Police Given Further Powers', *Thunder*, Vol. 5, No. 13, 26 June 1954, p. 3.

95　Killingray and Anderson, 'An Orderly Retreat? Policing the End of Empire', 12.

96　Lau, 'Decolonization and the Cold War', 45–7.

97　TNA, FCO 141/14772, Singapore Intelligence Committee, Report for the Period 14 to 27 September 1956; TNA, CO 1030/187, Sir Roger Black, the Governor of Singapore, to, Alan Lenox-Boyd, Secretary of State for the Colonies, 9 September 1956.

98　For official accounts of the riots see TNA, FCO 141/15167, Singapore Riots October 1956, Report to His Excellency Sir Robert Black, Governor and Commander in Chief Singapore, from D. D. C Tulloch and N. G. Morris, Commissioner of Police; TNA, WO 252/1212, Report on the Military Action in Singapore Riots, 25 October–2 November 1956; *Annual Report of the Singapore Police Force for 1956* (Singapore: Government Printer, 1956), 42–55.

99　TNA, CO 1030/187, Note on Singapore Riots, 13 November 1956.

100　TNA, FCO 141/15167, Sir R. Black, Governor of Singapore, to Alan Lenox-Boyd, Secretary of State for Colonies, 10 December 1956.

101　TNA, FCO 141/14773, Director of Special Branch to Chief Secretary, 31 October 1956.

102　TNA, WO 252/1212, Report on the Military Action in Singapore Riots, 25 October to 2 November 1956.

103　In the aftermath of the riots, Lim Chin Siong was accused of making a speech during which he encouraged the crowd to 'beat the police'. However, Thum Ping Tjin has uncovered evidence to the contrary, suggesting that Lim pleaded with the crowd not to attack the police. Thum's discovery is a significant intervention in the debate on the role of the left during Singapore's struggle for independence and challenges established narratives regarding the willingness of leftist activists to resort to violence. See Thum Ping Tjin, 'Lim Chin Siong was wrongfully detained', available at: http://www.theonlinecitizen.com/2014/05/lim-chin-siong-was-wrongfully-detained/(accessed: 21 January 2016).

104　The emergence of the PPP-PNC rivalry in British Guiana and the Anglo-American role in stoking these tensions has attracted a considerable body of scholarship. Standout examples include Stephen G. Rabe, *U.S. Intervention in British Guiana: A Cold War Story* (Chapel Hill: The University of North Carolina Press, 2005) and Spencer Mawby, *Ordering Independence: The End of Empire in the Anglophone Caribbean, 1947-1969* (Basingstoke: Palgrave Macmillan, 2012), 182–204.

105　On Grey's initial refusal to intervene see TNA, CO 1031/4034, Use of Military and Naval Force in Support of the Civil Power, Statement by the Governor of British Guiana, Sir Ralph Grey, February 1962.

106　*Report of a Commission of Inquiry into Disturbances in British Guiana, 1962* (London: HMSO, 1962), 42–3.

107　Robert Waters Jr. and Gordon O. Daniels, 'The World's Longest Strike: The AFL-CIO, the CIA, and British Guiana', *Diplomatic History* 29 (2005): 279–307.

108　Mars, 'Colonialism, Political Policing', 78; Robert Anthony Waters Jr. and Gordon Oliver Daniels, 'Striking for Freedom: International Intervention and the Guianese Sugar Workers' Strike of 1964', *Cold War History* 10, no. 4 (2010): 537–69.

109　International Institute of Social History (IISH), Amsterdam, ICFTU Papers, Folder 5266, Report on British Guiana by Gene Meakins of the AFL-CIO, 2.

110　IISH, ICFTU Papers, Folder 5266, Report on T. S. Bavin's Visit to British Guiana, 31 July to 8 August, 1964.

111 Drayton, 'Anglo-American "Liberal" Imperialism', 334.
112 *Report of the Wismar, Christianburg and Mackenzie Commission*, available at: http://www.guyana.org/features/wismar_report.html#chapter1 (accessed: 21 January 2016).
113 Ibid.
114 Killingray and Anderson, 'An Orderly Retreat? Policing the End of Empire', 13.
115 Mars, 'Colonialism, Political Policing', 79.
116 David M. Anderson and Øystein Rolandsen, 'Violence as Politics in Eastern Africa 1940-1990: Legacy, Agency, Contingency', *Journal of Eastern African Studies* 8, no. 4 (2014): 548.
117 TNA, CO 1037/9, Colonial Office Circular Despatch, August 1953, 'Police Service Commission, Nigeria 1956-7', quoted in Anderson and Killingray, 'An Orderly Retreat', 13.
118 Anderson and Killingray, 'An Orderly Retreat', 13.

5

'A Litigious Island': Law, Rights and Counter-insurgency during the Cyprus Emergency

Brian Drohan[1]

During Britain's decolonization wars, colonial authorities criminalized insurgent behaviour and contrasted it with the government's apparent lawfulness in an effort to enhance the colonial regime's political legitimacy.[2] Sir Robert Thompson, a civilian defence official during the 1948–60 Malayan Emergency, embraced the notion that promoting the 'rule of law', winning the population's 'hearts and minds' and restricting the use of force to the minimum necessary would increase government legitimacy in the eyes of the local population. His 1966 book *Defeating Communist Insurgency* has since come to represent a mythologized and idealized approach to counter-insurgency based on the notion that British forces obeyed the rule of law.[3] In actuality, however, the law was less benign than Thompson acknowledged.

When the Cyprus Emergency began in 1955, colonial officials based Cypriot Emergency laws on those already being used to combat the Mau Mau rebellion that had erupted in 1952 in Kenya.[4] But despite the existence of harsh legislation in Cyprus, including what one legal scholar called 'a more extensive liability to the death penalty than had existed in either Malaya or Kenya', the effects of legalized state coercion in Cyprus paled in comparison to the notorious brutality inflicted in Kenya.[5] One statistic is particularly illustrative: Through almost four years of conflict, colonial officials executed nine Greek Cypriots for Emergency-related offences. This makes for a ratio of 1 person executed for Emergency-related offences out of every 40,111 Greek Cypriots. In Kenya, it was 1 out of every 1,284.[6] Circumstances in Cyprus differed from Kenya in many ways, but the role of Greek Cypriot lawyers is chief among these differences. In Cyprus, the local legal elite established a vocal advocacy network that defended the rights of Greek Cypriots from the effects of repressive Emergency regulations. These advocates challenged counter-insurgency laws, which transformed the colonial legal system into a contested space in which British authorities had to justify their actions to Greek Cypriots, domestic British audiences and in the international arena.

Law, empire and the Kenya Emergency

By the late eighteenth century, colonialism's moral rationalization was based on the 'rule of law'. The applicability of law to all imperial subjects, regardless of status, therefore formed a core justification of the legitimacy of colonial rule.[7] But such equality before the law did not occur in practice. Historians understand colonial legal systems as plural spaces in which law often applies to different groups in different ways. In addition, various actors – including imperial agents, cultural intermediaries and colonized subjects – can assert agency and contest the colonial order through legal processes. In this sense, 'ordinary' colonial legal regimes could offer a degree of flexibility and room for negotiation between colonizer and colonized. As a result, colonial legal regimes were hybrid justice systems in which the application of law was always contested and based on mixtures of metropolitan and local ideas.[8] The idea that colonized peoples required instruction in the rule of law in order to become 'civilized' also became part of the justification for colonial rule constructed upon racial hierarchies. In colonies with large white settler populations, such as Kenya, settlers resisted equal application of the law to whites and indigenous populations.[9]

When faced with the imperative of preserving the colonial state, however, officials could exercise whatever discretionary authority was necessary to ensure the survival of the colonial regime. During the nineteenth century, British officials developed a series of imperial legal precedents which granted the state broad emergency powers. Measures such as the 1818 Bengal Regulation permitted detention without trial. The Bengal Regulation later formed the basis for similar legislation in Ireland. Emergency laws therefore allowed colonial officials to place insurgents beyond judicial inquiry.[10] The application of violence during emergencies applied to civilians as well as insurgents. By the twentieth century, in colonies as far-flung as Malaya, Palestine and Nyasaland, colonial governments regularly employed forced resettlement, curfews and collective punishments.[11] The most documented – and extreme – case of the 'rule of law' run amok, however, is the 1952–60 Kenya Emergency.

After the outbreak of the Mau Mau rebellion, colonial authorities implemented emergency laws that transformed Kenya's legal system into a particularly coercive counter-insurgency apparatus. Since the insurgency gained support from the colony's 1.4 million Kikuyu, emergency legislation permitted the detention of much of the Kikuyu population in a 'gulag' where they were deprived of basic rights and subjected to physical and psychological abuse in abhorrent living conditions. In addition, colonial authorities manipulated the law by changing rules of evidence and expanding the use of capital punishment. Taking a Mau Mau oath became a capital offence. Ultimately, the colonial government executed 1,090 people for Emergency-related offences.[12] Tens of thousands died in the detention camps.[13]

Although broad social factors such as institutionalized racism and the influential white settler community in Kenya contributed to the Emergency regulations' viciousness, the Kikuyu also lacked a strong indigenous legal elite. In 1953, one year after the insurgency began, there was only one African lawyer in Kenya. He was Chiedo Argwings Kodhek, and he defended Mau Mau suspects along with a handful of lawyers from Kenya's South Asian community. These lawyers, however, often faced harassment from officials and white settlers. Many lawyers would only represent Mau Mau clients if they received an assignment through the system of 'pauper's briefs' designed for defendants who were too poor to afford legal fees. White lawyers in Kenya overwhelmingly sided with the colonial administration and showed little interest in defending Mau Mau suspects. Lacking a cohesive legal advocacy network to represent their interests, the Kikuyu remained vulnerable to a predatory colonial legal system operating with what historian David Anderson has called a 'culture of impunity'.[14] In Kenya, the 'rule of law' translated into perhaps the most repressive regime in the British Empire. In Cyprus, however, Britain's legalized repression faced a concerted challenge from Greek Cypriot lawyers.

The Cypriot legal elite

According to British expatriate newspaperman Charles Foley, Cyprus was 'a litigious island'.[15] This litigiousness was an unexpected by-product of British imperial rule. For many middle- and upper-class Cypriots fortunate enough to study in Britain, the legal profession was a popular choice. Once called to the bar in Britain, Cypriot lawyers from the Greek and Turkish communities often returned home to practice, where they helped administer law and order. Colonial authorities relied on the indigenous elite's social connections and status to reinforce imperial rule. In exchange for their cooperation with colonial rulers, local intermediaries benefited from imperial connections to increase their social status.

Before the insurgency, Greek Cypriot lawyers who actively supported the enosis movement, such as John Clerides, worked closely with the colonial government. From 1946 to 1949, Clerides served as mayor of Nicosia. In 1952 the governor appointed him to the Executive Council. He was also appointed a Queen's counsel.[16] During the Second World War, John's son Glafkos volunteered for bomber duty in the Royal Air Force and spent several years as a German prisoner of war.[17] From 1944 to 1952, another barrister, Stelios Pavlides, served as the first and only Greek Cypriot attorney general under British rule. Pavlides was also appointed to the Legislative Counsel and, like Clerides, was named a Queen's counsel.[18]

The 1955 Advocates Law regulated the structure, qualifications and organization of the Cypriot legal profession. The law established the Cyprus Bar Council as an association to which all practising attorneys on the island were required to belong. Intended to provide lawyers with a forum for organizing the Cypriot legal profession, the Bar Council maintained close relations with the colonial administration. The attorney general held the title of Bar Council president, while the solicitor general served as vice president. Both officials also sat on the board of directors. Whereas the president and vice president positions were largely symbolic, the council functioned on a daily basis under the direction of the chairman, elected by council members to serve a fixed term.[19]

The Greek Cypriot legal elite existed because of British rule – some had even gone to war for the empire – but they did not embrace the colonial regime. Repressive policies following a 1931 revolt and persistent British opposition to *enosis* – union with

Greece – after the end of the Second World War alienated many Greek Cypriots. The post-war creation of the United Nations seemed to herald a coming of age of national self-determination and international human rights, yet Britain insisted on retaining the control of Cyprus. On 1 April 1955, when the pro-*enosis* insurgent group EOKA launched a guerrilla campaign against the British, Greek Cypriot lawyers also had to choose sides. With the November 1955 declaration of a State of Emergency and the strict emergency legislation that followed, many Greek Cypriot lawyers' opinions tilted decisively in favour of EOKA and *enosis*.[20]

The Emergency regulations

In response to the EOKA threat, colonial officials enacted harsh emergency laws designed to enhance the authorities' ability to conduct counter-insurgency. The legislation established non-jury special courts to try Emergency-related offences. The laws also permitted the Security Forces to stop, search and question any person suspected of acting or intending to act in a manner 'prejudicial to public safety, or public order'. Security personnel could arrest without warrant and detain without trial any person believed to have acted 'in a manner prejudicial to public safety or public order'. Any officer in the rank of a major or higher could order a suspect's detention without trial for up to twenty-eight days. The governor, Field Marshal John Harding, could authorize it indefinitely. He could also designate 'Danger Areas' in which 'no one was allowed to enter, or remain' other than Security Forces, who were authorized to shoot anyone in an off-limits area.[21] Harding could also impose fines on entire villages, confiscate property, and order the whipping of juveniles for offences such as throwing stones at soldiers or disseminating EOKA propaganda.[22]

Emergency laws also facilitated government control over civilian daily life. Colonial authorities could censor the Cypriot press and restrict or suppress news reports from outside the island. Propaganda such as signs, slogans, graffiti, banners and flags bearing political messages was also prohibited. The Curfew Law permitted district commissioners to prohibit the population of a designated area from leaving their homes for a set period of time. The commissioners could determine where and for how long the curfew would apply. Persons wishing to move about during the curfew had to obtain a pass from the police.[23] Legislation also prohibited persons under age twenty-seven from riding bicycles, which EOKA fighters often employed as 'get-away' vehicles.[24]

Two of the most notorious regulations were enacted in November 1956, a year after the declaration of a State of Emergency. The Firearms Law required judges to sentence to death anyone convicted of carrying, possessing or using firearms or explosives.[25] The Public Officers' Protection Regulation shielded members of the Security Forces and Colonial Civil Service from prosecution. Public servants could only face charges on a case-by-case basis if the attorney general consented. Such prosecutions were rare. As one EOKA leaflet complained, the Public Officers' Protection meant that 'if you have been unjustly treated or ill-treated … you have no right to take the persons responsible to court'.[26]

To the Greek Cypriot legal community, these draconian laws violated the most fundamental concepts of justice. 'British justice is fair in England, but not abroad,' recalled barrister Renos Lyssiotis. To him, the Emergency laws perverted hallowed principles of justice – innocence until proven guilty, the freedom of speech and association, and respect for individual rights – by creating a repressive system in which the government wielded absolute power. Such a system also undermined fundamental elements of human dignity and human rights upon which the post-war international order was supposedly based.[27] Seeing the authoritarian effects of British rule, another barrister, Lellos Demetriades, expressed his derision: 'Cyprus had the philosopher Zeno, we had a civilization of our own – Greek civilization – when the British were still in caves.'[28] No longer a group of loyal imperial intermediaries, many Greek Cypriot lawyers instead embraced EOKA and *enosis*.[29] Knowledgeable of domestic and international law and well organized under Bar Council auspices, these EOKA lawyers wielded the colonial legal system as a weapon against British authority.

Waging 'lawfare'

Applying what has since been termed 'lawfare', EOKA lawyers turned the colonial legal system into an arena where they challenged the colonial state's arbitrary authority.[30] This legal advocacy focused on the protection of detainees' civil rights, particularly the right of detainees to legal representation and the confidentiality of attorney–client relationship. In addition, the lawyers staunchly defended EOKA fighters in capital punishment cases.

The protection of detainees' access to lawyers served several purposes – it allowed lawyers to keep family members informed of their loved ones' whereabouts, provided an opportunity to build a case for trial defence and enabled lawyers to convey messages from EOKA leaders to captured fighters. As soldiers and police began making arrests, EOKA lawyers complained to the attorney general that Security Forces often prevented them from speaking with detainees. Family members ran into difficulties, too, as parents and spouses of arrested persons often spent several days seeking to learn the whereabouts of their loved ones.[31]

By February 1956, only three months after Harding's declaration of Emergency, officials responded to the lawyers' complaints by reaffirming the right of a detainee to consult an attorney. Deputy Attorney General Nedjati Munir reminded security officials that 'it is a fundamental principle of British justice, almost dating back to the Magna Carta, that a person in custody must be given reasonable facilities for obtaining legal advice and for arranging his defence'. This right was enshrined in Cyprus law – the Detention of Persons Laws associated with the Emergency stated that visits by attorneys to detainees 'will be allowed at all reasonable times'. To prevent future obstructions of this right, Munir informed the Chief of Staff that 'this principle and the statutory provisions in our law, should be drawn to the attention of Area and Unit Commanders'.[32]

On 18 February, Chief of Staff Brigadier J. S. Aldridge circulated a memorandum that established protocols governing arrest and detention procedures. He instructed the

Security Forces that upon making an arrest they were to notify the closest Divisional Police Headquarters. If a police station received inquiries from family members regarding the location of an arrested person, station personnel were to contact their Divisional Police Headquarters to obtain the information. The memorandum also stipulated that arrested persons had the right to legal representation. Aldridge ordered that when an interview between an attorney and detainee occurred, guards were to position themselves within eyesight of the meeting, but not within range of hearing. This procedure was intended to preserve the confidentiality of attorney–client discussions. The memorandum further proclaimed that powers of arrest and detention without warrant 'do NOT override the ordinary law of the colony in one important respect, namely that any arrested person must be given reasonable facilities for obtaining legal advice'. Soldiers and police who inhibited this right were therefore acting 'contrary to the spirit of the law'.[33]

Discussions between Bar Council leaders and government legal authorities continued throughout the summer. Eventually the participants agreed on three key points and recorded them in an 17 August memorandum. First, any person detained under the Emergency regulations should be allowed to see an attorney after 48 hours of interrogation. Second, the government will provide a liaison officer at a central office available to answer calls and inquiries from lawyers. The third point reiterated the February discussion that allowed attorney–client meetings to occur within sight, but beyond the hearing of prison authorities.[34] The memorandum was fundamentally a compromise. Greek Cypriot attorneys obtained concessions from the government, but had to accept the Security Forces' desire to interrogate detainees for 48 hours after capture before permitting lawyers to visit. Police and army commanders insisted on this measure so they could gather time-sensitive intelligence. The August memorandum also included an important caveat: 'Facilities for a lawyer to interview a person in custody may be withheld if, in the opinion of the officer in charge of the Police Division, they would be likely to hinder urgent enquiries or to prevent further arrests.' Senior police officers could therefore inhibit a detainee's defence in court by limiting lawyers' access to clients based on suspicion rather than evidence.[35]

Some Security Force officials chafed at the limitations imposed by the 17 August guidelines. The director of the detention camps, J. C. Piegrome, was one. He visited the solicitor general 'to obtain his opinion on refusing detainees permission to see their lawyers for the purpose of taking action against members of the Security Forces or Camp Staff'. Piegrome wanted to prevent detainees from meeting with attorneys if they intended to file charges against the detention camp staff. But the solicitor general insisted that Piegrome 'must grant permission for the detainees to see their lawyers and that we would only be justified in withholding this permission if we had sound grounds for thinking that the lawyer was likely to engage in some unlawful act while in the Camp'.[36]

Other officials, such as Attorney General Sir James Henry, followed the 17 August guidelines closely. In October 1956, British forces launched a major cordon-and-search operation called Sparrowhawk. On 17 and 18 October, several Greek Cypriot lawyers wrote to Henry complaining that the police had failed to answer repeated requests for a complete list of Greek Cypriots detained during the operation. The lawyers wanted to identify who was detained, find out where they were being held, provide them with legal advice, and inform their family members of the arrests. All of these requests fell within the remit of the 17 August memorandum, but the authorities had not yet provided the information. The lawyers asked for Henry's help in obtaining the desired information.[37] Within 24 hours, Henry provided a by-name list of detainees and their place of detention. The EOKA lawyers responded by expressing their 'deep appreciation' for Henry's quick reply.[38]

Despite opposition from some within the colonial administration, the 17 August memorandum chipped away at the colonial state's emergency powers. The lawyers' pressure paid off as Attorney General Henry instructed police and prison staff 'not to hold up visits longer than is absolutely necessary in the cases of persons detained for interrogation' and reminded the Security Forces that 'persons should be enabled to see advocates as soon as possible'.[39] But the lawyers' efforts depended on British authorities' willingness to follow the agreed-upon procedures. The aftermath of Operation Sparrowhawk, in which Sir James Henry scrupulously followed the tenets of the 17 August memorandum, reinforced the unequal balance of power between the colonial authorities and the Bar Council advocates. Without the attorney general's positive response to their complaints, the lawyers' efforts would have failed to produce their desired results.

Although the 17 August memorandum remained in effect throughout the conflict, EOKA lawyers continued to file complaints when British forces failed to abide by the memorandum's instructions. In February 1958, Special Branch headquarters chastised its subordinates because 'Special Branch Officers are not in all cases complying with the Rules issued on the 17th August 1956 setting out the procedure to be followed when persons are arrested and detained in custody'. Assistant Chief Constable Whymark, author of the memorandum, insisted that 'it is of the utmost importance that these rules should be observed strictly'. He reiterated that the police must allow lawyers to interview their clients 'out of hearing of the police'. Only in 'special circumstances' could this instruction be flaunted, and the officer doing so 'must be prepared to give cogent reasons for his action'.[40] When colonial officials disregarded policies, there was little the EOKA lawyers could do but complain. In these cases, however, the lawyers' complaints generated positive responses from some senior officials, particularly the attorney general.

Besides protecting detainees' rights to legal representation, the lawyers defended prisoners accused of capital offences. Michelakis Karaolis and Andreas Demetriou were the first of nine EOKA fighters to face the 'long drop' of the gallows. Demetriou's case was straightforward. He was caught after shooting and wounding a British civilian businessman. In normal circumstances Demetriou would have faced charges of attempted murder that did not carry the death penalty, but under the Emergency laws he was subject to capital punishment for discharging a firearm with intent to cause harm.[41] The Karaolis case was a different matter. The prosecution alleged that in October 1955, before Harding enacted Emergency legislation, Karaolis killed a police sergeant. His defence attorneys, Stelios Pavlides and Glafkos Clerides, argued that it was a case of mistaken identity. They discredited one prosecution witness by proving that the witness had not been on Ledra Street, the location of the crime, when the murder was committed. Another prosecution witness could not identify Karaolis at the suspect identification parade. The remaining two prosecution witnesses identified Karaolis, but they were both police officers who, according to the defence, 'had only a limited and momentary opportunity of seeing the murderer face to face'. Defence witnesses, however, insisted that Karaolis was not the man that they saw conduct the killing. Karaolis's attorneys also submitted evidence that Karaolis had an alibi – he claimed that he was at his uncle's house when the murder occurred.[42]

Karaolis was found guilty, but his lawyers appealed to the Cyprus Supreme Court. When the Supreme Court upheld the verdict, Pavlides and Clerides appealed to the Privy Council. The Privy Council also upheld the conviction. Finally, the lawyers appealed to Governor Harding. Harding had little sympathy for Karaolis. The governor wrote that 'in light of my experience over the past six months it seems to me that appeasement is not a course to which the Greeks whether Government or people are inclined to respond'. It was 'firm government', Harding believed, that would help Britain 'see this business through'.[43] Karaolis and Demetriou were hanged on the same day – 10 May 1956. In retaliation, EOKA killed two captured British soldiers.[44]

Despite failing to win their case, Pavlides and Clerides demonstrated to colonial officials that Greek Cypriot lawyers would challenge capital cases in every way possible. In addition, the outrage that the Karaolis and Demetriou executions incited across the island and overseas demonstrated that every execution would cause controversy. As one prominent legal scholar wrote, the executions 'had a significance which resembles that of the fifteen executions after the Easter Rising of 1916'.[45]

In capital cases, defence attorneys did all they could to save their clients' lives. The case of Michael Rossides illustrates the impact that Greek Cypriot lawyers could have. British forces arrested Rossides for killing one of the two soldiers who died as retribution for the Karaolis and Demetriou executions. Rossides confessed to the killing and was sentenced to death. His lawyers, Michael Triantafyllides, Stelios Pavlides and Glafkos Clerides, first argued that interrogators obtained Rossides's confession through coercion. When that defence failed to prevent Rossides's conviction, the attorneys turned to common law precedents. They argued that Rossides had only killed the British soldier because other EOKA members threatened to kill Rossides if he failed to follow their orders. In a clemency submission to the governor, Clerides and Triantafyllides cited *Kenny's Outlines of Criminal Law*, which states that 'fear of some lesser degree of violence, insufficient to excuse a crime, may nevertheless mitigate its punishment' and Professor Glanville Williams's *Criminal Law*, which states that 'if a man were placed in the agonising situation of having to choose between his own life and somebody else's and preferred his own no capital sentence would be carried out'. Harding acquiesced and commuted Rossides's sentence from death to life in prison.[46]

By battling death sentences through appeals and clemency applications, Greek Cypriot lawyers forced colonial authorities to justify judicial punishments. Even when the lawyers' efforts failed, as in the case of Karaolis, executions of Greek Cypriot fighters only inflamed public opinion among the Greek Cypriot population as well as in sympathetic foreign publics in countries such as Greece and Egypt. The attorneys' efforts ensured that the colonial legal system became a site of contestation where pro-EOKA lawyers challenged the exercise of arbitrary, unaccountable power – the kind of power upon which the colonial order was built.

Beyond colonial courts – the 'human rights committees'

From the beginning of the Emergency, EOKA lawyers consistently heard their clients report that they had suffered 'ill-treatment' – physical abuse, humiliation and torture – at the hands of British interrogators. These allegations included beatings, mock executions and more creative humiliations – one man claimed that he was forced to hold two large stones in his hands and run circles around a tree for two hours. Another detainee held for interrogation at Omorphita Police Station reported that his interrogators threw salt on the floor and forced him to lick it. The 'bucket torture' also proved popular. In this technique, interrogators would place a metal bucket on the detainee's head and beat the bucket with sticks.[47]

Officially, Security Force officials were prohibited from physically abusing any Cypriot. In 1956, the Acting Administrative Secretary declared that according to the law, 'no form of violence against any individual, except in cases of resistance to lawful arrest, is allowed, nor will ill treatment of a detained person be tolerated'. In April 1956, the government convicted two soldiers from the Gordon Highlanders – Captain Gerald O'Driscoll and Lieutenant Robin Linzee – for causing actual bodily harm and obstructing the subsequent investigation. Colonial officials cited the O'Driscoll and Linzee courts martial and another conviction of a police officer in Limassol on 'ill-treatment' charges as 'proof of the resolution with which Government and the military authorities deal with such cases'.[48] This conclusion was disingenuous, however, as the commander-in-chief of Middle East Land Forces decided not to confirm the findings against O'Driscoll and Linzee – essentially overturning the verdict – and commuted their sentences to dismissal from the army.[49]

As ill-treatment allegations persisted, in October 1956 the Cyprus Bar Council formed a 'human rights committee' led by John Clerides. Based in Nicosia, this loose network decided to investigate and document the abuses. Their remit included torture and cruelty during interrogation as well as the impact of curfews and collective punishments on villages and the civilian population. To the human rights committee lawyers, curfews amounted to human rights violations because people could not import food or water, buy goods at markets or work on their farms when British troops ordered entire village populations to remain indoors. Additional human rights committees were formed in many localities – from Famagusta to Paphos, every major city hosted a human rights committee. Thirteen barristers participated. Although the human rights committee lawyers documented dozens of abuse cases, none asked for payment.[50]

The human rights committees internationalized ill-treatment allegations by appealing to British opposition politicians and facilitating the Greek government's efforts to censure Britain before the European Commission of Human Rights at the Council of Europe. Human rights emerged as a major component of the post–Second World War international order with the proclamation of the Universal Declaration of

Human Rights in 1948. The European Convention on Human Rights came into being in 1951 in response to the challenge of Cold War communism. As anti-colonial nationalists sought liberation from colonial control, human rights came to represent a universal moral political language that could be used against European imperial powers.[51]

Human rights committee leaders' overtures to Parliamentarians found a receptive audience among the Labour Party's anti-colonial Left wing. One of Clerides's main contacts was a relatively obscure Labour lawyer named Peter Benenson. Later to earn international renown as a co-founder of Amnesty International, at the time Benenson was chairman of the Society of Labour Lawyers' Foreign Relations Sub-Committee.[52] In December 1956, Benenson joined the legal team retained by Charles Foley, the *Times of Cyprus* owner, to defend the newspaper against libel charges filed by the Cyprus government. Foley described Benenson as 'red-haired, rabidly energetic, and had a warm heart for lost causes'.[53] Through Foley, Benenson met John and Glafkos Clerides, who began corresponding with him over allegations that the Security Forces had 'ill-treated' Cypriots during interrogation. Benenson decided to help.[54]

On 17 December, John Clerides gave Benenson a letter listing a spate of complaints that he had recently filed with the Cyprus government. Clerides wrote that on 1 November, he filed six allegations of ill-treatment. The Administrative Secretary pledged that investigations would occur, but Clerides had not yet received news of the investigation results. By the end of November, Clerides had filed an additional thirty complaints, which colonial officials failed to answer. 'I have been submitting complaints', he wrote to Benenson, 'for the purposes of remedying a situation which discredits the prestige of British Administration.'[55]

Clerides's overture occurred when the British government was highly vulnerable. Prime Minister Anthony Eden's Conservative government was reeling in the wake of the Suez Crisis and Governor Harding had recently expanded the Emergency regulations in Cyprus to incorporate a mandatory death sentence for firearms offences and comprehensive restrictions on the press. Lord Listowel criticized the new press restrictions in the House of Lords. Lord Jowitt lamented, 'I do not think I have ever seen a more draconian set of rules than these regulations.' Liberal Party leader Jo Grimond argued that the curtailment of free speech in Cyprus amounted to a 'sad day for this great liberal country'.[56] On 21 December, Labour MP Kenneth Robinson condemned 'repressive government and draconian legislation' that amounted to an 'almost total denial of civil liberties'. James Callaghan expressed his concern that Clerides and Pavlides, whom he called 'persons of the highest repute in Cyprus', had documented thirty cases of 'prima facie brutality by security forces' that amounted to 'examples – I think I am not putting it too highly – of torture'. The government's failure to investigate the complaints only heightened suspicions of wrongdoing. 'There is a responsibility upon the Administration', Callaghan asserted, 'to ensure that every complaint of this nature is investigated.' Until then, Callaghan concluded, 'We are under a cloud of suspicion.'[57]

Repressive legislation and brutality in Cyprus remained an issue for British politicians throughout the conflict. In December 1956, Callaghan dispatched Benenson to the island with instructions to investigate. A furious Harding ordered Deputy Governor George Sinclair to 'keep Benenson on the rails'.[58] Labour MPs Fenner Brockway and Jennie Lee visited deported EOKA prisoners held in Britain and publicized the detainees' ill-treatment accusations. In July 1957, Callaghan, Brockway, Lee and Kenneth Robinson again reproached the government over ill-treatment allegations. 'The fact is', Labour MP Lena Jeger insisted, 'in the twentieth century we cannot, without an element of totalitarianism, hold down a country against the will of the people who live in it.'[59]

In addition to lobbying anti-colonial British politicians, human rights committees cooperated with the Greek government to use international legal agreements against Britain. But international law had its limits. Britain had little to fear from the United Nations as General Assembly debates would not necessarily result in an anti-British resolution. Even if such a resolution was passed, it would have lacked enforceability. Likewise, Greek Cypriot lawyers' complaints that the Cyprus government had violated the letter of the 1949 Geneva Conventions and the spirit of the Universal Declaration of Human Rights had not resulted in the revocation of Emergency legislation. The Universal Declaration articulated principles to which states should aspire, but it was not legally binding. In addition, Britain denied that the 1949 Geneva Conventions applied to internal security operations – to the War Office the Geneva Conventions only regulated conflict between sovereign states.

One avenue, however, remained open: Britain was a party to the European Convention on Human Rights. Britain played a major role in creating the Convention and was the first country to ratify it, doing so in March 1951. In 1953, Britain extended the Convention's protections to forty-two colonies and dependent territories, including Cyprus. The European Commission started work in 1955 and received 400 applications during its first four years – 360 were from individuals. The United Kingdom did not recognize the right of individual petition at this time, but did recognize the right of other states to submit applications concerning violations of the Convention.[60] Even so, the extension of the Convention to apply to Cyprus created a legal vulnerability. Britain was potentially exposed to formal international censure.

During 1956 and 1957, the Greek government submitted two applications alleging that Britain violated the European Convention on Human Rights. On 7 May 1956 – the day of Karaolis's and Demetriou's executions – the Greek government filed the first interstate application submitted to the commission. Officially termed 'Application 176/56', the Greek submission amounted to a 15-page assault on the Emergency regulations. The application asserted that emergency powers 'have meant the denial of nearly all human rights and fundamental freedoms in the island' and condemned arbitrary powers such as the forced closing of shops, collective fines and detention without trial. At the time, over 3,200 Cypriots were detained under the emergency powers.[61]

On 17 July 1957, the Greek government filed a second application alleging that Britain committed 'torture or maltreatment amounting to torture' in forty-nine cases.[62] John Clerides's human rights committees documented much of the evidence for the Greek applications. Many cases included complaints that Clerides had previously submitted to the Cyprus government. For example, in the case of Takis and Savas Kakoullis, Clerides documented the Kakoullis's allegations of being subjected to 'blows inflicted over a period of several hours' and 'frequent immersion in ice-cold water' while held in a house at Agios Amvrossios. Clerides filed a complaint with the colonial administration on 2 November 1956, but did not receive a response until he inquired five months later. Colonial authorities replied that they could not identify the perpetrators and did not pursue the complaint any further. Clerides also documented the case of Maria Lambrou, a pregnant woman who alleged that interrogators' beatings caused her to miscarry. Between October and November 1956, Clerides lodged three complaints on Lambrou's behalf. On 7 January 1957, Clerides finally received a reply. The findings of a police inquiry did not corroborate Lambrou's story, so the police refused to release her interrogator's name.[63]

The European Commission appointed a Sub-Commission to investigate the first Greek application. Hearings continued into March 1957 with the Sub-Commission hoping for an amicable solution between Greece and Britain. This soon proved impossible. In January 1958, much to the chagrin of senior colonial officials, the Sub-Commission proceeded with its inquiry into the Cyprus situation. After nearly two years of proceedings, the Sub-Commission finally concluded that Britain faced an emergency serious enough to threaten 'the life of the nation' and therefore justify the use of emergency powers to curtail rights and liberties. The European Commission considered appointing another Sub-Commission to investigate the second Greek application, but before a decision was made, the British and Greek governments jointly requested the termination of the proceedings. A political settlement among Britain, Greece and Turkey – the three states with a major stake in the conflict's outcome – was close at hand. Both sides believed that ending the dispute amicably would facilitate further negotiations.[64]

Despite the unfavourable outcome from the first Greek application and the early termination of the second, human rights committee lawyers' efforts in documenting abuses, filing complaints and lobbying British politicians contributed to an operational environment in which British actions faced constant legal scrutiny. For the first time, British officials had to justify their actions before not only Parliament, but also an international human rights organization that Britain had helped to establish. The administration of justice according to the 'rule of law' – a supposedly cherished principle of British counter-insurgency – emerged as a site of contestation, a site where the state's legitimacy was questioned rather than reaffirmed.

To colonial officials, the Conservative government and many other Britons, however, the EOKA lawyers were propagandists seeking to politicize the legal system and human rights ideals. Deputy Governor George Sinclair wrote that 'their objectives will be first to smear our name abroad and second to hold up the vital work of the Security Forces by directing their efforts into investigations of allegations'.[65] On 11 June 1957, the Cyprus government issued a White Paper entitled *Allegations of Brutality in Cyprus*. Governor Harding intended the White Paper as a countermeasure against the EOKA 'atrocity campaign'. EOKA lawyers countered that the White Paper undermined their integrity as members of the Bar.[66] They also doubted the document's accuracy. Citing the reduced sentences obtained by the court-martialled officers O'Driscoll and Linzee, Bar Council attorneys challenged the government's assertion that it punished those guilty of ill-treatment when allegations were proven. The lawyers' British detractors built their criticisms on the assumption that altruistic human rights ideals and calculated political objectives were separate motivations that existed in binary opposition to one other. But for the lawyers, idealistic principles and the politics of *enosis* were not mutually exclusive. The lawyers supported EOKA and *enosis*, but they also embraced the ideals of justice and human rights. To them, achieving the political goal of *enosis* and an end to colonial rule would result in a more just society. How the Turkish Cypriot community fit into this vision, however, was unclear.[67]

Conclusion

The British Army's two official after-action reports on the conflict recognized the impact of Greek Cypriot legal advocacy. Brigadier George Baker, author of the first report, concluded that 'the Cyprus Emergency differed from that in Malaya and Kenya, where the leaders of the legal profession were wholeheartedly in favour of a quick restoration of law and order'. Instead, in Cyprus 'every step in legal proceedings was fought inch by inch by the Bar, which searched throughout for any irregularity, technical or otherwise, which might have been committed either in the legislation or the legal processes which followed'.[68] The Bar Council's appeals to opposition politicians also had an impact: 'MPs with a strongly pro-Greek bias made singularly unhelpful remarks both in Cyprus and in Parliament'.[69] On the international level, European Convention on Human Rights proceedings had a tremendous effect on British officials. As Brigadier Baker wrote:

> The general feeling amongst the senior officers of the Government and the Security Forces … was one of disgust. That they should be called to account, at the bidding of the Greek Government, for the actions they had taken, which they believed were in accordance with the policy and interests of H.M.G. and the people of Cyprus, was a bitter and distasteful experience.[70]

The second report included an ominous warning for future counter-insurgency campaigns: 'In an Emergency it is very important that the wheels of justice should turn as quickly as possible, otherwise there is the danger that the Security Forces will lose faith in the judicial system and attempt to mete out rough justice themselves'.[71]

EOKA lawyers, drawn from an elite Greek Cypriot legal class, established a legal dimension to the war in Cyprus that did not exist in Kenya. In Kenya, the legal system was largely one-sided. Kenyans accused of crimes against the colonial government gained little solace from the few lawyers willing to aid their cause. In Cyprus, lawyers used the colonial legal system to pressure the government to justify its actions. Ultimately, Greek Cypriots could rely on legal advocates to guard their interests in a way that Kikuyu in Kenya could not.

Considering recent studies of colonial warfare, it is clear that scholars have decisively overturned the idealized view of British counter-insurgency by demonstrating that not only were British methods more brutal than previously believed, they were also not necessarily more or less effective than any other military's approach.[72] Broad studies examining the British Army's organizational culture explain how that culture influenced the military's conduct of counter-insurgency campaigns, but the application of a common doctrine does not fully explain the conduct or outcome of counter-insurgency wars. Enemy actions as well as social, political, cultural and economic circumstances specific to each conflict also play a role. In Kenya and Cyprus, British authorities applied a common legal approach, but local circumstances shaped the conduct and outcome of each war in unique ways. As the saying goes, 'All politics is local.'[73] So are insurgencies.

Notes

1 The views expressed here do not necessarily represent the official position of the US Military Academy, the US Army or the Department of Defense.

2 See David French, *The British Way in Counter-Insurgency, 1945-1967* (Oxford: Oxford University Press, 2011).

3 Sir Robert Thompson, *Defeating Communist Insurgency* (Westport: Praeger, 1966). For the mythologized view of British counter-insurgency, see Thomas R. Mockaitis, *British Counterinsurgency, 1919-60* (New York: St. Martin's Press, 1990). Other works that follow this line include John Nagl, *Learning to Eat Soup with a Knife: Counterinsurgency Lessons from Malaya and Vietnam* (Chicago: University of Chicago Press, 2005) and Robert M. Cassidy, *Counterinsurgency and the Global War on Terror: Military Culture and Irregular War* (Stanford: Stanford University Press, 2008).

4 This is particularly true of death penalty legislation. See The National Archives (TNA) FCO 141/4306 Governor to the Colonial Office, 21 November 56.

5 See Fabian Klose, *Human Rights in the Shadow of Colonial Violence: The Wars of Independence in Kenya and Algeria* (Philadelphia: University of Pennsylvania Press, 2013) for an analysis of how and why colonial violence in Kenya went through a process of radicalization. The best political overview of the Cyprus Emergency is Robert Holland, *Britain and the Revolt in Cyprus, 1954-1959* (Oxford: Clarendon Press, 1998). For an analysis of the military aspects of the campaign, see David French, *Fighting EOKA: The British Counter-Insurgency Campaign on Cyprus, 1955-1959* (Oxford, UK: Oxford University Press, 2015).

6 There were 361,000 Greek Cypriots according to the 1946 Census (see CO 927/68/4). In Kenya, there were 1.4 million Kikuyu according to the 1948 census. Of those, 1,090 were executed. See David Anderson, *Histories of the Hanged: Britain's Dirty War in Kenya and the End of Empire* (New York: W. W. Norton & Company, 2005), 4-7.

7 Nasser Hussain, *The Jurisprudence of Emergency: Colonialism and the Rule of Law* (Ann Arbor: University of Michigan Press, 2003), 3-5.

8 Lauren Benton, *Law and Colonial Cultures: Legal Regimes in World History, 1400-1900* (Cambridge, UK: Cambridge University Press, 2001); Benton and Ross, *Legal Pluralism and Empires, 1500-1850*, 2013; Jane Burbank and Frederick Cooper, *Empires in World History: Power and the Politics of Difference* (Princeton: Princeton University Press, 2011); Bonny Ibhawoh, *Imperial Justice: Africans in Empire's Court* (Oxford, UK: Oxford University Press, 2013), 118.

9 Hussain, *The Jurisprudence of Emergency*, 136; Diane Kirby and Catharine Colebourne (eds), *Law, History, Colonialism: The Reach of Empire* (Manchester, UK: Manchester University Press, 2010).

10 Hussain, *The Jurisprudence of Emergency*, 6.

11 A. W. B. Simpson, *Human Rights and the End of Empire: Britain and the Genesis of the European Convention* (Oxford: Oxford University Press, 2001), 276-322.

12 Anderson, *Histories of the Hanged*; Huw Bennett, *Fighting the Mau Mau: The British Army and Counter-Insurgency in the Kenya Emergency* (Cambridge University Press,

2012); Caroline Elkins, *Imperial Reckoning: The Untold Story of Britain's Gulag in Kenya* (London: Macmillan, 2005).

13   Elkins argues that 130,000–300,000 Kikuyu died in the British 'gulag', but hers is an inflated estimate. See Timothy Parsons, Review of David Anderson, *Histories of the Hanged* and Caroline Elkins, *Imperial Reckoning*, *The American Historical Review* 110, no. 4 (2005).

14   Anderson, *Histories of the Hanged*, 156, 160, 327.

15   Charles Foley, *Island in Revolt* (London: Longman's, 1962), 127.

16   Dimitrios H. Taliadoros, *An Album of Lawyers Who Defended EOKA Fighters, 1955-1959* (Nicosia, Cyprus: Department of Education and Culture, 2002), 45–6.

17   Niyazi Kizilyurek, *Glafkos Clerides: The Path of a Country* (Nicosia, Cyprus: Rimal Publications, 2010), 17, 25–35.

18   Taliadoros, *An Album of Lawyers Who Defended EOKA Fighters, 1955-1959*, 97–8. Turkish Cypriots also trained as barristers, most notably Rauf Denktaş, later president of the Turkish Republic of Northern Cyprus.

19   TNA FCO 141/4593 Notes from Meeting with Representatives of the Bar Council, 17 December 1958.

20   EOKA stands for *Ethniki Organosis Kyprion Agoniston*, or the National Organization of Cypriot Fighters.

21   TNA WO 106/6020 Report on the Cyprus Emergency, 1959, Annex 'T', 91–4.

22   TNA FCO 141/4459 Baker Report, 42.

23   TNA WO 106/6020 Annex 'T', 94–6.

24   TNA FCO 141/4459 Baker Report, 30.

25   TNA WO 106/6020 Annex 'T', 95.

26   French, *The British Way in Counter-Insurgency*.

27   Author interview with Renos Lyssiotis, 8 January 1914.

28   Author interview with Lellos Demetriades, 25 February 1914.

29   Taliadoros, *An Album of Lawyers Who Defended EOKA Fighters, 1955-1959*. Taliadoros identifies seventy-six lawyers who represented EOKA fighters or participated in the human rights committees.

30   Defined as 'the strategy of using – or misusing – law as a substitute for traditional military means to achieve an operational objective'. Law, in this sense, is a weapon of war: 'It is a means that can be used for good or bad purposes'. See Charles J. Dunlap, 'Lawfare Today: A Perspective', *Yale Journal of International Affairs* (Winter 2008): 146.

31   TNA FCO 141/4591 Munir to Chief of Staff, 15 February 1956; FCO 141/4591 Chief of Staff Memorandum, 'Arrest & Detention without Warrant', 18 February 1956.

32   TNA FCO 141/4591 Munir to Chief of Staff, 15 February 1956.

33   TNA FCO 141/4591 Chief of Staff Memorandum, 'Arrest & Detention without Warrant', 18 February 1956.

34   The agreement also upheld legal etiquette allowing junior barristers to accompany a Queen's Counsel in court. TNA FCO 141/4591 Munir to US (IS), 6 July 1956.

35   TNA FCO 141/4591 Administrative Secretary Memorandum, 17 August 1956.

36   TNA FCO 141/4591 Piegrome to Chief of Staff, 12 October 1956.

37   TNA FCO 141/4590 Telegram, Demetriades to Henry, 17 October 1956 and telegram, 18 October 56.

38   TNA FCO 141/4590 Pavlides and Triantafyllides to Henry, 18 October 1956.

39   TNA FCO 141/4591 Henry to Staff Officer-in-Charge, Nicosia, 10 December 1958.

40   TNA FCO 141/4592 Memorandum to Division-level Special Branch officers, 24 February 1958.

41   Simpson, *Human Rights and the End of Empire*, 920.

42 Cyprus State Archives (CSA) SA1/1096/1956, Petition for Special Leave to Appeal, Case of Karaolis and the Queen, 9 December 1955.
43 TNA FCO 141/4305 Harding to Colonial Secretary (repeated to Athens), 20 April 1956.
44 TNA FCO 141/4305 file note regarding telegrams no. 920, 921, 11 May 1956.
45 Simpson, *Human Rights and the End of Empire*, 921.
46 CSA SA1/1297/1957, Clerides and Triantafyllides to the Governor, 7 October 1957; and Acting Administrative Secretary to Triantafyllides, 16 October 1957.
47 TNA FCO 141/4592 Memorandum of Evidence Prepared by the Bar of Cyprus, not dated, but discussed on 9 January 1957.
48 TNA FCO 141/4591 Administrative Secretary Memorandum, 17 August 1956.
49 Nancy Crawshaw, *The Cyprus Revolt: An Account of the Struggle for Union with Greece* (London: George Allen & Unwin, 1978), 179.
50 Taliadoros, *An Album of Lawyers Who Defended EOKA Fighters, 1955-1959.*
51 Stefan-Ludwig Hoffmann, 'Introduction: Genealogies of Human Rights,' in *Human Rights in the Twentieth Century*, ed. Stefan-Ludwig Hoffmann (Cambridge, UK: Cambridge University Press, 2010), 16–17.
52 TNA FCO 141/4360 Governor to Colonial Secretary 21 December 1956.
53 Foley, *Island in Revolt,* 125.
54 Eric Baker Papers, University of Bradford, EB1/H2 'Notes on conversation with Peter Benenson after meeting with Sir Hugh Foot, 1.12.57'.
55 TNA FCO 141/4361 Clerides to Benenson, 17 December 1956.
56 'Press Decree to End "Slander"', 29 November 1956; 'Cyprus Editor in Court' and 'Press Decree in Cyprus: Mr. Grimond Horrified', 1 December 1956; and 'New Emergency Regulations in Cyprus Attacked', 7 December 1956, all in *The Manchester Guardian*. For Lord Jowitt's statement, see Hansard HL Deb. 6 December 1956, vol. 200, c.819.
57 Hansard, HC Deb. 21 December 1956, vol. 562, cc.1622–31.
58 TNA FCO 141/4360 Harding to DG, 22 December 1956.
59 Hansard, HC Deb. 15 July 57, vol. 573, c.869. See also Crawshaw, *The Cyprus Revolt,* 253–4.
60 Simpson, *Human Rights and the End of Empire,* 2–4.
61 Ibid., 909, 923–30.
62 TNA FO 371/130143/RG1073/51B, as quoted in Simpson, 1022. For details on the forty-nine cases, see CO 926/881-7, 504-30.
63 TNA LO 2/503 Cambalouris to the Commission of Human Rights, 16 September 1957.
64 Ibid., 996–1018; 1048–50.
65 TNA FCO 141/4495 Governor Cyprus to CO, 7 May 1958.
66 Here the lawyers reacted with false outrage – they regularly used their status as members of the Bar to support the EOKA insurgency.
67 Crawshaw assumes that politics and principle are mutually exclusive motivations. She writes that the lawyers were 'motivated by political aims rather than a desire to establish the truth and to ensure humane treatment for their clients'. See ibid., 251.
68 TNA FCO 141/4459 Baker Report, 34.
69 Ibid., 47.
70 Ibid., 64.
71 TNA WO 106/6020 Report on the Cyprus Emergency, 1959, 47.
72 French, *The British Way in Counter-Insurgency.*
73 Popularized by American Congressman Tip O'Neill. See *All Politics is Local: And Other Rules of the Game* (Holbrook, MA: Adams Media Corporation, 1995).

6

'A Battle in the Field of Human Relations': The Official Minds of Repressive Development in Portuguese Angola

Miguel Bandeira Jerónimo

A multifaceted *repressive developmentalism* was a distinct feature of the politics and policies of late colonialism in the Portuguese empire.[1] The intersections between particular developmental schemes, strategies of social engineering, and particular coercive repertoires of rule became fundamental to the Portuguese authorities' efforts to counterbalance the growing weight of domestic and international opposition they faced. This repressive developmentalism gathered further momentum after the outbreak of organized anti-colonial violence during the early and mid-1960s in the three major Portuguese overseas provinces (Angola, Guinea-Bissau and Mozambique).[2] The entanglements between the programmes and repertoires of development on the one hand and new strategies of coercive societal control on the other are pivotal to an understanding of the complex realities of late colonialism. The emergence of a 'welfare colonialism' embedded in the development projects of the 1950s, 1960s and 1970s is thus bound up with Portuguese strategies of counter-*subversion*, exemplified by schemes of forcible resettlement.[3]

This chapter deals with a particular debate among senior Portuguese colonial administrators, what might be termed the official mind(s) of late colonialism – one that demonstrates the importance of analysing strategies of development and counter-subversion holistically. The debate in question concerned the organization in Angola of a 'secret' symposium in March 1969 to review the *nature*, purpose and implementation of counter-subversion. It was here that the cross-fertilization between security policies and developmental rationales was most clearly articulated. The organization of the symposium was crucial moment in forging this connection.[4] The symposium's debates and conclusions reinforced and, in some aspects, changed the doctrines and actions of military and civilian actors, constraining their engagement with the conflicts in Portuguese Africa. The chosen topics were profoundly revealing: population regrouping, social promotion, rural development, psychological action, 'public information', civil defence and the organization of militias in the regedorias (a cluster of local administrative agencies).

Repressive developmentalism entailed two combined processes. The *securitization* of late colonial developmentalism – that is the ways in which developmental strategies of political, economic and sociocultural change, and processes of sociocultural engineering became governed by particular coercive (symbolic and material) repertoires of colonial rule – and the *developmentalization* of late colonial security – that is the ascendancy of developmental, socio-economic rationales in the formulation of programmes of coercive social control and in late colonial strategies of security, the social imagination permeating the late colonial economies of force.[5] All the interrelated doctrines of imperial reform in the post-war period – similarly crucial to late colonial developmentalism, despite their specific genealogies – were reassessed and put to use by these senior official mind(s), namely by those focused on the security and military dimensions of Portuguese counter-insurgency.[6] Two related processes were at work here: the promotion of developmentalism as a strategy of imperial legitimation; and the refinement of what might be termed late colonial securitization. The understanding of this intersection and interdependence requires much more than the mere mapping of the *military* ideation process on counter-insurgency – the autonomous formation of *military* doctrines and the prescription of related repertoires of action connected to processes of international and interimperial transfer, emulation or selective appropriation of norms and rules of intervention.[7] It also entails the acknowledgement and the assessment of multiple institutional spaces and ideational sources in which and from which *repressive developmentalism* emerged and evolved.

Programmes of rural development, community development, rural resettlement and welfare became central to colonial policymaking, and attendant efforts to disarm Portugal's anti-colonial opponents with tangible proof of rural lives improved. Colonial developmentalism was thus profoundly determined by security preoccupations rationales. Conversely, late colonial thinking about security policy embraced the language and practices of development and *welfar*ism, turning them into central instruments of counter-subversion policies. For instance, the emergence of schemes of forced native rural resettlement – *aldeamentos* – were designed to serve political and military purposes of counter-subversion, alongside their ostensible sociocultural purposes, the underlying aim being to strengthen the late colonial state.[8] These were instances of the 'spatialization of the colonial state of emergency', similar to analogous experiences in other colonies.[9] They were also concrete spaces of social engineering and economic planning, itself integral to developmentalist intervention.[10] Processes of late colonial development and social control (or coercion) were neither opposed nor physically separated: they were interdependent. Their histories intersected constantly, the thinking underpinning them cross-fertilized and the related institutions and protagonists cooperated and, sometimes, juxtaposed roles.

The point is an important one. In an influential analysis dealing exclusively with Angola, Gerald Bender identified a 'dilemma of development versus control' and 'opposed' perspectives on how to deal with the post-1961 nationalist uprisings. The reformers, he claimed, focused on the suppression of 'all forms of racial discrimination' and on improving social, economic and educational opportunities. Others, though, focused on the 'control' of local populations through forced resettlement. Security, they insisted, would pave the way for development. As a consequence, Bender argued, the policies that were actually implemented represented compromises between these 'opposing philosophies of development and control'. Contrary to this view, I consider that these dichotomies obscure more than they reveal. The co-constitution of these two strategies is more revealing.[11]

Thinking like a late colonial empire

In 1967, a General Council for Counter-Subversion (GCCS) was created, supervised by the commander-in-chief of the armed forces in Angola and comprised high officials of the colonial administration, some of whom were also serving military personnel.[12] From 1966, long-standing attempts to devise a solid policy of counter-subversion, involving the police apparatus – particularly the PIDE, the political police – and centred on intelligence and information gathering, finally came to fruition, especially in Angola. The constitution of the Eastern Military Zone, a response to new strategies of insurgency pursued by the MPLA (Movimento Popular de Libertação de Angola) and its UNITA (União Nacional para a Independência Total de Angola) rival, was one tangible outcome. A unified command was established, its operational boundaries more firmly delineated. By 1967 the *strategic* rationale of counter-subversion thus acquired an institutionalized and unified framework, coordinated by the GCCS. Local and district councils were created, their aim being to territorialize the new scheme. For instance, Luanda and its suburbs had their own Special Council of Counter-Subversion. In July 1968 a Council for the Orientation of Psychological Action and a Department for Psychological Action were also created, each working closely with the GCCS. The first GCCS meeting on 20 January 1968 immediately addressed the fundamental areas in which counter-insurgency should focus: civil administration; security; the regrouping of rural populations ('for their defence and social promotion'); tighter population control; settlement (*povoamento*); counter-propaganda; and the psychological reorientation of 'advanced populations'. The need to plan the 'regrouping and the resettlement of populations' occasioned the most number of comments: it being recognized that it was fundamental to 'avoid the resentment of the populations concentrated'.[13] On 7 February 1968 a further meeting reviewed a document produced by the Military Cabinet, 'Resettlement of Populations and their Self-defence'. Again, the focus was on the 'concentration of populations'.[14] The model for new villages, it was asserted, should be the 'successful' concentrations that had been undertaken in Uíge District after 1961.[15]

After important debates in the 1930s and the 1940s that placed native settlements at the core of the Portuguese political strategy of colonial reform as preconditions for an 'efficient' civilization – that went as far as to mobilize the example of the population settlements created by the Society of Jesus in Brazil and Paraguay, the *aldeamentos* (villages) and the *reduciones* (reductions), respectively – the Uíge experiment became the major point of reference.[16]

When violence broke out in Luanda and in the north of Angola in 1961, the Portuguese authorities took a series of strategic political decisions in response. Most urgent was to deal with a massive exodus of Africans from northern Angola, to pacify the worst affected regions and to rectify the grave disruption to the territory's valuable coffee industry.[17] A raft of measures were decreed on 6 September 1961, among them were the abolition of the *indigenato* system (the regime of dual citizenship), the creation of the Junta Provincial do Povoamento (Provincial Settlement Board, or JPP) and the creation of regedorias, which aimed to 'respect the tradition and the habits of populations', placing the local *traditional* elites under the supervision of the Portuguese lower administrative entities, the *chefes de posto*.[18] The formation of regedorias entailed gathering an average of '2000 to 3000 souls' in 133 'new settlements' (in fact, only eighty-three were actually formed by early 1964). The objective was to avoid the 'dispersal' of native populations, thereby combining security imperatives with the longer-term development of closely supervised new villages.[19] After this eruption of insurgency in 1961, an effective solution to population 'dispersal' thus became a reinforced top official priority. The early projects of rural resettlement provided the opportunity to achieve it, supported by the creation of a Comissão Técnica de Reordenamento Rural (Technical Commission for Rural Resettlement) in 1964 (but established as a goal since 1962).[20]

According to Rebocho Vaz, governor of Uíge District between 1961 and 1966, the adoption of rural resettlement was explained by the need to restore order to the populations that escaped the violence unleashed by the 1961 events. Despite the lack of solid information about its impact, or sufficient material and human resources to implement it, rural resettlement, as defined by Decree no. 3484 (25 April 1964), became a central *political* element of colonial counter-insurgency in Angola. It was seen as a way to promote the 'integral valorisation of rural communities', economic but also social and political, through 'techniques of community development.' In 1965, a total of 5,000 *contos* were spent on rural resettlement. This increased markedly in 1966 and 1967, with 19,638 and 19,591 *contos* disbursed, respectively.[21]

The policy (and the techniques) of community development was seen as combining three fundamental dimensions: one related to 'technical-financial' aspects, that is, the creation of socio-economic infrastructures, the transformation of agricultural production, the administration of credit and the promotion of cooperativism; the other related to 'social education', aiming at pushing the 'rural contexts towards progress and responsibilities'; and another to the means to 'foster an *adherence* and growing *active participation* by the African masses' (but also by the *évoluées*) in the efforts of 'promotion of rural communities.' In parallel with a 'campaign of social justice', a consistent 'preventive action' was needed, based on a 'scientific and systematic psychological work, premeditated and planned.' Among other goals, community development aimed at the regrouping or concentration of populations.[22]

In Uíge, the new policy of mobilizing rural development to foster improved security had multiple dimensions. Spending was certainly part of it, with investment in public works, in education (notably the creation of 263 'rural schools' of which forty-five were operated by military personnel) and in improved sanitation (with the help of Africans instructed in a course of 'rural assistance'). But there were other economic interventions as well, including the creation of regulated markets to assure fair prices for products grown for commercial sale by the local population (namely coffee) and the promotion of social security schemes designed to promote regular saving (about 6,000 depositors reportedly signed up). Other schemes were agronomic: the encouragement of fish farming, agricultural modernization and cattle breeding, plus the supply of stallions and of seeds, including rice, peanuts, corn and beans. Technical support was offered and reliance was placed on so-called 'lay missionaries' who were taught the basics of nursing and ethnography, and political geography.[23]

Carrying out social engineering on a grand scale, these ideas and practices were justified with the 'international language' of community development, partially calculated to appeal to international audiences.[24] Although these doctrines antedated the 1961 events, their enactment was part of the Portuguese regime's broader counter-insurgency strategy thereafter.[25] The avoidance of population dispersal was the key prerequisite to implementing the principles of community development. Without concentration and regrouping, what was described as the 'work of social promotion' would be impossible. The restoration of security and the regime's much-vaunted 'psychological action over the masses' would be equally unattainable. Moreover, these operations were meant to fulfil another declared policy objective: the strategic preservation of 'traditional socio-economic structures'. Despite some noteworthy obstacles – particularly, 'the existence of tribal quarrels and hate, succession crises within native authorities, and rivalries between the old and the "notable"' – the Uíge experience was judged a remarkable success, which could be shown 'with pride to any foreigner'. Accordingly, the Governor-General of Angola was praised as the great promoter of an 'exceptionally important enterprise ... in the field of [the] social advancement of native populations'.[26]

Rural resettlement played a similarly pivotal role in the broader marriage between security policy and development strategies pursued after 1961. Crucial here was the 1962 creation of a Technical Commission of Rural Resettlement at the JPP, a planning group whose rural resettlement policies expressed the official will to devise an integrated policy of socio-economic intervention in rural areas. Again, this meant regrouping populations to facilitate their acculturation to the tenets of Portuguese colonial development. Model villages were projected – with schools (including specialist arts and crafts and agricultural ones), chapels and churches, nurseries, administrative buildings, workshops and fountains – connecting *regedorias* and villages into an integrated socio-economic unit under a unified politico-administrative authority and tighter military control. Overcoming the particularism of the affected communities and changing their mentality (*mentalização*) towards Portuguese authority were further priorities. In April 1964 a new legal framework was promoted, which recognized rural resettlement as a crucial aspect of the programmes designed to promote 'social advancement, development and settlement' (article 1º), via the '*rational* intensification and spread' of education and 'sanitary-medical, social and techno-economic assistance'. The stated aim was to induce popular cooperation through improved administrative integration, the promotion of a market economy, better housing and welfare provision. The establishment of the regedorias was the means to reach that end (article 2º).[27]

Emulating international ideas and programmes of development, whether emanating from international organizations or from the emerging social science paradigms (including of development studies), the official ambition was to adapt such practices to rural Angola. The embrace of a policy of 'guided change', the 'acceleration' of 'the rhythm of evolution of rural communities' that previously was a result of a 'prolonged historical process', debated and promoted at the United Nations in one of its Cycle d'Études Européen (in Palermo, Sicily, 8–18 June 1958) and by social *experts* on community development, became a reality.[28] Notwithstanding its significant implications – the threat of social destabilization as a result of overhasty modernization and consequent (or apparent) disruption to local communities' *traditional* ways and customs – rural resettlement was considered the most appropriate instrument of development, one with clear potential security benefits.[29] As the governor general of Angola argued in 1964, rural resettlement was a priority among the 'global concerns of administration'.[30] Despite the reservations expressed by experts and at specialist conferences, such as the First Meeting of Social Workers in Luanda between 25 and 28 March 1968, rural resettlement became a cornerstone of the regime's much-vaunted policy of *integration*. The lack of qualified personnel to supervise it, the scarce access to agricultural credit and, most importantly, the absence of any 'broad, spontaneous and effective collaboration by the African population' were still to be overcome. The same went with the still prevailing 'excessive paternalism'.[31]

'Our new order'

For years afterwards, the Uíge experience was presented as the model on which to draw and improve. Some of its foundations – namely the logic of concentrating rural populations and the merging of welfarism and security imperatives, connected to multiplies modalities of coercion and control, with various types and degrees of violence – were to be built upon in later schemes. The preoccupation with population regrouping dominated the third meeting of the GCCS in March 1968. The organization of militias and the supervision of self-defence units were now included as a central element of the concentration policy.[32] In October, a revised version of an earlier GCCS study 'Resettlement of Populations and their Self-defence' was reviewed, and a further extraordinary GCCS meeting was scheduled to conduct a deeper analysis of the connections between population resettlement and counter-insurgency strategy at a 'national scale'.[33]

The official intention to roll out 'population concentration' nationwide was visible in the production of a further confidential report in March 1968. This document outlined 'instructions and basic principles' that should be observed by the military and administrative authorities in Angola. Following Decree no. 3484 of 25 April 1964, which regulated rural resettlement, the 1968 report reiterated that the concentration of populations was an 'effective counter-subversion weapon'. While rural resettlement strategies were meant to be permanent and were 'directed towards a market economy', the more urgent priority was to use population regrouping to insulate rural populations from insurgency, from 'subversive actions'. Intended to create self-supporting communities practising market agriculture, population regrouping was also regarded as the 'embryo of future resettlement', and the first step towards sustainable development. Its effectiveness was said to hinge on adaptation to local circumstances; no single, 'rigid doctrine' existed. Instead, the consultation of 'traditional chiefs' was required and tribal hierarchies preserved. Psychological warfare and *mentalização* described innocuously as 'persuasion' were also evident, resettled communities being made to recognize the socio-economic benefits of improved security provision.

The constitution of the new villages (*reagrupamentos*) was to follow a careful evaluation of key local features, including the exact location proposed, the villages' relationship with the regedorias, and, of course, the means and possibilities of population control. Specific instructions regarding the organization of self-defence of concentrated populations were also provided. A 6 January 1962 Decree (no. 3252), identified the militias of the regedorias as the key building blocks of local security.[34] Those who assigned the task of organizing the militias were also expected to serve as agents of 'social advancement'. Although the potential jurisdictional rivalries between local administrators and village chiefs were singled out as a potential difficulty, no problems were anticipated from the underlying conflation between basic development and security policy.[35]

A further GCCS meeting on 10 July 1968 agreed to convene a symposium to review the extent of the development effort and the results thus far obtained by the existing counter-subversion programme. A 'revision of doctrine' was in order. Although building on the Uíge experience remained important, heightened levels of local and international opposition indicated that much more was required.[36]

Between November 1968 and March 1969 the resulting symposium brought together senior figures from the Portuguese army, the Angolan police and numerous security and intelligence services to consider how to connect development and counter-insurgency more effectively. The 'plethora of bureaucracy' created and managed by the late imperial and colonial states with a view to articulating securitarian and developmental rationales was summoned.[37] Twenty-five reports on numerous aspects of the renewed planning of counter-subversion were to be prepared and debated. The goals were clear: to bring ideas about counter-insurgency into closer dialogue with thinking about social welfare, population regrouping and control, the recruitment of self-defence militias, propaganda and psychological warfare.[38] New confidential instructions on enhanced counter-insurgency building on past precedents and recent experience of forced resettlement were to be prepared.[39] This echoed the GCCS claim that 'regrouping and resettlement of villages' was now the main instrument by which to 'promote socio-economic welfare and organize [local] self-defence through militias'. The ambitions may have been boldly stated but the fact remained that counter-subversive action was, as the CGGS conceded, 'immensely hampered by its meagre administrative, political and military coverage' and also by 'the almost complete absence of [the] economic mainstays of regional development'. However, the answer to these problems, it was averred, was more forced population regrouping and rural resettlement, not less.[40]

A summary document, devised by the Group of Coordination and Inspection of Counter-Subversion (GCICS), and highlighting the general guidelines of the *new* strategy, laid particular emphasis on what it described as 'a vast information-gathering campaign'. This required the improvement of existing networks of informers capable of gathering information about local human, natural and material resources – an oversight that was frequently mentioned as a crucial shortcoming of the Uíge experience. More importantly, the report went on to stress the need to win the 'support of the population through social and psychological influence'. Once persuaded to comply, target populations were to be directed towards the reoccupation of abandoned regions. The final objectives of this step-by-step plan were now clearly articulated. First, identify the means to achieve effective social control within the villages as a prelude to the broader regrouping of the rural population in the target area. Then take steps to assure 'security' and to develop a sustainable, market-oriented economy. 'Psychological and social action[s]' were expected to proceed meanwhile as forced regrouping was progressively transformed into lasting rural resettlement, and the 'reordering of suburban areas (transition neighbourhoods)' was done. Last but not least, support was to be offered to 'local anti-subversive political organization' – in other words, to locally raised counter-insurgent militias. Once again, the combination of security goals and developmental projects informed the entire process.[41]

A further GCICS confidential report produced in October 1968 assessed the strategy's teething problems. The administrators who produced this document supervised the Huambo, Cuanza-Sul, Benguela, Huíla and Mossamedes districts, relatively peaceful areas that were perceived as being merely at the 'stage of subversive incubation'. The main goal was thus to ensure the allegiance, or, at minimum, the compliance of the local populations. Europeans in the area were problematic insofar as they were still 'unaware of the gravity of the situation', and therefore adhered to 'old concepts' that perpetuated unequal and discriminatory patterns of interaction. Reactionary settlers, in other words, were a barrier to the supposedly progressive policies that the counter-subversion strategists espoused. Aside from diminishing the consequent resentments felt by the African majority, the regrouping of communities and the constitution of self-defence units were seen as ways to prevent people from succumbing to insurgency. Upholding 'social justice', building respect for the colonial administration, raising living standards and pushing the benefits achieved were also underlined as vital. 'New rules of coexistence' were needed. Only then could what was described as 'our new order' successfully meet the challenge of colonial conflict.[42]

Other policy reviews of counter-insurgency strategy echoed these criticisms of both past political and administrative failings and unreconstructed colonialist attitudes. The critical appraisal of past (and more recent) wrongdoings, which were seen as leading to the African population's 'great level of receptivity' to subversive doctrines, warrants a long citation:

> Slavery, the wars of pacification, the abuses of power, the physical violence exerted by the authorities, forced labour and all attendant consequences that are so unpleasant to mention, the misuse and abuse of trusteeship during the *indigenato* regime, administrative security measures, land expropriation that under customary law belonged to the community and should not therefore have been appropriated individually, population displacement, the mandatory cultivation of certain crops, the numerous violations of traditional law and of a range of African values.

These countless abuses, it was admitted, had become central to 'family histories, legends and fantasies' shared among African communities. 'Whites', as a result, were portrayed as 'the sole origin of past disgraces, [and] perhaps the traditional enemy of the black.' The problem was that the 'tendency' [of the Europeans] to 'treat the African with a supremacy they believe is conferred by colour' was still a widespread reality.

Looking back at such embedded racism, a 'justificatory doctrine that could minimize its consequences' was correspondingly urgent.[43]

As José Henriques de Carvalho, administrator of the Council of Lubango, openly stated: counter-insurgency was the waging of 'a battle in the field of human relations'. The persisting 'antagonisms, misunderstandings and injustices', even if 'unintentional', committed by the 'the businessman, the foreman, the trader, the housewife, the civil servant, ... the labour recruitment agent, ... the producer of *cachipembe* [sweet-potato brandy]', were mighty obstacles to any counter-subversion strategy. Without the transformation of these attitudes and the pursuit of socio-economic reform, 'no programme of social advancement and population re-conquest' would work.[44]

Some of these hindrances were addressed more in detail. Unsurprisingly, alongside analyses of the damage done by the 'occupation and the concession' of lands, the labour regime was foregrounded as a factor leading to subversion. The labour question, which constituted such a fundamental source of division in colonial societies, generated abiding grievances that contributed to unrest and disorder. The imbalance between the salaries of African workers in rural and urban settings (the former represented three-quarters of Angola's active manpower but received six times less than their urban counterparts) was one aspect of this. The authorities' coercion of workers, which, it was admitted, included 'frequent' and 'extreme physical violence' both from government employees and private interests, was another. So, too, were the 'grave irregularities' committed by employers (for instance, the 'lack of payment' for work done), abuses which were made possible by the inadequacy and partiality of Labour Courts. Restrictions on rural workers' freedom of movement were also problematic, although such restrictions were, if anything, tightened for security reasons. Application of Decree no. 3819, of 4 April 1968, for instance, underlined workers' requirement for a mandatory certificate of residence. Finally, even putative reformist measures such as the rural Labour Code of 1962 had failed to eradicate either 'paternalism' or 'ethnic discrimination' (including unequal salaries). In sum, the structural causes of labour discrimination were many, varied and still largely intact. Moreover, 'native' labour mobilization and use, essentially of an enforced kind, were crucial to the ongoing developmental and securitarian dynamics and purposes: the erection of settlements and of their facilities, including the defensive ones, for instance, required local manpower. Reversing this state of affairs would not be easy.[45] The SCCIA spokesperson was similarly hard-hitting. A 'vigorous attitude' towards the transformation of this problem was imperative. Otherwise, the development side of counter-insurgency would get nowhere.[46] Another significant contribution came from a secret study prepared by Afonso Mendes, the head of the Institute of Labour, Social Security and Social Welfare of Angola (ITPASA). Trenchant criticisms from one of the most noteworthy Portuguese experts on the topic were particularly revealing.[47]

The meaning of the 'economic'

In addition to tackling labour discrimination head-on as part of the new development strategy, the analysts considered it equally important to raise rural living standards in both phases of counter-subversion (in other words, both before insurrection began and after it). Accordingly, technical assistance should be provided to enhance labour productivity, new agricultural techniques should be promoted and minimum market prices guaranteed. Rural credit facilities, enabling cultivators to invest in basic equipment and high-quality seeds, should be provided, not least to help combat the rural exodus towards Angola's urban centres.[48] Focusing on these basics, it was hoped that resettled agricultural communities would come to appreciate 'the meaning of the 'economic'; a patronizing but shorthand phrase for the anticipated transition from subsistence to farming for commercial profit. This transformation of social behaviour required fundamental changes to the colonial agricultural market, opening up greater possibilities for African cultivators. No 'psychological action' would be possible without this 'social action' triggered by the institutionalization of *strategic* economic initiatives.[49]

If development was the basis for security, some also argued that the emergence of conflict was the catalyst to development.[50] Widening colonial conflicts in Portuguese Africa impacted on colonial government policies in numerous sectors, from education and health to investment in infrastructure. These 'social operations' enacted as complements to military efforts were integral to the overall process of socio-economic development in Lusophone Africa from the 1960s onwards. According to some estimates, social and economic schemes constituted over 80 per cent of expenditure allocated to the war effort.[51] The governor of Angola's Zaire District could not have been clearer: 'The Zaire has progressed more since the beginning of the violent subversion than in all its history.' For all that, he insisted, even further 'accelerated promotion' was required, especially in rural areas, because 'time is a weapon of the insurrectionaries'. Agricultural modernization was imperative, as was the improvement of livestock farming. The rural education of Africans was considered mandatory, following the example of the Cuban *rebellious youth*'s motto 'education, labour, and riffle.' Dictums culled straight from the United Nations' Food and Agriculture Organization were invoked, and should be strictly embraced. The reoccupation of the 'empty spaces', that is the rural zones depopulated as a consequence of insurgent violence in northern Angola, was another concern, especially those near the frontier with the Congo. Resettlement with a 'diverse ethnic composition' would bring economic development and political–military benefits. This 'normalization' of occupation would bring the 'normalization of commerce', and a gradual restoration of political stability. The governor thus drew a direct equivalence, concluding that an increase in local agricultural production … enabled counter-insurgency.[52]

Social advancement was thus conceptualized as a strategic goal.[53] Ten fundamental areas of intervention were ambitiously proposed: a greater mixing of populations geographically, politically and reproductively; more educational opportunities for women, whose 'social influence' was pivotal; improved professional training in agriculture; enhanced civic education, including a stronger appreciation of the regime's corporatism paradigm; introduction to forms of cooperativism and associativism; religious assistance and Christianization; greater access to schooling in remote 'bush' areas; support for local enterprise initiatives by fixed price guarantees for any goods produced; a microcredit scheme to help foster local market economies; improved communications; and the elevation of living standards, in part to promote a sense of upward social mobility.[54] Socio-economic change, a 'total revolution in our economy', namely in agriculture, was the sine qua non for the solution of the problem of insurgency.[55]

Some of these ideas were further explored at the Congress on Settlement and Social Promotion in Luanda on 4–9 October 1970, a meeting that gathered the 'armed forces, the private and the public sectors.' The Congress's concluding remarks were telling: 'The pressing need to mobilize all moral and material resources to intensify the socio-economic advancement of the more underdeveloped communities and the occupation of the overseas territories characterized by a low demographic presence is a vital precondition of national survival.' Adding to economic (e.g. promotion of agricultural-livestock farming), financial (e.g. facilitation of access to credit), educational (e.g. enhanced teaching of the Portuguese language) and communicational (e.g. increase and improve maritime and terrestrial communications, which contained as well benefits regarding the 'security of population'), political–military rationales were also at work. Improved living standards were expected to 'hasten total pacification'. The crucial intersections and interdependence between (re)settlement, social promotion and counter-subversion were obviously addressed. Without the enforcement and improvement of such intersections, the 'Portuguese world' would vanish.[56]

The February 1971 creation of *Brigades for rural promotion and development* confirmed this direction of travel. Via 'informal teaching, locally provided, at home and in the fields', their action was designed to promote the 'acceptance of new patterns of technical and social behaviour that could lead to integral development'. Again, the 'solution of the overseas problem' was to be found in the 'intensification of social promotion of populations.' Experts on 'Household Economy', 'Agricultural Credit', 'Work with Rural Youth', for instance, would ensure such desired outcome.[57] A pilot project testing these ideas had been running in the district of Bié (in Angulo and Nharea) since October 1969, and was regarded as a success, given the positive local response, measured in terms of heightened demand for seeds, fertilizers and pesticides.[58] The role played by Hermann Possinger, the inspiration behind the application of these rural development programmes in Angola, was central. He coordinated the Bié pilot project, having worked in Angola's Central Plateau since 1963. Possinger conceptualized rural development as the reorganization of rural space and the 'modification of attitudes' of those who occupied it. Accordingly, 'material development' was the 'product of the action of a modified man'. The impact that his ideas and projects might have on combating insurgencies was obvious, as numerous senior officials understood. In a lengthy lecture given in July 1968, Possinger stated that economic stabilization was critical, promising 'more security than that provided by any army with planes and tanks.'[59]

In late 1971 his development scheme was rolled out further in Bié and Huambo. The decree officially creating the resultant Rural Development Mission stated that, on the advice of 'well-known national experts on issues of social balance', the government was convinced that 'economic welfare and the gradual extinction of tensions' were 'the most effective barriers to the infiltration of negative ideas.' The 'economic, social and cultural promotion of rural populations', the rational use of human and material resources available in rural contexts and the 'restructuring of rural communities with a view to achieving total societal integration' were indispensable. By 1973 fifty-six teams of *extensionalists* were supervising half a million people.[60]

'Eliminating "empty spaces"'

The entire rural development project was predicated on population regrouping and control. Population regrouping – taken as a synonym for the 'stabilization of agriculture and populations' through resettlement – was judged as the optimal means to assure social promotion and popular compliance. The goal was double-edged. On the one hand, it was meant to modernize agriculture, raise living standards and 'make the populations aware' of the fact. This would push them towards the rejection of a tribal life. It would also undermine tribal 'primitivism'. On the other, it was to make resettled communities responsible for their own defence against insurgents while monitoring their movements and interactions. But significant geographical obstacles and material shortages remained. In some places the anticipated transition to a market economy was painfully slow; in others 'tribal organization' persisted, as evinced by cultural practices such as polygamy, chiefly politics, and so-called 'fetishism'.[61] As important, communities rarely welcomed regrouping – given what they were obliged to leave behind, and the uncertainty that their new settlement would be more productive or secure. Insurgent groups were also quick to exploit these sources of discontent.[62]

Aside from its use as a vehicle for development projects and social promotion, population resettlement was integral to colonial schemes of population control. Decree no. 3819 (4 April 1968) highlighted the need for a proper 'identification' of the 'natives' and the active control of their 'residence', 'movements or circulation', 'commodities and luggage', and 'activities and jobs'. The existing practices and mechanisms of population control were reinforced and tentatively enhanced.[63] A confidential SCCIA 1967 memorandum on 'Control of Populations' highlighted the absence of population control as a major barrier to effective counter-insurgency. Initiatives to 'concentrate populations', particularly in frontier districts, and to 'control people and their movements' were imperative. The mandatory 'certificate of residence', already decreed in February 1964, needed to be effectively enforced.[64]

More effective measures to acquire, organize and exploit colonial knowledge (not merely intelligence) were also required. For some specialist administrators, the nature and scope of the population census changed after 1961. Its informational value decreased, failing to provide the variety, or the quality, of information previously gathered. Before 1961 the collection of a wide swathe of demographic and socio-professional data as well as detailed statistical evidence about agriculture and labour had been achieved. This made subjective indices such as 'idleness' measurable – and controllable. The situation was different after 1961. The revocation of the *indigenato* regime, the replacement of the 'native card' [*caderneta indígena*] (which contained detailed information about an individual's socio-economic profile) with a standardized 'identity card', itself the result of heightened bureaucratic centralization (of a 'convoluted formalism'), diminished the colonial state's capacity for sociological analysis of the Angolan population. The revocation of the *indigenato* regime also abolished the use of so-called 'transit permits' and therefore reduced previous restrictions on freedom of movement. Associated, as it was, with the legal imposition of free labour, which was connected to international pressures and dynamics, including the 1961 complaint made by Ghana against Portugal at the International Labour Organization, the new framework was also criticized for the loss of restrictive control over workers that it entailed. The new framework was perceived as leading to the 'spread of idleness, with no option for repression.'[65] To remedy this, the new proposals envisaged the multiplication of operations of control, new surveillance mechanisms, including a more comprehensive census, the 'rationing of commodities and foodstuffs', the actual introduction of residency certificates and a thorough restructuring of the government information service.[66]

This move towards an enhanced population control was also central to the administration of regrouped African populations. The presence of differing ethnic groups, the local disagreements generated by the upsetting of traditional hierarchies, and the unpopularity of resettlement in unfamiliar areas caused profound resentments.[67] It was fundamental to understand local realities and societies.[68] The fact was that forcible resettlement risked increasing local support for insurgent movements. Stricter population control measures were devised in response. For one thing, the precise location of newly concentrated settlements had to be carefully thought through: they should be located nearby existing settlements with a strong administrative and military presence. However, this policy preference ran up against another: namely, the tendency to use resettlement as a means to repopulate 'empty spaces' from which depopulation had previously occurred, sometimes as a result of rebel activity. This led those in charge of counter-subversion to warn that the fear of leaving such 'empty spaces' untouched should be confronted, and perhaps abandoned.[69] Despite this admonition, the policy of occupying such regions with 'ethnic groups dissimilar to those that previously occupied them' was consistently advocated as fundamental to success.[70] It continued to be promoted during the 1970 Congress. 'Emptiness', it was noted, was a 'positive factor for the adversary'. 'Eliminating "empty spaces"', reoccupying them 'urgently' and on a massive scale, should be 'a basic national concern.'[71]

The question of 'empty spaces' was, of course, connected to the issue of who actually filled them. Certain Protestant missions were, for example, criticized for 'promoting a false idea of nationalism': their 'deleterious action' was denounced, they were seen as responsible for 'the subversive or deviationist mentalization of unprepared masses.' They were, it was argued, the 'hotbed of the infection.' But they were also competing providers of basic development. Given their 'abundant material resources', they demonstrated a 'great potential for action that impresses and predisposes the native masses' towards cooperation with them. The erection of free schools, hospitals, infirmaries and basic healthcare centres along with qualified and highly committed personnel offered an alternative to the regime's doctrines and projects. Regime supporters, such as J. Figueiredo Fernandes, president of the Sá da Bandeira municipal chamber, pointed out that missionary development projects initiatives, which tended to be allocated far from 'more evolved population centres', were 'a fertile domain for comparisons that dishonour us'. The articulation between (re)settlement, social promotion and 'population concentration' was also important to counterbalance the influence of Protestant missions.[72]

Continuing population control measures once resettlement had occurred generated further arguments. One concerned the need to introduce Europeans in the *sanzalas* [native villages in the interior] as a safeguard against subversion. European settlers were also thought to be vital in generating greater local commercial activity, which would, in turn, increase interethnic contact and also contribute to the broader 'social advancement' that was being advocated as *the* powerful counter-subversion instrument.[73] In practice, though, the process of 'rural resettlement' was generating African-only villages, which, it was feared, might become easy targets for subversion. Moreover, the clear distinction between Africana and European villages would lead to 'racist localities.' The presence of 'whites' was seen as crucial. Otherwise, the beneficial results of socio-economic programmes associated with rural resettlement would be undermined.[74]

Conclusion

Given the perceived economic, political and military importance, not to mention the propaganda value of the *social* dimension to population regrouping and rural resettlement, it was no surprise that on 3 April 1972 a new policy was announced with the publication of the *Norms of Rural Resettlement and Population Regrouping*.[75] The culmination of the intense official debates between 1968 and 1969 among the Portuguese regime's colonial counter-insurgency strategists, this policy document, elaborated by the provincial council of counter-subversion, focused on the elements perceived as fundamental to success.[76] First among these was the need to promote development practices capable of inducing rapid social transformation by accelerating 'the rhythm of evolution of rural communities'. Community development (identified as *the* tool to provide an 'integral', 'harmonious' and 'progressive' development of 'countries or territories in which the population is still in a scarcely developed state'), rural *extension* (the instrument to foster the modification of mindsets and attitudes and therefore improve rural productivity) and 'closed supervision' (*the* means to identify those willing to cooperate, rewarding them with technical and financial assistance) were confirmed as pillars of the 'system.' A second priority was to pursue rural resettlement and population regrouping more vigorously. Both measures, it was claimed, enabled development to occur in otherwise 'unsafe zones' insulating the affected population from insurgent subversion.[77]

These measures could and did entail the forced removal and displacement of populations between regions, as occurred for instance under *Operação Robusta* between 1969 and 1974, in which 6,506 people were relocated from North Cuanza, the vast majority (5,183) to Zaire, the rest to Mossamedes.[78] 'Model villages' such as those in Banza Puto, Calambata, Madimba, Quiende and Quiximba were another crucial element of counter-subversion and were held up as exemplars of 'social promotion' and development. The construction of communal sanitary, religious, educational, economic, and social and associational infrastructures also built on the proposals set forth since the Uíge experience and reinforced since the 1968–9 debates. And Operation *Robusta*, too, became an example to be replicated, despite its inherent violence and disruptive, traumatic consequences.[79] In Mozambique and Angola, by the end of empire, some two million Africans were regrouped in *aldeamentos*, the frontlines of *progress*, population control, proselytization and counter-insurgency propaganda.[80] During the 1960s the intersection between the security precepts of counter-insurgency and the social engineering of development was fundamental to the political economy of Portuguese colonialism in southern Africa. Incorporating and generating multiple doctrines, methods and techniques that addressed political, social, economic dimensions of development and security, this cross-fertilization was a central component in the historical transformation of Portugal's African colonies into a particular 'repressive version of the developmentalist colonial state.'[81] The debates covered here among senior security officials, and the associated schemes of societal modernization they studied and recommended, reveal the ways in which the *securitization* of late colonial development and the *developmentalization* of late colonial security were two sides of the same coin in the endgames of empire. The triangulation between security, development and population in European late colonialism needs to be further investigated.

Notes

1 This chapter is a result of the research project 'Change to Remain? Welfare Colonialism in European Colonial Empires in Africa (1920-1975)', funded by the Portuguese Foundation for Science and Technology (Ref: IF/01628/2012). The general arguments behind this statement are developed in Miguel Bandeira Jerónimo and António Costa Pinto, 'A Modernizing Empire? Politics, Culture and Economy in Portuguese Late Colonialism', in *The Ends of European Colonial Empires*, ed. Miguel Bandeira Jerónimo and António Costa Pinto (Basingstoke: Palgrave Macmillan, 2015), 51–80.

2 Miguel Bandeira Jerónimo and António Costa Pinto, 'International Dimensions of Portuguese late colonialism and decolonization,' Special Issue of *Portuguese Studies* 29, no. 2 (2013).

3 In order to fully capture these historical co-constitutions and intersections, we need to recognize, and explore further, the interplay between international, transnational, interimperial, metropolitan, regional and colonial connections and dynamics. This process entailed more and more diversified processes than the ones captured by James C. Scott's *authoritarian high modernism* argument. See James C. Scott, *Seeing Like a State* (New Haven: Yale University Press, 1998), 87–102.

4 The fact that it was organized in Angola and assembled local forces and experiences is noteworthy.

5 Patricia Owens, *Economy of Force: Counterinsurgency and the Historical Rise of the Social* (Cambridge: Cambridge University Press, 2015), *maxime* 173–208.

6 The official mind(s) was (were) also formed, conditioned by and enacted in *peripheral* institutional spaces. Most analyses, with a clear metropolitan focus, fail to recognize this aspect. For a recent, multifaceted and rich collection of contributions about the advantages in exploring the colonial mind(s) in diverse scales of analysis, see Martin Thomas (ed.), *The French Colonial Mind* (Lincoln: University of Nebraska Press, 2011).

7   In the Portuguese case, the contact with the Intelligence Centre of the British
    Army (Maresfield Park Camp), which in 1958–9 welcomed five Portuguese officials
    and enabled the transmission of experiences and interpretations about Malaya,
    Kenya and Cyprus, and the presence at the *Centre d'instruction à la pacification
    et à la contre-guérilla* in Arzew (Algeria), which initiated six Portuguese officials
    in the potentialities of psychological war and the *guerre révolutionnaire*, were two
    crucial moments. For instance, the contact with the *Service d'Action Psycologique
    et d'Information* in Algeria was decisive to the introduction of *psico* strategies as
    pillars of the overall counter-insurgency project. The manual *The Army in Subversive
    Warfare* (*O Exército na Guerra Subversiva*) was one of the first outcomes of this
    international and interimperial engagements. For the doctrinal aspects of counter-
    insurgency see, among others, Hermes de Araújo Oliveira, *Guerra revolucionária*
    (Lisboa: s.n., 1960); the multivolume Estado Maior do Exército, *O Exército na
    Guerra Subversiva* (Lisboa: EME, 1963; 1966); and Joaquim Franco Pinheiro, Hermes
    de Araújo Oliveira and Jaime de Oliveira Leandro, *Subversão e contra-subversão*
    (Lisboa: JIU, 1963).
8   For Angola see Gerald Bender, *Angola under the Portuguese* (London: Heinemann,
    1978), 156–96. For Mozambique see Brendan Jundanian, 'Resettlement Programs:
    Counterinsurgency in Mozambique,' *Comparative Politics* 6, no. 4 (1974): 519–40; and
    João Borges Coelho, 'Protected Villages and Communal Villages in the Mozambican
    Province of Tete (1968–1982)' (PhD diss., University of Bradford, 1993). For
    general approaches see, for instance, John P. Cann, 'Portuguese Counterinsurgency
    Campaigning in Africa 1961-1974' (PhD Thesis, University of London, 1996); W. A.
    van der Waals, *Portugal's War in Angola* (Pretoria: Protea, 2011).
9   Fabian Klose, *Human Rights in the Shadow of Colonial Violence* (Philadelphia:
    University of Pennsylvania Press, 2013), 236.
10 To similar ideas see Nick Cullather, '"The Target is the People": Representations of
    the Village in Modernization and U.S. National Security Doctrine,' *Cultural Politics*
    2, no. 1 (2006): 29–48, and Nicole Sackley, 'The village as Cold War site: Experts,
    Development, and the History of Rural Reconstruction,' *Journal of Global History*
    6 (2011): 481–504. See also Frederick Cooper, 'Modernizing Bureaucrats, Backward
    Africans, and the Development Concept,' in *International Development and the
    Social Sciences*, ed. Frederick Cooper and Randall Packard (Berkeley: University
    of California Press, 1997), 64–92; Joseph Hodge, *Triumph of the Expert* (Athens:
    Ohio University Press, 2007), 207–53. See also Moritz Feichtinger's chapter in this
    collection.
11 Bender, *Angola Under the Portuguese*, 156–8.
12 Ibid, 157, and Waals, *Portugal's War in Angola*, 207–10.
13 'Memorial dos principais assuntos tratados no Conselho Geral de Contra-Subversão,'
    secret, *Contra Subversão em Angola 1968-01-01/1972-01-01*, AHD/MU/GM/GNP/
    RNP/56.
14 'Memorial dos principais assuntos tratados no Conselho Geral de Contra-Subversão.'
15 For the situation in Uíge, assessed by two important reports, see Services of
    Centralization and Coordination of Information of Angola (SCCIA), Uíge Section,
    'Relatório dos trabalhos de reordenamento rural e organização comunitária,
    empreendidos no distrito de Uíge a partir de Junho de 1962,' AHD/1/MU-GM/
    GNP01-RNP/S0413/UI06546; Joaquim Carrusca de Castro, 'Relatório dos trabalhos
    de reordenamento rural e da organização comunitária – distrito de Uíge, 1964,'
    AHD-UM-GM-GNP-RNP-0413-06592. See also Diogo Ramada Curto and Bernardo

Pinto Cruz, 'Cidades coloniais: fomento ou controlo?,' in *Cidade e Império: dinâmicas coloniais e reconfigurações pós-coloniais*, ed. Nuno Domingos and Elsa Peralta (Lisboa: Edições 70, 2013), 113–66.

16   For the appropriation of the model of catholic villages in the 1940s, see Miguel Bandeira Jerónimo and Hugo Dores, 'On the "efficiency" of Civilization: Politics, Religion and the Population Debates in Portuguese Africa in the 1940s,' *Portuguese Studies Review* (forthcoming, Spring 2017). For 'model villages' in the interwar period see Samuel Coghe, 'Population politics in the Tropics: Demography, Health and Colonial Rule in Portuguese Angola, 1890s-1940s' (PhD diss., EUI, 2014), 311–79.

17   See Alexander Keese, 'Dos abusos às revoltas? Trabalho forçado, reformas portuguesas, política "tradicional" e religião na Baixa de Cassange e no distrito do Congo (Angola), 1957-1961,' *Africana Studia* 7 (2004): 247–76; Diogo Ramada Curto and Bernardo Cruz, 'Terrores e saberes coloniais: notas acerca dos incidentes na Baixa de Cassange,' in *O Império Colonial em Questão*, ed. Miguel Bandeira Jerónimo (Lisbon: Edições 70, 2012), 3–35; Gerald Bender, *Angola under the Portuguese*, 165 (which mentions a mass exodus from northern Angola since the outbreak of the war with figures between 400,000 and 500,000).

18   For the regedorias see Government of Portugal, *Decree nr. 43.896. Decree organising local administrative bodies known as regedorias* (Lisbon: AGC, 1961). For the entire legislative package see *Providências legislativas ministeriais tomadas em Angola de 20 a 28 de Outubro de 1961* (Lisboa: AGU, 1961). See also a coeval political interpretation in João Pereira Neto, 'Política de integração em Angola e Moçambique,' *Estudos Ultramarinos* 2 (1962): 87–114.

19   Joaquim Carrusca de Castro, 'Relatório.'

20   SCCIA, Uíge Section, 'Relatório.'; Decree no. 3237, 2 May 1962 and Decree no. 3484, 25 April 1964; Alfredo J. de Passos Guerra, 'Reordenamento rural. Promoção Económico-Social das Populações Rurais de Angola,' *IV Colóquio Nacional do Trabalho da Organização Corporativa e da Segurança Social* (Luanda: JPPA, 1966), 1–9 (for a brief analysis of both decrees); Rosa Maria Serrão Ravara, *Contribuição para uma política de reordenamento rural no Ultramar* (Lisboa: Junta de Investigações do Ultramar, 1970), 84–5.

21   Camilo Rebocho Vaz, *Acção Governativa* (Luanda: Imprensa Nacional de Angola, 1971), 97–107.

22   A. Correia de Araújo, *Aspectos do desenvolvimento económico e social de Angola* (Lisboa: Junta de Investigações do Ultramar 1964), esp. 137–92, cit. at 142–3. See also A. Castilho Soares, 'Bem estar rural em Angola,' *Estudos Ultramarinos* 4 (1959): 127–186 (quoted by Araújo); idem, *Política de bem-estar rural em Angola (ensaio)* (Lisboa: Junta de Investigações do Ultramar/Centro de Estudos Políticos e Sociais, 1961), 17; and Hermes de Araújo Oliveira, *Guerra revolucionária* (mentioned in relation to the preventive actions).

23   Joaquim Carrusca de Castro, 'Relatório.'

24   The United Nations Economic and Social Council were the references, both in Joaquim Carrusca de Castro's report and in the thinking of Rebocho Vaz, for example. The book mentioned was Nations Unies Service de l'Assistance Technique, *Les principes généraux du 'social group work'* (Genève: Nations Unies, 1960).

25   See, for instance, Alfredo de Sousa, 'Desenvolvimento comunitário em África,' *Estudos Ultramarinos* 4 (1959): 7–17; idem, 'Desenvolvimento comunitário em Angola,' in *Angola* (Lisboa: ISCSPU, 1964), 421–40; Alfredo J. Passos Guerra, 'Reordenamento rural e desenvolvimento comunitário,' *Trabalho* 4 (1963): 83–128.

26 Joaquim Carrusca de Castro, 'Relatório'; Department of Political Affairs to Governor-General of Angola, 7 May 1964, AHD-UM-GM-GNP-RNP-0413-06592. For the ideas about the *psico-social* drives see Hermes de Araújo Oliveira, *A batalha da certeza: acção psicossocial* (Lisboa: Edição de autor/Tipografia Esmeralda, Lda., 1962) and the collective debate in Joaquim Franco Pinheiro, Hermes de Araújo Oliveira and Jaime de Oliveira Leandro, *Subversão e contra-subversão*, volume that was the result of a series of conferences at the Instituto Superior de Ciências Sociais e Política Ultramarina (School of Social Sciences and Overseas Policy).

27 The italic is ours. Decrees no. 3237, 2 May 1962, and no. 3484, 25 April 1964. Alfredo J. de Passos Guerra, 'Reordenamento rural,' 9-10, AHU-IPAD-08418.

28 *La recherche sociale et le développement communautaire dans les régions-problèmes en Europe* (Genève: Organisation des Nations Unis, 1958); Alfredo J. de Passos Guerra, *Reordenamento rural*, cit. at 8. See also Maurice Milhaud, 'L'assistance technique et la méthode du développement communautaire,' *Tiers-Monde* 2, no. 5 (1961): 108–12. Milhaud was an UN advisor for Social Affairs.

29 One of the important theses at the time, advanced by an important actor in colonial affairs, Silva Cunha (later Minister of Overseas between 1965 and 1973), stated that the 'cultural contact' with 'superior forms of civilization' did not obliterate the 'social structure' of African communities. To argue in such a way was considered an erroneous 'socio-political perspective'. Those communities 'adapted themselves, but did not surrender' to new circumstances. See Joaquim Silva Cunha, *Aspectos dos movimentos associativos na África Negra* (Lisboa: JIU, 2 vols., 1958). See also Georges Balandier, 'Déséquilibres socio-culturels et modernisation des "pays sous-développés,"' *Cahiers internationaux de sociologie* 20 (1956): 30–44. Both references were considered as fundamental in the definition of the policy of rural resettlement by Passos Guerra, president of the Technical Commission of Rural Resettlement, and many others. See his 'Reordenamento rural,' 16–18.

30 Silvino Silvério Marques, *O reordenamento rural integrado nas preocupações globais da administração* (Luanda: JPP, 1964), 5, 8.

31 'Relatório da Comissão Técnica de Reordenamento Rural da Junta Provincial de Povoamento de Angola – 1968,' AHU-Fundo IPAD-PT/IPAD/MU/DGE/RPAD/1408/06263, 1, 2, 61–65.

32 'Memorial dos principais assuntos tratados no Conselho Geral de Contra-Subversão.'

33 Minutes of the meeting of the General Council of Counter-Subversion, 9 October 1968, Secret, *Contra Subversão em Angola 1968-01-01/1972-01-01*, AHD/MU/GM/GNP/RNP/56.

34 'Concentração de populações,' confidential, circular n° 750, 21 March 1968, *Contra Subversão em Angola 1968-01-01/1972-01-01*, AHD/MU/GM/GNP/RNP/56.

35 'Deliberations in meetings,' Chief-command of Armed Forces in Angola, Executive Council of Counter-Subversion, circular no. 1894, secret, 9 July 1968.

36 'Esforço da Contra-Subversão,' reserved, 15 November 1968, *Contra Subversão em Angola 1968-01-01/1972-01-01*, AHD/MU/GM/GNP/RNP/56.

37 See Miguel Bandeira Jerónimo and António Costa Pinto, 'A Modernizing Empire? Politics, Culture and Economy in Portuguese Late Colonialism.'

38 These texts, like many other documents related to the symposium, clearly demonstrate the interdependence between these idioms of development and security rationales. Chief-Command of the Armed Forces in Angola, Military Cabinet, Executive Council of Counter-Subversion, circular no. 2345, 21 August 1968, reserved, *Relatório, conclusões e sugestões do Gabinete Militar do comando-chefe das*

Forças Armadas em Angola acerca do Simpósio da Contra-Subversão, 1968-1969, AHD/PT/AHD/MU/GM/GNP/RNP/0570/01234.

39   This 'secret' and 'confidential' collection of documents had been kept from public eye until late 1972. After that, the doctrine and the intents of the *new* counter-subversion strategy became internationalized, providing critical information to be used by those determined to expose the workings of the colonial empire to hostile attention. A non-governmental group based in Amsterdam, the Angola Committee, published the documentation in Dutch, in 1973. One year later, an English version was published by the Catholic, Rome-based, International Documentation and Communication Centre (IDOC), which contained commentaries by the members of both organizations. The Angola Committee was active in publishing documents that exposed many facets of Portuguese colonialism. The magazine *Facts and Reports* was the vehicle used, publishing information about Portugal and its colonies (and the Southern Africa context more broadly). See International Documentation and Communication Centre (IDOC), *Angola: Secret Government Documents on Counter-Subversion*, edited and translated by Caroline Reuver-Cohen and William Jerman (Rome: IDOC, 1974).

40   Minutes of the meeting of the General-Council of Counter-Subversion, 18 September 1968, secret, *Contra Subversão em Angola 1968-01-01/1972-01-01*, AHD/MU/GM/GNP/RNP/56.

41   João Craveiro Lopes, 'Plano de Contra-Subversão. Esquema sobre os aspectos fundamentais,' secret, 20 October 1968, *Contra Subversão em Angola 1968-01-01/1972-01-01*, AHD/MU/GM/GNP/RNP/56.

42   GCICS, 'Relatório Especial. Breves reflexões sobre os problemas da contra-subversão na zona do G.C.I. Nº3,' 20 October 1968, *Contra Subversão em Angola, 1968-01-01/1972-01-01*, AHD/MU/GM/GNP/RNP/56.

43   'Simpósio de Contra-Subversão. Comissão de Estudo da Secção I. Plano de Contra-Subversão. Relatórios, conclusões e sugestões,' 31 January 1969. This passage is also contained in Afonso Mendes, 'Aspectos relevantes da Contra-Subversão,' secret, both in *Relatório, conclusões e sugestões do Gabinete Militar do comando-chefe das Forças Armadas em Angola acerca do Simpósio da Contra-Subversão, 1968-1969*, AHD/PT/AHD/MU/GM/GNP/RNP/0570/01234.

44   José Henriques de Carvalho, 'Reagrupamento de populações e Promoção Social,' 25 September 1968, *Contra Subversão em Angola, 1968-01-01/1972-01-01*, AHD/MU/GM/GNP/RNP/56.

45   Ibid.

46   Ramiro Monteiro, 'Breves considerações sobre alguns dos aspectos focados no "Plano de contra-subversão do G.C.I., nº1,"' confidential, 6 January 1969, *Relatório, conclusões e sugestões do Gabinete Militar do comando-chefe das Forças Armadas em Angola acerca do Simpósio da Contra-Subversão, 1968-1969*, AHD/PT/AHD/MU/GM/GNP/RNP/0570/01234. For the centrality of labour question in Portuguese colonialism, see Miguel Bandeira Jerónimo and José Pedro Monteiro, 'Internationalism and the labours of the Portuguese colonial empire (1945-1974),' *Portuguese Studies* 29, no. 2 (2013): 142–63.

47   Afonso Mendes, 'Aspectos relevantes da Contra-Subversão.' See also Miguel Bandeira Jerónimo and José Pedro Monteiro, 'O império do trabalho. Portugal, as dinâmicas do internacionalismo e os mundos coloniais,' in *Portugal e o fim do Colonialismo*, ed. Miguel Bandeira Jerónimo and António Costa Pinto (Lisboa: Edições 70, 2014), 15–54.

48 'Simpósio de Contra-Subversão. Comissão de Estudo da Secção I. Plano de Contra-Subversão. Relatórios, conclusões e sugestões,' 31 January 1969.

49 José Henriques de Carvalho, 'Reagrupamento de populações e Promoção Social.'

50 The study of the impact of the developing colonial conflicts in the dynamics of the late colonial economy is yet to be done. The same happens with the instrumental use of the developmental drives and projects by the colonial war efforts.

51 See, for instance, Cann, *Portuguese Counterinsurgency Campaigning in Africa 1961-1974*, 276–95.

52 Carlos Santos, 'Missão dos serviços provinciais na promoção das populações afectadas pela subversão,' October 1968, in *Contra Subversão em Angola 1968-01-01/1972-01-01*, AHD/MU/GM/GNP/RNP/56. See also Anne Luke, 'Youth Culture and the Politics of Youth in 1960s Cuba' (PhD Thesis, University of Wolverhampton, 2007).

53 Júlio Costa, 'Promoção Social das populações,' 30 September 1968, *Contra Subversão em Angola, 1968-01-01/1972-01-01*, AHD/MU/GM/GNP/RNP/56.

54 Júlio Costa, 'Promoção Social das populações.'

55 Jorge Serro, 'A promoção sócio-económica das populações na base dos problemas da contra-subversão,' *Contra Subversão em Angola, 1968-01-01/1972-01-01*, AHD/MU/GM/GNP/RNP/56.

56 *Congresso de povoamento e promoção social, Luanda, 4 a 9 de Outubro de 1970* (Luanda: Associações Económicas de Angola, 1970), cit. at 517, 523. Hermes Araújo de Oliveira, 'Povoamento e promoção social armas fundamentais contra a subversão,' in idem, 311–21, cit. at 320–1.

57 Decree no. 17482, 2 February 1971. See JPP Angola, *Brigadas de promoção e desenvolvimento rural* (Luanda: JPP Angola, 1971), 3, 5–6, 17, 23.

58 JPP Angola, *Brigadas de promoção e desenvolvimento rural*, 12.

59 JPP Angola, *Brigadas de promoção e desenvolvimento rural*, 29–59, citations from pp. 34–35, 36, 39, 42, 58. For more information see *Relatório de Inquérito sobre Agricultura em Angola* (Luanda: Missão de Inquérito Agrícola de Angola, 1969). See also Gerald Bender, *Angola under the Portuguese*, 186–7, n. 77.

60 Missão de Extensão Rural de Angola, *Alguns elementos acerca da Missão de Extensão Rural de Angola* (Nova Lisboa: ERA, 1973), IPAD-09500, 1, 3. See also Gerald Bender, *Angola under the Portuguese*, 187.

61 Artur Carmona, governor of the District of South Cuanza, 'Reagrupamento das populações,' *Contra Subversão em Angola, 1968-01-01/1972-01-01*, AHD/MU/GM/GNP/RNP/56.

62 Much needs to be done to assess the impact of these policies on the ground. 'Simpósio de Contra-Subversão. Comissão de Estudo da Secção I. Plano de Contra-Subversão. Relatórios, conclusões e sugestões.'

63 Fernando Lisboa Botelho, 'Controle de populações,' *Contra Subversão em Angola, 1968-01-01/1972-01-01*, AHD/MU/GM/GNP/RNP/56. For the Decree no. 3819 see the *Boletim Oficial de Angola*, 1st Series, nº 81, 4 April 1968, 597–604. See also 'Projecto de diploma legislativo que estabelecerá os meios de controle do movimento das populações, 1967-1968,' in PT/AHD/MU/GM/GNP/RNP/0362/04514.

64 Memorandum on 'Control of Populations,' SCCIA, 22 November 1967, PT/AHD/MU/GM/GNP/RNP/0362/04514.

65 José Henriques de Carvalho, 'Reagrupamento de populações e Promoção Social.' For the Ghana complaint and respective international, national and colonial contexts

see José Pedro Monteiro, 'A internacionalização das políticas laborais 'indígenas' no império colonial português (1944-1962)' (PhD thesis, University of Lisbon, 2017).

66 Fernando Lisboa Botelho, 'Controle de populações.' All these efforts to rationalize the administration and the control of populations were confined to communities that tended to settle. The challenges posed by pastoral communities, such as the one dwelling in the south of the Huila District, were obvious, and required different approaches. See Carlos Morais, 'Controle das populações nos reagrupamentos,' 20 September 1968, and José Gonçalves Coelho, 'Condicionalismo do reagrupamento das populações pastoris da Huíla,' *Contra Subversão em Angola, 1968-01-01/1972-01-01*, AHD/MU/GM/GNP/RNP/56.

67 Carlos Morais, 'Controle das populações nos reagrupamentos.'

68 See, for instance, the work by Hélio Felgas, *As populações nativas do norte de Angola* (Lisboa: Tipografia da L.C.G.G. 1965).

69 Carlos Morais, 'Controle das populações nos reagrupamentos.'

70 Meeting, 20 January 1968, 'Memorial dos principais assuntos tratados no Conselho Geral de Contra-Subversão,' secret, *Contra Subversão em Angola 1968-01-01/1972-01-01*, AHD/MU/GM/GNP/RNP/56.

71 Hermes Araújo de Oliveira, 'Povoamento e promoção social armas fundamentais contra a subversão.' See also his *Povoamento e promoção social em África* (Famalicão: Centro Gráfico de Famalicão, 1971), 26.

72 J. Figueiredo Fernandes, 'Mentalização desviacionista de massas nativas,' 25 September 1968, *Contra Subversão em Angola, 1968-01-01/1972-01-01*, AHD/MU/ GM/GNP/RNP/56; 'Deliberations in meetings,' Chief-command of Armed Forces in Angola, Executive Council of Counter-Subversion, Circular no. 1894, Secret, 9 July 1968. For the religious dimension see Didier Péclard, *Les incertitudes de la nation en Angola* (Paris: Karthala, 2015), 245–314.

73 Horácio Nunes, Administrator of the Uíge Council, and Virgílio Morão, 'Necessidade de enquadramento das populações rurais com elementos evoluídos,' 28 September 1968, *Contra Subversão em Angola, 1968-01-01/1972-01-01*, AHD/MU/GM/GNP/ RNP/56.

74 José Correia, 'Constituição de localidades só com população Africana e sua possível influência futura na subversão,' *Contra Subversão em Angola, 1968-01-01/1972-01-01*, AHD/MU/GM/GNP/RNP/56.

75 The document was preceded by the publication of Norms about Militias and Regedorias and Population Self-defence. *Normas de Reordenamento Rural e Reagrupamento das Populações*, Reserved, PT-AHD-UM-GM-GNP-RNP-0163-01091.

76 The analysis of the political, military and socio-economic impact of the symposium's proposals needs to be further explored.

77 *Normas de Reordenamento Rural e Reagrupamento das Populações*, 4–5, 7, 9, 31–3.

78 Other estimates point to similar numbers: 5,988 persons. Report by the Council-General of Civil-Military coordination (GEC/QG/CCFAA), 21 October 1974, in 'Operação Robusta – Regresso das populações deslocadas do Distrito do Cuanza Norte para o do Zaire,' AHM DIV2/2/127/003. On this operation see Miguel Bandeira Jerónimo, *A Robust Operation* (forthcoming)

79 Report by the Governor of the District of Zaire, 11 November 1969, 'Retorno das populações deslocadas no Distrito do Cuanza-norte no Distrito do Zaire – Op. "Robusta"'; Report by the Council-General of Civil-Military coordination (GEC/

QG/CCFAA), 21 October 1974, in 'Operação Robusta – Regresso das populações deslocadas do Distrito do Cuanza Norte para o do Zaire,' AHM DIV2/2/127/003.

80   In Angola the figure, circa one million, is only related to the EMZ, where approximately 80 per cent of the communities were settled in *aldeamentos*. Waals, *Portugal's War in Angola*, 219; Thomas Henriksen, *Revolution and Counterrevolution* (London: Greenwood Press, 1978), 155. For a comparative assessment, see Christian Gerlach, *Extremely Violent Societies* (Cambridge: Cambridge University Press, 2010), 177–234.

81   Frederick Cooper, *Africa Since 1940* (Cambridge: Cambridge University Press, 2002), 62.

7

Strategic Villages: Forced Relocation, Counter-insurgency and Social Engineering in Kenya and Algeria, 1952–62[1]

Moritz Feichtinger

In 2012 and 2013 Kenya and Algeria, respectively, celebrated the 50th anniversary of the end of colonial rule. Official statements once again emphasized the unifying legacy of the wars of decolonization: 'We all fought for *uhuru*' in Kenya and '*un seul héros, le peuple*' in Algeria. Despite such evocations of a common and shared history, it is the memories of activists, freedom fighters and revolutionaries, often articulated through narratives of direct confrontation, that still predominate. Ambiguities, divided loyalties and the more complicated day-to-day experiences of ordinary people are rarely the subject of historiography and public commemoration. This absence is particularly shocking in the case of forced relocation of rural civilians, which was a major element of British and French counter-insurgency campaigns in Kenya and Algeria; indeed, perhaps the most common shared experience of colonial coercion. From 1952 to 1962, 1.1 million Kenyans and nearly 2.5 million Algerians were forcibly transferred into strategic villages and were compelled to remain there for between five and seven years.

At the time, British and French colonial military officials and administrators considered strategic resettlement a decisive turning point in their anti-guerrilla campaigns, while anti-colonialists denounced the camps and villages as 'concentration camps' and derided the entire strategy as a crime against humanity.[2] Historiography has not entirely ignored the phenomenon of forced resettlement, but there are few studies devoted exclusively to it.[3] Research on forced mass displacement and resettlement in late nineteenth-century colonial warfare has revealed the long tradition of this strategy to coerce and control colonized populations. Yet, the transformative and reformist incentives characteristic for post-1945 programmes of strategic resettlement were largely absent in earlier colonial 'concentration camps' run in Cuba, South-West Africa and the Philippines.[4] Most of the literature on post-1945 strategic resettlement is still written by scholars of counter-insurgency strategy (often with a military background), who are mainly interested in its tactical value and its practicability.[5] Marxist scholars of the 1970s on the other hand have analysed mass removal as just one element in the wider process of class formation and economic transformation during the shift from formal colonial rule to neocolonialism.[6]

This chapter combines three levels of analysis that signify a new direction in research on strategic resettlement. The work begins from the proposition that it is ethically and academically imperative to take the experiences and perspectives of the affected people into account. Local variations, complexities and contradictions should not be sacrificed to an abstract theory, but have to be taken seriously as crucial elements of the daily-life experience of the resettled.[7] Second, repressive and reformative aspects of strategic resettlement need to be analysed together. Neither the dynamics and processes of resettlement's implementation nor its scale and long-term effects can be wholly understood if the process is viewed exclusively from a military or economic perspective. Third, a comparative approach makes it easier to reach general conclusions about strategic resettlement and colonial counter-insurgency. Only systematic comparison enables us to distinguish specific local outcomes from generalizable elements and impacts that are structurally inherent to the strategy. The chapter follows this three-pronged approach by discussing three elements of strategic resettlement in Kenya and Algeria: social change and violence, control and social reconfiguration through the material and spatial outline of resettlement villages, and transformations of agricultural production and labour. The conclusion will briefly discuss the specific challenges that mass relocation posed to the colonial armies and administrations in their overall counter-insurgency strategy before finally returning to the difficult position of the resettled populations in postcolonial narratives on the wars of decolonization.

It is a fundamental and often noted logic of guerrilla wars that 'fence sitting' or 'free riding' – keeping an equidistance from both sides of the conflict – is the most important strategy of survival for civilians, while government forces as well as guerrillas try to make that very strategy untenable.[8] Strategic resettlement was the primary measure within British and French counter-insurgency by which a complete separation between guerrillas and the surrounding civilian population was enforced in Kenya and Algeria. The military logic behind it was quite simple: the removal of rural civilians from scattered homesteads in difficult terrain into controlled encampments would deprive the insurgents of their most important source of supplies of material, food, personnel and information.

Once this physical separation of insurgents and rural population was achieved, the second priority was less physical than psychological: to alienate those resettled from the aims and methods of anti-colonial militants. British and French colonial and civilian authorities did not consider the infamous *hearts and minds* measures to be the most attractive aspect of the resettlement for the affected populations – such amenities were provided only partially and often years after relocation; rather, it was the security offered by resettlement camps to war-torn rural civilians that was judged as their main selling point. This calculation was not unreasonable. Both the Mau Mau in Kenya and the FLN in Algeria resorted to violence against rural civilians in order to mobilize support and collect money, and both groups attacked real or supposed colonial collaborators within local communities. The massacres of entire village communities in Lari, Melouza and Wagram were exploited and exaggerated by colonial propaganda, but they illustrated nonetheless that rural communities could become targets of insurgent terror. Strategic resettlements offered protection from the operations of the security forces as well, because the countryside was also the theatre where military repression was most intensely felt. Rural civilians were exposed to security force operations such as aerial bombardments, search-and-destroy missions and, above all, collective punishment.[9]

Strategic resettlement in Kenya emerged from two different strategic objectives. In order to protect the labour lines of settler farms and the families of chiefs and loyalists, from early 1953 onwards the British colonial administration promoted the erection of guarded settlements and fortified posts.[10] At the same time, the colonial authorities declared restricted areas around the Mount Kenya forest and other strategically sensible regions, forcibly relocating the residents to fenced camps and new settlements.[11] A formal distinction between protective and punitive resettlements was established by a directive of April 1954, in which the acting governor recommended 'villagization' of the entire Kikuyu, Embu and Meru reserves.[12] The decision to extend forced relocation did not go uncontested. Various government agencies had discussed the matter since May 1953. While most commentators agreed on the tactical benefits in particularly critical areas around the Mount Kenya forest, they rejected the idea of concentrating the entire Kikuyu population in government-monitored settlements. District commissioners, with an eye to their already hard-pressed administrative staff, considered the idea 'impractical' and wanted to preserve the threat of forced resettlement as a disciplinary measure. Pro-government African advisers stated that life in villages was completely at variance with Kikuyu custom and pointed out that the civilian population would be even more exposed to Mau Mau agitators when concentrated in villages. Medical and agricultural experts warned of the possible detriment to health, sanitation and food production.[13]

Three countervailing factors may have led the colonial government's decision to resettle all Kikuyu in early 1954 despite the aforementioned concerns. First, military and civilian advocates of strategic villages repeatedly referred to the Malayan example, where the relocation of over half a million rural Chinese under the Briggs Plan in 1952, combined with strict food control, was lauded as decisive steps in defeating the communist guerrillas.[14] Although the circumstances in Kenya were quite different, forced relocation promised to isolate the Mau Mau fighters from any support among the population of the reserves. Second, the eviction of Kikuyu from European estates, cities and other parts of Kenya had caused mounting insecurity and heightened demand for food and shelter within the reserves. Rising numbers of displaced persons in the reserves was thus not only a problem of security but also of accommodation and welfare. A resettlement committee established by the Council of Ministers in July 1954 calculated that 150,000 people had been 'repatriated' to the reserves since the beginning of the Emergency.[15] The erection of more carefully planned permanent settlements promised a solution to this problem. Third and finally, the prospect of the entire population concentrated under firm administrative control appeared to promise the perfect preconditions for the implementation of an ambitious programme of land reform and agricultural modernization that was launched in 1954: the 'Swynnerton Plan'. Influential voices like Kikuyu expert Luis Leaky, ethno-psychiatrist Colin Carothers and the Minister of Community Development, Thomas Askwith, regarded village life as an ideal environment in which to work towards a profound transformation of customs, values and lifestyles.[16]

In Algeria, the first resettlement camps were an improvised measure devised to cope with the immense refugee streams created by the intense fighting in Eastern Algeria's Aurès mountains since 1955. General Gaston Parlange, civil and military commander of the Aurès-Nemencha region in 1955–6, established the first camps in 1955.[17] As an officer of the Affaires Indigènes (native affairs), he soon realized that the refugee camps, while creating an enormous humanitarian problem, would also provide an opportunity to build contacts with a population that had so far lived beyond the administrative reach of the state. However, despite Parlange's influential position as a technical adviser to Governor General Jaques Soustelle and, later, as prefect of Batna, he could not convince the government of the issue's significance and was denied the credits he demanded for permanently settling the refugees.

Official attitudes changed radically in 1957–8. Army commanders throughout Algeria had resorted to burning remote settlements and relocating the population from the war's inception, but it had not been until 1957 that Commander-in-Chief General Raoul Salan established strategic resettlement as a standard procedure of French counter-insurgency in Algeria.[18] Fortification of the borders with Tunisia and Morocco and the establishment of a net of military sectors and prohibited areas by his successor, Maurice Challe, a year later made a more elaborate approach towards the displaced populations inevitable. The new governor Paul Delouvrier promised to take charge of the resettlement problem personally.[19] He created a central office within the civil administration to investigate conditions within the '*camps de regroupement*' and ways to render them economically viable. He also named General Parlange head of the Inspection Générale des Regroupements de Populations (IGRP).[20]

The inspections conducted by Parlange's new office revealed that barely a half of the 2,000 camps scattered across Algeria had the potential to become permanent settlements, providing sufficient economic opportunities for their populations to survive. Those villages judged viable were to receive credits to improve infrastructure, housing and agriculture; the others were to be dissolved. Parallel to the amelioration of the better-equipped strategic villages, the government launched a propaganda campaign that highlighted the developmental efforts conducted within the new villages.[21] Rebranded by Delouvrier as the '*1,000 villages* programme', resettlement in Algeria was to become the major vehicle of rural development. As centres with higher living standards than the surrounding area, with their own internal markets, connections to main communications routes and welfare facilities, they were to serve as illustrations of the 'Algeria of tomorrow'.[22] Thus, in both the Kenyan and Algerian cases, the primary function of strategic resettlement as a tool of population control soon was complemented by a broader agenda of socio-economic transformation.

Social change and violence

Implementation of both aspects of strategic resettlement – repression and reform – required the active participation of segments of the resettled communities. The creation of village representatives and self-defence militias was therefore crucial to the process. It fell to these intermediaries to relax or intensify social control within the camps, and they, too, meted out assigned collective punishments. They were at once in an extremely powerful and highly vulnerable position.

In Kenya, villagization strengthened the power of preexisting administrative bodies, district commissioners and native affairs officers, chiefs and headmen.[23] With the concentration of so large a population into villages, the chiefs and headmen as local authorities were assigned responsibility for three to four villages at once. In addition, each Emergency village was required to form a village council, most often comprised of elders and other notables. Such positions conferred considerable power over the daily lives of villagers: chiefs controlled rationing and the distribution of food, they could issue permissions for temporary leave from villages, and they selected teams to perform public works obligations.[24] Corruption and abuse became widespread as a consequence.

At the same time, these intermediaries were exposed to pressure from both sides. The colonial administration demanded quotas of Mau Mau suspects to be rounded up for detention. Failure to present the required number could lead to suspicion of non-cooperation and, ultimately, to replacement.[25] Conversely, if chiefs and headmen were unable to explain collective punishment measures such as prolonged curfews, forced labour and fines to the population or if they failed to distribute such burdens equally, they lost support and could fall victim to acts of revenge.[26]

The French in Algeria also took steps to formalize the administrative structure of customary village councils (*djemaa*) and *caïds* (local officials) in the new settlements, but they went further than the British in Kenya in trying to create new hierarchies. It was a fundamental principle of French counter-insurgency that each person should be placed in at least two different lines of vertical parallel hierarchies. The system of naming responsible persons of contact for each family, each house, each housing block and each residential quarter, implemented during the infamous Battle of Algiers in 1957, was further refined in the rural resettlement camps.[27] The camp populations were also codified as members of particular representative bodies, whether by profession, age or gender. The results were comparable to the Kenyan case. Those assigned responsible positions might accrue influence or gain material benefits for themselves or their peers, but, at the same time, they risked being compromised in the eyes of the community. Social mobility consequently became more dynamic and inter-communal conflicts were more often fought out violently.

This last point is best illustrated by the example of the self-defence militias. As Daniel Branch has convincingly shown in his study of loyalism during the Kenyan Emergency, engagement in camp-guard units or pro-government militias was not necessarily an expression of political commitment to colonial rule. More often than not, it was a locally situated and opportunistic decision. In the Emergency villages of central Kenya, the Home Guard or Kikuyu Guard oversaw the process of relocation, guarded the encampments, and questioned and punished the resettled. Lightly armed, trained and commanded mostly by European officers, these men were selected by chiefs and headmen. In addition, the administration tried to revive the ancient system of spearmen (*githungati*), who were recruited by clans and families in order to control and defend sections of the resettled population.[28] There is no doubt that Home Guards committed various acts of violence inside the resettlement villages, especially against women and girls during communal labour.[29] The discussion of their role led to open conflict between the Criminal Investigation Department (CID) and the colonial administration, which culminated in the head of the CID resigning.[30] Yet former inmates of the Emergency villages have a surprisingly balanced view of the Home Guard's role. While some have verified allegations of indiscriminate beatings during communal work and widespread sexual violence, others felt protected by the Guards' presence.[31] There are even cases where the Home Guard seems to have collaborated with Mau Mau.

The main point is that by arming members of the resettled communities and placing them in the line of fire, violence was extended down to the level of individual households. Insurgents attacked family members of the Guards, while the latter regularly denounced and punished relatives of known or suspected Mau Mau adherents. Unattached girls had to navigate carefully in this climate of ubiquitous violence. To have a relationship with a militia member could offer protection against assaults from other Home Guards or villagers, but damaged the girl's reputation within the village community. Moreover, such relationships were sometimes arranged by the girls' families in the hope of profiting from greater security or material benefits.[32]

The Algerian *groups d'autodéfense* (GADs or self-defence groups) played an equally ambiguous role. They were recruited from the resettled population to release the army from static defence duties. Armed only with hunting rifles, they manned the watchtowers at night and controlled exits and entrances to the camps during the day. Only their leaders received limited military training.[33] Service in the GADs was intensely disliked, as it was unpaid and dangerous. The motivation for arming the GADs was consequently less a matter of military performance than of psychological impact. Recruitment and arming of GADs was often embedded in staged ceremonies. Their deployment followed the general pattern of French counter-insurgency to engage as many Muslim Algerians as possible on the side of colonial authority in order to portray the nationalists as isolated fanatics. Group leaders were sent to three-week courses at special training centres (Centres de formation des auto-défenses, CFAD). The curricula of these courses reveal that militia leaders were expected to become a vanguard of rural socio-economic transformation. Lessons in citizenship and modern farming techniques were assigned as much time as military training.[34]

The role of GAD members in the daily life of villages was double-edged, however. In order to compromise them and secure their loyalty, they profited from various privileges such as more comfortable houses or improved access to education for their children. Misbehaviour or willing participation in torture or collective punishment by an individual guard on the other hand could endanger his whole family. Fence sitting in this situation sometimes led families to position members on both sides.[35] There are cases of entire GADs deserting with their weapons or disappearing into the *maquis* with their families, and numerous long-lasting vendettas originated in the behaviour of individual GAD members during the war.[36]

Three elements of militia recruitment and deployment appear distinctive for late colonial counter-insurgency. Their function as a tool for elite formation and for compromising elements within the resettled communities was at least as significant as their tactical role. The selection and composition of such units initially drew upon ethnological knowledge about traditional self-defence structures, but then gradually shifted towards forming and rewarding 'progressive' elements of the respective societies. The militias' ambiguous role in counter-insurgency efforts and their participation in inter-communal violence not only determined their individual fate after the conflicts ended, but also explain the occlusion of resettled populations within postcolonial narratives. While those resettled claimed that they were the primary victims of violence from such 'traitors' or 'collaborators', they still confronted persistent prejudice, alleging that resettled populations collectively benefited or even collaborated with the colonial regime.

Housing between relief and reward

The spatial turn, which has triggered innovative ways of thinking in various fields of history, has registered less impact on the study of violence. However, as scholars of colonialism are well aware, space, geography and Europeans' perception of colonial terrain have had significant influence on the treatment of colonized populations.[37] Topographic and environmental factors of course play a fundamental role, particularly in guerrilla wars, because insurgents typically site their bases in remote areas in which regular forces find hardest to operate.[38] Spatial categories can be analytically useful not just at this macro level, but at the micro level as well. Closer investigation of the material forms, the spatial structure, and the discrete architecture of strategic resettlements helps unlock their purpose and their effects. Many former inhabitants of strategic villages identified the camps' densely packed housing as equally traumatizing as the experience of direct physical violence.[39] Colonial civil and military authorities, on the other hand, invested considerable funds, planning and technical support in the construction of strategic villages. Because many of them were conceptualized as model villages, they reveal the broader ideas of rural modernization and visions of social transformation that informed them.

While other counter-insurgency measures like torture, detention and state terror remained invisible to the public eye, strategic resettlements were an important and often photographed subject of British and French imperial propaganda. A common trope in such propagandist output was the before-and-after montage, which contrasted poor and chaotic traditional dwellings with clean and orderly new houses in neat rows. It is tempting to use such pictures for the analyses of material conditions inside resettlement villages, but they do not reveal what life was like. On the contrary, the pictures were taken and published in order to counter negative accounts about forced relocation and the living conditions of the displaced. In the quest for global political support, it was highly important for the British and French governments to challenge allegations that they – victorious over Nazi Germany only a decade earlier – were now running concentration camps in their colonies.[40] In reality, it was only after several years in improvised dwellings that some of the resettled could move into more stable habitations.

At its outset, strategic resettlement was an unplanned, often ad hoc affair. Decisions about what regions to depopulate and where to resettle the affected communities were guided by military and strategic considerations alone. In Kenya the removal and resettlement of 1.1 million people was completed in little over a year; in Algeria local commanders were initially able to authorize the removal of groups and the creation of camps until the civil government sought to impose a more uniform resettlement policy after 1958.[41] Consequently, the resettled lived in dreadfully inadequate conditions during the war's first years.

In the Emergency villages of Kenya's Central Province, most of the huts were made out of local materials, but, until the construction of huts had been completed, people had to sleep in public buildings, such as schools and churches. The resettled were obliged to build their own Emergency village with communal labour during the first months after their relocation. They were instructed to dig a trench around it and to collect building materials from the forest or from the remains of their former homes. A more elaborate approach was required once the administration began to favour villages as a permanent feature of the Central Province. Town-planning specialists were consulted during the process of layout and construction; medical officers conducted inspections to oversee the sanitary situation. Finally, the British colonial administration issued a number of by-laws to enforce these improved housing and sanitation standards.[42] Probably the most absurd outcome of this consolidation effort was a village competition organized by the Ministry of Community Development. The inhabitants of the tidiest village in an administrative unit could win a week's release from communal labour obligations.[43]

Meanwhile, the hardest time for Algeria's resettled populations was the bitter winter of 1958–9. Most resettlement camps at that point were nothing more than refugee camps surrounded by barbed wire. The army and non-governmental relief agencies had provided tents to accommodate some of the resettled, but most of them had to improvise their own *gourbis* – small dwellings made of branches and bark. It remains unclear how many people died during the winter due to the harsh camp conditions, but the available statistics indicate markedly increased child mortality rates.[44] An investigative report compiled by socialist politician Michel Rocard revealed that among every thousand camp residents one child per day died from starvation or disease.[45] When this secret government report was leaked to the metropolitan press, the resultant public pressure to deal with the problem of the resettled populations made reforms inevitable. Consequently, the resettlement camps became integral to the ambitious Constantine Plan, a five-year scheme for Algeria's economic development, announced by Charles de Gaulle in late 1958.

The head of the planning commission and de Gaulle's new appointee, Governor Paul Delouvrier, delineated the Constantine Plan's ambitious objectives in 1959. Delouvrier represented the scheme as social engineering on a massive scale: 'We are dealing with the project to raise the standard of living of five to six million individuals, scattered over the whole surface of Algeria – a mainly poor and arid soil – with a soaring birthrate and a pervasive outlook which is not only pre-capitalist but positively medieval.'[46] In fact, the funds allocated to the development of the *mille villages* were insufficient to allow more than the realization of a few model projects. It is, though, important to acknowledge that the average living conditions of the displaced populations did improve marginally during 1959 and 1960. Houses were constructed using solid material and medical services and a basic sanitary infrastructure were installed in the more established camps.[47]

A first step towards consolidation in both Kenya and Algeria was to dissolve the big camps and create smaller settlements. In contrast to the overcrowded camps, in which 2,000 people and more were typically crammed together, colonial planners set a maximum of 500 inhabitants for an ideal new village in Kenya, and 1,000 for its Algerian equivalent. 'A village of 900 inhabitants is not only a very common type in the Mediterranean, it is the ideal size [of community] to learn the habits of democracy', a French directive stated in 1960.[48] Newly planned, permanent villages were to contain basic sanitary and administrative infrastructure, such as a water supply and sewerage systems, plus connection to road communications. Designated spaces and buildings for commercial and social activities, including sport facilities, shops and communal halls, also typically featured in the plans. In both Kenya and Algeria the resettled were expected to build their new houses, though they could obtain credits for the necessary funding.[49] In Kenya the traditional round huts constructed of local materials prevailed, and technical or financial assistance was only provided to the poorest landless families.[50] In Algeria several different types of houses were constructed, but the commonest was a standard building of the Commissariat à la Reconstruction et à l'Habitat Rural (C.R.H.R) costing 2,500 francs.[51]

That being said, the central administrations never wielded complete control over the resettlement policy in either colony. Both, the Minister for Community Development in Kenya, Thomas Askwith, and the French IGRP found their progressive vision of village consolidation frustrated by the overriding demands of the security forces and the local administration. Gaston Parlange, the head of the IGRP and father of Algeria's resettlement policy even resigned in December 1960, exasperated by local French army commanders who undertook 'wild resettlements', a practice only halted in 1962.[52] Security considerations were equally predominant in Kenya, affecting the planning and location of new villages even after the state of emergency was lifted in 1960.[53] More importantly, local availability of resources and expertise varied enormously between regions within both colonies, which placed greater onus on the commitment and capability of the regional administrative authorities, the district commissioners and district officers in Kenya and their Algerian equivalents – the prefects and sub-prefects (sous-préfets) at the head of local government.[54] Naturally, the planning and construction of so many new settlements at once required major increases in trained personnel. The problem here was not so much a lack of technical experts in town planning and construction, but the limited knowledge of the societies for which the villages were to be built. In their preliminary calculations of how many houses and new villages to construct in Kenya, for instance, colonial town planners worked on the basis of one house per head of family. Among several Kikuyu clans in central Kenya, however, it was still commonplace for a man to have several wives, meaning that actual demand could only be met by allocating one house per wife. This, of course, increased the number of houses to be built.[55] There is also evidence that fake marriages were arranged by some resettled in order to secure more dwellings for their families.[56] This explains why the District Commissioner of Nyeri noted in a secret letter to his successor that, 'One trained anthropologist would be worth several Agricultural and Medical Officers in the District Team.'[57]

In Algeria, increased political pressure to produce visible progress in the resettlement policy led to the construction of Potemkin villages, which fulfilled the modernist fantasies of enthusiastic planners and politicians but paid no attention to the economic viability of the new settlements and the needs of their inhabitants. One financial inspector proclaimed in 1959: 'To build has become a sort of a myth. ... The new villages create the impression of "mission accomplished"; that's why there are construction sites everywhere. However, apart from a few noteworthy achievements, the overall impression is that [settlements are] being constructed no matter where, no matter how and no matter what.'[58]

More than anything else, the counter-insurgency technique of combining repression and reward made housing in the strategic villages such a delicate affair. On the one hand, militia members, government employees and other loyal segments of the resettled population had to be rewarded for their service. Providing them with more comfortable houses was a simple way to do so. On the other hand, it was reasonable to build permanent houses only for people who would definitely remain in situ. In both Kenya and Algeria those who had either lost their land or didn't possess any were most likely to stay in the villages, while members of families that retained access to land were the most likely to leave. The resettled in Kenya and Algeria also devised discrete strategies to advance their interests. Fake militia membership was widespread in Algeria because of the privileges for the whole family conferred.[59] In Kenya even those who planned to leave the permanent settlements applied for plots there. 'The "town house and country house" principle is upon us,' the district officer of Kiambu in central Kenya informed his successor in 1957.[60]

Housing policy in Kenya and Algeria cannot, however, be reduced to a reaction to the humanitarian crisis provoked by mass relocation. It was also an instrument of social engineering.[61] Attempts to alter the position of women in the strategic villages serve to illustrate this point.[62] Many of the architects of the villages expressed the hope that the new settlement patterns and the distinct environment created would promote changes in the role of women. Some French planners, for example, designed the houses of some resettlement villages in Algeria without courtyards, traditionally, the gendered household spaces for Muslim women, in order to 'accelerate their emancipation'.[63] In practice, this measure did not result in greater freedom of movement for its intended beneficiaries; the women concerned were, on the contrary, forced to stay inside the houses under the constant control of their male family members. Another widespread measure sought to relieve rural Algerian women from carrying water over long distances by providing the new villages with central water supplies. Again, settlement planners considered this a practical step towards female emancipation. In reality, however, fetching water not only offered opportunities for social interchange with other women but was also essential in offering private space for female hygiene. A report on the impact of resettlement on the role of the women in Kabylia explained the problem: 'Even running water inside the houses – progress at first sight – can become a reason for the isolation of women who can no longer use the walk to the fountain to get some fresh air, to exchange information and to groom themselves.'[64]

To sum up, housing developments and the spatial outlines of resettlement villages mirror their double function as disciplinary spaces and laboratories of social transformation. If control and repression remained their primary function, once the concentration of the rural population was an established fact, housing – like strategic resettlement in general – gradually became an instrument of social engineering.

Transformations of land use and labour

Forced migration and resettlement of huge parts of the rural population had a devastating impact on the agricultural system of the affected colonies. At the same time, late colonial planners perceived the tabula rasa left by forced resettlement as a unique opportunity to introduce new forms of agricultural production and rural commerce. Locked up in strategic resettlements, Kenyan and Algerian small farmers could no longer cultivate their fields. They also lost the surplus income of the seasonal work typically performed by one or several family members. As a result, malnutrition and dependency on external aid figured among the immediate consequences of forced relocation. In order to deal with this problem, British and French colonial authorities devised plans for land reform and the rationalization of agricultural production.

Throughout the Kenyan Emergency, the Nairobi government's resettlement committee repeatedly debated how to reabsorb the displaced Kikuyu from the Rift Valley and Nairobi without further aggravating the situation in the overcrowded Kikuyu reserve. The Swynnerton Plan of 1954 purported to offer a comprehensive long-term solution.[65] Thomas Askwith summarized its main elements in 1955:

> All African areas will benefit by the Swynnerton Plan financed by the loan of £5,000,000 provided by her Majesty's Government and to be sent to Kenya at the rate of approximately £1,000,000 per year. This plan seeks, among other things, to raise the level of production of African farming to a point at which something like 600,000 families can be carried on intensive and semi intensive holdings. It also seeks to provide the foundation on which ultimately African cash crops will be pushed up so that coffee acreage would be increased eighteen times, the acreage of pyrethrum forty times, that under pineapples eight times, while the acreage under tea would grow from almost nothing at present to 12,000 acres and under sugar cane from 200 acres to 45,000.[66]

Villagization was a crucial precondition to the plan's implementation. First of all, it provided the administration with valuable statistics about the actual number of inhabitants of the districts, locations and sub-locations in central Kenya. Secondly, the compulsory communal labour of the resettled was used to undertake forest clearance, earth works for pioneer cultivation, and the opening up of new land. And thirdly, with their disciplinary features, the strategic villages helped to curb potential protests against the results of land demarcation.[67] After the redistribution of tribal land among members of subtribes and clans, some Kikuyu found themselves allocated poor quality land or plots of subeconomic size (less than three acres according to Roger Swynnerton's calculations).[68] Sometimes, this parcelling up of land was a result of the government policy to reward loyal elements of the population, but other times it was simply the product of corruption among chiefs and clan elders.[69] That this process would inevitably create winners and losers and would sooner or later lead to the emergence of a landless class in the countryside was openly stated by Swynnerton in his plan: 'Energetic or rich Africans will be able to acquire more and bad or poor farmers less, creating a landed and a landless class. This is a normal step in the evolution of a country.'[70] In practice, villagization not only helped to push through demarcation without public unrest, it also presented a possible future for the landless class as village dwellers:

> The establishment of villages also has undoubtedly helped in providing shelter and useful occupation for landless repatriates. If villages become a permanent part of Kikuyu life, which is still uncertain, considerable numbers may be able to make a living in the villages partly by their earnings as labourers or craftsmen or petty traders, and partly from pigs, chickens and vegetables on small plots around the village. If this happens on large scale, it will introduce a new facto into the tables, which will have the effect of increasing the 'population potential' of the district. It is, however, impossible to estimate how many people may be able to live in this way as 'villagers'.[71]

The introduction of wage labour as the principal source of income for a majority of the rural population was of course difficult as long as they found themselves confined to the strategic villages. Furthermore, the obligatory and unpaid communal labour of up to six days a week that all inhabitants of the Kenyan Emergency villages had to perform made a mockery of free labour itself. With the loss of their livestock and their homes, the resettled were forced to earn money in some way or another to pay taxes, to buy food and to finance their new dwellings. Those of the resettled Kikuyu still in employment after resettlement often found that travel to their workplaces contravened curfew regulations. Exceptional authorization to travel was hard to come by, granted only after intense interrogation and an officially testified declaration of loyalty.[72]

French measures in Algeria to increase the number of non-agricultural employees in the countryside were equally double-sided. French planners in Algeria envisioned new and more rational forms of agricultural production that could be more readily introduced with the majority of the rural population confined to the strategic villages. This underpinned much of the thinking behind the Constantine Plan.[73] It made provision for the acquisition of new land and non-agricultural employment for a substantial part of the resettled population. Central to this was the creation of agricultural cooperatives (akin to those of France's wine producers), which was the cornerstone of the planned transition to bigger units and export-oriented production.[74] As in the Swynnerton Plan, so, too, in the Constantine Plan the creation of a rural working class was envisioned, not only as a result of accelerated industrialization but also through a new division of labour, and the rationalization and mechanization of agricultural production within the ambit of cooperative farming.

Several French directives stipulated that it would be 'counter-educative' to give away food and building materials for free in the strategic villages.[75] Wherever possible, the resettled were employed for road construction and other infrastructural projects. Additionally, the civilian administration could hire them for small communal jobs on a monthly basis, the *travaux dans l'intérêt communal* (TIC).[76] However, these temporary employments occasioned bitter dispute. For some commanders and administrators responsible for resettlement camps, they offered remedies to a starving population.[77] Planners and higher-level authorities, however, feared that these jobs would create a bubble of artificial employment: 'These jobs will be nothing but a form of indirect assistance if they don't lead to recovery and expansion of the local economy and will not help the population to make its living without external aid.'[78]

As the examples of elite formation, housing and economic transformation have shown, the contradictions between repression and reward in British and French counter-insurgency, while having several unintended consequences, also opened up a field of agency for the resettled that reached from collaboration and partial adaptation to outright subversion.[79] At the same time, the control-collaboration dynamic affected inter-communal tensions over social status or group solidarity and turned more violent, resulting in lasting conflicts and tensions, some of which persist to the present day.[80]

Conclusion

Civilian bureaucrats and military strategists within the British and French colonial apparatus shared the assumption that poverty was the main breeding ground for participation in violent nationalist movements. They considered the 'anachronistic' social structure of rural societies the main cause of such poverty, not the injustices of colonialism.[81] Anticipating later American modernization theory, these officials attributed the emergence of anti-colonial rebellions after the Second World War to the 'transitional phase' they deemed colonized societies to be traversing. Rural populations knew of the amenities of modern consumerism – mainly in the cities – but the majority nonetheless remained stuck in the endemic hardship of traditional culture.

Commandant Florentin, a French army inspector of the resettlement policy, wrote in 1960 that it took only a few minutes by helicopter to get from people who lived in a 'neolithic' fashion to citizens who enjoyed TV and all the luxuries that modern life had to offer.[82] The same ideas are to be found in the preambles of British government reports on the causes of Mau Mau. 'This society has rarely adjusted itself to the changed conditions, and has in some important instances steadily disintegrated. We have seen the logical result of such disintegration in the movement known as Mau Mau, which seeks to re-establish the primitive way of life of the Kikuyu forefathers as an alternative to the western way of life which the British have attempted to introduce.'[83] With their disciplinary features, the strategic villages were considered the perfect environments to guide the rural societies through the critical phase of accelerated socio-economic transition. British and French authorities alike praised them as instruments to turn 'backward' rural populations into 'citizens of the 20th century'.[84]

Research on comparable cases of strategic resettlement indicates that it can be considered a global paradigm. The Malayan 'new villages', the 'agrovilles' and 'strategic hamlets' of the wars in Vietnam, and the 'aldeamentos' erected by the Portuguese in Angola and Mozambique can all be interpreted as manifestations of a similar logic or even a parallel ideology.[85] As the most paradigmatic example for late colonial counter-insurgency, strategic resettlement combines repressive elements like collective punishment and population control with reformist schemes such as community development and basic welfare provision.[86] Military violence was used systematically to transform the way of life of whole communities; war thus became a catalyst of social change. Michael Shafer has pointed at this congruence of revolutionary aims of insurgents and counter-insurgents:

> Each, however, assumes the malleability of the masses and, despite reference to an overarching process of change, focuses on tactical measures for 'helping history'.

In other words, both revolutionaries and counterrevolutionaries identify their role as manager of modernization. … Hearts-and-minds analysts attribute insurgency to the trauma of modernization, the revolution of rising expectations, and Communist meddling. Thus, their prescriptions call for the rapid incorporation of the vulnerable periphery into the modern center. The aim is to transform the passive parochial into at least a subject, if not a true citizen, of a modern state.[87]

Community development as an element of strategic resettlement is in this view more than a mere side effect or ex post facto justification for this extremely harsh measure of population control. It is instead one of its core functions. What came after the shooting war – whether pacification as the French called it or stabilization as the British named it in Kenya – went far beyond the containment of the original anti-colonial uprising. The reconstruction of rural societies through coercive means was an important element in creating political and economic structures that were expected to endure beyond eventual political independence. As this observation suggests, on the eve of decolonization the counter-insurgent state tended to shape colonized societies in its own image.[88] While civilian and political authorities equipped with special powers and emergency regulations resorted to increasingly coercive means to implement socio-economic reforms, the military was confronted with new tasks. Selection and training of militias and village representatives, and the provision of material and technical assistance for housing, agriculture and education generated wider networks of contact with social science expertise about the civilian population.[89] Aside from such new tasks and skills in dealing with civilian populations, late colonial armies also had to communicate their actions to a critical global audience.[90] In the increasingly anti-colonial international climate of the 1960s, it required considerable propagandistic efforts from the colonial military to prove it was on the right side of history. Strategic resettlements and new villages were crucial in this regard – considered manifestations of the benevolent, constructive aims of late colonialism by those who created and run them.

The social hierarchies of the colonized also became more militarized – in the sense that they echoed the strict hierarchy of military formations and that the social changes with which they were confronted were often accompanied by violence. For the rural civilians in Kenya and Algeria who were subjected to these social engineering operations, the measures described above brought more death, suffering and violence than the hot war military conflict ever did. Additionally, the experience of constant surveillance and the absence of liberty and privacy for up to seven years forged social identities that were distinct from the rest of the rural population. The pressure to act in a tense spectrum of cooperation and resistance proved to be hard to explain to those without experience of the constraints of camp life. Indeed, many camp inhabitants feared that returning fighters would condemn them as beneficiaries of the colonial regime.

There were also profound differences in the long-term effects of strategic resettlement in Kenya and Algeria. For example, only a few of the Kenyan Emergency villages are still inhabited – most of them as markets and rural trading centres. The settlement policy of the Kenyatta government and the rapid growth of the cities created new opportunities for the former resettled after independence.[91] This contrasts starkly with the situation in Algeria where almost all of the 1,000 villages still exist, although, there too, the flight from the land increased after independence.[92] Some of Algeria's resettlement centres were integrated within postcolonial land-reform programmes, but most are still inhabited by those who lost everything during the war. For all these differences, there are also similarities in the long-term effects in both countries. For one thing, the changes imposed on patterns of rural settlement and economic structure became irreversible. Though postcolonial governments in Kenya and Algeria continued with land reform after independence – making use of former settler-owned land for redistribution – neither sought a return to the pre-war structures. The almost complete disappearance of smallholder farming in the countryside is a lasting legacy of strategic resettlement. The same might be said about the inter-communal frictions that stem from participation in violence during the time of forced colonial resettlement. On the one hand, traditional social groups and relationships such as clans and extended families have lost their former importance. On the other hand, individuals and entire rural communities are still stigmatized for their role in the late colonial counter-insurgency campaigns. These are issues too important to neglect.

Notes

1   Some sections of this chapter draw on an article published in the *Journal of Contemporary History*. The author is grateful to the editorial board and the anonymous reviewers for their comments on this material.
2   Mathew Connelly, *A Diplomatic Revolution. Algeria's Fight for Independence and the Origins of the Post-Cold War Era* (New York: Oxford University Press, 2002), 89.
3   Caroline Elkins has devoted an entire chapter of her book *Imperial reckoning* to the fate of the women in Kenya's Emergency villages, based on an impressive number of interviews. However, her interpretation of resettlement as a purely repressive measure and her lack of interest in ambiguities and the daily lives of villagers can be – and indeed has been – criticized: Caroline Elkins, *Imperial Reckoning: The Untold Story of Britain's Gulag in Kenya* (New York: Henry Holt and Company, 2005), 233–74. Critical reviews are: Bethwell A. Ogot, 'Review Article: Britain's Gulag', *Journal of African History* 46 (2005): 493–505; Susan L. Carruthers, 'Being Beastly to the Mau Mau', *Twentieth Century British History* 16, no. 4 (2005): 489–96; see as well the discussion of villagization in Kenya in: Daniel Branch, 'Footprints in the Sand: British Colonial Counterinsurgency and the War in Iraq', *Politics & Society* 38, no. 1 (2010): 15–34. The only two monographs so far on French resettlement policy in Algeria, *Le déracinement* by Pierre Bourdieu and Abdelmalek Sayad and *Les camps de regroupement de la guerre d'Algérie* by Michel Cornaton, have been written and published during or shortly after the war and came from sociologists, not historians: Pierre Bourdieu and Abdelmalek Sayad, *Le déracinement: la crise de l'agriculture traditionelle en algérie* (Paris: Les Éditions de Minuit, 1964); Michel Cornaton, *Les camps de regroupment de la guerre d'Algérie* (Paris: L'Harmattan, 1998). A recently completed PhD thesis provides an elaborate and systematic account of resettlement policy in Algeria: Fabien Sacriste, 'Les Camps de "regroupement". Une histoire de l'État colonial et de la société rurale pendant la guerre d'indépendance algérienne, 1954–62' (unpublished PhD thesis, Université de Toulouse 2 Le Mirail, 2014).

4   Aidan Forth and Jonas Kreienbaum, 'A Shared Malady: Concentration Camps in the British, Spanish, American and German Empires', *Journal of Modern European History* 14, no. 2 (2016): 245–67; Andreas Stucki and Ian R. Smith, 'The Colonial Development of Concentration Camps (1868-1902)', *The Journal of Imperial and Commonwealth History* 39, no. 3 (2011): 419–39; Sibylle Scheipers, 'The Use of Camps in Colonial Warfare', *Journal of Imperial and Commonwealth History* 43, no. 4 (2015): 678–98.

5   For the military view on strategic resettlements see Robert Marston, 'Resettlement as a Counter-revolutionary Technique', *Royal United Services Institute for Defense Studies Journal* 12, no. 4 (1979): 46–50; Kalev I. Sepp, 'Resettlement, Regroupement, Reconcentration: Deliberate Government-Directed Population Relocation in support of Counter-Insurgency Operations' (MA Thesis, Fort Leavenworth, Kansas, 1992).

6   Gavin Kitching, *Class and Economic Change in Kenya. The Making of an African Petite Bourgeoisie, 1905-1970* (New Haven: Yale University Press, 1980); Hartmut Elsenhans, *Frankreichs Algerienkrieg. Entkolonisierungsversuch einer kapitalistischen Metropole* (Stuttgart: Carl Hanser Verlag, 1974).

7   Some of the findings in this article are based on interviews with the former resettled, conducted during fieldwork in Kenya and Algeria between 2010 and 2012. In order to protect the informants, only initials and the place and time of the interview are given in the references.

8   Stathis N. Kalyvas, *The Logic of Violence in Civil War* (Cambridge: Cambridge University Press, 2006), 87–110; Stathis N. Kalyvas and Matthew Adam Kocher, 'How "Free" Is Free Riding in Civil Wars? Violence, Insurgency, and the Collective Action Problem', *World Politics* 59, no. 2 (2007): 177–216; Benjamin Valentino, Paul Huth and Dylan Balch-Lindsay, '"Draining The Sea": Mass Killing and Guerrilla Warfare', *International Organization* 58, no. 2 (2004): 375–407; Neil MacMaster, 'The "Silent Native": Attentisme, Being Compromised, and Banal Terror during the. Algerian War of Independence, 1954–1962', in *The French Colonial Mind, Volume 2: Violence, Military Encounters, and Colonialism*, ed. Martin Thomas (Lincoln: University of Nebraska Press, 2011), 283–303.

9   Huw Bennet, *Fighting the Mau Mau. The British Army and Counter-Insurgency in the Kenyan Emergency* (Cambridge: Cambridge University Press, 2013) 220–25; Moula Bouaziz and Alain Mahé, 'La Grand Kabylie durant la guerre d'Indépendance algérienne', in *La Guerre d'Algérie 1954–2004. La fin de l'amnésie*, ed. Mohammed Harbi and Benjamin Stora (Paris: Robert Laffront, 2004), 227–65.

10 The National Archives, Kew/London – United Kingdom (henceforth: TNA), CO 822/481: D. O'Hagan, Provincial Commissioner, Central Province, press-statement, 19 March 1953.

11 Kenya National Archives, Nairobi – Kenya (henceforth: KNA) DC/MRU/2/1/4: District Commissioner Nyeri, Memorandum on Kikuyu Village Settlement [secret], 11 February 1954.

12 TNA FCO 141/6247: F. Crawford (Acting Governor), The Governor's Directive No. 3 of 1954, 26 April 1954.

13 KNA CS/1/14/25: Movement of Kikuyu/Concentration of Kikuyu into Villages – Correspondences and Debates 1953-5.

14 TNA CO 822/481: Saving from Secretary of State of the Colonies, Resettlement and New Villages, 5 May 1953. On positive references to the Malayan Emergency as textbook-counter-insurgency, see Karl Hack, 'The Malayan Emergency as Counterinsurgency Paradigm', *Journal of Strategic Studies* 32, no. 3 (2009): 383–414.

15 TNA CO 822/797: Council of Ministers – Resettlement Committee, Long Term Absorption of Displaced Kikuyu, Absorption in Kikuyu Districts, 15 February 1955.

16 KNA MAA/7/787: Thomas Askwith, Report and Recommendations – Resettlement and Rural Development, 31 August 1953.

17 Service historique de l'armée de terre, Vincennes/Paris – France (henceforth: SHAT), 1H 2032: Inspection Générale des Regroupements à Délégué Général, Inspection dans le Département de l'Aurès, 28 July 1960.

18 SHAT 1H 2030: Directive Générale 654/SC/RM.10/S., Regroupement de Populations, 20 September 1957.

19 SHAT 1H 2030: Directive 2.445 CC., regroupement de populations, 24 April 1959.

20 SHAT 1H 2030: Inspection Générale des Regroupemens – Fiche résumant les principaux points du rapport sur les regroupements, [no date]; SHAT 1H 2032: Inspection Générale des Regroupements à Délégué Général 200/C/I.G.P.R. Inspection dans le Département de l'Aurès, 28 July 1960.

21 Archives nationales d'outre-mer, Aix-en-Provence – France (henceforth: ANOM) 81F/444: 146/IGRP, 4 July 1960; ANOM 81F/454: Documents Algériens 1959, Naissance de Mille Villages – Algérie.

22 See as well: Keith Sutton, 'Army Administration Tensions over Algeria's Centres de Regroupement, 1954-1962', *British Journal of Middle Eastern Studies* 26 (1999), 243–70.

23 For a detailed discussion of the administrative structure in Kenyan Central Province during the Emergency, see Bruce Berman, *Control & Crisis in Colonial Kenya. The Dialectic of Domination* (London: James Currey, 1990), 301–76.

24 Daniel Branch, *Defeating Mau Mau, Creating Kenya. Counterinsurgency, Civil War, and Decolonisation* (Cambridge: Cambridge University Press, 2009), 65.

25 Branch, *Defeating Mau Mau*, 108.

26 Interview S. K, Ndumberi, Kiambu, Kenya, 22 March 2012.

27 SHAT 1H 2575/D4: Colonel Trinquier, Note de service 126, Controle des populations rurales, 8 September 1959.

28 TNA FCO 141/6236: Deputy Director of Operations, Post Anvil Operations, 22 June 1954.

29 TNA FCO 141/5921: Allegations of brutality by the Home Guard brutality, 1954; Caroline Elkins, *Imperial Reckoning*, 244–50; Branch, *Defeating Mau Mau*, 82–4.

30 FCO 141/5921: Commissioner of Police A.E. Young to Governor Baring, 28 December 1954.

31 Interview N. K, Kjanjakoma, Embu, Kenya, 27 November 2012.

32 Interview Z. N., Kibogi, Embu, 27 November 2012.

33 The most comprehensive account on auxillary forces of the French in Algeria is François-Xavier Hautreux, *La Guerre d'Algérie des Harkis, 1954-1962* (Paris: Éditions Perrin, 2013).

34 SHAT 1H 2575/D1: Centres de Formation des auto-défense, Programme du Centre Dicisionnaire du Kreider, 8 October 1960.

35 Interview S. S. Sidi Bakhti, Bou Thilis, Algeria, 14 October 2010.

36 SAHT 1H 2575/D4: Autodéfense des Populations – Rapports de Desertion, 10 July 1961; Interview S. M., Sidi Amar, Tiaret, Algeria, 8 November 2010.

37 See for example William Gallois, *A History of Violence in the Early Algerian Colony* (Basingstoke: Palgrave Macmillan, 2013).

38 For an overview of the use of spatial categories in conflict studies, see Sven Chojnacki and Bettina Engels, *Material Determinism and Beyond: Spatial Categories in the Study*

of Violent Conflict, SFB-Governance Working Paper Series, No. 55, Collaborative
Research Center (SFB) 700, Berlin, June 2013; as examples see Maureen Sioh, 'An
ecology of Postcoloniality: Disciplining Nature and Society in Malaya, 1948–1957',
Journal of Historical Geography 30 (2004): 729–46; Kalyvas, *The Logic of Violence*,
210–45.

39 Bourdieu, Sayad, *Le Déracinement*, 151–6; Cornaton, *Les camps de regroupment*,
225–9; Interview J. S., Kabare, Kirinyaga, 29 November 2012.

40 Fabian Klose, *Human Rights in the Shadow of Colonial Violence. The Wars of
Independence in Kenya and Algeria* (Philadelphia: University of Pennsylvania Press,
2013).

41 KNA DC/MRU/2/1/4: Chief Native Commissioner (E.H. Windley), to District
Commissioners 'Villagisation', 20 May 1954; SHAT 1H 3865/D2: Delouvrier à
Commandants de Corps d'Armée, N°2445 CC, Regroupement des popualtions, 31
March 1959.

42 KNA AB/2/53: Memorandum on the Aggregation of the Population into Villages in
Rural Areas, 12 April 1954.

43 KNA OP/EST/1/986: District Commissioner Nyeri to Provincial Commissioner,
Village Settlement Report 4 November 1954.

44 SHAT 1H2032: Rapport sur les regroupements de population dans les
arrondissements Nord du département de Setif, 30 November 1960.

45 Michel Rocard, *Rapport sur les camps de regroupement et autres textes sur la guerre
d'Algérie*, ed. Silvy Thénault (Paris: Fayard, 2003), 103–53; reactions of the press can
be found in ANOM 81F/107.

46 ANOM 81F107: Exposé de M. Delouvrier aux Equipes itinérantes au Palais d'Eté, 29
Mai 1959.

47 Sixteen million new francs were attributed to the development of the new villages
in the 1961 budget, but this was still criticized as far too little; see SHAT 1H 2030:
Délégué Général (Morin) à Général Commandant en Chef les Forces en Algérie
(Crepin), No 80 CAB/SG, Financement des centres de regroupement en 1961, 4
January 1961. About one half of the population of the accredited definite camps
was housed in standardized maisonnettes by 1962, see ANOM 81F951: Rapports
de l'Inspection Générale des Finances sur l'utilisation des crédits des centres de
regroupement.

48 ANOM 81F 950: Contribution de l'inspection générale des regroupement au raport
d'information generale, 13 August 1960. A similar directive for the Kenyan case can
be found in KNA OP/EST/1/986: Provincial Commissioners Office, Central Province
to The Permanent Secretary, Ministry of Local Government and Health, Village
Planning – Central Province, 2 October 1959.

49 SHAT 1H 3865/D2: Ministre Résidant à Prefets d'Algérie, Amélioration de l'habitat
traditionnel des popualtions rurales d'Algérie, 25 September 1956.

50 KNA DC/MRU/2/1/4: Medical Officers Conference, Notes of a Discussion on Village
development in African Reserves 25 May 1954.

51 The army had developed its own version of prefabricated houses, as well as the
Bureau d'aménagement rural: SHAT 1H2030: J. Florentin, IGRP, Les Regroupements
de Population en Algérie, 11 December 1960; SHAT 1 H2030: IGRP, Fiche au sujet de
la construction dans les Nouveaux Villages, 2 February 1960.

52 SHAT 1H 2030: ACP agency report 22 December 1960.

53 KNA DC/MRU/2/1/4: Provincial Commissioner, Central Province (C.M: Johnston)
to Minister of African Affairs, Construction of Villages Meru, Embu, Nyeri, Fort Hall
Districts, 8 July 1954.

54   ANOM 81F/951: M. Auboyneau, Inspecteur Général des Finances, Rapport de l'Inspection Générale des Finances sur l'utilisation des crédits des centres de regroupment; TNA WO 276/511: Report by General Sir George W.E.J. Erskine, The Kenya Emergency June 1953 to May 1955.

55   TNA CO 822/1257: Council of Ministers, Memorandum by the Minister for African Affairs, 2 July 1957.

56   Interview with F.K., Kagumo, Kirinyaga, 28 November 2012.

57   KNA DC/NYI/2/2: Handing over Report Nyeri District, O.E.B. Hughes to J.M.B Butler, December 1954.

58   ANOM 81F444: Commission départementale de la Réforme Agraire d'Orleansville, Réunion de 17 Juillet 1959.

59   SHAT 1H 2032: Service d'Action Psychologique, Zone Sud Oranais No 11/PSY, Considérations générales sur les regroupements, 9 November 1958.

60   KNA DC/KBU/2/1: Githunguri Division Handing Over Report February 1957 by A.N Savage.

61   Alfonso Castro and Kreg Ettenger, 'Counterinsurgency and Socioeconomic Change: The Mau Mau War in Kirinyaga, Kenya', *Research in Economic Anthropology* 15 (1994): 63–101.

62   On late colonial interventions in gender relations see Cora Ann Presley, *Kikuyu Women, the Mau Mau Rebellion and Social Change in Kenya* (Boulder, CO: Westview Press, 1992); Marina E. Santoru, 'The Colonial Idea of Women and Direct Intervention. The Mau Mau Case', *African Affairs* 95 (1996): 253–67; Neil MacMaster, *Burning the veil: The Algerian war and the 'emancipation' of Muslim women, 1954-62* (Manchester, 2009); Djane Sambron, 'La Politique d'Émancipation du Gouvernement Français à l'Égard des Femmes Algériennes pendant la Guerre d'Algérie', in *Des Hommes et Femmes en Guerre d'Algérie*, ed. Jean-Charles Jauffret (Paris, 2003), 226–42.

63   SHAT 1H 2032: Inspection Générale des Regroupements, Fiche au sujet de la construction dans les Nouveaux Villages, 2 February 1960.

64   SHAT 1H 2032: Rapport établi par Professeur Jean-Jaques Denonain sur les regroupements dans les Régions d'Orléansville et de Tizi-Ouzou, 17 May 1960.

65   Anne Thurston, *Smallholder Agriculture in Colonial Kenya: The Official Mind and the Swynnerton Plan* (Cambridge: Cambridge African Studies Centre, 1987); Gary Wasserman, 'Continuity and Counter-Insurgency: The Role of Land Reform in Decolonizing Kenya, 1962-70', *Canadian Journal of African Studies* 7, no. 1 (1973): 133–48.

66   TNA CO 822/794: Report from Commissioner for Community Development and Rehabilitation, Thomas G. Askwith, Rehabilitation Programmes in Kenya, 6 January 1954.

67   M. P. K. Sorrensen, *Land Reform in the Kikuyu Country: A Study in Government Politics* (London: Oxford University Press, 1967), 113–34.

68   KNA DC/NYI/2/2: Nyeri District, Mathira Division Handing over Report 1957.

69   TNA FCO 141/5920: District Commissioner Nyeri Directive, Closer Control of the Population, 13 May 1955.

70   TNA CO 822/966: Roger Swynnerton, Plan to intensify the development of African agriculture, 8 December 1953.

71   TNA CO 822/794: Council of Ministers – Resettlement Committee, Long Term Absorption of Displaced Kikuyu, Absorption in Kikuyu Districts, 15 February 1955; see as well: Kitching, *Class and Economic Change*, 315–74.

72   TNA FCO 141/6125: Memorandum by the Internal Security Working Committee on KEM Passbook regulation, 10 July 1959.

73 Daniel Lefeuvre, 'L'échec du plan de Constantine', in *La guerre d'Algérie et les Français*, ed. Jean-Pierre Rioux (Paris: Fayard 1990), 320–4; Daniel Lefeuvre, *Chère Algérie. Comptes et Mécomptes de la tutelle coloniale, 1930–1962* (Paris: Flammarion 1997), 366–425; Elsenhans, *Frankreichs Algerienkrieg*, 543.

74 SHAT 1H 4063/D3: Minitre de l'Algérie, Regroupement de populations – councours de la caisse d'accession à la propriété et à l'exploitation rurales, 6 January 1958; ANOM 81F/443: Documents Algériens N. 128, 5 January 1960, Le programme de développement agricole en 1960, 5.

75 Grégor Mathias, *Les Sections Administratives Spécialisées. Entre Idéal et Réalité* (Paris 1998), 75.

76 SHAT 1H 2030: Colonel Vaudrey, Commandant le Secteur de Collo, Note de Service, 'Résorption du chômage', 15 January 1960.

77 ANOM 81F/444: Centre de Hautes etudes Administratives sur l'Afrique et l'Asie Modernes, Groupe d'etudes, Stage 1959–60.

78 SHAT 1H 2030: Note de Service Z.N.C No 5 131/SCO/5/PY, Colonel Vaudrey, Commandant le Secteur de Collo: 'Résorption du chômage', 15 January 1960.

79 On the inherent contradictions of population centric counter-insurgency, see Daniel Branch and Elisabeth Jean Wood, 'Revisiting Counterinsurgency', *Politics & Society* 38 (2010): 3–14.

80 Stathis Kalyvas, 'Micro-Level Studies of Violence in Civil War: Refining and Extending the Control-Collaboration Model', *Terrorism and Political Violence* 24, no. 4, 1 (2012): 658–68.

81 Frederick Cooper, 'Modernizing Bureaucrats, Backward Africans, and the Development Concept', in *International Development and the Social Sciences. Essays on the History and Politics of Knowledge*, ed. Frederick Cooper and Randall Packard (Berkeley: University of California Press, 1997), 64–92, here 70.

82 SHAT 1H 2030/D1: J. Florentin, Les Regroupements de Population en Algérie, 11 December 1960.

83 TNA CO 822/655: Community Development Organisation, Kenya: establishment and annual report, 26 February 1953.

84 SHAT 1H 2026: General Jean Olie, Directive No 7, Phase de Consolidation de la Pacification, 12 October 1959.

85 For an overview on strategic resettlement and anti-guerrilla warfare after 1945 see Christian Gerlach, *Extremely Violent Societies: Mass Violence in the Twentieth-Century World* (Cambridge: Cambridge University Press, 2010), 177–234.

86 Eqbal Ahmad, 'Revolutionary Warfare and Counterinsurgency', in *National Liberation. Revolution in the Third World*, ed. Norman Miller and Roderick Aya (New York: Free Press, 1971), 137–213; Ben Oppenheim, 'Community and Counterinsurgency', *Humanity: An International Journal of Human Rights, Humanitarianism, and Development* 3, no. 2 (2012): 249–65.

87 Michael D. Shafer, *Deadly Paradigms. The Failure of U.S. Counterinsurgency Policy* (Princeton: Princeton University Press, 1988), 108, 116.

88 *The Counter-insurgent State: Guerrilla Warfare and State Building in the Twentieth Century*, ed. Paul B. Rich and Richard Stubbs (New York: Palgrave Macmillan, 1997).

89 Moritz Feichtinger and Stephan Malinowski, 'Transformative Invasions: Western Post-9/11 Counterinsurgency and the Lessons of Colonialism', *Humanity: An International Journal of Human Rights, Humanitarianism, and Development* 3, no. 1 (2012): 35–63.

90 Susan L. Carruthers, *Winning Hearts and Minds: British Governments, the Media and Colonial Counter-Insurgency, 1944–1960* (London: Leicester University Press, 1995).

91 There have been, however, schemes of forced resettlement after decolonization in Kenya; see Hannah Whittaker, 'Forced Villagization during the Shifta Conflict in Kenya, ca. 1963–1968', *International Journal of African Historical Studies* 45, no. 3 (2012): 343–65.

92 Keith Sutton, 'Algeria's Socialist Villages – a Reassessment', *Journal of Modern African Studies* 22, no. 2 (1984): 223–48.

8

Reconsidering Women's Roles in the Mau Mau Rebellion in Kenya, 1952–60

Katherine Bruce-Lockhart

On 12 September 2015, a new statue was unveiled in downtown Nairobi.[1] Two figures stand across from each other: a man, carrying a rifle, and a woman, who is handing him a basket of food. Their faces are turned from each other, signifying the secret and forbidden nature of the interaction. Built as a memorial to the Kenyans tortured and killed by the British during the Mau Mau Rebellion, the two figures are meant to represent the heroes and heroines of this movement. Unlike previous monuments, the statue highlights an important feature of this conflict: the significant contributions of Mau Mau women.

The relative lack of attention to women's participation in the Mau Mau Rebellion is surprising given the dense scholarly literature on this particular colonial counter-insurgency. As Daniel Branch argues, 'Few such tightly defined periods of time in the history of such a small area of the world can have been subjected to such intensive scrutiny as Kenya's Central Highlands for the years between the end of World War II and independence in 1963.'[2] The Rebellion, which took place during the state of Emergency in Kenya between 1952 and 1960, was one of the most violent uprisings of the late colonial period. The 'Mau Mau' was a group of rebels drawn from the Kikuyu, Embu and Meru ethnic groups in central Kenya, who launched a violent rebellion as a result of a combination of economic, social and political grievances. The issue of land was paramount. Many Kenyans in the Central Province had lost their land to white settlers, and were left to work as squatters with no rights to land of their own. Responding to this and other issues, the Mau Mau launched a guerrilla style insurgency in the forests of central Kenya in 1952, which ended with a British victory in 1956. The situation had by that point, however, extended far beyond a military conflict. Recognizing the importance of civilian support to the Mau Mau fighters, the British directed their efforts to the broader population, resulting in an unprecedented expansion of confinement in Kenya. During the Emergency period, at least 80,000 Kenyans were put into detention camps without trial, while over a million other civilians were forcibly resettled into government villages with conditions similar to the detention camps.[3]

There have been several valuable studies of Mau Mau women, but they are somewhat limited in their scope and are largely outdated.[4] In the last decade, topics such as capital punishment, the detention camp system, and the civil war between the Mau Mau and the Kenyan loyalists supporting the government have all received considerable attention, but a corresponding comprehensive study of women's roles is still lacking.[5] Caroline Elkins' study of the detention camp system provides one of the most extensive discussions of Mau Mau women, utilizing oral histories to illuminate female experiences.[6] However, her work, like the research of the earlier generation, does not benefit from the recent release of the Hanslope Park Disclosure archival material. These archives, discovered in 2011 by historians working on a London High Court case between the Foreign and Commonwealth Office and Kenyan plaintiffs who were detained during the Emergency, have yielded fresh information on women's involvement in the Mau Mau and the government's response to it.[7] The court case – which ended with a settlement in favour of the Kenyans in 2013 –featured female plaintiff Jane Muthoni Mara, whose testimony has also provided new insight into women's experiences.

As the statue in Nairobi symbolizes, women made significant contributions to the Mau Mau Rebellion: they engaged directly in combat and supporting roles in the forests; played a crucial part in the 'passive wing' that supplied Mau Mau troops with food, ammunition and information; occupied positions in the Mau Mau leadership hierarchy; experienced forced resettlement into government villages; and were held in detention camps and prisons. Others contributed to the British counter-insurgency efforts, serving as members of the loyalist 'Home Guard', taking part in the government-run women's clubs, or working in the detention camps. The discourses shaping the British response to women's involvement in the Rebellion were deeply gendered, drawing on particular conceptions of femininity.

This chapter will explore the diverse ways in which women supported, opposed and experienced the Mau Mau Rebellion, arguing that gender considerations are central, rather than peripheral, to our understanding of this counter-insurgency. Although gendering refers to a 'set of practices and discourses that constitute "men" and "women" *and* masculinities and femininities',[8] this chapter focuses on women and femininity in the Mau Mau context.[9] It will consider this specific case within the broader literature on counter-insurgencies, offering some preliminary comparisons with colonial and contemporary cases, such as the South African War of 1899–1902, the Algerian War of 1954–62, the Malayan Emergency of 1948–60, and the ongoing American-led counter-insurgency in Afghanistan. While there are marked differences between these cases, gender has shaped the spaces, practices and discourses of each of these counter-insurgencies.

Beyond the scholarship on the Mau Mau Rebellion, counter-insurgency research has traditionally neglected gender analysis, focusing instead on theory, strategy and methods from a military perspective. Gender analysis is largely confined to specific case studies which foreground the role of women in counter-insurgencies.[10] However, this is beginning to change. In the last decade or so, there has been a major expansion and reconsideration of counter-insurgency in academic literature,[11] focusing particularly on contemporary cases such as Afghanistan.[12] Within this new wave of literature, there have been some attempts to think through the theoretical implications of the relationship between gender and counter-insurgency at a comparative level.[13] While this trend is encouraging, gender largely remains a specialist topic within the literature, rather than an integral element of counter-insurgency research. Thus, significant scope remains for studying the intersections of gender and counter-insurgency, in terms of case studies, comparative works, and as a tool for deepening theoretical understandings of counter-insurgencies. Such research can go beyond the work of 'gap-filling', and can instead open up new ways of understanding counter-insurgencies.

This chapter explores two key elements of counter-insurgency that are shaped by gender: the sites in which counter-insurgencies are waged, and the emphasis on winning the 'hearts and minds' of civilian populations.[14] First, as an asymmetrical, nontraditional mode of warfare, counter-insurgencies cross boundaries, invade spaces and impact people normally left out of more conventional military conflicts.[15] The dyad of male combatants and female civilians is disrupted, as is the demarcation between the front line and the home front.[16] As Laleh Khalili argues, 'Counterinsurgency doctrine and practice directly bring those bodies and spaces previously coded as "private" or "feminine" – women, non-combatant men, and the spaces of the "home" – into the battlefield.'[17] This is evident in the Mau Mau case, as forced villagization and detention brought a large number of Kenyans in contact with counter-insurgency measures. Similar methods were used in the South African War, in which concentration camps were constructed to sever the links between military and civilian elements of the population, and the Malayan Emergency, where the British forcibly resettled over 500,000 Chinese into government-controlled settlements.[18] In each of these cases, counter-insurgency strategies disrupted the private sphere, bringing it within the remit of war.

Gender shapes not only the physical terrain of counter-insurgency but also the somatic one. The focus on civilian populations demands a set of practices that extend beyond combat and aim at building cooperation and loyalty among locals, commonly referred to as 'hearts and minds' campaigns. During the Mau Mau Rebellion, winning the 'hearts and minds' of Kenyans was a major priority. As Thomas Askwith, the director of Community Development and Rehabilitation in Kenya at the time, wrote, 'It is our task to re-educate these Africans and to convince them that our plans are better and hold promise of a brighter future than those of the Mau Mau.'[19] To do this, the government placed significant emphasis on community development programmes for women. Similar patterns are evident in the Algerian War, where Muslim women were major targets of French propaganda and development efforts, as well as the contemporary American counter-insurgency in Afghanistan, in which medical and social services are provided to local women in part to gain their support.[20] Ultimately, as the Mau Mau Rebellion and other cases demonstrate, gender shapes the contours of counter-insurgencies in myriad ways, and should be a focal point of any counter-insurgency analysis. Foregrounding gender also shifts the focus away from military tactics, opening up new lines of inquiry into the social dimensions of counter-insurgency, the relationship between counter-insurgency and the wider practices of colonial governmentality, and finally the interplay between local and imperial histories.

Warriors, 'spies' and 'eyes': Women in the Mau Mau

Upon declaring a state of emergency in Kenya in 1952, the British government was not concerned about Kenyan women's participation in the Mau Mau. Adopting traditional androcentric views about warfare, the British assumed that men would be fighters and women supporters. Philosopher Jean Bethke Elshtain argues that such views are embedded in long-standing Western approaches to war, which rest on 'an affinity between women and peace, between men and war'.[21] Women are seen as 'beautiful souls' who are in need of protection in times of conflict; they are considered to be victims of violence rather than agents.[22] In Kenya, this approach was adopted by the British government despite the growing trend of women's involvement in more radical political movements in the preceding decades.[23] Even when evidence of women's involvement in the Mau Mau did emerge early on, some colonial officials dismissed it as a product of male persuasion. This was the view expressed by Askwith, who wrote: 'The women have, of course, far less knowledge than the men and have been easily swayed by the Mau Mau leaders.'[24]

By 1954, this perception was changing. A memorandum from the Kenya Intelligence Committee in November of that year revealed the importance of women's contribution. The memorandum explained that, while women had initially done little more than 'feed and harbor their menfolk', they had come to 'assume a more important role' as the Emergency period went on.[25] The committee argued that the punitive and aggressive counter-insurgency strategies adopted in the initial years of the Rebellion had severely undermined male participation in the movement from civilian areas, thus enhancing women's importance. One such example is Operation Anvil, which was launched in 1954, and involved the roundup and screening of over 50,000 Kenyans.[26] As a result of this operation, more than 20,000 Kikuyu males were detained.[27] Women, including the wives of detainees and those who were 'unattached', were forcibly moved back to the reserve areas where they could be more closely monitored and controlled.[28]

With men behind bars, it was left to women to take a leading role in the 'passive wing'. This civilian network coordinated the provision of food, supplies and intelligence to the forest fighters. The Kenya Intelligence Committee noted that 'more and more responsibility was placed on the shoulders of the women' as punitive measures undercut male participation in the passive wing, with the result that women became 'the mainstay of the passive organisations in the Reserves'.[29] By acting as the 'eyes and ears' of Mau Mau, women were vital to the sustainability and survival of the Rebellion.[30]

Women undertook a range of activities in the passive wing. One woman by the name of 'Beatrice' had 'devoted her energies to fostering Mau Mau', visiting different parts of her district to organize oathing ceremonies and collect funds.[31] Oath-taking, a long-standing practice used by the Kikuyu to generate unity, was transformed for more militant purposes during the Rebellion to bind new recruits to the Mau Mau.[32] Thus, women's participation in these ceremonies helped to spread support for the movement. In official correspondence on Beatrice, it was noted that 'persons such as this have played an important part in the Mau Mau organisation by bringing the women into the movement, who are often more vicious than their menfolk'.[33] In an Embu District Intelligence Summary, it was reported that thirty-five women from

Nyeri had 'infiltrated' the region and were organizing women to 'help gangsters in this area'.[34] Jane Muthoni Mara, the female plaintiff in the High Court case, was responsible for coordinating 'the women and girls in the village to provide the Mau Mau with food, water and wash their clothes'.[35] A final example is Wambui Waiyaki Otieno, who has written one of the only memoirs on the Mau Mau Rebellion from a female perspective. As a passive wing leader, she obtained government records to enhance Mau Mau intelligence, smuggled weapons into the forest, and recruited house servants to help gain access to information and firearms held by their employers.[36]

Women's importance in the passive wing was enhanced not only by the realities of counter-insurgency but also by British gender stereotypes. Overall, women were considered less suspicious than men, and were thus ideal for carrying out this kind of covert work. As the Kenya Intelligence Committee commented, the government had initially displayed a 'reluctance' to 'deal with women in the same manner as it had dealt with the men' and the Mau Mau had taken advantage of this.[37] In her memoir, Otieno reflects on the importance of gender considerations in passive wing strategies. 'A typical Mau Mau scout', she wrote, 'was a young, smartly dressed woman'[38] who had 'perfected the art of assuming an innocent young girl's expression'.[39]

This trend is apparent in other colonial counter-insurgency cases. In Malaya, women were at the heart of the Communist Party's underground communication network because they were 'less likely to be subjected to close searches by the police or the army'.[40] In Algeria, the National Liberation Front (FLN) strategically utilized French assumptions about Muslim women to their advantage.[41] Women in traditional dress were viewed as 'passive' and 'submissive', while those in Western dress were seen as civilized and pro-French, with both groups being left alone as a result.[42] Women were thus a vital component of the 'bomb network' in Algiers, which waged war in the city 'through planting bombs, gathering intelligence or transporting arms, medicine and messages'.[43]

Along with their contributions to the passive wing, Kenyan women went into the forests to join the militant groups. Like their counterparts in Malaya or Algeria, women became combatants in their own right during the Emergency period.[44] Women had various reasons for going to the forest: some, especially those who were not married, went voluntarily; others went to escape government persecution or were abducted by the Mau Mau.[45] Although there were far fewer women than men in the forests, women nonetheless had a presence throughout the various gangs. The Kenya Intelligence Committee revealed that 'the majority of gangs' in the Aberdares Forest region had 'always contained a number of women'.[46] In November 1954, it was estimated that there were over one hundred women in the forest gangs to the areas south and west of Mount Kenya.[47] Historian Tabitha Kanogo estimates that women made up 5 per cent of forest fighters overall, while others have suggested the percentage was higher.[48]

Although there is a lack of clarity around the scope and extent of women's involvement in combat, it is clear they played a part in the military struggle. While women were initially relegated to domestic tasks such as cooking and cleaning, in 1953 Mau Mau leaders decided that they could be promoted up to the rank of colonel.[49] One woman, Muthoni wa Kirima, rose to the rank of Field Marshal, and remained in the forest until after independence was achieved in 1963.[50] Female fighters did take part in violent activities,[51] such as the Lari Massacre of 1953, which was one of the worst attacks by the Mau Mau on Kenyan civilians, leaving over 120 people dead.[52] Other women involved in the militant wing took a leading role in organizing oathing ceremonies.[53]

Women's presence in the forest was controversial, as it challenged traditional gender roles within Kikuyu society. As historian John Lonsdale argues, Mau Mau was not only a conflict over 'land and freedom' but also involved internal cleavages of generation and gender.[54] Women's entry into the forest intensified these debates, particularly over marriage and sexual relations. Ultimately, Mau Mau leaders had to abandon Kikuyu norms prohibiting sexual intercourse in the forest, but they still tried to regulate relations between men and women to avoid jealousy between male fighters.[55] Policing such relationships proved difficult and was inconsistent, a reality that spoke to the intensity of wider contests over gender within the Mau Mau movement. For some women, these debates created space for new roles and opportunities that challenged male authority.[56] More research is necessary to understand the internal gender dynamics of the Mau Mau, especially from the perspective of its female participants. As Zoe Marks argues, 'A contextualized understanding of gender relations in war impels researchers to account not only for the violence and destruction,' but also 'the interpersonal and productive dimensions of conflict', recognizing the importance of 'social and gender norms' in shaping the structures of armed groups.[57]

'Better than a course of beauty treatment': Punishing women

As the British recognized the growing contribution of women to the Mau Mau, they decided to act. In 1954, the Kenya Intelligence Committee wrote, 'It is emphasized that unless the Kikuyu, Embu and Meru women receive attention similar to that accorded to their menfolk, the operational aspect of the Emergency will be prolonged unnecessarily.'[58] Action to stem women's contribution took two main formats. First, those women considered particularly 'hardcore' in their devotion to the Mau Mau Rebellion were detained without trial. Second, women were disproportionately affected by the government's policy of 'villagization', through which Kikuyu, Embu and Meru were forced into newly created government villages to cut off support for Mau Mau fighters. This represented the strongest attempt to undermine women's contribution to the Mau Mau, as it sought to cripple the passive wing supply networks. In both these policies, gender perceptions played a central role in determining punitive strategies.

The decision to detain women on a large scale was not taken lightly. There was considerable unease among government officials about locking up women without trial, as they were concerned that the metropolitan population would view this as uncivilized. Such wariness was heightened by awareness of the concentration camps controversy of the South African War, in which the death of 28,000 Boers – the vast majority of them women and children – created a major scandal in Britain.[59] Indeed, these misgivings proved to be accurate, as the detention of Kenyan women and girls became one of the most controversial elements of the government's counter-insurgency strategy.[60]

In the autumn of 1954, debates ensued over how to deal with Mau Mau women. At that point, small groups of female detainees were being held at predominantly male detention camps such as Athi River, a policy that was not sustainable if women were to be detained on a larger scale. In September 1954, a Kiambu District official proposed building a camp on the 'Manyani model' for 'hard-core Mau Mau women'.[61] Manyani, a notorious male detention camp, was an isolated site where Mau Mau leaders were held, and thus the idea was to create a similarly remote camp for female Mau Mau leaders. However, the Minister for African Affairs expressed his concern that creating such a camp would result in even more 'political agitation' than had been the case during the South African War.[62] Debates also emerged over who should be detained. Some colonial officials felt that they should focus on the 'two or three hundred female leaders of the passive wing', while others proposed building an 'extensive system of detention camps for women'.[63] Consensus was reached on the 'most dangerous categories of women', which were identified as the 'young unmarried girls who, for the sake of excitement and in order to gain some local repute, joined gangs and, in some cases, married young gangsters', the 'mothers, wives and sisters of gangsters, prisoners and detainees', and the 'widows of dead terrorists'.[64]

Focusing on these 'dangerous' groups, the government decided to build one major detention camp for women. Towards the close of 1954, Kamiti Detention Camp was operational as a women's only camp. Located on the edge of Nairobi, this camp was built at the existing site of Kamiti Maximum Security Prison, which remains one of the largest and most notorious prisons in Kenya's penal landscape. Over the course of the Emergency period, Kamiti was home to the majority of the approximately eight thousand women detained.[65]

British conceptions of femininity were pivotal in shaping the detainees' treatment at Kamiti. Eileen Fletcher, a British Quaker woman who was brought over to design the rehabilitation programme, focused on enhancing women's roles as mothers and homemakers. Consequently, women's rehabilitation emphasized their domestic and maternal roles. While female detainees were provided with training in hygiene, gardening, embroidery, childcare and cooking, male detainees were taught skills in carpentry, farming, cobbling, tailoring and animal husbandry, thus reinforcing and reproducing a gendered division of labour.[66]

Initially, Kamiti was viewed as a major success story. Reports by media outlets and visitors to the camp extolled the rapid progress of female detainees. A rehabilitation officer who visited the prison in 1955 commented, 'A job worthy of note is being done here and will certainly bear results in the future.'[67] Katherine Warren-Gash, the officer-in-charge of screening at Kamiti, described the rehabilitation process as 'better than the course of beauty treatment', commenting that it turned 'sullen, sour, unpleasant, and downright ugly' detainees into 'really pretty' women.[68] Warren-Gash's language illuminates the extent to which British officials conceptualized detainees at Kamiti in highly gendered terms. Similarly, some officials at Kamiti initially thought that women could simply be rehabilitated through 'friendly cups of tea', rather than a systematic rehabilitation programme.[69]

By the mid-1950s, it was clear that these assumptions were misguided. Although many women were 'rehabilitated' through detention, this was not because of their malleability or passiveness. Many women at Kamiti had been swept into the violence of the Emergency involuntarily, either coerced into joining the movement or put into detention for infractions of the Emergency Regulations. Fletcher would later write about the unjust incarceration of women following her departure from Kamiti in 1956.[70] She shared the story of a headmistress in Nairobi, whose student had been taken to Kamiti after she had gone 'into Nairobi without a pass to ask her Aunt to lend her money to pay her school fees for the upcoming term!'[71] Failure to carry these mandatory identity documents resulted in many women being detained at Kamiti.[72] Women could also end up behind Kamiti's walls after being falsely accused of involvement in the Mau Mau by community members trying to settle individual scores. For example, a woman by the name of Elizabeth Wanjiro was detained at Kamiti after refusing to marry a prominent loyalist chief.[73] This heterogeneity shows the extent to which detention affected a wide range of women in Kenya, irrevocably changing their lives.

While many innocent women were caught up in the tide of the Emergency punitive policies, other detainees were devoted to the Mau Mau. As discussed at length in the *Journal of Eastern African Studies*, these 'hardcore' women greatly troubled the British, who had not expected female detainees to resist rehabilitation.[74] By August 1957, a group of 162 female Mau Mau devotees remained at Kamiti.[75] With the release of the Hanslope Park files, we now know that the British set up a satellite camp just a few miles from Kamiti to deal with these women. At this camp, Gitamayu, the British applied the 'dilution' technique, a policy that explicitly permitted the use of 'compelling force' in the handling of detainees, as well as isolation in small groups to allow for more intensive rehabilitation.[76] This technique was also applied to male hardcore detainees, but at Gitamayu it took on a specifically gendered character.

The treatment of hardcore women was shaped by discourses of madness. Between 1958 and 1959, the colonial administration made several attempts to classify the women at Gitamayu as insane. The connection between female deviancy and madness was evident throughout British colonial Africa, and stemmed from the belief that sane women would not engage in violence.[77] At Gitamayu, the discourse of madness was a useful way to cover up violent abuses in the camp. Throughout the archives on this camp, there are repeated accounts of women who appeared to be unable to walk or speak. In the archival materials, these issues were diagnosed as symptoms of insanity. However, these physical behaviours were much more likely due to the use of 'compelling force' at the camps. Letters from female detainees detail such abuse, explaining that they were 'beat much' and that 'we cannot walk because we are hurt'.[78] In her testimony for the High Court case, Mara also described how she found it 'difficult to walk' due to the beatings and treatment she received.[79] Thus, while it is clear that women were subjected to violence at Gitamayu and Kamiti, the British were – to a degree – able to cover up this treatment by claiming that the women were mad, leveraging stereotypes of female deviancy to their advantage. In this case, notions of malleability and domesticity were replaced with discourses of deviancy, specifically those of madness.

Violence was not only a feature of life at Gitamayu, or even the detention camps. For Mara, violence had begun in a government village through physical abuse, and it continued in the screening camp to which she was brought before going into detention.

Along with being whipped and 'stepped on' by guards, Mara and the other women at the screening camp were subjected to sexual torture.[80] She recounts how small groups of women were brought into tents for questioning, and if they denied their involvement in Mau Mau, a glass filled with hot water was forced into their vagina as punishment.[81] As Mara recalled, 'This manner of sexual torture was used on most of the women. ... Many of the women died from this torture.'[82] Similar accounts of this type of sexual abuse emerge from Caroline Elkins' oral histories of former female detainees, who describe having 'various foreign objects thrust into their vaginas, and their breasts squeezed and mutilated with pliers'.[83] Along with torture, women were also raped in the camps. In her memoir, Otieno recounts her experience at Lamu Detention Camp, where she was 'brutally raped' multiple times by an officer-in-charge, leaving her pregnant.[84] British soldiers who were fighting the Mau Mau were also the perpetrators of rape against Kenyan women, a reality that was largely ignored by the army.[85]

Targeting women's bodies in a sexualized way has been part of the punitive repertoire in many counter-insurgencies. Historian Raphaëlle Branche outlines how women detained in Algeria were subjected to sexual torture involving the burning of breasts and the use of electrodes on women's sexual organs.[86] Rape was also used to terrorize female detainees, as it was especially useful in threatening women's position within the family.[87] Outside of detention, Branche argues that French soldiers inflicted rape on civilian women as a form of collective violence.[88] In this and other cases, women's bodies were part of the terrain on which war was waged.

The experiences of women in screening and detention camps were often horrific, but it was not only detainees who encountered violence. Many more women were affected by villagization than detention. Inaugurated in June 1954, villagization involved the forcible transfer of over one million Kikuyu out of the reserves and into over 800 newly constructed, government-controlled villages,[89] a policy that had been used earlier by the British in Malaya to counter the communist threat.[90] Some villages were designed as punitive sites for Mau Mau supporters, while others were constructed as protective sites for the Home Guard, a Kenyan militia loyal to the government.[91] These sites were disproportionately female, as much of the male population was either in the forests, in detention or part of the Home Guard. For example, of the 1,360 inhabitants of the loyalist Kabare village in Embu District, only 176 were men.[92]

In the punitive villages, the population was tightly controlled by the Home Guard, often through violent means. Mara recounts how Home Guards would go around to each house in the village and 'ask them if they had seen the Mau Mau', and would 'beat them' if they replied that they had not.[93] Elkins' informants recount how Home Guards would rape women in the villages or inflict various forms of sexual torture on them as punishment.[94] A series of files on Ndithini Camp reveal allegations of women being raped by an officer-in-charge at a location used to house village populations engaged in compulsory labour.[95] The statement of one of the alleged victims illuminates the various forms of abuse experienced by women and girls in the villages:

> They took me to the camp where I found a lot of girls being detained. ... We all went on making roads under orders of Headman. ... We were not being paid for the work and no food was being given to us, everyone had to get food from her

home as they had no food at all in the camp. ... I did not go back to the camp because of the ill-treatment we had been given in the camp. ... Working too hard without food or pay and being beaten all the time, also the T.P's [Tribal Police] troubling us throughout each night to have sexual intercourse by force.[96]

Along with sexual violence, women in the punitive villages suffered in other ways. Their homes were burnt down – often without warning – as part of the forced removal procedures.[97] Once they were moved to the new villages, they were forced to participate in communal labour.[98] Village inhabitants operated in an environment of intense surveillance and control, which included curfews, barricades and policing by Home Guards.[99] Famine, malnutrition and disease were widespread in the villages, often leading to death among village inhabitants.[100] Finally, Elkins describes how women were subjected to a range of punishments for alleged allegiance to the Mau Mau, including beatings, sexual assault and various forms of torture.[101] As Elkins argues, 'Villagization was intended as a punitive strategy to contain, control, and discipline Mau Mau women.'[102]

Loyalist women

Daniel Branch's seminal study of loyalism in the Mau Mau Rebellion has prompted scholars to reframe this conflict as a civil war.[103] Although Branch's book provides some insight into the experiences of women supporting the government, it only forms a small part of his study. As was the case with the Mau Mau movement, women made important contributions to the loyalist cause. They took on a range of roles, including rehabilitation officers, Home Guards, and leaders and participants in government-run women's clubs.

Loyalist women directly engaged with members of the Mau Mau, either to punish them or persuade them to leave the movement. David Anderson notes that women were often important witnesses in the trials against Mau Mau.[104] Women also took a leading role in encouraging Mau Mau fighters to surrender. Branch cites the example of Nancy Njarua, a loyalist Kikuyu woman, who urged her female counterparts, 'To save your life and save your children's lives you should try in whichever way possible to see that the few remaining gangsters have surrendered.'[105] Some women were involved in the Home Guard, engaging in activities such as seizing Mau Mau suspects and performing anti-Mau Mau songs.[106] Other women formed part of the staff at screening and detention camps. Loyalist female elders and Athi River detainees who had confessed their Mau Mau involvement regularly visited Kamiti to encourage female detainees to follow suit.[107] At Gitamayu, 'forthright, loyal women' were integral to the 'dilution' technique, and were used to 'encourage the detainees by friendly persuasion to abandon their sullen and aggressive attitudes'.[108] Those detainees who responded well to rehabilitation were then able to spend more time with the loyalist female staff, permitted to 'talk and sew and make baskets' with these women as part of their rehabilitation process.[109]

Along with this direct engagement, the government scaled up their community development efforts to dissuade others from joining the Mau Mau. Elkins argues that

Kikuyu women were the primary targets of liberal reform in this period.[110] Such efforts had a dual purpose: they contributed to the counter-insurgency efforts, but they also fit into the government's desire to buttress the discourse of the civilizing mission, which was facing a barrage of criticism by the 1950s. Providing development opportunities for women was a way of making counter-insurgency more palatable. It also reflected the wider reorientation of the colonial administration in the post-war period, often referred to as the 'second colonial occupation' due to the more interventionist approach adopted.[111] As historians John Lonsdale and Donald Anthony Low argue, this new approach was characterized by two goals: making Africans 'fit for self-government', and providing state-directed social welfare in order to ameliorate the effects of 'detribalisation'.[112] Thus, although the counter-insurgency measures were a response to the Mau Mau Rebellion, they were interwoven with the broader policy agenda of the British colonial administration.

Central to these efforts were the Maendeleo ya Wanawake – progress among women – clubs. Launched in 1952, the clubs were meant to provide women with opportunities for training and development, while also solidifying their opposition to Mau Mau.[113] The movement expanded rapidly, reaching over five hundred clubs by 1954.[114] Women were barred from being members unless they had pledged to oppose the Mau Mau.[115] Through Maendeleo ya Wanawake women were trained in domestic skills such as hygiene and childcare.[116] Askwith praised their widespread impact on females and communities:

> These clubs proved an enormous success and multiplied fast. Some people felt that they had a greater impact on African life than the courses for men, and this may well be so. After all, it was the women who stayed at home. … They had to rear the children, to cultivate, to sell their produce and keep the home intact.[117]

For many women, these clubs offered tangible benefits. They were an avenue for personal advancement and helped women to provide for their households.[118] While colonial accounts depict these clubs as saving women, Branch acknowledges the agency of those who took part in these initiatives. Facing poverty and food shortages, women turned to Maendeleo ya Wanawake and 'used its brand of modernity to consolidate control of households and their budgets'.[119]

Similar initiatives are apparent in other counter-insurgency cases. In Algeria, teams of women undertook 'in-depth actions' to 'penetrate the local Muslim population through the female population' by providing medical and educational services.[120] The most significant groups were the Equipes Médico-Sociales Itinérantes, which were composed of a medical doctor, a European female assistant and two Muslim female assistants.[121] Their primary role was to provide medical care, social assistance and education in domestic matters.[122] Contemporary parallels can be drawn, to some extent, in Afghanistan where similar strategies have been employed in the counter-insurgency operations. This is particularly true in regard to the use of Female Engagement Teams (FETs): groups of marines who run medical, educational and leadership projects to help secure the loyalty of local women.[123] From Kenya to Afghanistan, gender has played a key role in shaping the focus and framing of 'hearts and minds' campaigns in counter-insurgencies.

Although loyalist women in Kenya benefited from some of the development opportunities provided by the government, they also faced challenges. Many women were killed as a result of Mau Mau attacks such as the Lari Massacre of 1953.[124] For example, Embu District intelligence reports note numerous instances of loyalist women being murdered by the Mau Mau.[125] Furthermore, while moving into protected villages enhanced women's security, it also brought its own set of problems, including curfews, limited economic opportunities, controls on movement and communal labour.[126] Lives were therefore changed in profound ways by the counter-insurgency, providing both challenges and opportunities for loyalist women.

Conclusion

As symbolized by the statue in Nairobi, the significance of women's involvement in the Mau Mau has recently been brought into greater focus. Women in Kenya played a crucial part in the Rebellion, whether as active participants or as loyalists supporting the government. Acknowledging women's roles is important, but examining their experiences goes beyond recognition, yielding important insight into the effects of gender on counter-insurgency practices. Numerous elements of the Emergency period in Kenya were influenced by gender dynamics, such as the internal struggles within the Mau Mau movement, the punitive policies adopted by the British and the development strategies designed to win over the 'hearts and minds' of civilians. By bringing gender into the foreground of the Rebellion, we not only rectify the empirical gap in scholarly considerations of women's roles, but we are also able to probe more deeply into the gendered nature of counter-insurgency discourse and practice.

The centrality of gender in shaping counter-insurgencies extends beyond the Mau Mau case, with similar patterns evident in both colonial and contemporary examples. The spaces and means by which counter-insurgencies are fought unsettle the traditional divide between combatants and civilians, bringing women more directly within the realm of conflict. Gender binaries are at once destabilized, as women assume more direct roles in carrying out and supporting insurgent combat, and hardened, as feminine tropes of domesticity and victimization are used to legitimize counter-insurgency actions and design hearts and minds campaigns. Thus, the nature of this form of warfare means that gender must be a pivotal rather than a marginal part of academic research in this field. In considering gender, scholars deepen their understanding of particular cases and also explore how social constructions and categories shape the parameters of conflict. Such a perspective broadens the relevance of counter-insurgency research beyond military history and strategic studies. This shift is urgent and necessary as we confront the legacies of past counter-insurgencies and grapple with the challenges of those in the present.

Bringing women's experiences into the foreground of the Mau Mau Rebellion also shifts our understanding of colonial counter-insurgencies by recasting the relationship between crisis and everyday colonialism. The concepts and practices that shaped Britain's response to Mau Mau women were embedded in the wider workings of colonial rule, from assumptions about women's domestic and docile nature, which undergirded much of the imperial project in Africa and beyond, to the Maendeleo ya Wanawake clubs, which represented the broader welfare-centred approach of the colonial state after the Second World War. Thus, rather than exceptionalizing the counter-insurgency measures enacted in response to the Mau Mau Rebellion, we can recognize them as an extreme manifestation of the wider ideas and strategies of colonial governmentality. The declaration of a state of Emergency – whether in Malaya, Nyasaland or Kenya – marked an increase in the scale and intensity of colonial tactics of control and repression, but was ultimately representative of more long-standing approaches and beliefs.

Thus, the study of counter-insurgencies offers many possible avenues of insight beyond military and strategic studies. Through examining multiple dimensions of colonial counter-insurgencies – the leveraging of certain gender stereotypes, the impact on households and families, the agendas of 'hearts and minds' programmes and the resistance to or participation in counter-insurgency campaigns – we can learn much about both local histories and broader imperial ones. As Anderson and Branch argue in relation to the study of loyalist counter-insurgency forces, 'Recovering such histories requires a local perspective, but understanding the significance of these struggles demands an awareness of global processes and connections.'[127] Examining counter-insurgencies using multiple historical lenses and scales of analysis opens up new critical possibilities for this field of study.

Notes

1　'UK-funded Mau Mau monument unveiled in Kenya,' BBC News, 12 September 2015, http://www.bbc.co.uk/news/world-africa-34234812 (accessed 27 October 2015).

2　Daniel Branch, *Defeating Mau Mau, Creating Kenya: Counterinsurgency, Civil War, and Decolonization* (Cambridge: Cambridge University Press, 2009), xv.

3　David M. Anderson, 'British Abuse and Torture in Kenya's Counter-Insurgency, 1952-1960,' *Small Wars & Insurgencies* 23, nos. 4–5 (2012): 702. For the debate on detainee figures David Elstein, 'The End of the Mau Mau,' Letter to the Editors, *The New York Review of Books*, 23 June 2005, http://www.nybooks.com/articles/archives/2005/jun/23/the-end-of-the-mau-mau/ (accessed 25 October 2015).

4　See Tabitha Kanogo, 'Kikuyu Women and the Politics of Protest: Mau Mau,' in *Images of Women in Peace & War: Cross-Cultural and Historical Perspectives*, ed. Sharon MacDonald, Pat Holden and Shirley Ardener (Basingstoke: Macmillan Education, 1987), 78–99; Cora Ann Presley, *Kikuyu Women, The Mau Mau Rebellion, and Social Change in Kenya* (Boulder: Westview Press, 1992); Marina E. Santoru, 'The Colonial Idea of Women and Direct Intervention: The Mau Mau Case,' *African Affairs* 95 (1996): 253–67. While not a formal scholarly work, Muthoni Likimani provides important insight into women's roles through fictional accounts in *Passbook Number F.47927: Women & Mau Mau in Kenya* (London: Macmillan, 1985).

5　On capital punishment, see David Anderson, *Histories of the Hanged: Britain's Dirty War in Kenya and the End of Empire* (London: Phoenix, 2006); for detention camps see Caroline Elkins, *Britain's Gulag: The Brutal End of Empire in Kenya* (London: Jonathan Cape, 2005); for the civil war see Daniel Branch, *Defeating Mau Mau, Creating Kenya: Counterinsurgency, Civil War, and Decolonization* (Cambridge: Cambridge University Press, 2009).

6   Elkins, *Britain's Gulag.*
7   See David M. Anderson, 'Mau Mau in the High Court and the "Lost" British Empire Archives: Colonial Conspiracy or Bureaucratic Bungle?' *Journal of Imperial and Commonwealth History* 39, no. 5 (2011): 699–716.
8   Laleh Khalili, 'Gendered Practices of Counterinsurgency,' *Review of International Studies* 37, no. 4 (2011): 1473.
9   More research is also necessary for understanding the ways in which ideas about masculinity impacted the Mau Mau Rebellion. For some discussion of this, see Luise White, 'Separating the Men from the Boys: Constructions of Gender, Sexuality, and Terrorism in Central Kenya, 1939-1959,' *The International Journal of African Historical Studies* 23, no. 1 (1990): 1–25.
10 Examples include Mike Kesby, 'Arenas for Control, Terrains of Gender Contestation: Guerrilla Struggle and Counter-Insurgency Warfare in Zimbabwe 1972-1980,' *Journal of Southern African Studies* 22, no. 4 (1996): 561–84; Mahani Musa, 'Women in the Malayan Communist Party, 1942-89,' *Journal of Southeast Asian Studies* 44, no. 2 (2013): 226–49; Paula M. Krebs, '"The Last of the Gentlemen's Wars": Women in the Boer War Concentration Camp Controversy,' *History Workshop Journal* 33, no. 1 (1992): 38–56.
11 David Kilcullen, 'Counter-insurgency Redux,' *Survival* 48, no. 4 (2006–07): 111.
12 Synne Laastad Dyvik, 'Women as "Practitioners" and "Targets": Gender and Counterinsurgency in Afghanistan,' *International Feminist Journal of Politics* 16, no. 3 (2014): 410–29; Charles Hirschkind and Saba Mahmood, 'Feminism, the Taliban, and the Politics of Counter-Insurgency,' *Anthropological Quarterly* 75, no. 2 (2002): 339–54.
13 See Khalili, 'Gendered Practices.'
14 Ibid., 1471.
15 Ibid., 1471–3.
16 Ibid., 1473.
17 Ibid., 1474.
18 Karl Hack, '"Iron Claws on Malaya": The Historiography of the Malayan Emergency,' *Journal of Southeast Asian Studies* 30, no. 1 (1999): 99.
19 Tom Askwith, *From Mau Mau to Harambee* (Cambridge: African Studies Centre, 1955), 101, http://www.african.cam.ac.uk/images/files/titles/maumau (accessed 1 November 2015).
20 See Ryme Seferdjeli, 'The French Army and Muslim Women During the Algerian War (1954-62),' *Hawwa* 3, no. 1 (2005): 40–79; Keally McBride and Annick T. R. Wibben, 'The Gendering of Counterinsurgency in Afghanistan,' *Humanity* 3, no. 2 (2012): 199–215.
21 Jean Bethke Elshtain, *Women and War* (Chicago: University of Chicago Press, 1995), 4.
22 Ibid.
23 See Kanogo, 'Kikuyu Women,' 81–5.
24 Askwith, *From Mau Mau to Harambee,* 107.
25 The National Archives of the United Kingdom (TNA), Public Record Office (PRO), Foreign and Commonwealth Office (FCO) 141/6244, 'Female Mau Mau Terrorists: Memorandum by the Kenya Intelligence Committee,' 4 November 1954.
26 Anderson, *Histories of the Hanged,* 205.
27 Ibid., 204.
28 Ibid.
29 TNA PRO FCO 141/6244, 'Female Mau Mau.'

30 Quoted in Elkins, *Britain's Gulag,* 222.
31 Kenya National Archives (KNA) JZ/7/24/7, 'Re: Detention No. 281 Beatrice, Your Detn. P.281 of 2 December, 1953.'
32 Anderson, *Histories of the Hanged,* 30.
33 KNA/JZ/7/24/7, 'Re: Detention No.281.'
34 TNA PRO FCO 141/5676, 'Embu District Intelligence Committee Summary for week ending 7th January 1954.'
35 Royal Court of Justice, *Ndiku Mutua and Others and the Foreign and Commonwealth Office. Witness Statement of Jane Muthoni Mara.* 4 November 2010. Case No. HQ09X02666.
36 Wambui Waiyaki Otieno, *Mau Mau's Daughter: A Life History* (Boulder: Lynne Rienner Publishers, 1998), 37–43.
37 TNA PRO FCO 141/6244, 'Female Terrorists'
38 Otieno, *Mau Mau's Daughter,* 38.
39 Ibid., 43.
40 Musa, 'Women in the Malayan Communist Party,' 238–9.
41 Natalya Vince, *Our Fighting Sisters: Nation, Memory and Gender in Algeria, 1954-2012* (Manchester: Manchester University Press, 2015), 81.
42 Ibid., 81–2.
43 Natalya Vince, 'Colonial and Post-Colonial Identities: Women Veterans of the "Battle of Algiers",' *French History and Civilization* 2 (2009): 155.
44 Kanogo, 'Kikuyu Women,' 88.
45 Ibid., 87.
46 TNA PRO FCO 141/6244, 'Female Mau Mau.'
47 Ibid.
48 Kanogo, 'Kikuyu Women,' 78; John Lonsdale, 'Authority, Gender and Violence: The War within Mau Mau's Fight for Land and Freedom,' in *Mau Mau and Nationhood: Arms, Authority and Narration,* ed. E. S. Atieno Odhiambo and John Lonsdale (Oxford: James Currey, 2003), 63.
49 Kanogo, 'Kikuyu Women,' 88.
50 'Historic hair,' *The Economist,* 6 April 2013, http://www.economist.com/news/middle-east-and-africa/21575787-female-veteran-mau-mau-laments-new-order-historic-hair (accessed 25 October 2015).
51 TNA PRO FCO 141/6244, 'Female Mau Mau.'
52 Anderson, *Histories of the Hanged,* 126.
53 TNA PRO FCO 141/6244, 'Female Mau Mau.'
54 Lonsdale, 'Authority,' 60.
55 Ibid., 63.
56 Kanogo, 'Kikuyu Women,' 78.
57 Zoe Marks, 'Sexual Violence in Sierra Leone's Civil War: "Virgination," Rape, and Marriage,' *African Affairs* 113, no. 450 (2014): 87.
58 TNA PRO FCO 141/6244, 'Female Mau Mau.'
59 Krebs, 'The Last of the Gentlemen's Wars,' 41.
60 Katherine Bruce-Lockhart, 'The "Truth" About Kenya: Connection and Contestation in the 1956 Kamiti Controversy,' *Journal of World History* 26, no. 4 (2016): 815–38.
61 TNA PRO FCO 141/6324/12, R.G. Turnbull to C.M. Johnston, 10 September 1954.
62 Ibid.
63 TNA PRO FCO 141/6244, 'Extract from War/c 375 of 22 November 1954.'
64 Ibid.

65 Anderson, *Histories of the Hanged*, 313.
66 KNA AH/4/26/11/A, 'Rehabilitation of Detained Persons,' 1953.
67 KNA AB/1/112/34, 'Official Visit to Kamiti Prison,' 13 June 1955.
68 KNA AB/1/112/92, 'The Mau Mau Women at Kamiti – Christian cleansing oaths successfully used,' *The Sunday Post*, 1 April 1956.
69 School of Oriental and African Studies (SOAS) Conference of British Missionary Societies (CBMS) 278, Eileen Fletcher, 'Proposed Scheme for the Rehabilitation of Women and Girls in Prisons and Camps,' February 1955.
70 SOAS CBMS 278, Eileen Fletcher, 'The Truth About Kenya: An Eyewitness Account by Eileen Fletcher,' 4 May 1956.
71 Ibid.
72 KNA AB/1/112/8, Eileen Fletcher to Mr Morrison, 8 February 1955.
73 KNA AB/1/112/5, John Mukiri Githendu to The Women's Rehabilitation Officer, 18 January 1955.
74 Katherine Bruce-Lockhart, '"Unsound" Minds and Broken Bodies: The Detention of "Hardcore" Mau Mau Women at Kamiti and Gitamayu Detention Camps, 1954-1960,' *Journal of Eastern African Studies* 8, no. 4 (2014): 590–608.
75 TNA PRO FCO 141/6324/25/1, Kathleen Warren Gash to Secretary for Community Development, 2 August 1957.
76 Anderson, 'British Abuse,' 707.
77 See Stacey Hynd, 'Deadlier than the Male?: Women and the Death Penalty in Colonial Kenya and Nyasaland, c. 1920-57,' *Stichproben. Wiener Zeitschrift für kritische Afrikastudien* 12 (2007): 13–33; Tapiwa B. Zimudzi, 'African Women, Violent Crime and the Criminal Law in Colonial Zimbabwe, 1900-1952,' *Journal of Southern African Studies* 30, no. 3 (2004): 499–518.
78 TNA PRO FCO 141/6324/93/4, 'ALL Woman detainees' to Mr Patrick Gordon Walker, 26 November 1958.
79 Royal Courts of Justice, 'Witness Statement.'
80 Ibid.
81 Ibid.
82 Ibid.
83 Elkins, *Britain's Gulag*, 226–7.
84 Otieno, *Mau Mau's Daughter*, 81.
85 Huw Bennett, *Fighting the Mau Mau: The British Army and Counter-Insurgency in the Kenya Emergency* (Cambridge: Cambridge University Press, 2013), 210.
86 Raphaëlle Branche, 'Sexual Violence in the Algerian War,' in *Brutality and Desire: War and Sexuality in Europe's Twentieth Century*, ed. Dagmar Herzog (London: Palgrave Macmillan, 2009), 250.
87 Ibid.
88 Ibid., 251–2.
89 Keith M. P. Sorrenson, *Land Reform in the Kikuyu Country: A Study in Government Policy* (Nairobi: Oxford University Press, 1967), 110–12.
90 Huw Bennett, '"A Very Salutary Effect": The Counter-Terror Strategy in the Early Malayan Emergency, June 1948 to December 1949,' *Journal of Strategic Studies* 32, no. 3 (2009): 438–9.
91 Branch, *Defeating Mau Mau*, 108.
92 Ibid., 112.
93 Royal Courts of Justice, 'Witness Statement.'
94 Elkins, *Britain's Gulag*, 244.

95   TNA PRO FCO 141/6205, Ndithini Camp, Provincial Commissioner Southern
      Province to MAA, 13 December 1955.
96   TNA PRO FCO 141/6205, Yula d/o Muthoks, Konza, Kibauni Location, Machakos.
97   Elkins, *Britain's Gulag*, 238.
98   Ibid., 241.
99   Anderson, 'Mau Mau in the High Court', 705–6.
100   Elkins, *Britain's Gulag*, 259–65.
101   Ibid., 233–74.
102   Ibid., 240.
103   Branch, *Defeating Mau Mau*.
104   Anderson, *Histories of the Hanged*, 74–6.
105   Branch, *Defeating Mau Mau*, 143.
106   TNA Colonial Office (CO) 1066/12, 'Women's Home Guard: Kikuyu Guards, Forest
      Guards, Buffs and Home Guards displaying skills,' 1953–4.
107   KNA AB/1/92/155, Henry Kuria to Secretary for Community Development, 31 July
      1957.
108   TNA PRO FCO 141/6324/82, J. S. Simmance to Special Commissioner, Central
      Province, 26 November 1958.
109   TNA PRO FCO 141/6324/77/1, J. S. Simmance to Minister for African Affairs,
      3 October 1958.
110   Caroline Elkins, 'Detention and Rehabilitation during the Mau Mau Emergency:
      The Crisis of Late Colonial Kenya' (PhD diss., Harvard University, 2001), 229.
111   D. A. Low and J. Lonsdale, 'East Africa: Towards the new order 1945-1963,' in *Eclipse
      of Empire*, ed. D. A. Low (Cambridge: Cambridge University Press, 1991), 174.
112   Ibid., 173.
113   Daniel Branch, *Defeating Mau Mau*, 142.
114   Ibid.
115   Ibid.
116   Ibid.
117   Rhodes House, Mss.Afr.s. 1770 (1), Thomas Askwith, 'Memoirs of Kenya, 1936-61,'
      41.
118   Branch, *Defeating Mau Mau*, 144.
119   Ibid.
120   Seferdjeli, 'The French Army,' 42.
121   Ibid., 45–6.
122   Ibid., 47.
123   McBride and Wibben, 'The Gendering of Counterinsurgency,' 206–7.
124   Anderson, *Histories of the Hanged*, 127.
125   TNA PRO FCO 141/5767, 'Kenya: Embu District Intelligence Committee
      summaries,' 1953–4.
126   Branch, *Defeating Mau Mau*, 112–14.
127   David M. Anderson and Daniel Branch, 'Allies at the End of Empire – Loyalists,
      Nationalists and the Cold War, 1945-76.' *The International History Review* (2016),
      http://dx.doi.org/10.1080/07075332.2016.1230770.

9

The Art of Counter-insurgency: Phase Analysis with Primary Reference to Malaya (1948–60), and Secondary Reference to Kenya (1952–60)

Karl Hack

The search for the recipe for counter-insurgency success and the attempt to describe a distinctive 'British way' of counter-insurgency have characterized much counter-insurgency literature from the 1960s to the present: from classics by practitioners such as Sir Robert Thompson to David French's magisterial 2011 work, *The British Way in Counterinsurgency*.[1] For articles no less than books, the debate has often been about the relative importance of supposedly opposed principles: for instance, minimum versus demonstrative and punitive force.[2]

The reality, however, is that any description of a single campaign, or formula for lessons drawn from it, is likely to be seriously misleading if treated as if it is applied to the whole campaign cycle. To take just one example, incipient and early stages are very likely to be characterized by inadequate intelligence and poorly suited security force structures, presenting radically different challenges and possibilities to a mature campaign phase. It seems extremely unlikely that the same policies would be feasible, let alone as effective, in phases as contrasting as the build-up to insurgency, its early stage, the stage of fully mature counter-insurgency policies and the rundown (or exit or transitional) stage. Different campaign stages (with contrasting bundles of resources, and of civilian, military and political attitudes) manifest in sharply contrasting needs and approaches.

Yet this point, which once named seems so glaringly obvious, has for the most part remained hidden in plain view. It receives very limited attention in the conclusions to many counter-insurgency articles and surveys, which instead tend to talk as though 'lessons' and techniques might be broadly applicable across campaigns. Though more recent comparative works are increasingly sensitive to differences of place and context, and so to the dangers of assuming 'lessons' are easily transferable across campaigns, they usually take little cognisance of the equally significant difference between types of campaign phase.[3] Works which compare campaigns for a particular phase, or techniques with attention to their lifecycle changes, are much rarer than they should be.[4]

This chapter explores the nature of phases, and their vital role in comparative counter-insurgency analysis, in two main stages. The first section analyses in detail how phases can be defined and demonstrates just how contrasting various phases in the Malayan Emergency of 1948–60 were. By identifying the distinctive weighting and interrelationship of approaches in each phase, it characterizes these as 'counterterror', 'geodemographic control' and 'optimisation', followed by normalization and deep transition. It also uses this framework to identify roadblocks to, and causes of, change between periods. This in itself, however, is not sufficient to demonstrate the utility and difficulty of phase-based analysis for *comparing* insurgencies, so a shorter subsequent section then demonstrates how phases for the Kenyan counter-insurgency of 1952–60 might be identified, and used to generate contrasts and comparisons to Malaya. While not suggesting that any exact matching of phases is possible, it shows that thinking about comparability of phases remains vital. The conclusion then seeks to draw out more general points about phases and their place in the wider art of comparative counter-insurgency analysis.

Malayan phases

Summations of the Malayan Emergency at trough and peak demonstrate just how important it is to recognize qualitatively different periods of counter-insurgency. The most dramatic contrast can be demonstrated by contrasting earliest phase (the first six months of June to December 1948) with the latest (from 1957 to the formal end of Emergency in 1960).

The first six months saw limited Security Forces (SF) numbers. The mainly Malay police force of 9,000 (for a population of five million, of which 38 per cent or two million were Chinese) had only three Chinese officers and twenty-seven inspectors.[5] They were unprepared to deal with a 90 per cent plus Chinese insurgent force that grew to about 4,000 by the year's end.[6] This necessitated a strategy that could work with very limited SF, scarce intelligence, and a largely un-administered jungle-fringe population of Chinese 'squatters'. Consequently a police force that nominally directed the campaign ceded the initiative to the army. The latter conducted sweeps often netting few 'bandits', but helping to break down typical insurgent bands from 100 to 200 plus in 1948 to 40 or less by mid-1949. But communist support and numbers increased despite this, and the insurgents could return to rural areas after SF patrols, creating a liminal danger area between Malaya's central north-south spine of mountain and forest (that covered four-fifths of the country) and the plains.

This policy of constant pressure, partly with the aim of intimidating rural inhabitants into withdrawing insurgent support, encouraged army shooting in liminal areas when in doubt whether those fleeing might be consorting with bandits. No fewer than seventy-seven people were shot while running away in 1948 to early 1949.[7]

By the late period of 1957–60, however, Special Branch (SB) had a strong core of Chinese-speaking officers. Well before Independence Day (31 August 1957) it knew the name, and broad location, of most of the remaining 1,800 Malayan National Liberation Army (MNLA) members, and controlled many Surrendered Enemy Personnel (SEP).[8]

Propaganda and operations could now be targeted against specific individuals. Furthermore, most of Malaya's rural population were now reasonably well protected. More than 430,000 Chinese were among 540,000 resettled in New Villages with a police station and armed Home Guard, fences, gates and amenities, and often piped water and electricity. Increasing numbers had 'Good Citizens Committees' (GCCs) as well.[9] Where there was still a threat, the local military–police–administrative war executive committee (WECs) could call in blended operations. These combined village protection, strict food controls and curfews, propaganda involving leaflets, voice aircraft, SEP and GCCs, and sometimes a squeeze between troops airlifted or dropped into deep jungle to drive bandits out, and a backstop of police and army at the jungle fringe.[10] Within the jungle even *orang asli* had been brought onside from 1953, by developing Jungle Forts from where the SAS and Police Field Force could dominate the surrounding area and provide medical and trading facilities, and arms to local auxiliaries.[11]

One example can give the flavour of blended operations in that late period, and a taste of how entirely different they look to early counter-insurgency. This is the campaign against Ah Hoi's small group upriver of coastal Kuala Selangor. In 1957 the SF offered an amnesty (17–21 July), gave voice and leaflet warnings and then had the area pounded by bombers and artillery from the 22nd before jungle patrols commenced. On 27 July nearby Sekinchang GCC arranged for a minister and Ah Hoi's wife to address 3,000 New Villagers, and led a procession carrying effigies of her husband, before burning them. Yet Ah Hoi remained steadfast from February to April 1958. Then B Squadron 22 SAS was parachuted into the jungle and marsh, pushing the gang towards a police backstop at the jungle edge, and eventually inducing the group's surrender.[12]

Over 1956–9 other such operations netted from a few 'CT' a time to tens or even over 100 when surrenders snowballed. On 16 February 1959 the entire State of Selangor was declared a 'White Area'. From their introduction in 1953 such White Areas involved lifting curfews and food controls. What mattered in this late British policy was thus maximizing the gap between bad consequences for villagers of continued incidents, and the good consequences of cooperation and compliance.[13]

Contrasting these two extremes brings out two points. First, the late-stage counter-insurgency in Malaya, as a blend of techniques, was cumulative in its origin and compound by nature. It was cumulative in that some tactics – such as leaflets and voice messages utilizing SEP to address ex-comrades – were dependent on earlier change, and in the sense that combined food–intelligence–military operations were predicated on effective prior resettlement. They were compound in that they blended tactics that included intimidation, 'winning hearts and minds' (rewards for helping procure surrenders, White Areas, amenities and elections), control (fences, curfews, rations) and force (bombing, artillery, patrols). The key to explaining counter-insurgency in any one period is to describe the recipe that combined these ever-present types of ingredient in particular proportions and ways.

Secondly, understanding the very different nature of each phase is the vital precursor to any meaningful counter-insurgency analysis. If we want to understand how counter-insurgency changed (or failed to change) across time, we need to define phases each typified by a particular context and blend of techniques. This will avoid a 'one thing after another' chronological account that implies causation from mere correlation; or a 'one model' non-chronological approach that emphasizes only optimized late-stage operations, or a particular tactic without tracing its changing relationships with other tactics over time.

This chapter identifies campaign phases, in each of which a particular blend of techniques predominated. These are used in a heuristic way, in full realization that periods are fuzzy and overlap, and that definition is only half the job. The other half is to ask questions about *stasis* and *transition*. What, for instance, were the roadblocks to moving from early sweeps and killings of civilians towards a more discriminating form of counter-insurgency? The rest of this section addresses these concerns, commencing with a detailed analysis of Malayan Emergency phases, and the 'roadblocks' to change in each of them.[14]

Counterterror in its first (1948) and second (1949) manifestations

British policy in Malaya started as 'an approach to counter-terror'.[15] Killings of unarmed Chinese in ones, twos and small groups resulted from a policy that was loose in controlling lethal force, and that emphasized pressuring Chinese.[16] The lurch towards 'counterterror' was fuelled by pressure from fearful Europeans, desire to punish rural Chinese for nearby major incidents, and army emphasis on large-scale actions to disrupt the enemy. While the police expanded, and raised Auxiliaries and part-time Special Constables for static duties, the army emphasized relentless patrols and sweeps. After Sir Henry Gurney arrived as the new High Commissioner in October, he told the Colonial Office (in December) that the Chinese 'are … notoriously inclined to lean towards whichever side frightens them more'.[17]

This 'counterterror' holds for 1948–9 as a whole, but with a shift from early 1949 from episodic violence to more systemic, bureaucratized forms. This can be characterized as a change from the frequency with which people were 'shot running away' to the more bureaucratized and controlled use of collective detention and deportation.

Between June and December 1948 the SF utilized tactics that could be described as 'episodic counter-terror'. 'Counterterror', including burning huts from where insurgents had been assisted, reflected the belief that squatters would only assist government if they feared it more, and knowledge that insurgents groups used rural villages as logistics bases. Clusters of villages might therefore be regarded as requiring military reoccupation. Take Batu Arang, the mining town north of Kuala Lumpur that communists briefly held on 12 July 1948. On 31 July, police and soldiers detrained nearby and swept inland clearing the area and two alleged 'camps'. No shots were returned despite pistols being found. Between twenty-two and thirty people were killed – critics claimed many were civilians. Elsewhere, in Pulai and Gua Musang in July, the insurgents held the area for a week. Afterwards some Pulai villagers were detained, others resettled and their village burnt. The early months established a pattern of areas being contested, *liminal space*, where troops might assume villagers were potential informants and that pressure or demonstrative punishment might yield results.[18]

While Batu Arang showed how SFs might see an area as hostile, the most infamous killing was more cold-blooded. At rubber plantation labour lines near Batang Kali a 2nd Battalion Scots Guards patrol gunned down twenty-four male Chinese estate workers on 11–12 December 1948. Villagers were detained overnight, searched and subjected to mock executions, and women and children separated for trucking off. The patrol reported '26 bandits killed', before the puncturing of that lie led them to claim the workers had been trying to escape. In January 1949 the state retrospectively 'legalised' what the Guards claimed with Emergency Regulation (ER) 27A, which allowed shooting people escaping custody if they ignored a clear warning. In fact, when this shooting started, there appears to have been no warning, and it degenerated into cold-blooded finishing off of victims.[19] The situation had arisen because the platoon believed villagers had been visited by bandits and were withholding information.

There was also poor administrative control over patrols. For instance, instead of hut destruction being targeted only at buildings used as accessories to insurgency, they were sometimes burnt en masse, as at Kachau on 2 November 1948.[20] Such burnings, large-scale screening of villagers, and occasional shooting of people innocently running away (alongside patrols and sweeps) were perhaps most typical of this period. Batang Kali and Batu Arang thus constituted grimly extrapolated bookends on 1948–9, as a counterterror period characterized by relentless SF pressure on rural populations, and by small-scale, episodic killing of civilians.[21]

Following the initial period of episodic violence, the counterterror strategy became more systemic, a phase that started in January 1949 and lasted until at least December 1949. In 1949 the government attempted to hold troops more to the rules, and bureaucratized pressure on squatters, while the army continued mass sweeps and screenings. The MCP responded since February 1949 by moving to smaller groups and reorganizing its Min Yuen (mass organization), so they could supply insurgents regardless of patrols.

Changed MCP tactics led to reduced number of incidents in 1949 but not to lessening of government pressure on jungle-fringe villagers. In September 1948 a Local Defence Committee paper demanded urgent action against select squatters, who had 'No real inducement' to give information. Adequate protection was 'difficult' to provide.[22] The administration believed that only removal of hard-line communists would free squatters from fear, unlocking cooperation.[23]

Gurney also wanted to reassure allies, and appease Malay anger at rural Chinese, some of whom were illegally squatting on Malay reservations.[24] Gurney additionally wanted to intensify operations without overburdening detention camps. Nearly 6,000 detention orders were issued for 1948, with less than a tenth of the detainees being released that year.[25] One palliative appeared to be to arrest 'bad' villagers en masse, with the option for deportation without appeal. The majority of rural Chinese were not citizens (though most had been born in Malaya or arrived in the 1920s and 1930s), meaning they could be 'repatriated'. Yet so far only a handful had been, as objections had to be heard first.[26] Gurney's solution was ER17D, as part of a wider move towards more systemic but also more controlled pressure. This featured the following: collective detention and also optional deportation under ER17D; simultaneously insisting ERs limits were adhered to, alongside select trials of transgressors; and looking into protective settling of the remaining squatters. ER17D, issued on 10 January 1949, allowed for collective detention of all the inhabitants of an area for which a significant part was deemed to have been assisting insurgents, or withholding information. Any persons thus detained could be repatriated if they were neither British subjects nor federal citizens. There was – as opposed to ER17D for individual repatriation – no recourse to objection. The year 1949 saw sixteen 17D operations, featuring predawn swoops, and destruction of fixed property with compensation. Several thousand were removed in 1949, with repatriations reaching 10,262.[27]

At the same time as mass action against groups and areas was made possible, uncoordinated SF action was reined in. As early as the army burning of Kachau village on 2 November 1948, the administration made clear destruction was to be only against specific huts used to aid insurgents (ER18B of 13 November 1948). There was a gradual attempt to ensure the army adhered to limits. Paradoxically, its de facto discretion was reigned in even as ER17D regularized wholesale burning of selected villages. In 1949 at least two widely reported trials confirmed abuses, yet signalled action against excess. On 1 June 1949 three policemen tortured a Chinese suspect. In September 1949 they were found guilty of 'causing hurt', and given prison sentences. Then there was Police Sergeant Frederick Ewin, who burst into a hut on 8 June 1949 expecting to pump bullets into bandits, and killed the sleeping five-year-old Lai Ah. He was sentenced in July for 'culpable homicide not amounting to murder'.[28]

A longer-term 'solution' to the problem of rural villagers and squatters supplying the insurgents was also pursued meanwhile. Chinese-speaking administrators argued since 1948 that squatters had been abandoned. A committee on the squatter question reported in January 1949.[29] This recommended they generally be resettled roughly where they were, even if on forest or Malay reservations.[30] In May 1949 Gurney told state authorities they must act on the report, or he might stop ER17D operations. Chinese leaders' suggestions for resettling some detainees at Mawai in Johore went ahead as early as 1949.[31] In reality, resettlement was limited up to March 1950, by when 18,500 had been resettled, which leads to additional points about phases. First, there can be *latent, developing* or *de jure policies*, significant for the future, but with limited immediate traction. Secondly, there may be policies, which '*roadblocks*' inhibit. Understanding roadblocks is crucial to explaining what did not happen, and for being alert to how they were later removed.

Some early phase roadblocks have been hinted at above. Targeting in detentions was limited until police and SB could recruit more Chinese, and use SEP to better effect. Furthermore, early SF and administrator numbers were insufficient to protect squatters, let alone estate labourers and miners. All of which emphasizes the need for comparative counter-insurgency work specifically targeted on the dilemmas of incipient and early counter-insurgency phases.

Policies that would work later would have been almost impossible to implement effectively in this early period. Hence breakneck police expansion was a prerequisite for later comprehensive resettlement. The police expanded from around 9,000 to 67,000 over 1948–51 (under 30,000 being full-time, the rest part-time Special Constables for more static duties). This provided the platform for Lieutenant-General Briggs' transformative 1950 'Briggs' Plan', which would see 380,000 people resettled in twenty-one months from June 1950 to December 1951, in 423 Resettlement Areas (later rebranded New Villages). By the latter date these settlements had an average of seventeen policemen or Special Constables per village (totalling 6,250). Resettlement on this scale without a sufficient police force would have courted disaster.[32]

Additional roadblocks applied to earlier resettlement. Malay-dominated state governments resented allocating land to what many saw as illegal, hostile aliens, while many Malay *kampongs* (villages) remained impoverished. Even some Chinese leaders were anxious that squatters on commercially valuable land should be moved.[33] Federal revenue had also been tight until after the Korean War broke out, after which soaring tin and rubber prices provided a temporary bonanza. The federal government made no large-scale financial provision for resettlement until 1950.

The more general implications of these roadblocks are twofold. First, physical constraints such as in SF numbers and intelligence may offer a limited menu of effective actions early on. Secondly, any attempt to accelerate movement out of an earlier phase – where, for instance, detentions and screening are likely to be of a larger scale and less discriminatory – requires addressing how the likely physical, institutional, fiscal and political constraints can be overcome.

Geodemographic control (April 1950 to June 1952)

From December 1949 to March 1950 the roadblocks described above eroded. The Communities Liaison Committee (of Malay, Chinese and Indian leaders) was coming towards agreement, by early 1950, that more Chinese should get citizenship. In return Malays were to get a development board.[34] It also helped that SB had expanded. But another key solvent was the gathering sense of crisis, which partly stemmed from British misreading of 1949. After mid-1948 there had been no more significant MCP attempts to seize towns or establish liberated areas, and the size of insurgent groups and number of attacks had fallen. So by October 1949 it looked as if pressure, intimidation and ER17D operations were working.

From October 1949, however, a reorganized MNLA returned to the charge, with 'counterterror' having fuelled its recruitment. Major incidents swelled from a 1949 low of around 100 a month to 500 by March 1950, and the MNLA assembled larger forces. Most famously, on 23 February 1950, around 120 insurgents overran the isolated Johore police post of Bukit Kepong, killing twenty-one police and Home Guards.[35] The fact that a Malay leader took a prominent role highlighted the danger that the MCP might recruit more Malays, swelling their proportion above the roughly 5 per cent of insurgents they then constituted. This crisis propelled Gurney to boost federal funding for resettlement, request more troops, and ask for a Director of Operations (DOO) to coordinate all SF. The new DOO was Lieutenant-General Harold Briggs, and by his taking office in April the ground was thus ready for a new kind of campaign.

The 'Briggs' Plan' went into full operation in June. Its centre of gravity lay in *geodemographic control:* of people and space in order to provide administration, protection and to coerce behaviour, in a way that framed the space between villages and insurgents as an SF-friendly contact zone. The plan included four major elements:[36]

1. Population movement and spatial control; featuring resettlement of around 500,000 squatters, and regrouping 600,000 estate and mine labourers by clustering their huts in defensible groups. DOO Directive 13 of February 1951 envisaged a police post, fence, community hall, youth groups, vegetable plots inside the fence, medical visits and more. A development (later 'aftercare') committee was appointed in October. By December 1951 there were Resettlement Officers (ROs) for groups of villages, a Chinese Assistant Resettlement Officer (ARO) in most of them and Home Guard units in 280. In short, the plan envisaged moving 20 per cent of Chinese into resettlements and regrouping 10 per cent of the population into defensible labour lines.

   The rationale was to extend *administration* and *protection* to villagers, who would be given *confidence* to give information. This would isolate insurgents and provide 'live' intelligence about future MNLA actions, enabling more *contacts* (SF-induced meetings). It involved cutting links between insurgent and villagers, but also a blended administrative-security approach with simultaneous protection (fences, police posts, Home Guard), reward (for giving information leading to surrenders and kills, plus in facilities and ultimately land rights) and tightened coercion. Hence DOO Directive 17 on Food Control (June 1951) was highly coercive (rationing, searches at gates, controlled commodities and food movements) but also protective (villagers could tell insurgents they could not smuggle supplies out).
2. Security force framework. SF units would be attached to dominate particular areas, providing a comprehensive framework.
3. Civil–military coordination. Existing committees provided a comprehensive network from Federal War Council, through State WECs (SWECs) to Districts (DWECs). Each was chaired by the highest civilian administrator (from High Commissioner down to a District Officer for a DWEC), and included requisite police and army commanders. This meant separate activities could be coordinated. While an individual army unit could experience its role as mere patrol and ambush, the local SWEC might have requested the precise pattern of patrols to back up combined food control–police operations.
4. Strike forces. Briggs hoped resettlement would happen fastest in priority states, which would then successively be targeted by additional striking forces to clear them state by state. This element would take much longer than anticipated to become effective.

The result was that by December 1951, in twenty-one months, resettlement soared from 18,500 to over 400,000 in 410 New Villages. Resettlement eventually covered more than 540,000 (80 per cent Chinese) in around 480 New Villages. But the first 80 per cent of these were completed in just twenty-one months, during which the police strength peaked at nearly 70,000 (including 40,000 part-time Special Constables).

The result was a double crisis in late 1951. First, the colonial state suffered a crisis. SF were overstretched by the scale of resettlement, and the administration suffered a leadership crisis. Gurney was ambushed and killed on 6 October 1951, Briggs retired and commissioner of police Colonel Gray was removed in December. There was dismay that resettlement was accompanied by a peak of incidents in 1951, and at setbacks including Mawai resettlement's abandonment in late 1951. In response, the incoming Conservative government appointed General Sir Gerald Templer as combined DOO and High Commissioner in February 1952. Templer's increased powers, combined with the effect of the crisis on people's willingness to tolerate more drastic action, now saw policy continued with renewed energy.

Secondly, the insurgents suffered a crisis, which it turned out was even more fundamental than the administration's. The MNLA issued *October 1951 resolutions*, based on its reading that it could not reverse resettlement.[37] These reduced MNLA numbers to provide more support to villagers and divert resources to cultivation. They reduced incidents that harmed the people such as infrastructure attacks, and increased subversion. The hope was to take one step back to take two forward later. This programmed in reductions of incidents, civilians deaths and insurgent numbers. In 1952 many categories of incident halved or more. Average insurgent strength fell from 7,294 in 1951 to 5,765 in 1952.[38] Geodemographic control had persuaded the MNLA to scale back activity, despite many New Villages being leaky, and having Min Yuen (the insurgent's workers attached to the masses) inside. The MNLA headquarters retreated to the Thai border in 1953, and the challenge increasingly became how to hunt down remaining MNLA units.

A repeat health warning on the heuristic nature of 'phases' is warranted here. I am defining a phase by which of many persistent types of tactics are predominant, and which core ideas flavoured their combination. Hence the early, 'counterterror' phase featured broad sweeps, constant pressure, mass screenings and a belief that many squatters required intimidating. The more mature and bureaucratized 'counterterror' phase of 1949 saw limitation of ad hoc abuses, but substituted draconian ER17D operations against entire villages. Then in 1950–2 – the phase when geodemographic control came to the fore – the centre of gravity became rapid resettlement of a significant percentage of the population.

The fact that one type of activity became central, however, did not mean older tactics ceased. Although resettlement dwarfed other activities in 1950–2, repatriations of non-citizen Chinese reached a second high of 9,782 in 1951. In addition, collective punishment was regularized in ER17DA of late 1949, which allowed an area that had supported bandits to be collectively subject to punishments including fines and longer curfews. The village of Pusing, in January 1951, following a nearby murder, was fined $40,000.[39] Punitive action meant measures more draconian than the standard ones such as night-time curfews, and even more draconian than the stricter operational measures such as reduced rice rations. Government continued to believe that 'bad' villages should be subject to demonstrative, if short-term, punitive action. Into 1952, Chinese leaders complained that rural Chinese still felt caught between two terrors, that of the 'people inside' and of the government forces outside.[40]

This means that people who want to emphasize a particular tactic may find evidence for it throughout campaigns, without entitling them to assume it was predominant. Hence in this period plans were already laid to improve New Village conditions.[41] On 3 October 1951, three days before he was killed, Gurney told the Colonial Office that aftercare must soon come to the fore.[42] Yet scarce resources had so far been concentrated on the physical act of removal. ROs and over 300 Chinese Assistant Resettlement Officers (AROs) had been appointed, but most of their effort initially focused on security and basic infrastructure. Thus *roadblocks* to planned aftercare had remained overwhelming until late 1951. By December 1951 some villages still had inadequate fences, most no perimeter lighting, and though 280 Home Guard units were established, this had to be extended in number and responsibilities.[43] The principal roadblock to increasing 'hearts and minds' measures was thus the prior need to achieve resettlement and adequate security on a comprehensive scale.

Optimization (February 1952 to June 1954)

Once New Villagers were more adequately protected and controlled, amenities could be improved. The person who inherited this situation was the new combined DOO-High Commissioner Sir Gerald Templer. Templer's wide powers helped optimize the campaign. Changes instituted in 1952 included improving Special Branch, appointing more Military Liaison Officers at combined HQs and translating intelligence into operational form for the army, and removing ineffective personnel.

The most crucial improvements centred on refining operations around clusters of New Villages, and concentrating them on degrading MNLA committees – the nerve centres of each district. Following a DOO directive on intelligence in December 1952, emphasis was placed on achieving this by acquiring 'live' intelligence and agents, in the form of SEP and turned Min Yuen or suppliers.[44]

Take for example Bentong district, Pahang. During 1952–3 this hosted the MCP Central Committee. By 1953 resettlement was well established, SEP information providing for occasional kills.[45] Pahang SWEC generated a two-phase plan. In the first SB studied CT suppliers' routes, incidents, features such as tracks and harvest dates, and *orang asli*, and intensified aerial photoreconnaissance. They drew up a 'strategic supplies chart' for everything from Singer sewing machine spare parts to batteries. This allowed them to close '90%' of supply avenues and control the rest, which in turn allowed them to identify and turn two more suppliers. Phase two then saw more than a hundred arrests for quick screening, with sixty-two (the innocent and turned) released. This allowed Phase 2 SF operations (patrols and ambushes) to be structured around live intelligence. Through 1953–4 CT strength was ground down from seventy to twenty-two, the area being declared white by 1955.[46]

By 1954 this sort of multiphase, intelligence-centred, resettlement-focused operation was set out as a model, with food control close to its core.[47] DOO Instruction 36 of June 1954 suggested three phases: Phase I of one to two weeks' intelligence gathering, Phase II of intensified food lift and patrols and Phase III of exploitation of resulting enemy demoralization and entry into the pre-prepared killing zone between jungle and forest.[48] By 1956–8 the biggest such operations were able to net tens of, or even a hundred or more of, MNLA fighters over several months.

'Optimisation' thus built on prerequisites, including comprehensive resettlement and regrouping, an expanded and refined SB, controls including of food and a range of non-food restricted items, and a framing of demographics and space to create vulnerable MNLA-people lines of communication that could be identified and then exploited.

17D and punishment elements of older policy nevertheless persisted, despite becoming less salient. Templer inherited 17D, but used it only three times before its abolition in 1953. Templer also inherited 17DA powers to levy collective punishment. 17DA action was usually sparked by the killing of an unarmed government officer, such as a District Officer, or RO. Templer adopted use of 17DA almost immediately in March 1952. Tanjong Malim's Assistant DO was killed along with much of a water pipe repair party. Templer arrived with armoured cars, berated town leaders, and imposed a two-week-long twenty-two-hour curfew, closing schools and transport. The emphasis was on the town not having provided information despite persistent proximate insurgent incidents. But Templer converted the process from merely punitive to additionally offering concrete transformation mechanisms. In Operation Questionnaire – subsequently applied to other settlements – he provided questionnaires to be filled in during curfew, and placed in sealed boxes to be opened only in his presence. The curfew was subsequently eased to normal levels (curfews were also used for general security) after arrests, the dicey implication being that significant information had been forthcoming.[49]

Templer drew a storm of criticism in Malaya and *The Guardian*. The pipe had been cut near a Malay village, which was only subsequently resettled, and townspeople were effectively punished by both MNLA and government, as their water supply was cut multiple times before Templer's intervention. But when the MCA and UMNO (United Malays National Organisation – the main Malay party) petitioned against the action, Templer invited MCA representatives to advise how to make the 'question' element more effective. They suggested getting government officers or MCA leaders to visit houses individually, since information could then be offered freely even by the illiterate and frightened.[50]

A process emerged over 1952–3, by which a SWEC would invite Templer to visit a 'bad village'. He would sweep in with armoured cars and dignitaries, call village leaders to a public space and berate them for not providing information despite improving security. He would order specific actions such as cutting *lallang* (tall grass) outside the fence, or improved security. At the end he would say that he had told them what was wrong with the village, now they should tell him what they needed the government to do. Improvements might be delivered – one of the advantages of him coming with senior administrators – within days.

By mid-1953 it is clear that even when controls were imposed, the prospect of additional help was also kept very clearly in view. For instance villagers at Sepang were told their neighbouring village would receive help with pig breeding, and they could too if they improved.[51] The carrot of becoming a White Area might also be dangled from 1953. 'Ginger' operations were also added, in Perak for instance, whereby on improvements the SWEC called in Templer or other leaders, to thank the village, further explain policies and identify additional areas for rapid improvement. Templer nevertheless remained ambivalent about collective punishment and 17DA, which he visited on about twenty villages.

What is the point of this detail? First, transformation, once basic infrastructure and control of people and space were in place, was about continual refinements. Secondly, against 'bad' villages elements of 'punitive' and 'reward' and 'operational' and 'protective' action became blended in an increasingly sophisticated mix after 1952. This was further helped by the MCA, whose branches appeared in New Villages and whose officials sat on advisory committees to SWECs and DWECs.[52] By contrast, exaggerated debates over whether 'winning hearts and minds' and minimum force, or coercion and demonstrative force, dominated in British counter-insurgency fail to engage in the minutiae and subtleties of how different blends of *all* of these were created, and nuanced from period to period, and even from place to place within a single phase.

Normalization and deep transition (1953 to 1960)

In terms of building local force capacity, and transferring counter-insurgency responsibility, Britain practised 'deep transition' with crucial changes beginning early, and advancing incrementally. This means that the roots of this phase – almost better thought of as a 'strand' or theme – went back deep into and even beyond older phases.

Elections proliferated from late 1951, by when the first municipal elections had been held and Malayans appointed to quasi-ministerial posts on the Executive Council. In 1952–3 New Villages started electing committees, and over time some converted into village councils with powers to charge rates. Likewise, Resettlement Officers and AROs were to be gradually replaced by more Chinese as District Officers or Assistant DOs. Land titles were also offered to villagers from 1952 on leases of between twenty and thirty-three years, though take-up was slow. Citizenship rules also changed in September 1952, so potentially 50 to 60 per cent of Chinese – those born locally and with modest residence qualifications – could apply for citizenship.

In the WECS, meanwhile, there was movement from attaching 'advisory boards' of local representatives, through having local representatives on SWECs/DWECS as unofficials, to promoting locals as DOs, and Officer in Charge of Police District (officers who sat on the DWEC). At the highest level, Templer's merging of the Federal War Council and Executive Council in 1952 meant Asian unofficials were involved with federal Emergency policy.

Involvement of elected Asians increased with the march of elections. Kuala Lumpur's 1952 elections saw the 'Alliance' between the MCA and UMNO. That swept state elections in 1954–5 and federal elections in 1955, after which an Alliance Chief Minister and ministers were appointed. In 1956 a local Emergency Operations Council took over 'direction' of the Emergency, while a separate 'Operations Committee' beneath it exercised 'operational' control. By independence little change was required, and British continued to serve in diminishing numbers as senior police, SB and administrative officers into the early years of independence.[53]

'Deep' transition thus centred on ensuring Emergency control was an integral part of local government structures. Simultaneously, efforts to develop a British style service ethos in the police started in earnest from 1952, and efforts to develop a 'Malay' regimental ethos from inception in 1933. Rather than bursting the vessels of state with multiples of new funding, or insisting on foreign models of 'nation-building', parsimonious Britain went with the grain of local governance and society, even when that meant compromising aspirations, such as for the development of powerful cross-communal parties.

Kenyan 'phases' and comparative counter-insurgency analysis

It is all very well to articulate the nature of phases and their utility for analysis for a single case study, but comparative counter-insurgency demands that we go beyond that. What would it look like if we began to compare phases and strands of action across insurgencies? A brief look at the Kenyan campaign against 'Mau Mau' can help to suggest how this approach might be used both to ensure comparison of similar phases and to highlight similarities and contrasts across campaigns.

First, as for Malaya, we can sharply contrast early and mature phases of the campaign. At the outset the colonial government faced insurgents supported by a portion of 1.4 million Kikuyu (out of a population of five million) angry at land shortage and the lack of significant political advance for Africans. From October 1952 to early 1953 operations saw often futile army sweeps amid an intelligence drought, white settler expulsions of Kikuyu, arrests of moderate Kenyan politicians and inability to dominate areas. 'Mau Mau' support grew.

By contrast, by January 1955 'villageization', improved Home Guard supervision, and expanded rewards for 'loyalists', combined with larger SF dominating areas in smaller patrols, had pushed Mau Mau gangs into the forests, with prohibited areas around their edges, and property cleared from a one mile strip outside. The army now concentrated on the killing zone at and in the forest edge, and on pushing deeper into the forests. As with Malaya, this later phase offered radically different challenges and possibilities to the first.[54]

Furthermore, the campaign in Kenyan can be broken into overlapping phases in much the same manner as Malaya can. Two sources can be used to show how this can be used analytically. The first is Huw Bennett's *Fighting the Mau Mau*. The second is a 1957 report by the Operational Research Unit (Far East), entitled 'A Comparative Study of the emergencies in Malaya and Kenya'.[55] Taking these two sources, a number of issues arise.

Bennett's work identifies four main phases, this time for army involvement in the Kenyan Emergency. It is therefore possible to start to map 'phases' from the two campaigns onto each other. The Malayan phase one of 1948–9 maps onto the phase Bennett describes as stretching from 1952 to 1953.[56] Extended also to additional conflicts, this could be the beginning of an analytical approach that emphasizes identifying comparable phases.

Both Malaya and Kenya featured a core of 'villageization' and geodemographic control in mature phases (Malaya from 1950, Kenya from 1954), but also demonstrate how that core approach could have different manifestations according to local social dynamics (of the state, SF, and insurgent ideology and host communities), geography and demography.[57] There were differences in mature operation type, and in detention and rehabilitation outcomes. A comparative study, for example, shows a marked contrast when it comes to resettlement and the control of food supplies. Both campaigns employed large-scale resettlement (over one million in Kenya's New Villages and over 500,000 in Malaya's). But the control of food and supplies to create a kill zone between forest and village was a more specifically Malayan feature.

In the Kenyan case, however, it argued that honey and plants would keep forest groups thriving, so food control around villages was less central in mature phases. Before villageization there was an emphasis on patrolling the 'contact' zones between forest and villages as well as the forest fringe, as in Malaya, before driving tracks into the forest itself.[58] Once villageization was complete, the operational emphasis became twofold.[59]

First, for normal operations battalions were allotted a forest area to cross-grain patrol, while an ambush line of police and tribal police set up fringe ambushes, and Special Forces-operated versus specific targets. Secondly, for deeper operations in the Aberdares forests and Mount Kenya forests in 1955 a five-stage model was adopted:[60]

- Stage I – Intensive forest fringe operations to drive 'gangs' into the forests.
- Stage II – Establishing a stop line of SF to guard the forest fringe.
- Stage III – Clearing the high-altitude areas.
- Stage IV – Sweeps and patrols downward through the forest.
- Stage V – Intensive ambush programme in the forest and its fringe.

The latter looks more like some of the vice-like operations in Malaya of 1956–60, where the SAS or other troops deployed deep into jungle and drove insurgents out towards a stop line nearer populated areas. There was a huge amount of similarity, but also key differences, in that Kenya lacked the more intense food–intelligence–military operations around resettled areas of the Malayan mature phase.

Marked differences were also apparent when it came to rehabilitation and detention. As with Malaya, early lack of intelligence resulted in poorly targeted mass sweeps, arrests and detentions, with selectivity improving over time. In later phases Kenya attempted to adapt aspects of the Malayan model (graded prisoners, and a stress on rehabilitation prior to release), but similar approaches resulted in vastly different results, due to Kenya's different insurgent nature, higher settler component, and possibly also due to different racial stereotyping. The 1957 study merely noted the Malayan 'safety valve' of mass repatriation (ultimately over 30,000 inclusive of voluntary, family and all races). But it failed to discuss the social dynamics of race, and the impact of counter-insurgent models of the enemy. Hence the assumption that Mau Mau oathing was premodern, if not semi-magical, led to a determination to get renunciation even if 'psychological shock' (beating, 'confrontation' or dilution of new inmates with those who had already confessed) had to be employed in the post-1956 programme, and 'compelling force' to make detainees obey orders. In Malaya, by contrast, the belief emerged that hard core could be left believing in communism, providing they renounced violence. For the majority, the assumption was that once surrendered or captured they merely had to be persuaded of the hopelessness of the cause, and possibility of rehabilitation, or to take rewards for betrayal. In Malaya the result appears to have been limited abuse, in Kenya a high degree of coercion against 'recalcitrant' prisoners, culminating at Hola Camp in March 1959 in the death by beating of eleven detainees, and serious assault on seventy-seven more.[61]

We do not know enough about Malaya to be sure of the extreme there, but the indications are that most camps had more the nature of British POW camps of the Second World War combined with regular prison discipline, with added rehabilitation sections emphasizing education and securing a job before release. Life in wired-in compounds of several hundred people, with their canteens, vegetable plots and often basketball courts may have been depressing and constrictive, but violence was the exception and more likely to start from intra-insurgent disputes (loyalist vs. 'running dog' in Ipoh Detention Camp in 1955, or in detainee riot or beating of visitors) than from guard barbarity or policy.

This brief comparative foray points to potential for analytical, phase-sensitive comparative counter-insurgency analysis; as well as for comparing techniques and strands of policy that developed across phases. The questions of why phases take on particular natures and of why one particular tactic or model (such as resettlement in Malaya, Kenya and Algeria) worked out so differently in two or more campaigns are as or more interesting than any attempt to oversimplify in pursuit of modular 'lessons' to be transferred in simplistic ways.

Conclusions

This chapter makes the case for a sophisticated analysis and comparison of insurgencies. Phases are defined by what the core concepts and centre of gravity or particular blend of policies is. Hence, early campaign phases are likely to be characterized by limited intelligence deficient resources, and so greater temptations to use relatively indiscriminate and/or punitive measures. Early campaign strategy is a topic in itself, as are mature optimization and transitional phases. To the accusation that these are heuristic toys that oversimplify, the reply is that *not* acknowledging such phases is more oversimplified. If the latter involves assuming that an optimum strategy, plucked from later a campaign period, can inform all types of period, then it threatens a degeneration into cartoonish stereotyping.

Issues of stasis and transition are critical to meaningful counter-insurgency analysis. What stops counter-insurgency adopting more targeted measures at earlier stages? What are the roadblocks to strategies that are latent, and what conditions overcame roadblocks? How far, for instance, was the changing of political positions, or the ability to use crises to leverage change, vital to paradigm shifts in Malaya? Even if you identify a policy that works in one context, its transferability is likely to be related to understanding how that policy became implementable, that is, what roadblocks had to be removed and how, and how domestic and international support was gained for new policies.

Prerequisites for later changes mattered in Malaya, and will matter elsewhere. For instance, the sort of intense administration of New Villages cumulatively achieved after 1952 and the intensification of civil hearts and minds elements were dependent on prior achievement of basic security, and build-up of resources including more than 40 ROs from overseas, and 300 Chinese-speaking AROs.

Phases can be conceptualized as made up of bundles of tactics with a particular blend constituting each one's core identity. But individual tactics or policy *threads* persist over periods, and need to be plotted for scope, intensity and detail in their own right. Hence collective action and/or punishment (most notably 17D group detentions) existed across periods, but only constituted a preponderant influence around 1949. This ebbing and flowing of threads over qualitatively different phases has implications. Notably, anyone can point to one type of tactic across periods and construct a fake narrative in which their chosen type is pre-eminent. But the real skill comes in recognizing what is preponderant and what ancillary in each period, how the blend in each phase is interrelated in distinctive recipes, and how each thread develops in itself.

Such finely tuned phase analysis can also help us when assessing the relative weight of kinetic action versus 'winning hearts and minds' in turning campaigns around, and the degree to which the military has led in the latter. The US Army/Marine manual FM3-24 emphasized the role of 'population-centric' approaches and winning hearts and minds, but this has been questioned more recently.[62] Some critics have suggested the Army/Marines should stick more to kinetics and degrading and decapitating the enemy, and de-emphasize the nation-, state-building and restraint side and 'big COIN'. The Malayan example suggests that it was the civil government that directed, provided police intelligence through SB, and achieved resettlement. However, it also suggests that any simplistic kinetic versus civil distinction can prove artificial. The SWECs and DWECs, in coordinating the food–intelligence–SF blended operations, integrated army actions into overall plans. This was acknowledged as vital, since on average it might take 1,000 hours of patrolling to encounter an insurgent, or 300 to carry out an ambush, but a multiple without information.[63] An individual army patrol might, therefore, *experientially* see its role as kinetic, while in reality being tightly integrated into a blended approach. That said, FM-3-24 (in its 2006 and notably its 2014 versions) appears more pliable than the debate about it sometimes is. Hence for instance the latter emphasizes the combined civil, political and kinetic elements in operations such as the winning over of Anbar region in Iraq in 2007.[64]

The main message of this chapter, however, is that phases matter, and that comparative counter-insurgency analysis demands both thoughtful periodization for each insurgency, and comparing similar periods with each other across insurgencies. Hence in this case the slightly chaotic and less discriminatory 'counter terror' period of 1948–9 might be compared to Kenya in 1952–3, and the mature or optimization phase with Kenyan operations from 1954 to 1955. Such a rigorous, chronologically disciplined approach to comparing only commensurate phases is a sine qua non for penetrative comparative counter-insurgency analysis.

Notes

1   David French, *The British Way in Counterinsurgency, 1945-1967* (Oxford: Oxford University Press, 2011). Sir Robert Thompson, *Defeating Communist Insurgency: The Lessons of Malaya and Vietnam* (London: Chatto & Windus, 1966). Richard Stubbs, *Hearts and Minds in Guerrilla Warfare: The Malayan Emergency 1948-1960* (Singapore: Oxford University Press, 1988). See also Paul Dixon, '"Hearts and Minds?" British Counter-Insurgency from Malaya to Iraq', *Journal of Strategic Studies* 32, no. 3 (2009): 353–82.

2   Huw Bennett, 'The Other Side of the COIN: Minimum and Exemplary Force in British Army Counterinsurgency in Kenya,' *Small Wars and Insurgencies* 18, no. 4 (2007): 638–64. Thomas Mockaitis, 'The Minimum Force Debate: Contemporary Sensibilities Meet Imperial Practice', *Small Wars and Insurgencies* 23, nos. 4–5 (2012): 762–81.

3   French, *The British Way in Counterinsurgency*, 247–55, for instance, concludes with an excellent discussion on the difficulties of 'learning' across campaigns, which nevertheless ignores the issue of phasing within campaigns. Likewise, Andrew Mumford's interesting *The Counter-Insurgency Myth: The British Experience of Irregular Warfare* (London: Routledge, 2012), especially pp. 147–55 does not directly integrate phases into analysis.

4   For a focused example of comparing a similar phase across campaigns, see Robert Johnson and Timothy Clack (eds), *At the End of Military Intervention* (Oxford: Oxford University Press, 2015).

5   Leon Comber, *Malaya's Secret Police 1945-1950: The Role of the Special Branch in the Malayan Emergency* (Singapore: ISEAS, 2008), 60.

6   For a good survey see Director of Operations (R. H. Bowen), 'Review of Emergency in Malaya, June 1948–August 1957', 12 September 1957, Henceforth DOO Review 1957.

7   Huw Bennett, '"A Very Salutary Effect": The Counter-Terror Strategy in the Early Malayan Emergency', *Strategic Studies* 32, no. 3 (2009): 436. The National Archives (henceforth all documents are from this source unless stated otherwise), TNA CO537/3688, Local Defence Committee, Federation of Malaya, 'Paper on the strategical and tactical measures to deal with the internal security problem …', October 1948 version; TNA WO106/5884, 'Report on Operations in Malaya, 1948-1949', Sir Neil Ritchie, 5–6.

8   DOO Review 1957, 4. By this point most MNLA were in southern Thailand.

9   *Straits Times*, 22 January 1959, 1; *Straits Times*, 17 April 1955.

10 *Straits Times*, 23 July 1957, 9; 28 July 1957, 8.

11 The *orang asli* suffered from earlier resettlement. John Leary, *Violence and the Dream People: The Orang Asli and the Malayan Emergency, 1948-1960* (Athens, OH: Ohio University Press, 1995).

12 *Straits Times*, 23 July 1957, 9; 28 July 1957, 8; 22 Jan 1959, 10.

13 From 1948 CEP could be executed. From June 1951 you could be executed for being a supplier. But post 1950, CEP cooperation might help secure deportation, rehabilitation or release, if not rewards.

14 See also my 'The Malayan Emergency as Counter-Insurgency Paradigm', *Journal of Strategic Studies* 32, no. 3 (June 2009): 383–414.

15 Anthony Short, *In Pursuit of the Mountain Rats* (Singapore: Cultured Lotus, 2000), 160–9.

16 Bennett, '"A Very Salutary Effect"', 415–44.

17 TNA CO537/4242, Gurney to Lloyd, 19 December 1948. Commissioner-General Malcolm Macdonald, 27 September 1948, saying Chinese were 'governed by the propaganda of force', TNA CO537/3688, BDDC (FE) 12, meeting of 27 September 1948, minutes.

18 TNA WO268/603 for '27 bandits' claimed killed. *Straits Times* 31 July 1948, 1, 'Great Army Success at Batu Arang, 47 taken prisoner'. *Straits Times*, 31 July 1948; Imperial War Museum, Davis Papers, Box 6. Don Sinclair, 7 September 1949. TNA CO717170/1, Farelf SitRep 4, 28 July to 10 August. The year 1948 claimed 22 bandits killed, 18 captured.

19 'Judgment in the case of Keyu et al. versus Secretaries of States for Foreign and Commonwealth Affairs and of Defence', 4 September 2012, http://www.judiciary.gov. uk/Resources/JCO/Documents/Judgments/keyu-sec-state-foreign-commonwealth-affairs-judgment-04092012.pdf. Norma Miraflow and Ian Ward, *Massacre at Batang Kali* (Singapore: Media Masters, 2012).

20 Short, *In Pursuit of the Mountain Rats*, 163.

21 Nick Turse, *Kill Anything That Moves* (Metropolitan, 2013) for the Vietnamese case of false classifiers (they ran, they stood, wrong clothes) of guilt being used to justify persistent shootings.

22 TNA CO537/3688, Local Defence Committee, Federation of Malaya, 'Paper on the strategical and tactical measures to deal with the internal security problem …', October 1948 version.

23 Over 1948–57 3,268 civilians were murdered (2,461) or missing (807), compared to 1851 SF deaths.

24 Kevin Blackburn and Karl Hack, *War Memory and the Making of Modern Malaysia and Singapore* (Singapore: NUS Press, 2012), 112–21, 278–85.

25 TNA WO291/1670, H. S. Lee Papers Folio 87, and TNA CO1022/132.

26 Federation of Malaya 33 of 1952, 'Resettlement and the Development of New Villages in the Federation of Malaya, 1952'. TNA CO1022/132. Short, *In Pursuit*, 185. TNA CO717/717/5, Creech Jones to Foreign Secretary, 17 January 1949.

27 Federation of Malaya 33/1952, 'Resettlement and the Development of New Villages'.

28 *Straits Times*, 28 October 1949, 3 December 1949, 25 February 1950.

29 TNA CO717/177/5, *Report of Committee Appointed by his Excellency the High Commissioner to Investigate the Squatter Problem*, Federal Legislative Council Paper 3, 1949.

30 Tim Harper, *The End of Empire and the Making of Malaya* (Cambridge: Cambridge University Press, 1999), 173–4.

31 Mawai was closed in late 1951 after an unresisted MNLA attack, when 25 young men absconded. It had poor land, straggled out and lacked a proper fence.

32 For figures see TNA CO1022/29.

33 Institute of Southeast Asian Studies, Singapore (henceforth ISEAS): Tan Cheng Lock Papers, Folio 23, CLC minutes, Ipoh meeting, 18–19 March 1949.

34 ISEAS: Tan Cheng Lock Papers, Folio 23.

35 SB interrogations of Mat Indera and others released for *Utusan Malaysia* versus Mohamad Sabu, Penang High Court, 8–9 October 2012 and 17–18 February 2014, in the author's possession.

36 TNA CAB 21/1681, MAL C(50)23, 24 May 1950, Appendix, 'Federation Plan for the elimination of the communist organisation …', COS for Cabinet Malaya Committee.

37 C. C. Chin and Karl Hack, *Dialogues with Chin Peng* (Singapore: NUS Press, 2004), 150–64.

38 TNA Air 20/10377, Director of Operations (R. H. Bowen), 'Review of Emergency in Malaya, June 1948 – August 1957', 12 September 1957.

39 *Straits Times*, 22 January 1951.

40 Karl Hack, 'Between Two Terrors': People's History and the Malayan Emergency', in *A People's History of Insurgency*, ed. Hannah Gurman (New York: Free Press, 2013), 17–49; and Hack, 'Everyone Lived in Fear', *Small Wars and Insurgencies* 23, nos. 4–5 (2012): 671–99.

41 Federation of Malaya 33 of 1952, 'Resettlement and the Development of New Villages', 6.
42 Durham University: MacDonald Papers 25/2/56-62, Gurney to Sir Thomas Lloyd, 3 October 1951.
43 Short, *Mountain Rats*, 292–4.
44 TNA CO1022/57, DOO Malay, Directive No. 21, Special Branch Intelligence Targets.
45 Arkib Negara Malaysia (henceforth ANM) 1957/0470566.
46 Derek Hatton, *The Tock Tock Birds* (Subang Jaya: Pelanduk, 2008), 230–3.
47 ISEAS: H. S. Lee Papers 7.44/1-19, DOO 36 of 26 June 1954.
48 Ibid.
49 Templer Papers (courtesy of Miles Templer), private letter from Templer to Lyttelton, 7 May 1952.
50 ISEAS: HS Lee Papers, 7.49 Petition from MCA, *passim*.
51 ANM 1957/0537074, SWEC Selangor, 114 meeting, 11 September 1953. National Army Museum, Templer Papers 7410-29-1-78, 'Speech at Sepang', August 1953.
52 ISEAS: H. S. Lee Papers 74/8, 1-36, for the Selangor State Chinese Consultative Committee.
53 Hack, 'Iron Claws on Malaya', *JSEAS* 30, no. 1 (1999): 115–25; and 'Tropical Transitions in Colonial Counterinsurgency', in *At the End of Military Intervention*, ed. Robert Johnson and Timothy Clack (Oxford: Oxford University Press, 2015), 61–85.
54 For 'distinctive if "overlapping" Kenyan phases (Oct. 1952-June 1953, June 1953-April 1954, April 1954-Dec. 1954, Jan. 1955-November 1956)', see Huw Bennett, *Fighting the Mau Mau: The British Army and Counter-Insurgency in the Kenya Emergency* (Cambridge: Cambridge University Press, 2013), 11–32.
55 TNA WO291/1670, ORU (FE) 1957/1, 'A Comparative Study of the emergencies in Malaya and Kenya', Lt Col. J. M. Forster, 1957.
56 Bennett, *Fighting the Mau Mau*, 8–30 (12–19 for 1952–3).
57 The experience of settlement was very different, Malayan Chinese were used to villages; many Kikuyu were more dispersed (Ngũgĩ wa Thiong'o, *In the House of My Interpreter* (London: Vintage, 2013), 4–5, 36–8, 53, 58–62). Kenya also had 'punishment' villages versus Malaya's briefer 'operational' or punitive measures.
58 'A Comparative Study', 52.
59 Ibid., 51–4.
60 In the earlier period the phases were: I – Ops in jungle-fringe and *contact zones* between gangs and supporters to build information; II – On information from I penetrate fringe to 7 miles to find gang hides; III – Tracks driven into forests, bases established for further operations, while fringe posts established to intercept movement out, and surprise raids made into Reserves and Settled Areas.
61 See TNA CO822/1459 for Kenya's 'dilution' technique, 'psychological shock' and foot on throat/mud in mouth to stop the 'Mau Mau moan in 1957, going up to Lennox Boyd; and Karl Hack, 'Human Rights in the Shadow of Colonial Violence', *Journal of Imperial and Commonwealth History* 42, no. 2 (2014): 357–62.
62 Gian Gentile, *Wrong Turn: America's Deadly Embrace of Counterinsurgency* (New York: New Press, 2013), Douglas Porch, *Counterinsurgency: Exposing the Myths of the New Way of War* (Cambridge: Cambridge University Press, 2013). Fred Kaplan, *The Insurgents: David Petraeus and the Plot to Change the American Way of War* (New York: Simon & Schuster, 2013). See also http://smallwarsjournal.com/blog/debate-on-counterinsurgency-gentile-vs-nagl (accessed 9 February 2015).
63 DOO Report 1957, 21.
64 FM3-24, US Army Manual, *Insurgencies and Counterinsurgencies*, http://armypubs.army.mil/doctrine/DR_pubs/dr_a/pdf/fm3_24.pdf.

10

Rebel Sanctuaries and Late Colonial Conflict: The Case of West Germany during Algeria's War of Independence, 1954–62

Mathilde von Bülow

Historians are increasingly studying late colonial conflicts from the perspective of internationalization, whether this is the relationship between decolonization and the global Cold War or the importance of diplomacy in shaping the process of national liberation.[1] Among the most influential studies in this new international history of decolonization has been Matthew Connelly's *A Diplomatic Revolution* in which he argues that the Algerian National Liberation Front (FLN) won its long and bitter struggle for independence from France not as a result of armed action but through sustained and multipronged diplomatic and propaganda campaigns on the international stage. 'For weapons', Connelly argues, 'the Algerians employed human rights reports, press conferences, and youth congresses, fighting over world opinion and international law more than conventional military objectives.'[2] The FLN's 'diplomatic revolution' of 1954 to 1962 proved successful, for although the French military won virtually every battle it fought against the Algerian insurgents, the latter won the war. In doing so, Connelly argues, the FLN prompted another, more radical 'diplomatic revolution', one that undermined the diplomatic edifice of the Westphalian system according to which only territorially defined, sovereign states were permitted to engage in international politics. To Jeffrey J. Byrne, meanwhile, Algeria's liberation struggle ultimately constituted a deeply conservative phenomenon: far from subverting the sovereign state model, it helped universalize it.[3] Either way, Algeria's decolonization had a profound impact on global politics, stoking East–West tensions as well as North–South ones, and setting a precedent for liberation movements around the world.[4]

If diplomacy served as a 'secret weapon' against French colonialism,[5] it was not the only manner in which the FLN used the international arena to its strategic advantage. As Guy Pervillé reminds us, the FLN's exterior organization 'always comprised more than a simple diplomatic apparatus', nor was its action ever 'the prerogative of a corps of [diplomatic] specialists.'[6] Though it started with only a handful of representatives, this organization grew into a disparate network of politico-administrative and military institutions comprising a government-in-exile (GPRA), the chief bases and headquarters of the National Liberation Army (ALN), as well as the offices of auxiliaries such as the General Union of Algerian Workers (UGTA), General Union of Muslim Algerian Students (UGEMA) and Algerian Red Crescent (CRA). The expansion of the FLN's international network of agents and activities was not lost on the French intelligence services. 'It is certainly the [external] organization, once of secondary but today of prime importance, which constitutes the rebels' principal force' and most 'coherent machine of war', the deuxième bureau (military intelligence) concluded in 1961.[7]

While much has been written about the FLN's diplomatic initiatives, the literature on Algeria's independence struggle often takes for granted the insurgents' use of external space. Even the close relationships between the FLN and countries such as Morocco, Tunisia, Libya or Egypt, which all came to serve as safe havens, logistical platforms, operational headquarters and recruitment grounds, remain surprisingly under-explored. Equally little is known about the FLN's networks in countries neighbouring mainland France, which by 1958 had come to constitute the 'second front' in Algeria's independence struggle. Whether in Western Europe or the Maghreb, the insurgents' ability to pursue their war effort from beyond the confines of French territorial jurisdiction exasperated the French security forces to no end. As Jean Verdier, director general of the Sûreté Nationale, avowed to German officials in November 1958, 'The total liquidation of terrorist activities in the metropole would be much more advanced today if the rebels did not possess safe havens situated on foreign territories that bordered France.'[8] His military colleagues in Algeria thought similarly. Being 'certain that the rebellion finds its force in the aid it receives abroad', one situation report concluded as early as November 1956, 'measures must be taken to try to isolate Algeria from the rebellion's external bases of support.'[9]

This chapter explores some of the ways in which 'external bases' in contiguous states factored into the FLN's insurgency and French counter-insurgency. In doing so, it draws attention to an aspect of the FLN's independence struggle that remains poorly developed in the existing literature: the role of external safe havens, or 'rebel' sanctuaries.[10] The chapter starts by outlining the scholarship on 'rebel' sanctuaries before returning to Algeria's independence struggle. It will then survey one particularly unusual 'rebel' sanctuary: the Federal Republic of Germany (FRG). The chapter's aim is to highlight the difficulties of sanctuary denial. As shall be seen, French efforts to achieve this end resulted in failure. They did so even when dealing with France's closest ally in the Algerian War, the FRG. The FLN had managed to turn even the most seemingly hostile external space to its strategic advantage.

Sanctuary and irregular warfare

Notions of sanctuary are deep-rooted, ubiquitous and multifarious both in Christian and in non-Christian societies. They are often associated with holy places, the physical space of worship, or consecrated ground. They also refer to the spaces of refuge and asylum where fugitives have been granted immunity and shelter both by law and by custom. And they denote the practice of granting that protection. Notions of sanctuary have been incorporated into legislative, political, and religious norms and conventions the world over. They play an important role in manifold codes of honour and cultures of hospitality.[11]

More recently, notions of territorial and non-territorial sanctuary have come to be associated with the rise of irregular conflict. Many theorists and practitioners of guerrilla and revolutionary warfare have highlighted the vital importance of safe havens and rear bases to insurgent movements. To the leader of the Chinese Communist Party, Mao Zedong, they constituted one of seven fundamental steps to securing victory in a people's war.[12] Võ Nguyên Giáp, the Viet Minh's military leader and architect of France's notorious defeat at Dien Bien Phu in 1954, believed 'a strong rear is always the decisive factor for victory in a revolutionary war'.[13] As 'a physical location, at arm's length from hostile forces, from which to organize, train, plan, and possibly launch operations, untroubled by the vicissitudes of war's fickle design', base areas constitute a type of territorial sanctuary.[14] Without them, Mao Zedong argued, 'There will be nothing to depend on in carrying out any of our strategic tasks or achieving the aim of the war'.[15] Territorial sanctuaries offer insurgent forces the time, space and security required to create durable politico-administrative structures, train military recruits and political cadres, and develop stable logistical networks and lines of communication. Based in secure, often inaccessible terrain, they make it possible for insurgent groups to launch (para-)military operations against conventional armies, expand their links to local populations and create a durable 'insurgent-state-in-waiting' with all the structures and institutions that entailed.[16] Territorial sanctuaries, then, are force multipliers. They make it possible for insurgent movements to engage a more powerful and territorially entrenched authority.[17] An insurgent movement's ability to secure safe havens and rear bases will have a significant impact not only on the duration, scope and intensity of a war but also on the way in which it ends. As such, counter-insurgency strategies and manuals frequently emphasize the pivotal need for combating, undermining and denying an insurgency territorial and other forms of sanctuary.[18]

Research on the impact of territorial sanctuaries in irregular warfare has generally concentrated on the post-Cold War era. Some scholars have focused on the ethnic and identity conflicts that proliferated during the 1990s, especially in Africa, where civil wars frequently spilled over territorial boundaries, affecting entire regions. Others have directed their attention to more contemporary conflicts still: namely, the US-led wars in Afghanistan and Iraq, as well as the Global War on Terrorism of which they were a part. The transnational nature of these conflicts has shifted scholarly attention to the vital importance of *external* sanctuaries – those located beyond the territorial confines of the state against which an insurgent force or a terrorist group is fighting. These conceptions of external sanctuary are bound up with thinking about the sovereignty and the role of states that harbour foreign combatants. Many sanctuary-states are considered to be ideological or political allies of the foreign insurgent force or terrorist group they host. Many more are deemed to be failing or failed states too weak to prevent an insurgent force or terrorist group from operating on their territory. Much of the literature has focused on the attendant challenges these two types of external sanctuary have posed to counter-insurgent strategies, especially in the context of the Global War on Terrorism.[19]

Contrary to what one might assume from the existing literature, however, the phenomenon of external sanctuary is not new to irregular warfare. Nor is it intrinsically linked to state failure or state fragmentation. Even a cursory glance at the era of decolonization and of the global Cold War reveals that external sanctuaries played a pivotal role in the process of state-building, helping to sustain anti-colonial struggles waged by a succession of national liberation movements.[20] For example, over the course of several decades the ANC directed and orchestrated its struggle to end Apartheid from exile in Zambia and Tanzania, with additional bases at various points in time in Angola, Botswana, Lesotho, Mozambique, Swaziland and Uganda.[21] The Tanzanian capital Dar es Salaam alone became a base for multiple liberation movements during the 1960s and early 1970s.[22] Extraterritorial sanctuaries were also a strategic asset in South East Asia, where external safe havens, rear bases and supply lines helped sustain the VietMinh during the Indochina War against France between 1946 and 1954, and to an even greater extent during the subsequent American phase of the conflict.[23]

Although external sanctuaries were not always essential to insurgents' success during the Cold War, insurgent failure often coincided with an inability to secure safe havens and bases in contiguous territories.[24] Accounting for the British triumph in the Malayan Emergency, one of the chief theorists of British counter-insurgency, Robert Thompson, wrote: 'Perhaps the greatest advantage of all was that Malaya was completely isolated from outside communist support, having only a 150-mile frontier with friendly Thailand in the north (with whom there was a border agreement under which Malayan police forces could operate across the border) and a 1,000-mile seacoast, which could easily be controlled.'[25] The absence of external sanctuaries also facilitated British counter-insurgency operations in Kenya. The Mau Mau, Andrew Mumford argues, was 'perhaps the most isolated insurgent group to fight the British in the postwar era.'[26] These examples underline the fact that the absence or loss of external bases and supply lines could have a detrimental, even devastating, impact on insurgencies. In other words, the presence, or absence, of sanctuaries situated across an inviolable (or theoretically inviolable) frontier constituted a significant factor in shaping the nature, duration and outcome of many irregular conflicts during the Cold War era.[27]

Algeria's independence struggle

External sanctuaries were certainly critical to the FLN's strategy during its war of independence from France between 1954 and 1962. In February 1957 at the height of the Battle of Algiers, which aimed to expunge the FLN from the colonial capital, the movement's leaders began directing their war effort from safe havens in neighbouring Morocco and Tunisia. Both countries had only just gained their independence from France the year before. The former protectorates became, as FLN militant Mohamed Lebjaoui later wrote, 'the principal bases of our political, diplomatic and military action'.[28] The ALN, too, established bases, training camps, and weapons depots on either side of the Algerian border (as well as in Egypt and Libya). In a similar vein, the Algerian provisional government, or GPRA, depended on external sanctuaries.

Founded in September 1958, it was headquartered first in Cairo, then Tunis, though its ministries and agencies also operated in Morocco and Libya.[29] As Hocine Aït Ahmed, one of the FLN's founders asserted, 'The government will be both inside and outside' Algeria; close enough to maintain communications with the internal insurgency, yet safely beyond the French authorities' reach.[30]

Extraterritoriality allowed the FLN to develop more sophisticated governmental structures, enhancing the movement's effectiveness, authority, and legitimacy. External sanctuaries in states contiguous to Algeria proved even more valuable because the host governments, while remaining non-belligerent, actively supported the insurgents' cause, providing not just passive shelter and asylum but active logistical and material support, military training, diplomatic backing and economic aid.[31] By providing succour to the FLN, Morocco and Tunisia along with Egypt and Libya proved invaluable allies.[32] To Lebjaoui, that solidarity constituted the FLN's 'most precious trump', for it kept the Algerian revolution alive.[33] Though political calculation certainly influenced each state's decision to support the FLN, other factors proved equally decisive, not least the shared history, culture and ideology that created bonds of solidarity with a fellow Arab, Muslim and Third World nation seeking liberation from colonial oppression.

The FLN's West German sanctuary

These affinities did not exist in the case of the FRG, making the country a most implausible external sanctuary for the FLN.[34] West Germany was neither a failing nor a failed state characterized by ineffective governance and insecure international borders in which an insurgent group could move with freedom and impunity; quite the contrary.[35] Subjected to occupation and division in the aftermath of the Second World War, the country was anxious to reassert its territorial sovereignty and return to the fold of the community of nations. Nor was West Germany likely to become a passive, let alone active host, which tolerated the presence of Algerian insurgents, turning a blind eye to their subversive activities.[36] After all, the country's security against Soviet-led attack was still guaranteed by the three Western allies, which maintained a military presence in West Germany and West Berlin even after the abrogation of the Occupation Statute in May 1955. These allies included France, the very nation against which the FLN fought. Allied support remained vital for the survival of the Bonn Republic, especially in the context of the second Berlin crisis that began in late 1958. Nor were the FRG's strategic alignments likely to change. To secure its goal of international rehabilitation, the government of Chancellor Konrad Adenauer pursued a foreign policy that anchored the Bonn Republic firmly within the Western alliance system.[37] It also engaged in a policy of reconciliation with Germany's 'historic enemy', France. The Franco-German rapprochement formed the cornerstone of Bonn's policy of *Westbindung*. The growing partnership between the two neighbours was a driving force of European integration, culminating in the historic Élysée treaty of Franco-German friendship of January 1963.[38]

These reasons alone made it inconceivable that the Bonn government would condone the FLN's presence on federal territory, let alone endorse the movement's objectives. Even so, the Algerians came to use West Germany as an external sanctuary and operational base. Abdelhafid Keramane, who headed the GPRA's external delegation in Bonn between 1958 and 1961, rated the country's contribution to the FLN's independence struggle as 'very positive': 'In Western Europe, [the FRG] was the country that did the most for the Algerian cause, for the refugees, for the FLN and for the External Delegation.'[39]

Keramane's assertion seems paradoxical in light of Bonn's alliance with France, so how was it that the country transformed into such an important sanctuary? In seeking answers, the first point to recall is that the FLN exploited the contradictions intrinsic to France's juridical characterization of the Algerian conflict, especially the fiercely upheld principle that France was not 'at war' with the FLN. While policymakers in Paris were willing to declare a full state of emergency in Algeria, they refused to do so in metropolitan France. This made it impossible for the French authorities to seal the country's borders. More importantly, since French official rhetoric and constitutional legislation postulated that Algeria was an integral part of France, on paper at least, Algerians enjoyed the same rights, responsibilities and privileges as any other French citizen. In Western Europe, where societies had become increasingly open, pluralistic and humanitarian in outlook, the 'paradoxical citizenship' of Algerians impeded French counter-insurgency efforts – although repressive COIN strategies were indeed pursued on the mainland as Emmanuel Blanchard and Neil MacMaster's chapter in this book reveals.[40] Considering the fact that France was not 'at war', these repressive strategies could hardly be pursued beyond the metropolitan frontiers. Any attempts to do so risked internationalizing the conflict, turning it into the 'real war' the authorities were so intent on avoiding. Moreover, since repressive COIN strategies rarely differentiated between 'innocents' and 'insurgents', their pursuit beyond French territorial frontiers risked exposing before world opinion the hypocrisy of French claims that Algerians were French citizens and that repression targeted a mere minority of 'outlaws' and 'rebels'. This, in turn, would have undermined one of the key arguments for which the French fought – that Algeria *was* and *wanted to remain* part of France – while at the same time bolstering the FLN's international legitimacy and standing. Even the French authorities thus recognized that Algerians arriving in the FRG would have to benefit from the same principles of hospitality as French citizens of 'European' extraction. Whether the authorities in Paris or Bonn liked it or not, Algerians could not be denied entrance to the FRG without good reason.

In addition to the inconsistencies inherent in France's juridical position on the war and the citizenship rights of Algerians, a number of other factors facilitated the FLN's implantation in West Germany. Uppermost among these was geographical proximity. The common frontier comprised long stretches of poorly patrolled forest spanning the Ardennes and Eifel regions. This facilitated illegal border crossings by militants on the run from the French police. Meanwhile, West Germany's freshly minted democratic and constitutional order enshrining freedoms of speech and assembly, as well as rights to political asylum, enabled the consolidation of a rebel sanctuary. The country's federalist state-structures further facilitated this process. With their powers devolved to the local level, the decentralized police and security service proved uneven in their commitment to track down Algerian insurgents. Finally, the rapid growth of West

Germany's export-oriented economy was threatened by labour shortages, making local enterprises especially amenable to hiring foreign workers.

The FLN moved quickly to maximize these advantages. It built up a network of allies in West Germany willing to provide moral, material, logistical and operational support, including most of the Arab diplomatic corps in Bonn. By March 1959 the French security service acknowledged the danger: 'Although the federal government carries no responsibility for it, West Germany has become the theatre of manifold intrigues, where Soviet agents, neo-Nazis, FLN delegates and Arab diplomats mingle their tracks.'[41] Although hyperbolic in tone, the assessment proved sound, for the insurgents could indeed count on the protection, and assistance of a range of civil society actors whose motives differed widely. While some were inspired by a desire to spite the former French occupier, others – especially arms dealers – were driven by the prospect of financial gain. More typical were those individuals or organizations, which – in view of Germany's own recent past – felt obligated to provide humanitarian aid. Still others were inspired by a genuine sense of solidarity with those fighting colonialism and other forms of political oppression. Without these allies, the FLN would have found it difficult to consolidate its sanctuary in West Germany or to use the country as a staging point for a range of insurgent activities from recruitment and political mobilization to fundraising and arms trafficking.[42]

While these factors help to explain West Germany's appeal as a refuge and base, they do not wholly explain why that sanctuary became necessary. After all, colonial conflicts rarely spilled over into Europe's imperial heartlands, let alone the territory of near neighbours.[43] Algeria's independence struggle proved the exception as metropolitan France acquired a pivotal role in FLN strategy. Early in the war, the FLN's Fédération de France set out to harness the sizeable Algerian migrant community to its cause. These migrants, better-educated and more highly politicized than Algerians back home, represented desirable recruits and a steady source of income for the insurgency. The metropolitan security services and the FLN's bitter rival, Messali Hadj's Algerian National Movement, each fiercely resisted these recruitment efforts.[44] The resultant environment of escalating police repression and relentless internecine violence prompted several thousand Algerians, both innocent refugees and nationalist activists, to seek shelter in neighbouring countries, thus mirroring developments in North Africa. As partly francophone countries, Belgium and Switzerland initially represented the favoured destinations. Belgium was already home to a small Algerian migrant community, which at its height during the Algerian War numbered 4,000.[45] The Algerian community in Switzerland was considerably smaller, never surpassing 800. But the country had a reputation of harbouring dissidents and was a preferred meeting place for Arab nationalists.[46] The Belgian and Swiss security services, pressed by the French authorities, soon cracked down on these communities, prompting many to relocate to the FRG. By 1959, the country had become the preferred destination for Algerians in Western Europe with an estimated 8,000 having taken refuge in the country.[47]

The FRG thus became the insurgency's prime sanctuary in Western Europe. Just as the FLN began to direct its war effort in Algeria from external sanctuaries in

Tunisia and Morocco, so the leaders of the *Fédération de France* began organizing their metropolitan 'second front' from hideouts in and around the city of Cologne.[48] With the help of the FLN's European support networks, the Federation created a clandestine network of safe houses and rendezvous points in West Germany. Weapons depots and workshops were established, and even a 'school' for new recruits and cadres. The GPRA's Foreign Ministry meanwhile maintained a permanent mission within the Tunisian Embassy in Bonn. Enjoying the cover of diplomatic immunity proffered by the FLN's Arab sponsors, this bureau first became active in late 1957 and helped orchestrate the movement's diplomatic and propaganda campaigns in West Germany and beyond. The bureau also served as the hub of a clandestine Europe-wide recruitment network helping Algerian draft-dodgers, deserters, and other volunteers join the insurgency's ranks. The GPRA's Ministry of Armaments and General Relations was another to maintain a covert permanent office in West Germany. According to French intelligence, it was the only such mission outside of the Arab world.[49] As this observation implies, the FRG became a logistical hub in the FLN's efforts to procure modern armaments and other war materiel to sustain its armed struggle in France and in North Africa.[50] Finally, with so many Algerians seeking refuge and work in West Germany, the FLN bureau in Bonn, assisted by representatives from the UGTA and UGEMA, established a loose-knit '*Fédération d'Allemagne*' to exert tighter social control over the Algerians and levy monthly taxes on them.[51]

The French response

By April 1959 French military intelligence analysts were sounding the alarm. One *deuxième bureau* officer concluded that 'the FLN made very good use of the advantages offered by the FRG: a sanctuary; a link to rebel forces [in North Africa and France]; and a not insignificant faction of public opinion sympathetic to its propaganda'.[52] Mirroring the course of events in North Africa, these developments, as Blanchard and MacMaster's chapter demonstrates, ran counter to everything the authorities were trying to achieve through the application of counter-insurgency techniques in metropolitan France. By leaving France in large numbers, Algerians were rendered immune to the 'constructive' aspects of the French security forces' brand of 'revolutionary warfare', which included social welfare, educational programmes and propaganda. Isolating the FLN and winning over Algerians for 'the establishment of a new order', always improbably difficult tasks, became harder still.[53] In seeking refuge across the border, the insurgents also undermined the effectiveness of the 'destructive' side of 'revolutionary warfare', a term connoting those repressive operations designed 'to uncover, dismantle, and suppress the rebels' politico-administrative framework and their guerrilla units'.[54] In addition, the resort to external sanctuaries impeded the collection of reliable intelligence, weakening the system of 'human management and control' upon which the French security forces had come to rely in their fight against the FLN.[55]

With the FLN's safe havens and base areas in West Germany now constituting a threat to national security, sanctuary denial became crucial. 'As long as this considerable war potential [on foreign territory] is not neutralised', Colonel Roger Trinquier, one of the foremost theoreticians of 'revolutionary warfare', wrote, 'peace, even if completely restored within our own borders, will be precarious and in continual jeopardy.'[56] Accomplishing this objective proved remarkably complicated, however, for as *New York Times* journalist Michael Clark noted in 1959, 'It is singularly difficult to destroy an enemy enjoying the sanctuary of an inviolable frontier.'[57] Armed operations beyond France's border, such as the Suez intervention of 1956 or the bombing of the Tunisian town of Sakiet-Sidi-Youssef in February 1958, proved counterproductive, resulting 'in little military gain, while costing a great deal in diplomatic complications and unfavourable public opinion.'[58] Rooted in a tradition of colonial warfare that largely ignored matters of sovereignty and legality, the military was willing to pursue the FLN across North African territorial boundaries, especially since the states affected were too weak to retaliate (and were still deemed to be in the French 'sphere of influence'). In Europe, as we have seen, such methods were ruled out on legal and political grounds to avoid internationalizing the war.

So was the tactic of border interdiction. Although the heavily defended 'Morice line' along the Tunisian frontier and its analogous barrier along the Moroccan border effectively stemmed the flow of men, arms and provisions into Algeria, the authorities never contemplated sealing France's territorial frontiers, having never declared a full-blown emergency in the metropole.[59] Border guards were instead instructed in September 1957 to intensify inspections of Algerians 'with judgement, avoiding vexatious measures, notably with regards to known Muslim personalities, and with a maximum of discretion in order to prevent unfavourable commentaries by foreign witnesses'.[60] The same incongruities of French policy that had enabled the FLN to establish external sanctuaries in Western Europe now prevented the security services from closing France's borders to prevent the insurgents' return. Outwardly at least, Algerians' freedom of movement had to be respected, notwithstanding the protests of Paris police prefect Maurice Papon, who considered it 'inconceivable that in times of war an enemy can cross the border just like all inoffensive individuals'.[61]

With a transparent approach to sanctuary denial precluded, the French security services resorted to more covert methods. The FRG became a prime target of the 'permanent secret war conducted by the special services' against the FLN's supply networks.[62] Between 1956 and 1961, the country was hit by a wave of assassination attempts against FLN agents such as Améziane Aït Ahcène or Abdelkader Nouasri and the West German arms dealers with whom the movement did business, including Otto Schlüter, Georg Puchert, Wilhelm Beißner and Walter Heck. Meanwhile, frogmen sabotaged at least two West German cargo vessels suspected of delivering arms to the FLN, while arsonists supposedly started a fire at one of the plants of *Telefunken*, a company accused by the French authorities of supplying radio transmitters and receivers to the insurgents.[63] Heavy-handed and illegal, the resort to covert action also proved ineffective. By December 1960, the deuxième bureau concluded that Eastern Bloc governments had replaced Western European merchants as the FLN's chief arms suppliers. This aid proved harder to track and interdict.[64] More remarkably, instead of highlighting the illegal and unethical activities of shady German (and other) gun runners, French tactics transformed these men into romanticized heroes, 'on the whole sympathetic, who had placed [their] skills and courage in the service of a good cause, in this case the fight by the Algerian insurgents for their liberty'.[65] The 'secret war' against the FLN's supply networks in West Germany thus reinforced the image of France as the villain of the Algerian War. Even French intelligence concluded that the campaign of sabotage and assassinations had rendered 'the greatest of services' to the FLN.[66]

This left the French authorities with one further option. Allies, or proxies, might be recruited to neutralize the FLN's external sanctuary in West Germany while circumventing the strictures imposed by national boundaries. Although legally and politically obliged to tolerate Algerians on federal territory – not least to prevent these refugees from formally requesting political asylum, and thereby legitimizing the FLN's claim that Algerians were not French – the German authorities had to be persuaded to thwart Algerian subversion of their own volition. French governments consequently exerted strong diplomatic pressure on the authorities in Bonn. In February 1959, Prime Minister Michel Debré cautioned the ambassador in Paris 'that the solidarity of the accord between France and Germany was linked to a community of views that must, for the moment, manifest itself principally in Algeria'.[67] Thanks in part to the protracted crisis over Berlin, this French pressure spurred the German authorities into action. Confident of the Adenauer government's support, the metropolitan security services collaborated closely with their West German counterparts, sharing top-secret intelligence that would enable local police to clamp down on insurgent activities. The West German authorities responded by stepping up surveillance and imposing tight conditions on Algerians seeking residence and work permits, not least a strict ban on 'political activities'.[68] In December 1959, the judiciary initiated a nationwide inquiry with a view to indicting the FLN for conspiracy, subversion, and developing a criminal, or terrorist organization in contravention of articles 128 and 129 of the West German criminal code.[69]

Having assembled over twenty-three evidence dossiers, on 20 April 1961 the federal prosecutor issued an arrest warrant against the FLN bureau in Bonn. This clampdown marked the climax of joint Franco-German efforts to eradicate the FLN's most vital sanctuary in Western Europe. 'It goes without saying', the French Foreign Ministry observed, 'that we cannot but congratulate ourselves for the measures taken by the German judiciary against the FLN's principal agents in Bonn'.[70] Their timing, however, could not have been worse. The arrests came just as French head of state, General Charles de Gaulle, acknowledged France's readiness to withdraw from Algeria and conceded negotiations with the FLN. Made to appear both draconian and pointless, the German crackdown sparked a wave of protest in the FRG and beyond. Bonn's ambassador in Tunis (and soon-to-be ambassador in Algiers) called the arrests so 'grotesque' that 'even a few hundred million [DM] in development aid will not wipe away the bad impression' they left on the developing world, let alone on Algeria's future leaders.[71] Anxious to limit the fallout, the authorities in Bonn backpedalled. Ultimately, the clampdown was exposed for what it was: the product of French attempts to neutralize the FLN by proxy. Once again, these efforts had backfired, for the arrests heightened public awareness of the discriminatory and oppressive nature of France's treatment of Algerians.

Conclusion

This chapter has argued that external 'rebel' sanctuaries are not purely a recent phenomenon of transnational terrorism, ethnic conflict, or state fragmentation but also played a decisive role in the context of decolonization and state-building. The FLN sustained its independence struggle by taking refuge in regions beyond France's territorial control. Whether in North Africa or in Western Europe, external 'rebel' sanctuaries came to constitute vital strategic, operational and logistical bases for the insurgency. The freedom of manoeuvre proffered by an inviolable frontier enabled the FLN to recruit and mobilize, to propagandize and raise funds, to procure essential military supplies and create an 'insurgent-state-in-waiting'. Although these external activities did not produce military victory in Algeria's independence struggle, they were of tremendous political, diplomatic and psychological value.[72] Indeed, external sanctuaries constituted a vital precondition for the FLN's 'diplomatic' victory. As in other wars of decolonization, they helped counterbalance the colonial powers' preponderance of coercive force, thereby reducing the asymmetry of power between colonizer and colonized. Paying closer attention to insurgents' use of external space thus helps to shed light on the transnational nature of the state-building projects of many movements of national liberation, which continued into the postcolonial era.

The chapter has also argued that contrary to received wisdom, active support or passive toleration on the part of host governments is not essential to the creation of external 'rebel' sanctuaries. The case of West Germany reveals that these can emerge even in states closely allied to a counter-insurgent power. Algerian militants were able to operate relatively freely inside an open, democratic and pluralistic society, the more so as the FLN won the sympathy of the wider West German public. Faced with an unfriendly, even hostile, host government, the FLN depended on civil society actors and Arab diplomats to secure its position in the FRG. Domestic allies constituted additional pillars of support, or force multipliers, that helped to sustain the insurgents in this sanctuary-state. These transnational networks, too, deserve closer scrutiny if we are to understand how they sustain insurgent (or terrorist) forces and transform relations to host governments.

Finally, this chapter has outlined the extent to which external 'rebel' sanctuaries create substantial, perhaps even insurmountable challenges for counter-insurgencies. In the context of the Algerian War, they thwarted French efforts to destroy the FLN's politico-administrative organization and fighting potential. Direct interventions and border interdiction were rarely successful in dismantling the FLN's external safe havens and base areas. Even covert and indirect methods relying on proxy actors proved ineffective. On the contrary, efforts at sanctuary denial generally backfired because they contradicted the moral and political goals for which the French supposedly fought in Algeria: the defence of sovereignty, democracy, freedom, civil liberties and social justice. Whatever the methods deployed, operations to deny sanctuary reinforced the image of an imperialist France defending an unjust cause, which in turn shored up the FLN's international legitimacy. In sum, it is not necessarily the military usefulness of external 'rebel' sanctuaries that matters most to insurgents; their psychological and diplomatic value may be greater still.

Notes

1 Key examples of this extensive and growing literature include Mark Philip Bradley, 'Decolonization, the Global South, and the Cold War, 1919-1962,' in *The Cambridge History of the Cold War,* Vol. I, ed. M. P. Leffler and O. A. Westad (Cambridge: Cambridge University Press, 2010), 464–85; Cary Fraser, 'Decolonization and the Cold War,' in *The Oxford Handbook of the Cold War,* ed. R. H. Immerman and P. Goedde (Oxford: Oxford University Press, 2013), 469–85; Marc Frey, R. W. Pruessen and T. T. Yong (eds), *The Transformation of Southeast Asia: International Perspectives on Decolonization* (New York: Routledge, 2003); C. E. Goscha and C. Ostermann (eds), *Connecting Histories: Decolonization and the Cold War in Southeast Asia* (Stanford, CA: Stanford University Press, 2009); Leslie James and Elisabeth Leake (eds), *Decolonization and the Cold War. Negotiating Independence* (London: Bloomsbury, 2015); K. Fedorowich and M. Thomas (eds), *International Diplomacy and Colonial Retreat* (London: Frank Cass, 2001).
2 Matthew Connelly, *A Diplomatic Revolution: Algeria's fight for independence and the origins of the post-Cold War era* (Oxford: Oxford University Press, 2002), 4.
3 Jeffrey J. Byrne, *Mecca of Revolution: Algeria, Decolonization, and the Third World Order* (New York: Oxford University Press, 2016), 9–10, 291–3; Jeffrey J. Byrne 'Africa's Cold War,' in *The Cold War in the Third World*, ed. Robert J. McMahon (New York: Oxford University Press, 2013), 101–23.
4 Westad, *Global Cold War,* 106.
5 Matthew Connelly, *L'arme secrète du FLN. Comment de Gaulle a perdu la guerre d'Algérie* (Paris: Payot, 2011).
6 Guy Pervillé, 'L'insertion internationale du FLN algérien,' *Relations internationales* 31 (1982) : 374.
7 First citation: Notice de renseignement no.1937/EMI/2, 1.6.1961; second citation: Fiche, EMI/2, 17.5.1960, Service Historique de la Défense, Armée de Terre (SHD-T), Vincennes, 1H/1743/D1 (unless stated otherwise, all translations from French or German are the author's).
8 Compte-rendu de la conférence entre représentants français et allemands au sujet de l'activité des rebelles algériens en RFA, 18.11.1958, Archives du Ministère des Affaires Étrangères (MAE), Paris, MLA/2.
9 Note d'information no.1053/INS/AFN/EM sur la situation en Afrique du Nord, 16.11.1956, SHD-T, 1H/1101/D3.
10 The term is taken from Idean Salehyan, *Rebels without Borders: Transnational Insurgencies in World Politics* (Ithaca, NY: Cornell University Press, 2009).
11 *The Oxford English Dictionary*, online edition. Also: R. Lippert and S. Rehaag (eds), *Sanctuary Practices in International Perspectives: Migration, Citizenship and Social Movements* (Abingdon: Routledge, 2013).
12 Mao Tse-Tung, *On Guerrilla Warfare,* trans. S. B. Griffith (New York: Praeger, 1961), 107.
13 Võ Nguyên Giáp, *People's War People's Army* (Hanoi: Foreign Languages Publishing House, 1961), 93.
14 Michael A. Innes, 'Protected Status, Sacred Sites, Black Holes and Human Agents: System, Sanctuary and Terrain Complexity,' *Civil Wars* 10, no. 1 (2008): 2.
15 Mao Zedong, 'Problems of Strategy in Guerrilla War against Japan, May 1938,' in *Selected Military Writings of Mao Tse-Tung* (Peking: Foreign Languages Press, 1967), 167–8.

16	Rex Brynen, *Sanctuary and Survival: The PLO in Lebanon* (Boulder, CO: Westview Press, 1990), http://prrn.mcgill.ca/research/papers/brynen2_01.htm (accessed 25 November 2014).
17	Rem Korteweg, 'Black Holes: On Terrorist Sanctuaries and Governmental Weakness', *Civil Wars* 10, no. 1 (2008): 66; Michael A. Innes, 'Deconstructing Political Orthodoxies on Insurgent and Terrorist Sanctuaries', *Studies in Conflict & Terrorism* 31 (2008): 62, 255; David Kilcullen, 'Counter-insurgency Redux,' *Survival: Global Politics and Strategy* 48, no. 4 (2006): 118.
18	Hannes Artens, 'Sanctuary State – Insurgency Relations in Ethnic Conflicts: A New Explanatory Model,' *Oficina do CES* no. 392 (2012): 1.
19	Examples include Daniel Byman, *Deadly Connections: States that Sponsor Terrorism* (Cambridge: Cambridge University Press, 2005); Joseph D. Celeski, 'Attacking Insurgent Space: Sanctuary Denial and Border Interdiction,' *Military Review* 86, no. 6 (2006), 51–7; Jeffrey T. Checkel (ed.), *Transnational Dynamics of Civil War* (Cambridge: Cambridge University Press, 2013); Kristian S. Gleditsch, 'Transnational Dimensions of Civil War,' *Journal of Peace Research* 44, no. 3 (2007): 293–309; Michael A. Innes (ed.), *Denial of Sanctuary: Understanding Terrorist Safe Havens* (Westport, CT: Praeger, 2007); Michael A. Innes (ed.), 'Protected Status, Sacred Sites, Black Holes and Human Agents,' Special Issue of *Civil Wars* 10, no. 1 (2008): 1–6; David Kilcullen, 'Countering Global Insurgency,' *Journal of Strategic Studies* 28, no. 4 (2005): 597–617; David A. Lake and Donald Rothchild (eds), *The International Spread of Ethnic Conflict: Fear, Diffusion, and Escalation* (Princeton, NJ: Princeton University Press, 1998); Sarah K. Lischer, *Dangerous Sanctuaries: Refugee Camps, Civil War, and the Dilemmas of Humanitarian Aid* (Ithaca, NY: Cornell University Press, 2005); James A. Piazza, 'Incubators of Terror: do Failed and Failing States Promote Transnational Terrorism?' *International Studies Quarterly* 52 (2008): 469–88; Jeffrey Record, *Beating Goliath: Why Insurgencies Win* (Washington, DC: Potomac, 2007); Idean Salehyan, *Rebels without Borders*; Paul Staniland, 'Defeating Transnational Insurgencies: The Best Offense is a Good Fence,' *The Washington Quarterly* 29, no. 1 (2005–6): 21–40; Paul Staniland, 'Organizing Insurgency: Networks, Resources, and Rebellion in South Asia,' *International Security* 37, no. 1 (2012): 142–77.
20	Examples include John P. Cann, 'Securing the Borders of Angola, 1961-1974,' *Revista Militar* 2495 (2009); Bruce Hoffman, Jennifer M. Taw and David Arnold, *Lessons for Contemporary Counterinsurgencies: The Rhodesian Experience* (Santa Monica: RAND Corporation, 1991); Thomas H. Henriksen, 'Lessons from Portugal's Counter-insurgency Operations in Africa,' *The RUSI Journal* 123, no. 2 (1978): 31–5; Washa G. Morapedi, 'The Dilemmas of Liberation in Southern Africa: The Case of Zimbabwean Liberation Movements and Botswana, 1960-1979,' *Journal of Southern African Studies* 38, no. 1 (2012): 73–90; Michael G. Panzer, 'Building a Revolutionary Constituency: Mozambican Refugees and the Development of the FRELIMO Proto-state, 1963-1968,' *Social Dynamics* 39, no. 1 (2013): 5–23.
21	Stephen Ellis, *External Mission the ANC in Exile, 1960-1990* (London: C. Hurst and Co., 2012); Tom Lodge, 'State of Exile: The African National Congress of South Africa, 1976–86,' *Third World Quarterly* 9, no. 1 (1987): 1–27; Hugh Macmillan, *The Lusaka Years: the ANC in Exile in Zambia, 1963-1994* (Johannesburg: Jacana Media, 2013); Filipe Ribeiro de Meneses and Robert McNamara, 'The Last throw of the dice: Portugal, Rhodesia and South Africa, 1970-74,' *Portuguese Studies* 28, no. 2 (2012): 201–15.
22	George Roberts, 'Politics, Decolonization, and the Cold War in Dar es Salaam, c.1965-72' (PhD dissertation, University of Warwick, 2016).

23 Christopher E. Goscha, *Thailand and the Southeast Asian Networks of the Vietnamese Revolution, 1885-1954* (Richmond: Curzon Press, 1999); Michel Lux, *La guerre d'Indochine, au 3e escadron monté du Cambodge, 1949-1951* (Nantes: Odin, 2009); J. J. Zasloff, 'The Role of the Sanctuary in Insurgency: Communist China's Support to the Vietminh, 1946-1954,' RAND Memorandum (May 1967); Thomas Briggs, *Cash on Delivery: CIA Special Operations during the Secret War in Laos* (Rockville, MD: Rosebank, 2009); John Prados, *The Blood Road: The Ho Chi Minh Trail and the Vietnam War* (New York: Wiley, 1999); Richard L. Stevens, *Mission on the Ho Chi Minh Trail: Nature, Myth, and War in Viet Nam* (Norman: University of Oklahoma Press, 1995); William Shawcross, *Sideshow: Kissinger, Nixon, and the Destruction of Cambodia,* 3rd edn (New York: Simon and Schuster, 1979); Roger Warner, *Back Fire: The CIA's Secret War in Laos and its Link to the War in Vietnam* (New York: Simon and Schuster, 1995).

24 Eqbal Ahmad, 'Revolutionary Warfare and Counterinsurgency,' in *Guerrilla Strategies: An Historical Anthology from the Long March to Afghanistan*, ed. Gérard Chaliand (Berkeley: University of California Press, 1982), 253.

25 Robert Thompson, *Defeating Communist Insurgency: Experiences from Malaya and Vietnam* (London: Chatto & Windus, 1966), 19.

26 Andrew Mumford, *The Counter-Insurgency Myth: The British Experience of Irregular Warfare* (Abingdon: Routledge, 2012), 67.

27 Bruce J. Reider, 'External Support to Insurgencies,' *Small Wars Journal* 10, no. 10 (2014): 1–17.

28 Mohamed Lebjaoui, *Vérités sur la Révolution algérienne* (Paris: Gallimard, 1970), 105.

29 For an overview of the FLN's structures and institutions: Gilbert Meynier, *Histoire intérieure du FLN, 1954-1962* (Paris: Fayard, 2002).

30 Étude envoyée au C.C.E. de la prison de la Santé (April 1957), in *La Guerre et l'Après-Guerre,* Hocine Aït Ahmed (Paris: Minuit, 1964), 17–18, 38–43.

31 Reider, 'External Support,' 2.

32 See Meynier, *Histoire,* 557–80; Amira Aleya-Sghaier, 'La Tunisie: base-arrière de la révolution algérienne,' *Revue d'Histoire Maghrébine* 118 (2005) : 155–60.

33 Lebjaoui, *Vérités,* 109.

34 This section draws on: Mathilde von Bülow, 'Franco-German Intelligence Cooperation and the Internationalization of Algeria's War of Independence (1954–62),' *Intelligence and National Security* 28, no. 3 (2013): 397–419. For a fuller view, see Mathilde von Bülow, *West Germany, Cold War Europe and the Algerian War* (Cambridge: Cambridge University Press, 2016).

35 Korteweg, 'Black Holes,' 60–2; Reider, 'External Support,' 2.

36 Byman, *Deadly Connections,* 219–23.

37 On foreign policy under Adenauer: Ulrich Lappenküper, *Die Außenpolitik der Bundesrepublik Deutschland 1949 bis 1990* (Munich: Oldenbourg, 2008).

38 On the Franco-German rapprochement: Ulrich Lappenküper, *Die deutsch-französischen Beziehungen, 1949-1963. Von der 'Erbfeindschaft' zur 'Entente élémentaire',* Bd.1-2 (Munich: Oldenbourg, 2001).

39 'Entretiens, Alger, 21.9.2000', in Nassima Bougherara, *Les Rapports franco-allemands à l'épreuve de la question algérienne (1955-1963)* (Bern: Lang, 2006), 214.

40 Alexis Spire, *Étrangers à la carte: L'administration de l'immigration en France (1945-1975)* (Paris: Grasset, 2005), 195.

41 Bulletin d'information, anon., Mar.1959, SHD-T, 1H/1164/D2.

42 On the FLN's implantation in the FRG, see von Bülow, *West Germany,* chs. 3 and 7.

43   Jim House and Neil MacMaster, *Paris 1961: Algerians, State Terror and Post-Colonial Memories* (Oxford: Oxford University Press, 2006), 5, 15, 25.
44   Rabah Aissaoui, 'Fratricidal War: The Conflict between the Mouvement national algérien (MNA) and the Front de libération nationale (FLN) in France during the Algerian War (1954-1962),' *British Journal of Middle Eastern Studies* 39, no. 2 (2012): 227–40; Linda Amiri, *La Bataille de France: La guerre d'Algérie en Métropole* (Paris: Robert Laffont, 2004); Ali Haroun, *La Septième Wilaya: La Guerre du FLN en France 1954-1962* (Paris: Seuil, 1986).
45   Jean L. Doneux and Hugues Le Paige, *Le Front du Nord. Des Belges dans la guerre d'Algérie (1954-1962)* (Bruxelles: CRISP, 1992), 35.
46   Marc Perrenoud, 'La Suisse et les accords d'Évian: la politique de la Confédération à la fin de la guerre d'Algérie,' *Politorbis* 31, no. 2 (2002), 4. Also: Damien Carron, *La Suisse et la guerre d'indépendance algérienne (1954-1962)* (Lausanne: Antipodes, 2013).
47   Auswärtige Amt an Bundesministerium des Innern und Bundesministerium für Arbeit, 6.10.1959; Bundesministerium des Innern an Auswärtiges Amt, 26.11.1959, Politisches Archiv des Auswärtigen Amts (PA/AA), Berlin, B25/11.
48   Omar Boudaoud, *Du PPA au FLN. Mémoires d'un combattant* (Alger: Casbah, 2007), 162–8; Mohammed Harbi, *Une Vie debout: Mémoires politiques 1945-1962*, vol. I (Paris: Découverte, 2001), 222.
49   Fiche no.8007/10R.M./EMI/2, 4.12.1958, SHD-T, 10T/531/D3*.
50   Mathilde von Bülow, 'Myth or Reality? The Red Hand and French Covert Action in Federal Germany during the Algerian War, 1956-61,' *Intelligence and National Security* 22, no. 6 (2007): 787–820.
51   'Entretiens avec Keramane, et avec Omar Boudaoud, Ali Haroun et Kaddour Ladlani,' Alger, 19.9.2000,' in Bougherara, *Les Rapports franco-allemands*, 206–24; Daho Djerbal, *L'Organisation Spéciale de la Fédération de France du FLN: Histoire de la lutte armée du FLN en France (1956-1962)* (Alger: Chihab, 2012).
52   Présentation sur les activités FLN en Allemagne, CCFFA/2, Apr.1959, SHD-T, 10T/528/D2*.
53   Peter Paret, *French Revolutionary Warfare from Indochina to Algeria: The Analysis of a Political and Military Doctrine* (New York: Praeger, 1964), 31–2.
54   Ibid., 30–1.
55   Ibid., 59.
56   *Modern Warfare: A French View of Counterinsurgency,* trans. Daniel Lee (London: Pall Mall, 1964), 97.
57   *Algeria in Turmoil: A History of the Rebellion* (New York: Praeger, 1959), 309.
58   Paret, *French Revolutionary Warfare*, 33–4.
59   Haas, 'Operations at the Border,' 33–4.
60   Instruction no.4085/SN.RG.RAF du directeur des Renseignements Généraux, 12.9.1957, Service des archives et du musée de la préfecture de police (SAMPP/P), Paris, Ha/66*.
61   Quelques suggestions sur la lutte à mener contre le FLN en France, undated, SAMPP/P, Ha/68*.
62   Plan de protection de l'Afrique du Nord contre la guerre froide, INS/AFN, 4.6.1955, SHD-T, 1H/1103/D1.
63   See Bülow, 'Myth or Reality?'
64   Note, EMG/2, 6.12.1960, SHD-T, 1R/352/D3*.
65   Dépêche no. 630 de l'ambassadeur Seydoux à Bonn, 26.3.1959, MAE, MLA/3.

66 Notice no. 31389/SDECE, 24.5.1960, SHD-T, 10T/523*.
67 Note a.s. de l'entretien du Premier Ministre et de M. Blankenhorn, 17.2.1959, MAE, EU/RFA/1261*.
68 Schreiben Nr.13514, Bundesministerium des Innern an Landesministerien des Innern, 13.11.1958, Bundesarchiv, Koblenz (BA/K), B106/15779.
69 Schreiben Nr.1310, Landeskriminalamt Baden-Württemberg an Bundeskriminalamt, 22.2.1960, BA/K, B131/214.
70 Télégramme no.1738 de la mission de liaison pour les affaires algériennes à l'ambassade de France à Bonn, 28.4.1961, MAE, MLA/7.
71 Schreiben Botschaft Tunis, 12.5.1961, PA/AA, B25/2.
72 Ahmad, 'Revolutionary Warfare,' 252.

11

David Galula and Maurice Papon: A Watershed in COIN Strategy in de Gaulle's Paris

Emmanuel Blanchard and Neil MacMaster

In the history of colonial warfare research has focused mainly on the elaboration and testing of counter-insurgency methods in the far-flung corners of Western empires. Far less is known about the way in which techniques developed within the colonial theatre were 'imported' back into the metropolitan heartland. One reason for this is that imperial centres, not often confronted by internal 'terrorism', had little cause to harness COIN methods to those of conventional domestic police and intelligence operations. One can, however, identify moments when developed states have had recourse to methods that were elaborated overseas, as in the case of the British army bringing methods tried and tested in colonial wars to counter the IRA in Northern Ireland, or the deployment by the Argentinian government of French counter-insurgency methods to crush left-wing insurgents.[1] More recently, the USA has quietly adapted COIN techniques developed in Iraq and Afghanistan to the domestic 'war' on terrorism and the policing of civil 'disorders'.[2] However, such 're-importations' have remained unexplored, in part because of the high level of state secrecy surrounding the introduction of techniques developed in Kenya, Vietnam, Algeria and elsewhere where there was little legal or political protection of basic human rights, into parliamentary democracies that still subscribed to the rule of law.

The Algerian War of Independence was unusual in the extent to which it saw colonial warfare flowing across the Mediterranean into the imperial centre. This case study makes a contribution to this little understood field by investigating the way in which the Fifth Republic under de Gaulle recruited David Galula, regarded by many as one of the leading COIN theorists of the twentieth century, to help organize anti-FLN operations in mainland France.

The year 1958 was a tumultuous one in the entangled histories of France and Algeria. As the Algerian conflict entered its fourth year, political impasse in Paris suggested to many that a fundamental change of French regime was required. As is well known, senior military figures in Algiers, working in combination with General Charles de Gaulle's political supporters, took decisive action to break the deadlock. The eight-month period between the revolt of the generals in Algiers on 13 May 1958, the collapse of the Fourth Republic and de Gaulle's return to power, first as prime minister (1 June) and later as president of the Fifth Republic (8 January 1959), represented one of the most significant watersheds in the history of modern France. During this tense transition de Gaulle rapidly moved to consolidate his power base against a fractious army. Although the military had supported de Gaulle's comeback through a coup against the civil powers in Algeria, the general wished to marginalize them by installing a new, carefully selected body of close advisers in his cabinet and the Sécrétariat général pour les affaires algériennes.[3] A few months after Colonel Lacheroy, the iconic and most influential exponent of counter-insurgency strategy, had been sidelined and forced to leave Paris for Algeria, the main defenders of the counter-revolutionary war against the Algerian Army of National Liberation (ALN) were in an ambivalent position. They had succeeded in overthrowing the Fourth Republic, but they were suspected by de Gaulle of pursuing their own political agenda.

By the late 1950s the security forces that fought France's wars of decolonization had acquired considerable experience in psychological warfare, notably during the Indochina conflict of 1946–54, when France's Vietnamese communist opponents used propaganda and brainwashing techniques to crushing effect. Nor was the extension of psychological action to metropolitan France a new phenomenon. It had been part of a police force agenda for more than three years, even if the practices involved were more difficult to implement on the French mainland. After 1954, as the violence in Algeria escalated, political warfare and psychological action also became the central preoccupation of an influential circle of French officers. In July 1957, an *Instruction provisoire sur l'emploi de l'arme psychologique (TTA 117)* was adopted and extended to cover metropolitan France, but without any specific reference to the 300,000 Algerians who lived mainly in Paris and the industrial regions. Despite de Gaulle's dislike of counter-insurgency ideologues and his distrust of its supporters in the armed forces, COIN seemed to be a necessary tool in the French capital from June 1958 onwards. Among the many pressing issues that confronted de Gaulle in the second half of 1958 was that of the growing strength of the FLN in the environs of greater Paris. There, the movement had developed a sophisticated clandestine organization, a parallel counter-state, the destruction of which presented a formidable problem for the police and the intelligence services. De Gaulle, sensitive to his personal and symbolic status as head of state and world leader, was outraged that armed nationalist militants were engaged in a fully fledged guerrilla war in the capital, immediately outside the walls of Matignon.

De Gaulle's response to the FLN French Federation has been investigated by historians in recent years largely through the figure of the prefect of police, Maurice Papon, and his role in the violent police repression that culminated in the massacre of 17 October 1961, when dozens of peaceful demonstrators were killed in central Paris.[4] Historians have shown how during the second half of 1958 de Gaulle's government developed a new counter-insurgency strategy, part of which was closely linked to the creation of two agencies dedicated to political surveillance: the Service de Coordination des Affaires Algériennes (SCAA), a central intelligence and policing unit, and the Service d'Assistance Technique aux Français Musulmans d'Algérie (SAT-FMA), a bureau that, under the cover of welfare, gathered information in the Algerian quarters of Paris.

Historians have tended to focus on Papon as the central actor in the operation of these new agencies. Papon was rushed from Algeria to replace the incumbent Police

Prefect Lahillonne on 15 March 1958 in order to resolve a crisis in the Paris force.[5] He is generally credited with the accelerated introduction of COIN strategies elaborated in North Africa into the capital, as well as the transfer of military specialists into the *préfecture*. What has received less attention was the role of de Gaulle himself as decision maker in shaping a new COIN organization for Paris during the potentially unstable and dangerous transition to the Fifth Republic. This was a period of considerable uncertainty during which the general created various working parties (*groupe de travail*) whose 'brain-storming' sessions were meant to devise ways and means to undermine the FLN's organizational network. Among these new working parties was the Committee for Psychological Action (CAP), which was established at de Gaulle's behest on 9 July 1958 and which was directly linked to the Army General Staff (*état-major*). It was headed by a high-ranking civil servant in charge of the Service de coordination des informations nord-Africaines (SCINA), an umbrella police network dedicated to the collection of intelligence on 'North-African terrorism' and Algerian nationalism.[6] The CAP was one of the many organizations created during these years that brought military and police officers into working partnership.

The CAP working party first met on 23 July 1958. Among its members were three army officers attached to de Gaulle's new cabinet team. One of these was Commandant David Galula who had been flown in from active service in Kabylia the day before. This chapter centres on Galula's role at this particularly sensitive moment in the elaboration of a COIN strategy. Galula was an unknown and relatively low-ranking officer at the time. Until quite recently he attracted little attention, even among specialist historians of COIN practices during the Algerian War.[7] Yet Galula has aroused enormous posthumous interest in recent years as the leading Western theorist of twentieth-century counter-insurgency doctrine. This chapter revisits the circumstances in which his appointment to the CAP occurred, its aim being to shed light on the security concerns of de Gaulle's cabinet in the summer of 1958.

David Galula: From Kabylia to Paris

David Galula (1919–67) was, until recently, largely unknown in France and elsewhere. His posthumous fame stems from 2007 when General David Petraeus commissioned a new and highly influential US Army COIN manual.[8] Developed from recent COIN experience in Iraq and Afghanistan, the publication in question saluted Galula as the most important theorist of counter-insurgency. His study, *Counterinsurgency Warfare. Theory and Practice*, first published by the RAND Corporation in 1963, was identified as the greatest influence on the team that prepared the new US doctrine.[9] This new-found interest in Galula generated a mass of publications, mainly by US military specialists, and gave rise to three full-length studies.[10] The military historian Douglas Porch, in a general critique of contemporary COIN doctrine, has exposed the myths surrounding Galula's inflated reputation as a genius, the 'Clauzewitz of the 21st century'.[11] This, however, still leaves open the question of why this minor figure was selected and plucked from relative obscurity as a field commander in the Algerian mountains to join de Gaulle's newly established cabinet team.

Galula had a long career in military intelligence, which allowed him to observe insurgents from China and Greece to Indochina and the Philippines. He volunteered to serve in Algeria where he was commander of a *sous-quartier* (sub-district) in Kabylia. So successful were his unit's operations there that they provided a showcase of COIN in action, attracting visits from numerous generals and ministers. Galula was also ambitious. A capable self-promoter, he won further attention through various reports he forwarded to senior figures in government, including the Minister of Defence Maurice Bourgès-Maunoury, and Generals Raoul Salan and Paul Ely.[12] Galula was also inspired by other French COIN theorists, including Jean Nemo, but his views differed from the most famous of them, Colonel Charles Lacheroy.[13] Although still relatively unknown, Galula's November 1956 memoir, *Notes on Pacification in Greater Kabylia*, reached Salan and the higher military command.[14] This account was later published in the restricted army journal *Contacts*, and it stirred considerable controversy when it was leaked to *Le Monde* and the communist daily, *L'Humanité*. Both critical of French colonial military practices, these newspapers cited Galula's work as evidence that 'fascism was guiding the French army in Algeria'.[15] Galula's operational techniques, which included his command of the *sous-quartier* of Djebel Mimoun in Kabylia, reflected COIN methods then being refined by fellow officers such as Jean-Yves Alquier. But Galula was able to combine his global expertise in revolutionary warfare with his Algerian experience of putting theory into practice. The result was a synthesis of theory and practice that amounted to a comparative model of counter-insurgency.[16]

On 22 July 1958 Galula was surprised to receive a telegram ordering his immediate transfer to Paris to join the Ministry of National Defence Psychological Action Branch.[17] There are conflicting accounts regarding whose initiative it was to summon Galula to France, but there is little doubt that Colonel Goussault, head of the Army's 5th Bureau of Psychological Warfare, endorsed it. Goussault corresponded frequently with Galula in Kabylia and nurtured his career.[18] Particularly interesting in the context of the political transition from the Fourth to the Fifth Republic over the summer of 1958 is the reason for Galula's transfer to Paris at this juncture and the specific duties he was expected to perform for de Gaulle's newly constituted cabinet.

During the seven-month interlude before de Gaulle's presidential system was enshrined in the Fifth Republic constitution, the general wrested the political initiative from the rebel officers who still held military power in Algiers. De Gaulle also edged closer to negotiations with the FLN, a long-term solution to the conflict likely to demand disengagement from Algeria. His more immediate dilemma was how to enter a dialogue with the FLN without triggering another military coup in reaction to it. To ease his path, de Gaulle assumed personal control of the armed forces, surrounding himself with a new cabinet team. Intensely loyal to de Gaulle, these appointees worked in total secrecy, immune to the tentacular networks of the right-wing generals and plotters. At a cabinet meeting on 9 June, a week after arriving at the prime minister's residence, the Hotel Matignon, de Gaulle announced his new ministerial and administrative team. Vice Admiral Georges Cabanier, a trusted Gaullist, was appointed Chief of Staff in the Ministry of Defence, a move that began the process of investing supreme military authority beyond the reach of Generals Raoul Salan, Jacques Massu and their associates in Algiers, commanders who were destined to be removed from

North Africa.[19] In July one of the most activist officers, Colonel Marcel Bigeard, was removed from the Centre d'entraînement à la guerre subversive (CEGS), a training centre for COIN officers in Jeanne d'Arc near Philippeville. The centre was then closed down, only months after its opening.

Coordinated by Cabanier, in the following two months, de Gaulle and his advisers overhauled the French armed forces, a reorganization that extended to the key area of counter-insurgency, including the fight against the FLN in France. It was during this relatively brief window of time between July and October 1958 that the new Gaullist regime first studied and then installed a new COIN organization for mainland France that remained substantially unchanged until the Algerian conflict ended. Put differently, a new COIN strategy was enacted in metropolitan France just as its forebear faced dismantlement in Algeria. Because of the high level of secrecy surrounding this reorganization – as much a matter of protecting the French state from its own *putchist* officers as from its external enemies – the structures put in place remain little known. Galula's biographer, A. A. Cohen, despite enjoying access to Galula's private papers and conducting interviews with his widow, remarks that Galula's life during this period is 'shrouded in secrecy'. However, enough is known to piece together some of the picture.[20]

On arriving in Paris Galula worked under the umbrella of the National Defence Staff (Etat-Major de la défense nationale – EMDN). He was responsible to the prime minister's office (recall that de Gaulle held this office before becoming president), working within the Division that, in August 1958, superseded the Service d'Action Psychologique et de l'Information (SAPIDNFA). Galula's role within the Information Division changed during his four years in Paris, but from his arrival in July 1958 he had two main responsibilities. One was as a specialist adviser to the Radio Broadcast Steering Committee, also created in July. There he was involved in the so-called 'war of the airwaves', which included the jamming of hostile radio transmissions, including those of the FLN, the dissemination of Arabic and Berber language propaganda, and the development of French shortwave transmissions.[21] His second and more pressing responsibility was to serve as a representative of the prime minister's cabinet on the CAP working party. Galula was flown in for the CAP's first meeting on 23 July, the committee having been established a fortnight earlier. It is with this body, on which Galula's presence had previously been unnoticed, that we are mainly concerned.

The CAP was chaired by F. X. Rousseau, head of the SCINA. It was an interdepartmental group comprising representatives from eleven bodies, including the Ministries of the Interior (Blanchard), Information (Massenet), and Armed Forces (Nesa), the Préfecture de police (Aubert), the Sûreté Nationale (Pimont), the General Secretariat for Algerian Affairs (Villeneuve), the Centre de Diffusion française (De Labastide) and the National Defence Staff attached to the Hotel Matignon (Galula, Casso and Brun).[22] The primary objective, as set out in Cabanier's directive of 9 July, was to recommend techniques of psychological action and counter-propaganda that could safeguard 'the mass of Muslims residing in metropolitan France from their domination by the separatists'.[23] The group thus began their deliberations from a flawed presumption, one shared by most of the armed and intelligence services in Algeria and France, that the majority of Algerians were essentially neutral and forced to pay the

FLN contributions. The mass of workers in France, it was claimed, was held in check by a small hard core of FLN terrorists, estimated at 5,000 men, and the objective was to find ways and means to insulate the vast majority from the tiny minority of violent militants. Another issue much in the minds of CAP members was the recent high-profile success of COIN operations, first during the 'Battle of Algiers' in 1957 and, second, in the so-called 'fraternisation' campaign in which Algerians and Europeans appeared alongside one another in Algiers demonstrations, meticulously orchestrated by the army, to demand de Gaulle's return to power in May 1958. Galula was witness to both – and they had left their mark. Both Papon (who did not attend CAP meetings but was represented by a deputy) and Galula were fascinated by the methods adopted by Jacques Massu's paratroopers during the counterterrorism campaign in Algeria's capital. Each knew that the same methods could not be transplanted wholesale to France without causing a major political crisis and an unparalleled media storm. Galula claimed that a mere 500 terrorists in Algiers had paralysed a city of 700,000 inhabitants. Even so, the army had dismantled the entire network within ten days. He liked to quote an unnamed paratroop colonel's chilling prediction, 'Give me one hundred resolute men and I will terrorize a city like Paris.'[24]

Although Galula had acquired most field experience in the mountainous interior of Aïssa Mimoun, he did spend a month conducting the 'pacification' of Tizi Ouzou, the regional capital of Kabylia. In common with other COIN specialists, he claimed to have found it relatively straightforward to adapt his skills in tracking down clandestine rural networks to the hunt for their urban equivalents. Indeed, Galula went further, claiming that the Kabyle capital was successfully 'cleansed' during his four-week operation and that counter-insurgency, contrary to expectations, had proved easier to carry out in towns.[25] Galula seems to have assumed, as did Generals Massu and Salan, that carrying out urban 'police' work posed no particular problems to a seasoned COIN specialist equally at ease in the mountainous *djebel* as in the packed *quartiers* of Algiers and Paris.

Galula made two main proposals to the CAP working group to penetrate the FLN's French network and separate the mass of workers from the militants. Both responded to the fact that the police confronted an FLN organization that was becoming increasingly watertight partly because of a 'growing shortage of informers'.[26] His first suggestion was to redeploy Algerians serving in the French army as undercover agents. Their task would be to worm their way into the FLN, paying dues and assisting at meetings, in order to identify lower-level organizers and provide a constant stream of intelligence about the movement's activities. These undercover operatives would also carry out propaganda work (*action psychologique*), among Algerian immigrant workers.[27] Galula's second proposal was to establish a '*centre de formation de cadres*' that would target Algerians previously threatened by the FLN and who lived in constant fear of reprisal. These individuals were to be recruited and offered civil affairs training, before being reinserted into the Algerian immigrant community as civic leaders around whom opposition to the FLN's demands might crystallize. Impressed with his proposals, the CAP asked Galula to produce a short report for the next, and what was possibly the last, working party meeting on 16 October. It was then that he delineated his plans to 'separate the leaders from the mass'. His scheme had three phases. In the first, leaflets, posters and other forms of propaganda would urge sympathetic Algerians to locate like-minded associates and 'trusted friends' (*des amis sûrs*). In the second, the security services would help these workers form into groups and, finally, in the third, these networks would be organized into active centres of opposition to FLN exactions. The production of propaganda could begin immediately, and would be disseminated by a so-called 'third force' movement: the Musulmans associés pour la défense des travailleurs FMA (Muslim Association for the Protection of French-Algerian Muslim Workers).[28]

Galula's '*centre de formation de cadres*' idea almost certainly derived from a secret plan devised by the ethnologist Jean Servier, which was adopted by Algeria's Resident-Minister Robert Lacoste in January 1957 and first tested during Operation *Pilote* in the western region of Orléansville (now Chlef).[29] Algerians were carefully selected in the region's rural hinterland and sent to the psychological warfare training centre at Arzew to conduct a crash-course in civil affairs. The trainees were then secretly reinserted back into their villages to serve as anti-FLN organizers in the rural communes. Galula had a long discussion with his patron, Colonel Goussault, the head of Operation *Pilote*, in January 1957 about this operation towards which Galula remained sceptical. He expressed his doubts both about whether agents of this type could be indoctrinated 'in our own ideology' and, if so, whether any such recruits could then be safely reintroduced to village *douars* without detection by the FLN. 'From my experience in China, I can assure you there is not much room for rival movements in clandestine situations'. Galula claims that six months later Goussault acknowledged the failure of his plan.[30] Evidently, though, Galula's earlier reservations did not prevent him from espousing something remarkably similar for Paris: specifically, the 'third force' initiative that would eventually come to fruition in 1960 as the 'Algerian front for democratic action' (Front algérien d'action démocratique – FAAD).[31]

Galula's agnosticism towards certain aspects of the 5th Bureau (the army's psychological warfare unit) served him well in gaining promotion to de Gaulle's cabinet team. De Gaulle was contemptuous of the psychological theories so fervently advocated by certain army officers, many of them veterans of the Indochina War who emerged traumatized from Vietminh prison camps, where they had been subjected to Vietnamese communist brainwashing techniques. De Gaulle had equally little time for the ideas of Russian theorist Serge Chakhotin about propagandist techniques. These, too, were venerated by 5th Bureau staff at the time. Perhaps more to the point, psychological warfare doctrine was closely associated with the right-wing officers who orchestrated the 13 May coup and who continued throughout late 1958 to present the greatest danger to de Gaulle's consolidation of power. Many disciples of Colonel Lacheroy, the pre-eminent advocate of psychological warfare in Algeria, went on to form the Organisation de l'armée secrete (OAS), the reactionary terrorist group devoted to keeping Algeria French, which eventually tried to assassinate the French president. It bears emphasis that one of the central tasks of de Gaulle's new cabinet team was to marginalize the doctrinaire exponents of psychological warfare. To that end, Pierre Guillaumat, the new Defence Minister, issued a directive on 18 July 1958 that marked a sharp break with the theories of *guerre révolutionnaire*.[32] It seems unlikely then that a minor figure such as Galula would have been handpicked for de Gaulle's inner circle if he had shown any leanings towards the Algérie française diehards. Quite the reverse: in November 1956 he had made clear his opposition to the 'psychologists' whose abstruse doctrines he dismissed as 'ridiculous' ideas bound to fail the acid 'test of reality in the field'.[33]

We could find no archival evidence of the continuation of the working group beyond its session on 16 October, and it seems probable that its activities were wound up, especially as the prefect of police seized the initiative in COIN operations from August 1958 onwards. The ambitious and domineering Maurice Papon resented any attempt, even by powerful figures or authorities, to trespass into what he viewed as his terrain as police chief, and he may well have viewed the CAP working party as a threat to his own plans.[34] Galula, only recently arrived from Kabylia and still finding his feet about the complex issues of policing Paris, was probably unaware of the extent to which Papon had already been experimenting with new COIN methods. Central to this was Operation *Meublés*, which began in June 1958. Principally an intelligence-gathering mission, the operation assigned police officers to the staff of the capital's housing inspectorate for hotels and lodging houses – always a point of contact with immigrant workers.[35]

It was no coincidence that Papon, on the very next day after the CAP working party's first meeting, wrote an important briefing document, *Note sur la répression du terrorisme nord-africain*, which was tabled at the next CAP session on 1 August.[36] On 23 August the government accepted Papon's ambitious proposal to create the SCAA-SAT organization that constituted the central apparatus of counter-insurgency in Paris until the war's end. Although Galula still presented his proposals to the (probably) final meeting of the working party on 16 October, he was undoubtedly sidelined by Papon's team and began to focus his attention instead on his Information Division work in radio and broadcasting.[37] By the end of August, Papon had thus seized the initiative in the fundamental restructuring of counter-insurgency by de Gaulle's new government.

Maurice Papon: Head of a Parisian COIN strategy

David Galula and Maurice Papon were unevenly matched in terms of their potential to influence COIN policy in metropolitan France. Admittedly, they agreed about some things. Papon, for instance, shared Galula's aversion to the doctrinaire partisans of counter-revolutionary war. Both men had advocated similar COIN strategies in Algeria, albeit at different levels. Papon enjoyed far greater influence as the civilian head (Inspecteur général de l'administration en mission extraordinaire – IGAME) of the Constantine region before he was appointed prefect of police in Paris. Ironic as it may seem, the two men also appeared to be less radical ideologues than some of their colleagues. Papon, for example, did not share the same obsessive anti-communism as one of his predecessors as prefect of police, Jean Baylot (in office from 1951 to 1955), under whom he had previously served as deputy. Galula, for his part, was a pragmatist who, as we have seen, dismissed the far-fetched ideas of those whom he labelled the 'psychologists'.[38] Yet, for all their similarities in terms of temperament and political priorities, the two men occupied quite different levels in their respective administrative hierarchies. Papon was one of the highest-ranking civil servants in France. He was directly responsible to de Gaulle and his ministers and he headed a 20,000-strong armed police force that was crucial not only to the control of Paris, but also to the defence of the regime itself, and which held the key to the defeat of the FLN in mainland France. Galula, by contrast, was but one officer among many who participated in the multifarious activities of the COIN working groups. He was an effective but little known intelligence officer who lacked the status to wield decisive influence on strategic planning and its implementation.

The Préfecture de police was the sole office of state able to implement an effective COIN strategy within France, full-blooded military operations being out of the question. Papon had no intention of sharing this role with other civil or military organizations. His cooperation with others was selective, contingent on his ability to subordinate them to his authority. Chance also played its part. It was the coincident timing of a significant change in FLN strategy in mainland France that provided Papon with the opportunity to impose his own agenda both within the CAP working party and upon the forms of intelligence-sharing and joint police and military strategies being discussed there.

On the night of 25–26 August 1958, the FLN *Fédération de France* launched attacks against economic and strategic targets throughout the mainland. The Paris and Marseilles regions were especially heavily hit with attacks on police headquarters, factories, military posts, state forests and the oil refinery at Mourepiane, which burnt for days.[39] The opening of this 'second front' shocked French public opinion and took the police services by surprise. For the Préfecture de police, it presented the perfect opportunity to impose new repressive measures such as deportations, detention without trial and 'residential banishment' (effectively, expulsion from France). These measures had already been under review by Papon's entourage before the FLN attacks, particularly among his newly appointed advisers, which included colonial army officers with long experience in Morocco and Algeria. The scale of FLN military operations, during which six police officers were killed and several others wounded in Paris, was to change the political situation dramatically, but until that moment it was difficult for the *préfecture* to win support for the kinds of repressive initiatives that were being discussed.

Although Papon was keen in the summer of 1958 to reinforce the legal and repressive powers of the Préfecture de police, his plans did not go unopposed. Although supported by the Minister of the Interior, he was challenged by other services that sought to protect the interests of Algerian migrants who, categorized as *Français Musulmans d'Algérie*, were legally French citizens. The FLN's attacks in Paris and other major French cities were therefore crucial, opening a window of opportunity for Papon to defeat his opponents in government. He was convinced that, as matters stood, his officers could not defeat the Algerian nationalists since they were, in principle, compelled to operate within the confines of criminal law. Its parameters were codified for times of peace, denying the police the sweeping powers needed to combat an organization engaged in a revolutionary war.

The scope of police powers had been widened somewhat in July 1957 with some extensions to France of the 'special powers' that had been applied to Algeria under the 'state of emergency' law enacted by the French National Assembly in April 1955. Papon, though, considered these legislative modifications woefully inadequate. He was determined to secure juridical authority to detain any and all Algerians suspected of supporting the FLN, rather than only those activists who had been sentenced for sedition or more petty offences. This was the context in which, during the summer of 1958 the Préfecture de police representative on the CAP went on the offensive in the working party demanding a more proactive COIN strategy spearheaded by tough police measures. At the CAP's first meeting on 23 July the main agenda item was counter-propaganda targeted at Algerian migrants and the working party's first job was to agree the necessary propagandist measures. The session was largely taken up with discussion of the content and distribution of pro-French leaflets and other forms of propaganda proposed by the various ministries and agencies present. The CAP minutes confirm that the Préfecture de police representative tried to shift the discussion to the more pressing problem of inadequate legal support for effective policing of the Algerian nationalists who were tightening their grip on thousands of migrants.[40]

The pressure applied by the Préfecture de police soon bore fruit, as reflected in the CAP's altered priorities. The report produced by the first CAP meeting was unequivocal in this regard, stipulating that psychological action, in order to be effective, must be preceded by a repressive campaign to 'neutralize' all the FLN terrorists. At the following meeting on 1 August the representative of the Sûreté Nationale, the central body for all police units outside the Paris region, backed the *préfecture's* analysis. He explained that it was vital to reinforce the legal arsenal available to the police in fighting the FLN, and he, too, supported measures such as preventive arrest, detention without trial, and expulsion from mainland France. The French government endorsed the proposed restrictions and they were included, alongside new powers for military courts, in the laws (termed ordonnances) promulgated on 7 and 8 October 1958. Like his colleagues in the Préfecture de police, the Sûreté Nationale representative was more engaged in lobbying for specific legal reforms than in devising a holistic COIN strategy. To sum up, while police complaints about insufficient legal powers and material means to defeat the FLN persisted throughout the war, their demands, especially those formulated by Papon, were largely satisfied during the autumn of 1958. The prefect of police succeeded in creating new units dedicated to the repression of the Algerian nationalists, a fact confirmed by the opening of detention camps for suspects in mainland France.

These developments notwithstanding, the CAP's counter-propaganda measures were not wholly abandoned, but Galula and other army representatives on the CAP lacked the support necessary to implement their strategy fully. They also underestimated the difficulties intrinsic to organizing operations in Algerian neighbourhoods, especially inside the shantytowns along the capital's outer rim. Their initial proposals to import into France certain methods used in Algeria were unsuccessful. A telling example was the use of adapted army trucks to project propaganda films in immigrant neighbourhoods, which came up against the reluctance of the shantytown's Algerian inhabitants to attend screenings. When propaganda films were also projected in commercial cinemas, spectators voiced their contempt.[41] Overall the CAP meetings produced few original ideas. Others seemed naïve, lacking consideration of the practical means necessary to achieve their declared counter-propaganda objectives. A typical example here would be the proposal discussed earlier to send leaflets to the home addresses of those Algerians thought to harbour pro-French sympathies asking them to supply the names of 'trusted friends'. In hindsight, it seems ludicrous that this idea, a measure that CAP members reckoned to be the most effective way to reach out to such loyalists, could possibly counteract the FLN's hold on the Algerian community.[42]

Thanks to the extensive manpower resources and enhanced legal powers at its disposal, the Préfecture de police was better placed to challenge nationalist hegemony over the migrants.[43] Having undermining the CAP working party's COIN strategy, Papon and his staff pursued their own agenda for psychological action.[44] Before August 1958 numerous internal police memoranda were headed 'The Algerian Muslim problem'. Revealingly, however, one such document was corrected by hand and changed to 'psychological and social action towards Algerian Muslims'. No trifling amendment, this indicated the broader change of direction within the Préfecture de police.[45] Over subsequent months a regular bunch of documents were exchanged on this issue and, in June 1959, Hippolyte Bérenguier, one of the colonial officers appointed by Papon to organize the new SAT units combining intelligence collection with welfare provision, wrote to Papon in very similar terms to those of the CAP working party.[46] He proposed the organization of a new training programme in psychological action for those Algerians, described as '*éléments sains*', who were thought to be waiting for the right moment to escape from the FLN's clutches. Beyond this, Bérenguier suggested sending letters to 5,000 Algerians urging them to support the French government and suggesting that the subscriptions collected by FLN activists from poor migrant workers were misappropriated to fund lavish lifestyles abroad. Yet he acknowledged that many of the intended recipients could not read French.[47] Conscious that the French authorities knew little about the Algerian community in France, Bérenguier further proposed an extensive 'sociological inquiry' to collect information on the Algerian immigrant population. This census was launched one year later and was symptomatic of something broader, a long-held desire within the Préfecture de police to gain an all-encompassing *panopticon* knowledge of a population that, despite numerous police raids on Algerian hostels and the dismantling of many FLN support networks, seemed ever more attached to militant nationalism.

These initiatives aside, the fact remained that the Préfecture de police undertook little in the way of psychological action. Papon preferred to collect intelligence through the administrative surveillance and welfare provision organized inside Algerian neighbourhoods by the *Bureaux de renseignements spécialisés* (BRS) of the SAT-FMA units. This remained the main source of intelligence gathered on the thousands of Algerians who were obliged to use the service each month since this was the only way to obtain administrative documents including identity cards and official authorization to travel to Algeria. The BRS was equally pivotal in providing assistance with housing, pensions, the remittance of savings and welfare rights. Furthermore, the FLN could not prevent Algerians making use of these services even when former colonial officers provided them. The SAT officers, who focused on this method of building up detailed biographical files on thousands of individuals, eventually paid less attention to the field of psychological action, despite taking pride in various initiatives they took in conjunction with their army colleagues on active service in Algeria. As time went on, the Préfecture de police restricted psychological warfare initiatives treating them as incidental to their overall activity. Most of the initiatives highlighted in police reports thus appear to be anecdotal and sometimes faintly ridiculous. By implication, they reveal the difficulties the police services encountered in trying to counter the FLN ideologically.[48]

For the Paris police psychological action was above all a rhetorical device, something that could be referred to highlight the ineffectual activities of other institutions that it wished to see brought under its wing in the mainland battle against the FLN. Typical in this vein, Papon dismissed the Seine *préfecture's* welfare specialists for *Français Musulmans* (referring to Algerian immigrants) as 'a form of free charity which refuses to engage in even minimal forms of psychological action, which, for them, represent a *"viol de conscience"* [literally, a violation of conscience]. In brief, this administration has, in classic style, sacrificed itself to bureaucratic routine … leaving the field open for the FLN'.[49] Moving beyond their jurisdictional rivalries, the analysts of the Préfecture de police remained wedded to the idea that the FLN had imposed itself on the Algerian immigrants through a policy of coercion. Yet, even those on Papon's staff willing to concede that the majority of Algerians in Paris were motivated by feelings of patriotism or nationalism continued to describe the immigrant population as a 'mass', which had to be won over by a subtle strategy of punishment and reward. Algerians were thus denied any agency in their own politicization, something that was instead depicted as the product of external pressures – of others acting upon them.

In this respect David Galula was no different from his military or civilian colleagues within the Préfecture de police. After the war ended, Galula continued to describe the Algerians of Paris as a mass that had been manipulated for decades, particularly by the French Communist Party (PCF), which made a point of propagandizing and recruiting among Kabyles long before the rebellion. Algerian Muslims, Galula misleadingly claimed, could move back and forth between France and Algeria without any visas or other travel restrictions and, once on the mainland, could vote in the same capacity as French citizens. The Communist Party, sensing the advantage to be won, would finance their trips just before election time, encouraging the returnee to register in constituencies where the contest was closest.[50] In fact, Galula's assertions were wide of the mark: voter registration had to take place well before an election and very few Algerians actually voted in France. Certainly, in the early 1950s, the description of Algerians as the 'shock troops of the Communist Party' was commonplace. But a dozen years later only the most doctrinaire anti-communist analysts still peddled this kind of myth. The example is a poignant one, pointing as it does to Galula's personification of a particular strand of counter-revolutionary warfare protagonists who remained blind to the complex dynamics of anti-colonial mobilization.

To conclude, Galula's contribution to French COIN activities in late-1950s Paris must be understood in the historical context. The increased media attention that Galula has attracted since 9/11, a phenomenon that is, in turn, attributable to his veneration by the

US military as a counter-insurgency genius, risks historical distortion. As we have seen, it would be a mistake to assume that he would have enjoyed any such preeminence when he served on the COIN working party in Paris. Galula the 'genius' is largely a twenty-first-century invention. Albeit recognized for some notable military achievements in Algeria, he came to Paris in 1958 as a relatively junior figure and his brief contribution to the three meetings of the short-lived CAP group was eclipsed by the burgeoning influence of the Préfecture de police. Under Papon's direction the *préfecture* consolidated its power as the one agency with the means to tackle the FLN in Paris. Police representatives quickly intervened to reorient the CAP agenda as part of a wider bid to secure the lead role in COIN operations and psychological action. That being said, the urgency with which Galula was recalled to Paris and his attachment to de Gaulle's inner cabinet at such a delicate political moment confirm that he enjoyed high-level military backing. But Galula's transfer, along with that of several of his army colleagues, must be set within the context of de Gaulle's transition to power, the urgent need to halt the FLN's advance among the French capital's Algerian immigrant population, and the consequent demand for an effective COIN strategy to do so. In this sense his presence in the CAP sheds light on a discrete phase, lasting from June to October 1958, during which de Gaulle and Papon laid the foundations for a new COIN structure in France. This new organizational apparatus, and the legal framework that supported it, enabled the government to combat the FLN's '*second front*' terrorist wave unleashed by its Organisation spéciale (OS) commandos in August 1958. Galula's Parisian story, then, is part of the Algerian War's expansion to the streets of mainland France.

However, in the final count, despite the ferocity of police repression and the sophistication of the counter-insurgency structures created in Paris, such measures failed to eradicate the FLN. Papon's flawed theory of revolutionary warfare that regarded the Algerian population as the passive victim of a minority of 'terrorists' failed to recognize the deep roots of nationalism among the majority of immigrants in France. No matter how often the police claimed to have 'decapitated' the FLN by the arrest of its leaders, the clandestine organization always sprang back. Even after the October 1961 massacre when thousands of activists were arrested and expelled to Algeria, the French Federation quickly rebuilt a strong organization and by early 1962 had fully restored the collection system. Contrary to the claims made by Papon in 1961, and repeated by him until his death in February 2007, Algerians immigrants remained resistant to most of the COIN strategies and tools deployed by the *préfecture*, and in the final count it was the FLN that won the 'battle of Paris'.

Notes

1 Brigadier Frank Kitson, a specialist in low-intensity operations in Kenya, Malaya and Cyprus, introduced COIN techniques to Belfast in 1970–1; see also Emma Bell, 'Normalising the Exceptional: British Colonial Policing Cultures come Home', *Cahiers du MIMMOC* 10 (2013), online at http://mimmoc.revues.org/1286; on Argentina see Marie-Monique Robin, *Escadrons de la mort, l'école française* (Paris: La Découverte, 2004).

2   Michael Gould-Wartofsky, '5 Tools the Police Are Using in Their War Against Activists', *The Nation*, 5 May 2015, https://www.thenation.com/article/5-tools-police-are-using-their-war-against-activists/

3   Eric Chiaradia, *L'Entourage du Général de Gaulle: juin 1958-avril 1969* (Paris: Publibook, 2011), 81–2.

4   For the extensive literature on this controversial episode, see the bibliographies in Jim House and Neil MacMaster, *Paris 1961. Algerians, State Terror, and Memory* (Oxford: Oxford University Press, 2006), and Emmanuel Blanchard, *La police parisienne et les Algériens 1944-1962* (Paris: Nouveau Monde éd., 2011).

5   Emmanuel Blanchard, *La police parisienne*, and 'Quand les forces de l'ordre défient le palais Bourbon (13 mars 1958). Les policiers manifestants, l'arène parlementaire et la transition de régime', *Genèses* 83 (2011), 55–73.

6   The documents of the CAP, mainly the minutes, are in the Archives de la Préfecture de Police (Paris) (APP), HA 59, subject to restricted access (*dérogation*).

7   The most detailed study by Paul and Marie-Catherine Villatoux, *La République et son armée face au 'péril subversif'. Guerre et action psychologiques 1945-1960* (Paris: Les Indes Savantes, 2005) makes no reference to Galula.

8   *The US Army and Marine Corps Counterinsurgency Field Manual No.3–24* (Chicago: Chicago University Press, 2007).

9   David Galula, *Counterinsurgency Warfare. Theory and Practice* (Westport, CT: Praeger Security International, 2006 edition). Galula only became widely known in France after 2008 following the publication of a translation, *Contre-insurrection: théorie et pratique* (Paris: Economica, 2008).

10 Ann Marlowe, *David Galula: His Life and Intellectual Context* (US Army War College, Strategic Studies Institute, August 2010), http://www.StrategicStudiesInstitute.army.mil/; A. A. Cohen, *Galula. The Life and Writings of the French Officer Who Defined the Art of Counterinsurgency* (Santa Barbara, CA: Praeger, 2012); Gregor Mathias, *Galula in Algeria. Counterinsurgency. Practice versus Theory* (Santa Barbara, CA: Praeger, 2011) a revised edition and translation of a 2010 French study.

11 Douglas Porch, *Counterinsurgency. Exposing the Myths of the New Way of War* (Cambridge: Cambridge University Press, 2013), 174–201.

12 David Galula's detailed account of his COIN actions and strategy in Kabylia, *Pacification in Algeria, 1956-1958* was first published by the RAND Corporation in 1963, and was released to the public in a new edition in 2006: available at www.rand.org/content/dam/rand/pubs/monographs/2006/RAND_MG478-1.pdf. Galula's original reports of November 1956 and spring 1957 are in appendix 2 and 3. On how he gained direct access to Generals Dulac, Salan and Ely and promoted his ideas through journalists, see *Pacification*, 178–9; Gregor Mathias, *Galula in Algeria*.

13 Gregor Mathias, 'David Galula et Jean Nemo, deux visons différentes des méthodes de contre-insurrection en Algérie?', in *Les maquis de l'histoire, guerres révolutionnaires, guerres irrégulières*, ed. Antoine Champeaux (Paris: Lavauzelle, 2010), 231–42.

14 The report is reproduced in *Pacification in Algeria* Appendix 2, 257–70; on its impact in the army see Cohen, *Galula*, 148.

15 David Galula, 'Observations sur la pacification en Grande Kabylie', *Contacts*, April 1957, 11–19; on *Le Monde*, see Galula, *Pacification*, 150. He remained anonymous as the 'Captain from Kabylia'.

16 Jean-Yves Alquier, *Nous avons pacifié Tazalt. Journal de marche d'un officier parachutiste rappelé en Algérie* (Paris: Robert Laffont, 1957).

17   Galula, *Pacification*, 238–9, recalls that the order was sent in 'mid-June', but Cohen, *Galula*, 183, has located in the Galula family archive a copy of the original order signed by Fourquet on 22 July 1958. The date is significant since Galula appeared the very next day at the first meeting of the CAP working party. The decision and his recall, to the dismay of his commander General Allard, was almost certainly related to de Gaulle's Cabinet decision to launch a new plan of Psychological Action in metropolitan France.

18   Galula, *Pacification*, 66–7, on Goussault, 'a brilliant officer'; Cohen, *Galula*, 170–2, correspondence between Galula and Goussault in the private archive of the Galula family. Goussault tried twice, without success, to get his protégé transferred to the 5th Bureau in April 1957 and April 1958. General Ely, chairman of the Joint Chiefs of Staff, was another of Galula's prominent supporters, see Cohen, *Galula*, 148, 186.

19   It was Cabanier's office that sent the order of 22 July 1958, signed by Brigadier Fourquet, for Galula's immediate transfer to Paris: see Cohen, *Galula*, 182–3.

20   Cohen, *Galula*, 184. Historian Gregor Mathias secured partial access to the secret archives of the division of information, see his *Galula in Algeria*, 73.

21   Service historique de la Défense (SHD), GR 5 Q 25-26. See also Mathias, *Galula in Algeria*, chapter 5: 'David Galula and the Battle of the Airwaves (1958-1962)', 70–91. It appears that from 1959 Galula was also attached to a 'crisis group', or *groupe opérationnel*, tasked with analysing intelligence on immediate strategic concerns and global hot spots and producing a daily briefing for de Gaulle.

22   All subsequent references to the working party are to APP HA59, consisting mainly of the agenda and minutes of three meetings held on 23 July, 1 August and 16 October 1958.

23   A further Ministry of Interior circular of 16 July 1958 stressed the importance, not just of repressing the FLN, 'but also [of] a psychological action and a co-ordinated, deep and continuous propaganda in all spheres and bringing into play the most diverse methods.'

24   Galula, *Pacification*, 143.

25   Ibid., 146–56, 280.

26   Minutes, 1 August 1958.

27   Ibid.: Galula was asked to report on this as quickly as possible. The idea of using Algerians attached to the army as undercover agents eventually came to fruition with the *Force de police auxiliaire* (*harkis*), established by Captain Montaner in 1959–60: see Rémy Valat, *Les calots bleus et la bataille de Paris* (Paris: Michalon, 2007).

28   Galula's proposals did not go unopposed. The representative of the *Service des affaires musulmanes* (SAMAS) thought, 'The conditions on the ground were not ready for a psychological action, as defined, to be fully effective', and more useful would be social welfare and other measures to alleviate the inequalities and difficult material conditions faced by migrant workers. This critique presaged a major conflict that later emerged between the police's repressive COIN operations and leading social workers in Paris, see House and MacMaster, *Paris 1961*, 144–6.

29   Neil MacMaster, *Burning the Veil. The Algerian War and the 'emancipation' of Muslim Women, 1954-62* (Manchester: Manchester University Press, 2009), 89–98.

30   Galula, *Pacification*, 66–7. This was not true, and the Pilote experiment was rapidly extended throughout Algeria. Galula probably confused this situation with Goussault's disillusionment with Jean Servier, who was soon removed. Goussault later offered Galula the directorship of the 5th Bureau in Orleansville, probably to replace Servier: see Cohen, *Galula*, 172.

31 On FAAD see House and MacMaster, *Paris 1961*, 142–3, 177–8.
32 P. and M.-C. Villatoux, *La République*, 553–4.
33 Galula, *Pacification*, 65–6; regarding Galula's promotion into the inner circle, see Cohen, *Galula*, 186–7.
34 See for example, Claude Paillat, *Deuxième Dossier Secret de l'Algérie, 1954-1958* (Paris: Presses de la Cité, 1962), 433–4, describing Papon's rejection, as IGAME of Constantine, of General Salan's directives to extend the COIN methods developed in Algiers to the eastern Algerian Constantinois.
35 House and MacMaster, *Paris 1961*, 72–3. The *Meublés* experiment was mentioned at the working party meeting of 23 July. So, too, were plans to replace the '*équipes itinérantes*' of the hotel inspectorate by permanent bureaux located in the densest Algerian quarters. The SAT implemented these plans from late August.
36 APP HA88, 'Note sur la répression,' 24 July 1958.
37 Mathias, *Galula in Algeria*, 77, Galula attended his first meeting of the Radio Steering Committee on 12 August.
38 Galula, *Pacification*, 52–3, 65.
39 Ali Haroun, *La 7e Wilaya. La Guerre du FLN en France, 1954-1962* (Paris: Seuil, 1986): chapter 5, 'Le second front', 85–111.
40 See the handwritten notes in APP HA 58, '*Convocation pour la réunion du 17 juillet 1958*,' describing 'insufficient judicial sentences' and 'inadequate repressive means'. The meeting was deferred to 23 July.
41 Minutes of 16 October CAP meeting.
42 Minutes of 23 July and 16 October CAP meetings.
43 Although no more than one in two Algerians resident in Paris paid dues to the FLN and Messali Hadj's MNA (*Mouvement national algérien*) was never totally defeated, the police found it difficult to collect intelligence on the Algerian community. Few Algerians were prepared to support the French government openly.
44 One conclusion of the third, and probably last, meeting of the CAP on 16 October was that 'The elimination of terrorism must of necessity precede any action intended to bring the two communities together.'
45 See APP HA 58.
46 Confidential note from Bérenguier to Papon, 'On the uses of psychological action in the fight against the FLN', 24 June 1959.
47 APP HA 58, Bérenguier added that their illiteracy was not a problem since these Algerians could ask for help from French colleagues or their employers.
48 APP HA 58, '*Note sur l'action psychologique menée par la Préfecture de police dans le département de la Seine*', undated but certainly September 1958.
49 APP HA 58, Maurice Papon note to Interior Minister, '*L'action sociale et psycho-sociale sur les FMA dans le département de la Seine*', 20 April 1959.
50 Galula, *Pacification*, 29.

12

Escaping the Empire's Shadow: British Military Thinking about Insurgency on the Eve of the Northern Ireland Troubles[1]

Huw Bennett

Soldiers stepped onto the streets of Northern Ireland on 14 August 1969, to help the civil authorities deal with the mounting disorder. Initially welcomed as peacekeepers, people came to question how long the soldiers would be hanging around. One day during these first months, soldiers were faced with a riot. Drawing equipment from the stores, they unfurled the banner normally used in these situations, with the phrase 'disperse or we fire' upon it. But the last time the banner had seen daylight was in Aden, and the inscription was in Arabic. The episode is seen to symbolize the British Army's 'importation of a "one-size-fits-all" strategy', profoundly colonial in character.[2] From the early entanglement in riot situations until at least the advent of police primacy in 1976, the army is portrayed as pivotal in the re-emergence of an old motif: Britain, the colonial power, bent on domination of Ireland.[3] The army is accused of reverting to a counter-insurgency approach developed in Palestine, Malaya, Kenya, Cyprus and Aden, applying tried and tested methods including mass arrests, internment without trial, the use of tear gas, and curfews.[4] For Douglas Porch, soldiers in Northern Ireland treated 'Catholics as just another criminal tribe on the fringes of empire'.[5] The notion was pervasive and persuasive, and remains so today.

Like much writing on counter-insurgency, the debate on the colonial legacy in Northern Ireland is primarily concerned with military tactics.[6] This chapter asks how far the colonial model illuminates British military thinking about insurgency just prior to its embroilment in Northern Ireland. Knowledge transfer from one campaign to the next has been a central theme in recent writing on British counter-insurgency.[7] Beyond low-level tactics, lesson-learning is unilluminating as a perspective on how armed conflicts evolved. The learning curve cannot be convincingly adhered to multiple conflicts because each possessed its own distinctive political attributes. Perhaps the most important insight to be gleaned from the learning genre is given by Georgina Sinclair, who succinctly points out how colonial policing was Irish in origin.[8] So if colonialism explains what happened in Northern Ireland, and Ireland explains what happened in the colonies, the result is a hollow circularity.

Counter-insurgency theory was most substantially elaborated in a colonial context, by such soldier-scholars as Hubert Lyautey, Joseph Gallieni and Charles Callwell.[9] So in its intellectual heritage and tactical content, all counter-insurgency thinking is colonial. This may be a truism, but it doesn't greatly illuminate how soldiers decided to act in the real world. However, the model cannot be entirely discarded because it does explain certain patterns, and because it shaped how many people read military behaviour at the time. Overall, the chapter argues the colonial framework is of limited value, and must be supplemented by placing the Northern Ireland conflict within a global context.

Colonialism has proven an influential idea in writings on the Northern Ireland Troubles. The historiography on the conflict falls into two broad traditions; the clash of cultures thesis, and the Republican tradition which attributes the conflict to British imperialism. The Republican tradition's truthfulness was, during the conflict's early stages at least, beside the point.[10] Many people ascribed to the interpretation and witnessed the British Army's acts through this lens. The colonial model, based upon ideological beliefs about the motives and character of policy, is often impervious to the evidence. It is influential enough for analysts based at the British military's own academies to espouse it.[11] Even leading unionist historians remarked how 'the British ruling class has always pursued an imperialist line'.[12] Colonialism is taken to be essential to understanding military conduct in Northern Ireland in the late 1960s into the mid-1970s. This chapter evaluates the colonial model's value in disclosing how the British Army thought about insurgency in the years immediately preceding the Troubles. Superficially, self-evidently true when events like the Falls Road curfew and Bloody Sunday are invoked, the model obscures the international dimensions to British military thought. Even more seriously, the model implies that attitudes and behaviour are transmitted without anyone noticing. Events in Northern Ireland in the 1970s happened because individuals made conscious decisions at the time.

Drawing on personal experience

Ideas cannot transport themselves. Scholarship on the Troubles often remarks upon the presence of men with colonial experience in Northern Ireland.[13] The necessary personnel records for an exhaustive analysis are closed, yet the overall picture is clear. Of those appointed General Officer Commanding-in-Chief Northern Ireland in the 1970s, General Sir Ian Freeland (GOC 1969–71) served in Cyprus in 1954–5.[14] General Sir Harry Tuzo (GOC 1971–3) spent his career in the Royal Artillery, winning a Military Cross for anti-tank fighting after Normandy. From 1963–5 he commanded 51st Gurkha Brigade in the Borneo Confrontation.[15] His successor, General Sir Frank King (GOC 1973–5), fought at Arnhem and then went on to hold appointments in Britain, the Middle East and Germany, none of them during a colonial counter-insurgency campaign.[16] Like Tuzo, Lieutenant-General Sir David House (GOC 1975–7) commanded 51st Gurkha Brigade in Borneo, from 1965 to 1967.[17] General Sir Timothy Creasey (GOC 1977–9) saw action in Kenya against the Mau Mau in 1955, in Northern Ireland in 1956 during the IRA's border campaign, in Aden from 1965 to 1967, and on secondment as the Commander of the Sultan's Armed Forces in Oman, 1972–5, during the Dhofar war. His obituary noted 'a reputation for toughness after a long record in colonial warfare'.[18]

Numerous individuals further down the command hierarchy can be found, and the histories of whole battalions recounted, to support the idea of knowledge transfer via personal experience. The 1st Royal Anglian Regiment, for example, participated in the Radfan operations in South Arabia from May to June 1964, and later in the year in Aden town. The battalion spent two years in Derry from July 1970.[19] Even some members of the Ulster Volunteer Force and the Provisional IRA boasted a personal history in the British Army's decolonization wars.[20] What inferences can be drawn from these connections? Aaron Edwards argues prior colonial experiences 'clouded the judgement of several Army commanders in Northern Ireland'.[21] We are left guessing as to whose judgement was clouded and how. According to Niall Ó Dochartaigh, 'The British army which came to Northern Ireland in August 1969 was very much a colonial army, experienced in colonial campaigns. It was therefore inclined to treat the situation as a colonial one.'[22] This is an incomplete representation. The army as an institution spent a great deal of time on matters quite unrelated to the colonies. Most junior officers and private soldiers sent to Northern Ireland lacked any colonial experience.

People form their outlooks from more than one experience, or learn from more than one teacher.[23] Returning to the senior commanders, apart from Creasey (who might be considered atypical), all these men spent the majority of their careers fighting or thinking about conventional warfare. Ian Freeland fought in Normandy, served in the British Army of the Rhine from 1946 to 1948, held several staff posts in Britain and commanded 12th Infantry Brigade in Germany from 1956 to 1957.[24] Harry Tuzo saw action in the Royal Artillery in France in 1940, and then in Normandy and Northwest Europe from 1944. He spent several spells in Germany after the war, including as Chief of Staff in the British Army of the Rhine (BAOR), 1967–9, as Commander-in-Chief of BAOR, 1973–6, and as Deputy Supreme Allied Commander Europe, 1976–8.[25] As noted above, Frank King had never fought in a counter-insurgency conflict before going to Northern Ireland. David House fought in Italy during the war, ran the British Commanders'-in-Chief Mission (BRIXMIS) in Berlin, 1967–9 (chiefly concerned with gathering intelligence on the Warsaw Pact), and was Chief of Staff to BAOR, 1971–3.[26] Even Timothy Creasey found himself devoted to conventional warfare at times; in Italy during the war, and commanding 11th Infantry Brigade in Germany, 1968–70.[27] Apart from Freeland, none of these men left private papers, so judging how far colonial experiences weighed on their decision-making in Northern Ireland is impossible. Claims about a person's professional background alone cannot establish any meaningful causal relationship between the colonies and Northern Ireland.

Oral history sources suggest those sent to Northern Ireland with prior knowledge about counter-insurgency were able to forget when necessary. The literature on organizational learning in war normally condemns forgetting as an impediment to military effectiveness.[28] However, forgetting can be beneficial. Terence Friend went to Northern Ireland in April 1970 with the Royal Artillery after undergoing 'very colonial' internal security training, so his unit ignored it.[29] John Cormack arrived in Northern Ireland in March 1971 with the Royal Engineers. He carried colonial baggage from the Cyprus Emergency, yet recalls the doctrine based on the colonies being discarded because it was 'totally inapplicable'.[30] Michael Gray commanded 1st Parachute Regiment in Belfast from October 1969. Facing riots, he devised his own procedures, finding the manuals useless. Gray 'spent a lot of time in the library in Belfast, looking up riot, insurrection, and the best guide I found was from the old Turkey, the way the Turks handled riots'. He also improvised, training his men in Aikido, so they could arrest people without having to hit them (too) hard.[31] Brigadier James Cowan, a seasoned counter-insurgent when he arrived to command 8th Infantry Brigade in Derry in January 1970, had fought in Kenya, Malaya and Aden. He commented how 'I can't imagine anything being similar to Northern Ireland. … It is utterly different from anything I've ever done in my life before.'[32] Asked why he thought things were unique there, he replied, 'The major difference is, one was operating in the United Kingdom. We were at home; these were allegedly our people, and I think it made a difference to the way people approached their jobs.'[33] Soldiers assessed the situation confronting them in Northern Ireland and understood that whatever lessons they had picked up elsewhere might be poorly suited to the strategic context.

Studying the colonial past to prepare for insurgencies in the future

The army certainly analysed the colonial past for lessons to apply in future insurgencies. Reports were routinely produced while operations were in progress, to guide units arriving mid-campaign, and assessments after they were finished. Written by the senior commander, these documents were produced for the campaigns in Palestine, Malaya, the Canal Zone, Kenya, Cyprus and Oman.[34] Whitehall twice attempted to capture lessons from South Arabia. Admiral Sir Michael Le Fanu, Commander-in-Chief Middle East, 1965–8, commented on the withdrawal from South Arabia, advocating a unified command structure and making recommendations on administration, but he noted the greatest lesson was that announcing a retreat two years in advance created immense difficulties.[35] These remarks were never disseminated. Nor were the lessons reached by the Foreign Office, who agreed on the disastrous effect of setting a deadline for independence, and queried whether anything could have been done to counter Arab nationalism.[36] Military commanders wrote about Aden in professional journals. Brigadier G. S. Heathcote, former Chief of Staff at Middle East Command, held that retaining the Aden base was counterproductive and an unjustified drain on Britain's resources.[37] Major Peter de la Billière, who spent time attached to the South Arabian Army, viewed Aden as likely to typify future guerrilla wars, and thus suitable for shaping counter-insurgency tactics. Aden exposed Britain's existing doctrine as too concerned with rural uprisings, whereas conflicts were likely to increasingly be urban-based. He also pointed to the National Liberation Front's skilful propaganda, successfully portraying the British as repressive to a global audience.[38] These were indeed themes to resurface in Northern Ireland.

The first doctrine publication on internal security to be produced after the Second World War was *Imperial Policing and Duties in Aid of the Civil Power*, in 1949. The manual drew on recent experience in Palestine, and gave detailed advice on how to conduct various tactical measures, such as road blocks, sweeps and village searches. Two theatre-specific handbooks were written in the 1950s: the *Conduct of Anti-Terrorist Operations in Malaya* (1952) and *A Handbook of Anti-Mau Mau Operations* (1954). They described how to conduct patrols and other drills in the jungle and forest conditions of Malaya and Kenya, and explained how to implement population control through such means as villagization and food denial. The general doctrine was updated in 1957 and 1963 in *Keeping the Peace. Operations in Support of the Civil Power*, the latter edition drawing on lessons from urban operations in Cyprus against EOKA, in addition to the earlier insights on the rural setting gleaned from Malaya. All these publications stressed the need to use the minimum force necessary, to gain the support of the population, and to build up an efficient intelligence machine. From 1949 there was a clear understanding of Maoist thinking on revolutionary war, and an appreciation that close civil–military cooperation was required to counter it.[39] The colonial doctrine upheld a clear separation between the military measures needed to counter civil unrest, such as riots and industrial action, and those for defeating serious insurrection, where a far more lenient attitude to the use of force was adopted.

The 1965 publication, *Quelling Insurgency*, designed to complement *Keeping the Peace*, contained elements from colonial settings, with synopses of the insurgencies in Palestine, Malaya, Cyprus and Kenya. Readers were advised to replicate the colonial committee system, to win the support of the people through fairness, and to move rural communities into protected villages.[40] The major publication written to inform counter-insurgency operations just as the army deployed to Northern Ireland was 1969's *Counter Revolutionary Operations*.[41] The publication has been criticized for being tainted by the Aden operations, and for ignoring relevant lessons from Aden due to a fixation with Malaya.[42] Brigadier Gavin Bulloch damned the publication for exuding 'the heavy scent of the jungle and rural operations in far away colonial territories'.[43] There are clear continuities with earlier doctrine, such as the need to secure popular backing for the government, coordination between civilian agencies and military commanders, and the use of minimum force and sound intelligence organization. Appropriate methods for tackling insurgency include population registration, resettlement, curfews, food denial and searches. The techniques adopted in Palestine, Malaya, Cyprus and Kenya are described in depth.[44] Part Two of *Counter Revolutionary Operations* gave specific tactical guidance for dealing with ambushes and other common problems, a number of them being illustrated with images from Aden. Many sections, such as that on screening operations, were almost identical to those from earlier manuals.[45] There is no mistaking the colonial imprint on the army's key doctrine publication as it went into Northern Ireland.

Military thought may be scrutinized by looking at what the army taught officers at the Staff College in Camberley, where they had time to consider the main strategic questions of the day. The 1966 course ran over five terms, from 15 January to 29 October. Students had a one-hour presentation on internal security and a ninety-minute presentation on psychological operations, before spending an hour and five minutes discussing internal security in their syndicate groups. They were shown the film 'Keeping the Peace', and heard talks on the Commonwealth and the Middle East situation (probably covering events in Aden).[46] The 1967 course introduced new studies of overseas operations, and used *Keeping the Peace* and *Quelling Insurgency* as core texts. In addition to 'Keeping the Peace', students were now shown films about Borneo and Aden too. Several colonial police officers were invited to offer advice.[47] To make the doctrine easier to digest, students were supplied with an aide memoire summarizing *Keeping the Peace*, and the relevant provisions from the *Manual of Military Law* and *Queen's Regulations*. The document reminded officers to maintain close liaison with the civil authorities, that the military commander alone could decide how to use force, and the procedures to be followed when opening fire.[48] Julian Paget's *Counter Insurgency Campaigning* and Robert Thompson's *Defeating Communist Insurgency* were suggested as readings.[49] They drew on the classic colonial lessons. Paget's book, for example, emphasized the need for good civil–military cooperation, command and control based on the committee system, sound intelligence, and gaining the support of the local population.[50] In 1969 Robert Thompson lectured the course on communist revolutionary warfare, before Lieutenant-General Sir Walter Walker lectured on the confrontation in Borneo.[51]

In syndicate discussions students were expected to 'be prejudiced, to some extent, by their own personal experience'. The Directing Staff were asked therefore to state the political characteristics were unique to each insurgency.[52] Class discussions on the 1967 course covered such counter-insurgency essentials as army–police relations, winning hearts and minds, and intelligence gathering. Yet the course also reached negative conclusions about colonial methods. The teaching notes reflected on the recent controversy surrounding interrogation methods:

> Some students may argue that the means justifies the end, and where the end involves human lives the means can be severe. In other words, torture = information = destruction of terrorists = saving innocent lives. However by denying the individual the basic human rights of justice and a free trial, we destroy the very principles which we are fighting to uphold or restore. It is interesting to see how the efforts of Amnesty International in Aden have resulted in an almost total abandonment of interrogation as a means of acquiring information.[53]

Students conducted three internal security exercises based on colonial scenarios. Exercise Rush Hour was set in Hong Kong, and required the students to think about handling serious riots in a large city.[54] The tasks involved planning joint police–military action, controlling vulnerable points, imposing a curfew, dispersing large crowds with troops, and imposing a cordon.[55] Guidance notes summed up how to conduct anti-riot operations – essential knowledge when soldiers came to support the police in Northern Ireland. For example, handling large crowds demanded advanced planning, military forces were best deployed 'before trouble starts', to deter potential rioters, the army needed to understand the unrest's political causes, and crowds must be given time and space to disperse.[56] The notes for 1968 added that CS gas should be used before resorting to firearms, that arrested rioters presented a valuable source of information and that helicopters were helpful as a command post, for observation, for dropping riot control agent and for communicating with crowds via loud speakers.[57]

These principles were grounded in extensive experience. That much of it was colonial does not detract from their validity.

The second internal security exercise taught at Camberley, Snake Bite, dealt with antiterrorism operations and their escalation into a confrontation of the type fought against Indonesia in Borneo.[58] To an extent the exercise was informed by colonial methods, but the campaign in Borneo involved British forces assisting the independent Malaysian government. The exercise considered the joint command of operations, intelligence matters, psychological operations and helicopter assaults. Students referred to Malaya, Kenya, Cyprus and Borneo when discussing intelligence organization. The Directing Staff emphasized how collective punishments (including curfews, fines and evictions) 'tend to punish simple people who have acted wrongly under threat of torture or death'. Officers were advised to avoid them as they alienated people, resulting in a diminished flow of intelligence. In addition, officers were told that brutal interrogation, rough searching and stealing from the population were counterproductive, even though 'we have been guilty of all on occasions in the past'.[59] These points portray the army as able to learn from the colonial past and embed the lessons into professional military education. But they clearly show the army rejecting common colonial methods, appreciating how a changing political environment rendered such techniques objectionable.

The final exercise inspired by the colonies was Seven Maids, referring to the Jebel Akhdar rebellion in Oman in the late 1950s and operations in the 1960s in the Radfan region of South Arabia. The aim was to study counter-insurgency in arid mountainous country and how it could develop into limited war in the desert.[60] The exercise was soon modified to draw heavily on events in Aden, to examine for the first time at Camberley urban terrorism – regarded as 'not a pleasant sort of op to deal with'. The essential challenges in these operations were the difficulty of identifying the terrorist, how to retaliate against terrorist attacks without harming innocent bystanders, and the terrorist's ability to quickly hide when being chased by the security forces. Commanders were likely to have to choose between following a 'Velvet Gloves' or a 'Mailed Fist' approach. The former was bound to please the United Nations, cause less suffering to civilians, produce fewer casualties to the security forces and gain support from the law abiding locals, but would be interpreted as weakness by the terrorists. Choosing the mailed fist stance promised to destroy the terrorist organization, but might be rendered impossible by 'the attendant publicity'. On balance the course favoured the hard line but expected the government to always prefer the softer policy.[61] The debate again highlights an awareness among the Directing Staff that military preferences, perhaps shaped by colonial experience, would have to give way in the future to political constraints that made a very tough security posture beyond the pale.

Searching globally for inspiration on insurgency

British Army officers looked for ideas about insurgencies from their closest allies. Richard Drayton points out imperial history's concentration on national perspectives, downplaying widespread cooperation between the major European empires over centuries.[62] His observation that states shared power beneath the surface is applicable to the counter-insurgency era after the Second World War. Jonathan Hyslop argues an international culture of military professionalism emerged in the nineteenth century: armed forces, despite their national differences, shared instrumental rationality as a core value. The concept of the concentration camp was disseminated among military officers around the world by the new forms of print media, resulting in armed forces adopting the method between 1896 and 1907.[63] Anthony King argues that since the Cold War's end, Western armed forces have formed a close professional network around NATO's operational headquarters.[64] These insights help in grasping the British Army's thinking about internal war, counter-insurgency and related topics in the 1960s, and are a welcome corrective to an over-concentration in strategic studies on national ways of war. The evidence presented here suggests that although a Western military network may have flourished most fully in the 1990s, the origins of this process can be found earlier, certainly influencing how armed forces thought about revolutionary war in the 1960s.

Doctrine took inspiration from beyond the British colonial world. *Quelling Insurgency* cited the French campaign in Algeria and American operations in Vietnam, and provided synopses on the conflicts in Vietnam, Algeria and Cuba. The decisive role played by external support in sustaining an insurgency, and the power of world opinion to undermine the counter-insurgents were analysed. Readers were advised to consult Bernard Fall's *Street without Joy* on the French in Indochina, T. N. Greene's *The Guerilla and How to Fight Him* (selected articles from the US *Marine Corps Gazette*, covering the conflicts in Greece, Malaya, Indochina, Russia, Cuba, Cyprus, Vietnam and Algeria) and F. M. Osanka's *Modern Guerilla Warfare* (an American volume covering guerrilla wars from the Second World War to 1962).[65] *Counter Revolutionary Operations* opened with a section on Vietnam, then the largest revolutionary war in progress in the world.[66] The doctrine writers wanted to develop the most effective methods to combat insurgency, and were ready to take good ideas from wherever they could be found.

Ideas about revolutionary war, incorporating age-old guerrilla tactics, emerged in the 1930s and were made famous by Mao Zedong.[67] An intensive debate took place in the French armed forces after their defeat in Indochina at the hands of the Vietminh. These writings informed militaries elsewhere and still colour doctrine today.[68] The first major study was General Lionel-Max Chassin's 1952 book, *La conquête de la Chine par Mao Tsé-Toung*. Revolutionary war was understood to be a decisive turning point in military history, where an inferior force could defeat a modern army by gaining popular support. Unified political-military organization and psychological operations were now critical elements in war.[69] *Guerre révolutionnaire* advocates closely studied Lenin and Mao, concluding the primary threat to Western security came from communist expansion in the Third World.[70] For Lieutenant Colonel Charles Lacheroy revolutionary war unfolded in five phases (compared to the three identified by Mao). First came shocking, random violence, such as bombings, intended to cause confusion and gain publicity. In the second phase assassinations were directed at those labelled traitors to the cause. Low-level individuals were killed, to intimidate the masses, who became too frightened to assist the police. In phase three military units were formed, and commissars began mobilising the masses. Phase four saw the rebel army organizing into larger units, while the civil section extended into fields such as justice. Finally, the rebel forces expanded into regular formations, and a complete shadow state was created.[71] Other writers broadly agreed with these five stages.

Revolutionary warfare theory denied rebellions stemmed from genuine grievances. They were believed to derive from indoctrination promoted by external actors. Violence caused by illegitimate forces therefore precluded negotiation – only total victory over the rebels would suffice. French theorists proposed five remedies: cutting the rebels off from their foreign sponsors, destroying the enemy's military formations (aided by psychological operations), protecting communications and economic centres, mobilizing the masses, resettlement or population control, and re-educating captured rebels. Administrative measures and psychological action were vital to winning, as was total backing from the government and nation to allow the army to prosecute a protracted campaign.[72] After the Algerian War ended, French military attention switched to nuclear deterrence and European security.[73] Yet the French contribution to strategic theory survived: French officers disseminated their ideas at American staff colleges, the Rand Corporation and Harvard University.[74] The Americans also possessed extensive experience in small wars.[75] The US Army's post-war doctrine was initially influenced by Axis methods during the Second World War, but in the 1950s took account of events in Malaya, Indochina and then of French thinking on revolutionary war and its application in Algeria. From December 1960 American doctrine blended ideas from the US, British and French armies. By 1964 the US Army possessed a complete family of COIN manuals, all couched within the revolutionary warfare perspective of a global struggle against communism.[76] President Kennedy's administration viewed insurgency as a serious threat to world order, brought about by communist manipulation of developing countries, which had to be confronted by the West.[77] Though containing many tactical ideas from colonial times, military thinking about insurgency in the 1960s assumed a changing political climate.

British military thought took a similar interest in revolutionary war. Students at the Staff College heard lectures on communist theory and revolutionary warfare.[78] Particular attention was paid to communist doctrine because even those who led nationalist rebellions tended to copy communist methods.[79] Echoing French ideas, the Directing Staff at Camberley painted communism as 'the greatest threat to law, order and peace in the world today'.[80] Students were exposed to lengthy discussions on communist 'gobbledegook' and warned its exponents wanted 'to spread the ideology to all countries of the world'.[81] The Commandant maintained links with staff colleges in NATO and the Commonwealth.[82] In March 1969 the Commandant visited staff colleges and combat development establishments in Canada and the United States, and sent his Directing Staff on liaison trips to the Far East, the Gulf, Germany, Canada and the United States.[83]

In 1966 students at Camberley had a lecture on French operations in Algeria from Lieutenant Colonel Pagès, and talks on Vietnam from Colonel Napier, the Defence Attaché in Saigon, Major Bickston from the US Infantry, and Major General Harry Kinnard, who pioneered airmobile tactics with the US Cavalry.[84] In 1967 a British liaison instructor in France returned to Camberley to present on 'French Higher Military Thinking'.[85] Students were recommended to read the writings of Mao Zedong and Che Guevara, Osanka's *Modern Guerilla Warfare*, C. N. M. Blair's *Guerilla Warfare* (by a British Army officer, chiefly about allied support for guerrillas fighting the Axis),

Virgil Ney's *Notes on Guerilla War* (a book about general principles with a focus on propaganda, by a US Army officer), M. W Brown's *The New Face of War* (covering American operations in Vietnam, 1961–4) and John McCuen's *The Art of Counter Revolutionary War* (an American text shaped by French theory).[86]

Students conducted exercises based on the insurgencies fought by other countries. Exercise Moulin Rouge simulated the position faced by the United States in 1961 when it began increasing military aid to South Vietnam. The exercise aimed to highlight the political background to all insurgencies and the challenges inherent in working with local allies.[87] Exercise Red Rice, introduced in 1967, also bore a resemblance to Vietnam in the early 1960s.[88] Students were asked to avoid the 'danger that our mil thinking will be over-influenced by the experiences of past campaigns', especially Malaya. The exercise covered basic counter-insurgency principles like the need to protect the population, to find a political solution and to forge effective civil–military cooperation.[89] These principles were seen to have universal validity, rather than deriving from a uniquely British approach. Red Rice was written by Directing Staff member Lieutenant Colonel James Glover.[90] He served in Malaya, going on to command 3rd Royal Green Jackets in Northern Ireland, 1970–1, and to serve as Commander Land Forces in Northern Ireland, 1979–80.[91] Senior officers were evidently capable of escaping from the confines of their own experiences when thinking about how to tackle internal security threats.

For the British Army, revolutionary warfare was defined as 'the process, which includes the use of political, economic and military measures, that militant communists or nationalists, working mainly within the country, employ to weaken and overthrow legally constituted governments'.[92] *Counter Revolutionary Operations* explained how

> the outbreak of insurrection, however deep the groundswell of disaffection, is never spontaneous. … Any insurrection therefore must have its roots in conspiracy, by definition the work initially of a close knit gang and it is at this conspiratorial stage of development that it is most easily checked, either by measures of political concession or by counter subversive action.[93]

By bracketing together attempts to weaken a government with a desire to overthrow a government, military thinking conflated disorder with insurrection – a dangerous exaggeration, prompting officers to find an existential threat to society where none existed. In the British interpretation, in contrast to the French position, unrest was believed to derive from 'social discontent, racial torment and nationalistic fervour'. Multiple potential sources for uprisings were acknowledged, avoiding categorical claims about communist conspiracy, but the belief remained that 'all revolutionary wars may ultimately have Communist backing'.[94] Where Charles Lacheroy found five phases in revolutionary war, British thinking discerned four. Doctrine described the phases as preparatory, active resistance, insurgency and counteroffensive (renamed 'open offensive' in 1969).[95]

During the preparatory phase, the rebels organized themselves in the community, recruiting new members, indoctrinating and training them. In the active resistance phase steps were taken to increase popular support for the revolutionary movement. The rebels killed people who refused to support the revolution, and anyone in a position of authority, to remove the state's leadership capacity. Propaganda discredited the government amid a 'climate of dissidence', and there would be waves of civil disobedience and industrial unrest. Terrorist attacks commonly occurred in the active resistance phase. The insurgency phase began when the revolutionary movement had gained enough military strength to launch guerrilla attacks on the government forces. The insurgents gradually came to achieve effective control over specific areas, displacing government agencies. Finally, the open offensive phase was launched when the insurgents judged the balance of power had swung in their favour. Large areas of the country were administered by the insurgents and guerrilla attacks on the state were complemented by mobile regular assaults. The government would eventually be defeated by conventional operations.[96] So British thinking shared the French penchant for categorizing insurgency into phases, but different slightly in how the categories were conceived.

Counter revolutionary warfare aimed to 'destroy totally the revolutionary movement'; this was 'not purely a matter of soldiers killing insurgents'. Patience was essential as these conflicts lasted for a long time.[97] British thinking stressed the need to win popular support by instituting political and economic reforms – after the military had brought an area under control.[98] Writing in the *Army Quarterly*, Major O'Ballance advised the military to take an interest in insurgencies at an early stage, and to concentrate on building up the intelligence machine. Auxiliary forces should be formed, to free up regular soldiers from guard duties for offensive operations. Above all, a reform programme boasting real material benefits was the most effective means for combating a communist uprising.[99] Major Tee concurred, warning against trying to destroy the enemy in an insurgency – instead the causes for rebellion had to be addressed.[100] Students at the Staff College were asked to ponder the negative consequences to taking a hard-line policy. For example, banning the revolutionary political party would only drive the movement underground, making it more difficult to monitor. Tough measures were only likely to work if a strong central government existed – a rarity in insurgencies – and risked prompting criticism at the United Nations. More positive methods included arresting ringleaders and confiscating guns.[101]

In common with French and American thought, psychological operations assumed a prominent part in British thinking, defining them as 'the planned use of propaganda in support of our military action or presence designed to influence to our advantage the opinions, emotions, attitudes and behaviour of enemy, neutral or friendly groups'.[102] Students at the Staff College were advised to avoid regarding psy-ops as a silver bullet, and rather to win over the local population with a long-term propaganda campaign.[103] Allowing a free press to exist during an insurgency was preferable to the inevitable condemnation that would come otherwise, though subversive propaganda could be banned. Creating a good working relationship with the press meant the government could communicate effectively with the people, boost security force morale and increase sympathy for the government's position abroad. Above all, psychological operations had to be carefully coordinated across all agencies to achieve a coherent and sustained message.[104] Special Forces could be deployed to acquire intelligence from the population, monitor hostile frontiers, locate guerrilla bases, attack guerrilla forces in cooperation with regular infantry and train local forces to fight the insurgency.[105] Whether these notions were especially innovative is questionable. Instead they highlight how many principles in counter-insurgency have a generic quality.

Counter Revolutionary Operations gave detailed guidance on the tactics to be applied in dealing with civil disobedience, unlawful assemblies, riots, urban terrorism and rural insurgency. The degree of force that could be used depended upon the political climate. Soldiers were expected to adhere to the minimum force principle 'most conscientiously' when confronted with civil disturbances not amounting to rebellion. When facing 'more violent threats with serious political undertones', commanders were allowed 'some latitude' to exert sufficient force. Indeed, armed rebellion may justify soldiers using more violence than immediately required, to 'show firmness of purpose to dissident elements'. On the other hand, an open display of force might do more harm than good; if possible, the commander should take advice from the civil authorities on the prevailing political circumstances. The doctrine described how to deal with unlawful assemblies and riots. Soldiers could only open fire against rioters if they were armed and 'in a position to inflict grievous injury'. Again reflecting on the connection between threat and response, the doctrine permitted firearms to be used 'as soon as the intention of the insurgents to carry out their purpose by force of arms is shown by open acts of violence'.[106] Any terrorist attacks – whether sabotage or assassination – could signify intensifying local violence, 'or could be part of the first phase of revolutionary war'.[107] By deciding violent incidents constituted an insurgency, the army therefore judged a violent reaction to be justified.

Conclusion

When the mass arrests, brutal interrogations, controversial shootings, curfews and internment without trial seen in Northern Ireland in the early 1970s are described, comparisons with earlier events in Palestine, Malaya, Kenya, Cyprus and Aden become almost automatic. The colonial model is seductive precisely because of its simplicity. Key figures in Belfast, like Frank Kitson, came to the conflict with knowledge about counter-insurgency acquired in the colonies, so does it not mean that they must have imposed a colonial strategy? To an extent the suggestion is irrefutable. The tactical repertoire displayed in Northern Ireland did replicate methods witnessed in the colonies. Whether these practices would have been applied against people in mainland Britain, without cultural assumptions about the Irish, is open to question. Military thinking suggests the response corresponded to the threat environment as much as it derived from beliefs about the opposing population. Conduct in Northern Ireland also replicated methods applied in Algeria, Vietnam, Afghanistan, Iraq and countless other insurgencies. Those mainstays of counter-insurgency – coordinated civil–military command arrangements, intensive intelligence gathering, trying to win popular support and so on – are generic military principles. They offer only limited insight into the actual conduct of war.

British Army officers reflected on their counter-insurgency heritage with serious intent – to beat insurgents in the future. The robotic importation of methods from the colonial era would have smacked of intellectual professional negligence. Instead, officers took forward those principles which seemed to have validity, such as ideas about riot control based on practice in Hong Kong. These could include highly destructive principles, such as the urge to exploit inter-communal tensions and manipulate societal divisions. Tolerating Home Guard abuses in Kenya and collusion with loyalist paramilitaries in Northern Ireland followed the same logic. At the same time, officers were aware that many colonial techniques were now unacceptable. Carefully examining contemporary conflicts, the army concluded that collective punishments and more broadly a 'mailed fist' approach was likely to prove counterproductive. Perhaps for this very reason several prominent colonial tactics were abandoned: the death penalty, mass forced resettlement and the free use of air power being central examples.

Great interest was taken in what allies were doing, or had done in the past, especially when it came to Algeria and Vietnam. Inspiration was found on the important part played by external backers in fuelling an insurgency and on seeing local conflicts in a global perspective. These ideas, and more besides, may have originated from within the British world, yet their framing in a comparative perspective shows how far the army saw counter-insurgency as a core task for all major Western armed forces. A significant shift in the global counter-insurgency era, shaped by French and American theory on revolutionary war, was to connect low-level civil unrest with large-scale insurrection. The British Army had long possessed tactical doctrine for handling riots on the one hand and rebellions on the other. But they were formally separated. New thinking on revolutionary war in the 1960s inserted the assumption that riots were always likely to descend into something worse, due to the machinations of communist troublemakers. The British Army thus entered the Northern Ireland conflict with an intellectual predisposition to expect escalation into full-blown insurgency. Western thinking on revolutionary war, rather than colonial methods, made the army ready to see a planned insurrection where chaotic communal violence existed. Some colonial methods were then applied in Northern Ireland, but only the wider international perspective explains why they were ever thought necessary.

Notes

1 Earlier versions of this chapter were presented at the universities of Exeter and Northampton. Thanks to Martin Thomas, Gareth Curless, Matthew McCormack, Jim Beach, David French, Richard Drayton, Aaron Cripps, Mike Rainsborough and Mike Finch for their kind advice and assistance.

2 Aaron Edwards, 'Misapplying Lessons Learned? Analysing the Utility of British Counterinsurgency Strategy in Northern Ireland, 1971-76', *Small Wars and Insurgencies* 21, no. 2 (2010): 312.

3 John Newsinger, 'From Counter-Insurgency to Internal Security: Northern Ireland 1969-1992', *Small Wars and Insurgencies* 6, no. 1 (1995): 90.

4 Paul Dixon, '"Hearts and Minds"? British Counter-Insurgency Strategy in Northern Ireland', *Journal of Strategic Studies* 32, no. 3 (2009): 445; Martin Thomas, *Fight or Flight: Britain, France, and their Roads from Empire* (Oxford: Oxford University Press, 2014), 365; Alexander Alderson, 'Britain', in *Understanding Counterinsurgency: Doctrine, Operations, and Challenges*, ed. Thomas Rid and Thomas Keaney (London: Routledge, 2010), 39; Caroline Kennedy-Pipe, *The Origins of the Present Troubles in Northern Ireland* (London: Longman, 1997), 54.

5   Douglas Porch, *Counterinsurgency: Exposing the Myths of the New Way of War* (Cambridge: Cambridge University Press, 2013), 282.

6   Porch, *Counterinsurgency*, 9.

7   Georgina Sinclair, *At the End of the Line: Colonial Policing and the Imperial Endgame 1945-80* (Manchester: Manchester University Press, 2006); Victoria Nolan, *Military Leadership and Counterinsurgency: The British Army and Small War Strategy since World War II* (London: I. B. Tauris, 2012); David French, *The British Way in Counter-Insurgency, 1945-1967* (Oxford: Oxford University Press, 2011), 200–18.

8   Georgina Sinclair, 'The "Irish" Policeman and the Empire: Influencing the Policing of the British Empire-Commonwealth', *Irish Historical Studies* 36, no. 142 (2008): 173–87.

9   Thomas Rid, 'The Nineteenth Century Origins of Counterinsurgency Doctrine', *Journal of Strategic Studies* 33, no. 5 (2010): 727–58. See also Beatrice Heuser, *The Evolution of Strategy: Thinking War from Antiquity to the Present* (Cambridge: Cambridge University Press, 2010), 387–437.

10 Richard Bourke, *Peace in Ireland: The War of Ideas* (London: Pimlico, 2012), xii.

11 Edwards, 'Misapplying Lessons Learned?', Rod Thornton, 'Getting it Wrong: The Crucial Mistakes Made in the Early Stages of the British Army's Deployment to Northern Ireland (August 1969 to March 1972)', *Journal of Strategic Studies* 30, no. 1 (2007): 73–107.

12 Paul Bew and Henry Patterson, *The British State and the Ulster Crisis* (London: Verso, 1985), 143.

13 David Benest, 'Aden to Northern Ireland', in *Big Wars and Small Wars: The British Army and the Lessons of War in the Twentieth Century*, ed. Hew Strachan (London: Routledge, 2006), 128; Tony Craig, 'From Countersubversion to Counter-insurgency – Comparing MI5's Role in British Guiana, Aden and the Northern Ireland civil rights crisis', *Journal of Intelligence History* 14, no. 1 (2015): 40–1.

14 'Sir Ian Freeland', *The Times*, 23 November 1979.

15 Toby Harnden, 'Tuzo, Sir Harry Craufurd (1917–1998)', *Oxford Dictionary of National Biography*, Oxford University Press, 2004, http://www.oxforddnb.com/view/article/70774 (accessed 11 November 2014; 'TUZO, Gen. Sir Harry (Craufurd)', *Who Was Who*, online edn, Oxford University Press, 2014, http://www.ukwhoswho.com/view/article/oupww/whowaswho/U182457 (accessed 11 November 2014).

16 'General Sir Frank King', *The Times*, 2 April 1998.

17 'Lieutenant-General Sir David House', *The Daily Telegraph*, 9 August 2012, http://www.telegraph.co.uk/news/obituaries/9465218/Lieutenant-General-Sir-David-House.html (accessed 11 November 2014).

18 'Sir Timothy Creasey', *The Times*, 7 October 1986.

19 Michael Barthorp, *Crater to the Creggan: A History of the Royal Anglian Regiment, 1964-1974* (London: Leo Cooper, 1976), 34–5, 98.

20 Michael Dewar, *The British Army in Northern Ireland* (London: Guild Publishing, 1985), 24; William Beattie Smith, *The British State and the Northern Ireland Crisis, 1969-73: From Violence to Power Sharing* (Washington, DC: United States Institute of Peace Press, 2011), 116.

21 Edwards, 'Misapplying Lessons Learned?', 314.

22 Niall Ó Dochartaigh, *From Civil Rights to Armalites: Derry and the Birth of the Irish Troubles* (Basingstoke: Palgrave Macmillan, 2005), 138.

23 Robert Gerwarth and Stephan Malinowski, 'Hannah Arendt's Ghosts: Reflections on the Disputable Path from Windhoek to Auschwitz', *Central European History* 42 (2009): 291.

24 'FREELAND, Lt-Gen. Sir Ian (Henry)', *Who Was Who*, online edn, Oxford University Press, 2014, http://www.ukwhoswho.com/view/article/oupww/whowaswho/U154617 (accessed 11 November 2014).

25 Harnden, 'Tuzo, Sir Harry Craufurd (1917–1998)'.

26 'HOUSE, Lt-Gen. Sir David (George)', *Who Was Who*, online edn, Oxford University Press, 2014, http://www.ukwhoswho.com/view/article/oupww/whowaswho/U20869 (accessed 11 November 2014).

27 'Sir Timothy Creasey', *The Times*, 7 October 1986.

28 For an excellent study, see Sergio Catignani, 'Coping with Knowledge: Organizational Learning in the British Army?', *Journal of Strategic Studies* 37, no. 1 (2014): 30–64.

29 Imperial War Museum Sound Archive [hereafter IWMSA]: 33124, Terence Friend (29 Commando Regiment, Royal Artillery), tape 5.

30 IWMSA: 21564, John Cormack (21 Field Engineer Regiment, Royal Engineers), tape 23.

31 IWMSA: 28362, Michael Gray (1st Parachute Regiment), tape 30.

32 IWMSA: 18802, James Cowan (8th Infantry Brigade), tape 25.

33 IWMSA: 18802, James Cowan (8th Infantry Brigade), tape 26.

34 French, *The British Way in Counter-Insurgency*, 201–2, 211.

35 The National Archives [hereafter TNA] DEFE 4/223: Chiefs of Staff meeting minutes, COS 85th Meeting/67, 5 December 1967.

36 TNA FCO 8/253: Minute by D. J. McCarthy to Sir Richard Beaumont, 20 November 1967.

37 Brigadier G. S. Heathcote, 'Aden – A Reason Why', *RUSI Journal* CXIII, no. 650 (1968): 139–42.

38 Major Peter de la Billière, 'The Changing Pattern of Guerrilla Warfare', *RUSI Journal* CXIV, no. 656 (1969): 42–4.

39 French, *The British Way in Counter-Insurgency*, 203–7.

40 Joint Services Command and Staff College Archive [hereafter JSCSC]: *Quelling Insurgency*, JSP 1, Supplement (QI), Joint Warfare Committee, 1 January 1965, especially 5-1 to 5-2, 7-1, 9-2.

41 TNA WO 279/649: *Land Operations. Volume III – Counter Revolutionary Operations. Part I – Principles and General Aspects*. Army Code No. 70516 (Part I), 29 August 1969.

42 Andrew Sanders, 'Northern Ireland: The Intelligence War 1969-75', *British Journal of Politics and International Relations* 13, no. 2 (2011): 4; John Bew, 'Mass, Methods, and Means: The Northern Ireland "Model" of Counter-insurgency', in *The New Counter-insurgency Era in Critical Perspective*, ed. Celeste Ward Gventer, David Martin Jones and M. L. R. Smith (Basingstoke: Palgrave Macmillan, 2014), 160.

43 Gavin Bulloch, 'The Development of Doctrine for Counter Insurgency – The British Experience', *British Army Review* 111 (1995): 23.

44 TNA WO 279/649: *Counter Revolutionary Operations. Part I*, 41, 45, 69, 85, 100, 119–30.

45 TNA WO 279/650: *Land Operations. Volume III – Counter Revolutionary Operations. Part 2 – Internal Security*. Army Code No. 70516 (Part 2), 26 November 1969.

46 JSCSC: Army Staff Course 1966, volume 1; Staff College Outline Programme 1966.

47 JSCSC: Army Staff Course 1967, volume 5; 'Overseas Operations 1. An introduction to the series'.

48 JSCSC: Army Staff Course 1967, volume 5; 'Instructions to Officers Acting in Aid of the Civil Power for the Preservation of Law and Order', Army Code No. 70014, 12 August 1964.

49 JSCSC: Army Staff Course 1967, supplementary records; 'Annex B to Geo-political studies 3. Recommended books'.

50 Julian Paget, *Counter-Insurgency Campaigning* (London: Faber and Faber, 1967).

51 JSCSC: Army Staff Course 1969, Provisional Programme Third Term.

52 JSCSC: Army Staff Course 1967, volume 5; 'Overseas Operations 2. Internal Security. DS Notes'.

53 JSCSC: Army Staff Course 1967, volume 5; 'Overseas Operations 2. Internal Security. DS Notes'.

54 JSCSC: Army Staff Course 1966, volume 12; 'Exercise Rush Hour. General Instructions'; Army Staff Course 1967, Volume 10; Army Staff Course 1968; 'Exercise Rush Hour. Introductory Note. DS Only'.

55 JSCSC: Army Staff Course 1966, volume 12; 'Exercise Rush Hour. DS Notes to Problem 1'; 'Exercise Rush Hour. DS Notes to Problem 2'; 'Exercise Rush Hour. DS Notes to Problem 3. Conduct of Problem'; 'Exercise Rush Hour. DS Notes to Problem 4'; 'DS Notes to Problem 5'.

56 JSCSC: Army Staff Course 1966, volume 12; 'DS Notes to Problem 5.b'.

57 JSCSC: Army Staff Course 1968; 'Exercise Rush Hour. DS Notes to Problem 4'.

58 JSCSC: Army Staff Course 1966, volume 12; 'Exercise Snake Bite. Gen Instr'.

59 JSCSC: Army Staff Course 1966, volume 12; 'Exercise Snake Bite. DS Notes to Problem 2'; 'DS Notes to Problem 3'; 'DS Notes to Problem 4'.

60 JSCSC: Army Staff Course 1966, supplementary records; 'Exercise Seven Maids. Gen Instrs'.

61 JSCSC: Army Staff Course 1968, 'Ex Seven Maids. DS Notes to Problem 5'.

62 Richard Drayton, 'Masked Condominia: Pan-European collaboration in the History of Imperialism, c. 1500 to the present', *Global History Review* 5 (2012): 308–31.

63 Jonathan Hyslop, 'The Invention of the Concentration Camp: Cuba, Southern Africa and the Philippines, 1896-1907', *South African Historical Journal* 63, no. 2 (2011): 251–76.

64 Anthony King, *The Transformation of Europe's Armed Forces: From the Rhine to Afghanistan* (Cambridge: Cambridge University Press, 2011), 65–102.

65 JSCSC: *Quelling Insurgency*, iv, 3–3, 3–4, 3–5.

66 TNA WO 279/649: *Land Operations. Volume III – Counter Revolutionary Operations. Part I*, 1–2, 119–30.

67 John Shy and Thomas W. Collier, 'Revolutionary War', in *Makers of Modern Strategy: From Machiavelli to the Nuclear Age*, ed. Peter Paret (Oxford: Clarendon Press, 1986), 817, 822.

68 Etienne de Durand, 'France', in *Understanding Counterinsurgency: Doctrine, Operations, and Challenges*, ed. Thomas Rid and Thomas Keaney (London: Routledge, 2010), 16.

69 Peter Paret, *French Revolutionary Warfare from Indochina to Algeria: The Analysis of a Political and Military Doctrine* (London: Pall Mall Press, 1964), 7.

70 Christopher Cradock and M. L. R. Smith, '"No Fixed Values": A Reinterpretation of the Influence of the Theory of *Guerre Révolutionnaire* and the Battle of Algiers, 1956-1957', *Journal of Cold War Studies* 9, no. 4 (2007): 74–6.

71 Mike Finch, 'The Dimensions of Totality in the French Theory of *la Guerre Révolutionnaire*', draft paper (King's College London, April 2015), 3, 6–8.

72 Paret, *French Revolutionary Warfare*, 22–4, 26, 32.

73 Martin Alexander, 'Seeking France's "Lost Soldiers": Reflections on the French Military Crisis in Algeria', in *Crisis and Renewal in France, 1918-1962*, ed. Martin Alexander and Ken Moure (Oxford: Berghahn, 2002), 247, 258.

74 Porch, *Counterinsurgency*, 163, 176.

75 See Andrew Birtle, *U.S. Army Counterinsurgency and Contingency Operations Doctrine 1860-1941* (Washington, DC: US Army Center of Military History, 2009).

76 Andrew Birtle, *U.S. Army Counterinsurgency and Contingency Operations Doctrine 1942-1976* (Washington, DC.: US Army Center of Military History, 2007), 132, 162–3, 166, 249.

77 Douglas Blaufarb, *The Counterinsurgency Era: U.S. Doctrine and Performance, 1950 to the Present* (New York: The Free Press, 1977), 52–88.

78 JSCSC: Army Staff Course 1966, volume 1; programme for 34th week.

79 JSCSC: *Quelling Insurgency*, iv; TNA WO 279/649: *Land Operations. Volume III – Counter Revolutionary Operations. Part I*, 1.

80 JSCSC: Army Staff Course 1967, supplementary records; 'Geo-political studies 1. DS Notes'.

81 JSCSC: Army Staff Course 1967, supplementary records; 'Geo-political studies 2. Communism. DS Notes'.

82 TNA WO 231/102: 'Study of Staff College Syllabus', Colonel W. Bate, for Major General, Commandant, Camberley, 20 September 1966. Annex A, 'The Army Staff Course. Directive to the Commandant Staff College, Camberley'.

83 JSCSC: Army Staff Course 1969, 'Staff College Report for 1969', by Major General J. A. T. Sharp, 18 December 1969.

84 JSCSC: Army Staff Course 1966, volume 1; course programme.

85 TNA WO 231/102: Letter from Major J. R. Weaver, for Director of Army Training, to Commandants of the Imperial Defence College, Joint Services Staff College Latimer, and Staff College Camberley, 6 February 1967; Letter to Ministry of Defence from Colonel M. E. Tickell, for Major General, Commandant, 17 February 1967.

86 JSCSC: Army Staff Course 1967, supplementary records; 'Annex B to Geo-political studies 3. Recommended books'.

87 JSCSC: Army Staff Course 1966, supplementary records; 'Exercise Moulin Rouge. DS Introduction'.

88 The exercise remained essentially the same in 1968 and 1969: JSCSC: Army Staff Course 1968, 'Ex Red Rice. DS Notes'; Army Staff Course 1969, 'Ex Red Rice. DS Notes. Introduction'.

89 JSCSC: Army Staff Course 1967, supplementary records; 'Ex Red Rice. DS Notes'.

90 JSCSC: Army Staff Course 1967, supplementary records; 'Ex Red Rice. DS Notes. Summing up'.

91 'GLOVER, Gen. Sir James (Malcolm)', *Who Was Who*, online edn, Oxford University Press, 2014; online edn, April 2014, http://www.ukwhoswho.com/view/article/oupww/whoswho/U178669 (accessed 31 May 2015).

92 JSCSC: Army Staff Course 1967, volume 5; 'Overseas Operations 1. An introduction to the series'.

93 TNA WO 279/649: *Land Operations. Volume III – Counter Revolutionary Operations. Part I*, 130.

94 JSCSC: Army Staff Course 1967, supplementary records; 'Geo-political studies 3. Revolutionary warfare'.

95   JSCSC: *Quelling Insurgency*, 1–2. The phases were taught at Camberley; see, for
     example, Army Staff Course 1967; supplementary records, 'Geo-political studies 3.
     Revolutionary Warfare. DS Notes'.
96   TNA WO 279/649: *Land Operations. Volume III – Counter Revolutionary
     Operations. Part I*, 23–7.
97   JSCSC: Army Staff Course 1967, supplementary records; 'Geo-political studies 3.
     Revolutionary warfare'.
98   JSCSC: *Quelling Insurgency*, iv, 4–1.
99   Major Edgar O'Ballance, 'Thoughts on Countering Communist Insurgent War',
     Army Quarterly and Defence Journal LXXXXIII, no. 1 (1966): 72–9.
100 Major W. S. Tee, 'Solutions in Counter-Insurgency', *Army Quarterly and Defence
     Journal* LXXXXV, no. 1 (1967): 70–3.
101 JSCSC: Army Staff Course 1968; 'Geo-political studies 3. Revolutionary warfare. DS
     Notes'.
102 JSCSC: Army Staff Course 1967, volume 5; 'Overseas Operations 1. An introduction
     to the series'.
103 JSCSC: Army Staff Course 1967, volume 5; 'Overseas Operations 3. Psyops. DS
     Notes'.
104 JSCSC: *Quelling Insurgency*, 4–2, 7–2.
105 JSCSC: Army Staff Course 1967, supplementary records; 'The Special Air Service'.
106 TNA WO 279/650: *Land Operations. Volume III – Counter Revolutionary
     Operations. Part 2*, 1, 2–3, 13, 75–7.
107 TNA WO 279/649: *Land Operations. Volume III – Counter Revolutionary
     Operations. Part I*, 14.

13

Shadow Warriors: The Phoenix Program and American Clandestine Policing in Vietnam

Jeremy Kuzmarov

Their boys did it for faith, ours did it for money.
Georgie Ann Geyer, 'The CIA's Hired Killers', *True Magazine*, February 1970

If the Union had had a Phoenix program during the civil war, among the targets were likely to have been Jefferson Davis, or the mayor of Macon Georgia.
Ogden Reid (D-NY), head of congressional fact finding mission

In November 1967, Frank Armbruster of the Hudson Institute drafted a policy brief which provided a blueprint for Operation Phoenix, whose goal was to dismantle the leadership of the Vietnamese revolutionary movement through improved coordination between police and intelligence agents. Written in cold, antiseptic language, the report included a favourable reference to a RAND Corporation study by Chong Sik-Lee on Japanese counter-insurgency during the Second World War and the US-led anti-Huk campaigns in the Philippines. Armbruster argued that current police operations were too lenient and badly organized to successfully infiltrate the VC apparatus, which had established shadow governments in villages and towns to rival the Government of Vietnam (GVN). In his view, the police should perform a similar function to the military in depleting enemy forces and weeding out the guerrilla infrastructure through effective intelligence collection, round-ups and interrogations allowing for a systematic classification of enemy operatives. Photography, Identity cards and fingerprinting, as well as paid informants, were crucial to the identification of VC cadres who easily blended into the civilian population. Defectors were needed to ensure the success of bounty-hunter operations. Effective counter-insurgents were best recruited from among the native population because they knew the terrain. Once identified, hard-core VC should be isolated and never allowed to return to their communities or executed outright. The rest of those detained could be won over through political indoctrination built around a counter-ideology.[1]Armbruster's writings provide a window into the mindset of shadow government operators who in plotting clandestine operations had little qualms about employing methods most Americans would consider morally repugnant. Named after a mythical all-seeing bird which selectively snatches its prey,

Phoenix was conceived as a clinically managed operation capable of reinvigorating counter-insurgency while minimizing 'collateral damage'. The programme was led for a significant period by Robert Komer, a PhD from Harvard Business School who embodied the cold managerial ethos of the Pentagon's Whiz Kids under Robert S. McNamara in their belief that statistical quantification and data management through use of computers could enable greater military efficiency like in the corporate world. As with the massacres in Indonesia following the 1965 coup, the United States could claim plausible deniability because of the reliance on local Provincial Reconstruction Units (PRU), or 'hunter-killer' teams recruited sometimes among criminal elements along with disaffected minority groups or religious sects.[2]

The Phoenix Program provides a quintessential example of *Parapolitics*, a set of observations which suggest a strange, powerful, clandestine and apparently structural relationship between state security intelligence apparatuses, terrorism and organized criminal activity, sustaining in the case of Vietnam a fundamentally illiberal social order.[3] Building off European colonial precedents, Phoenix originated in the top-secret 1290-d programme, which was instituted by the Eisenhower administration to train foreign police in counter-subversion and was expanded upon by Kennedy under the United States Agency of International Development's (USAID) Office of Public Safety (OPS). Embodying a US imperial style grounded in the quest for serviceable information but not deep knowledge of the subject society, these programmes were valued as a cost-effective means of suppressing radical and nationalist movements, precluding the need for military intervention, which was more likely to arouse public opposition or enabling the draw-down of troops. Many of the violent excesses were sanctioned as part of a counterterror doctrine which held that since insurgents did not typically abide by Western legal norms, neither should the United States or its proxies.[4]

Despite their centrality to American policy, most histories of the Vietnam War and American foreign relations neglect the police training programmes and give short shrift to Phoenix. The reasons may be psychological: the denial of a violent past is endemic to settler colonial societies.[5] The study of clandestine policing is essential however not only for its shock value but in understanding the instruments of statecraft deployed to advance US power. It casts important light, further, on the functioning of the American national security bureaucracy and Central Intelligence Agency (CIA).

'Suppressing dissidence before military-type action was necessary': 1290-d, the OPS and roots of Phoenix

After the Second World War, the United States pursued the creation of a stable international order dominated by American capital and open to free trade and foreign investment. Democratization was pursued if and only if it accorded with larger strategic interests.[6] Clandestine police operations were crucial in the attempt to strengthen client regimes and root out groups resisting American power, including radical nationalists and socialists promoting independent development and resisting the expansion of an American military base network. With remarkable continuity, the United States trained police not just to target criminals but to develop elaborate intelligence networks oriented towards internal defence, which allowed the suppression of dissident groups across a wide range and in a more surgical and often brutal way.[7]

Many of the techniques adopted under Phoenix were first applied during the US occupation of Japan as part of efforts to consolidate the pro-West Liberal Democratic Party (LDP) and suppress the Japanese Communist Party (JCP). Japan was considered the 'superdomino' by planners seeking to isolate China after the triumph of the Maoist revolution in 1949. The Supreme Command of the Allied Powers's (SCAP) public safety branch assisted former secret police (Tokkô) officers in compiling databanks on 'communist agitators' and 'subversives', and provided training in riot control and the use of tear gas to defuse protests against economic austerity measures (known as the 'reverse course'), resulting in mass layoffs and wage reductions. General Charles Willoughby, head of G-2 intelligence, forged ties with gangsters such as Hisayuki ('the Violent Bull'), Machii and Yoshio Kodama, a class-A war-criminal and Yakuza godfather to assist in breaking the power of the left, ensuring Japan's emergence as a junior partner in the Cold War.[8]

Orrin DeForest, a CIA counter-intelligence specialist and national police liaison who later sought to apply Japanese procedure in Vietnam, wrote in his memoirs that the Japanese were 'fanatic collectors of information, always exerting themselves to achieve a comprehensive understanding of a person and his activities before making any overt moves against him. ... Their goal was nothing less than total knowledge.'[9] These comments point to the striving of American advisers for total information control, which was subsequently applied in Vietnam.

South Korea and Thailand, where US policy contributed to the consolidation of military rule, was another model for clandestine policing operations. In 1948, two years before Harry Truman approved $5 million for the creation of a Thai constabulary, the CIA initiated a $35 million programme there through a front corporation, Sea Supply, which specialized in importing fruit and dairy products and tear gas for the military and police. Based out of Miami, Florida, Sea Supply was headed by Lt. Col. Willis Bird, deputy chief of OSS operations in China and Paul Helliwell, head of OSS Special intelligence in China who were known for combining moneymaking of an often illegal variety with anti-communism. The pair worked closely with Thai chief of police Phao Sinyanon, who used American aid to transform the police department into a quasi-military force of over 35,000 with its own mounted, mechanized, tank and seaborne divisions. As part of the quid pro quo, Phao established a 'special operations unit' in Burma, in violation of its sovereignty, to transfer arms to GMD commander Li Mi for an invasion of Yunnan province in Southern China.[10]

Operation Paper exemplified the intersection between American police training and covert operations in Southeast Asia which would again become manifest under Phoenix. In 1955, the NSC formally inaugurated the top-secret 1290-d programme (later Overseas Internal Security Program – OISP), whose central mission was to develop local police and security forces to 'provide internal security in countries vulnerable to communist subversion' and to 'aid in the detection of communist agents and fellow travelers' and 'suppress local dissidence before military-type action was necessary'. The 1290-d planning board included hard-liners from the Pentagon and CIA obsessed with 'the techniques of international communism', and was initially headed by Douglas MacArthur II, an ex-OSS operative and nephew of the famous general who later served as the ambassador to Japan and Iran. He was succeeded by Henry Villard, a silent movie actor and heir of a New York fortune, who was the first chief of the State Department's African Affairs Division in the Second World War and ambassador to Libya in the early 1950s.[11]

In an internal outline of 1290-d, Col. Albert R. Haney, an architect of the 1954 Guatemalan coup who ran secret agents into North Korea during the Korean War, stated that 'an efficient internal security system is a fundamental aspect of any growing society and contributes substantially to its orderly progress and development'. In his view, American support for undesirable political regimes, including dictatorships and juntas, was necessary to prevent the loss to neutralism or communist control.

> Confronted as we are against a deadly enemy who is highly disciplined and organized and dedicated to our capitulation, the U.S. cannot afford the moral luxury of helping only those regimes in the free-world that meet our ideals of self-government... . For those who decry efforts to make over others in our likeness and those who oppose helping undemocratic regimes to entrench themselves in power, let it be said that American methods *are in fact superior* to most others in the world and if we are to help them combat communism we can contribute greatly to the adoption of American democratic ways in achieving this end.[12]

These comments exemplify the ideological mindset underlying what social scientist Ola Tunander characterized as the 'deep state', in which clandestine, often-extra-legal tactics have been adopted to advance American global hegemony.[13] Staffed with men of like-minded views, the Kennedy administration convened a cabinet-level Special Group on Counter-Insurgency (CI), headed by his brother Robert and five-star general Maxwell Taylor, which championed the creation of police 'hunter-killer' squads serving as a prototype for Phoenix. Robert W. Komer of the NSC advised colleagues that 'while treaty arrangements and international law' were to be given careful consideration there was 'no overriding bar to [clandestine] action when overriding national interests prevail ... . When a government that is inimical to U.S. interests emerges, risks should be evaluated in encouraging and supporting the overthrow of that government.'[14]

In 1962, the Special Group established the OPS to 'develop the civilian police component of internal security forces in underdeveloped states ... identify early the symptoms of an incipient subversive situation', and 'maintain law and order without unnecessary bloodshed and an obtrusive display of the bayonet'.[15] Komer, a driving figure behind the organization and head of Phoenix, stressed that the police were 'more valuable than Special Forces in our global counter-insurgency efforts' and particularly useful in fighting urban insurrections. 'We get more from the police in terms of preventative medicine than from any single U.S. program,' he said. 'They are cost effective, while not going for fancy military hardware ... . They provide the first line of defense against demonstrations, riots and local insurrections. Only when the situation gets out of hand (as in South Vietnam) does the military have to be called in.'[16]

Echoing British imperial strategists such as Winston Churchill, who wrote in 1954 that an 'efficient police force and intelligence service are the best way of smelling out subversive movements at an early stage, and may save heavy expenditures on military reinforcements', these comments illuminate the geostrategic imperatives shaping the growth of the OPS, which is what accounted for significant human rights violations. Charles Maechling Jr., staff director of the Special Group on Counter-Insurgency, acknowledged years later that in failing to insist on 'even rudimentary standards of criminal justice and civil rights, the United States provided regimes having only a façade of constitutional safeguards with up-dated law-enforcement machinery readily adaptable to political intimidation and state terrorism. Record keeping in particular was immediately put to use in tracking down student radicals and union organizers.'[17] These remarks provide a striking admission of the repressive consequences of the police programmes, of which Vietnam and Phoenix was a paradigmatic example.

Containing the 'virus' of independent nationalism: Police training and 'nation-building' in South Vietnam

From 1955 to 1975, the United States spent over $300 million on police training in Vietnam – the largest total in the world – as part of the effort to build a client regime below the 17th parallel following the partition of the country under the Geneva accords. Bent on integrating Vietnam's economy with Japan and stamping out the 'virus' of independent nationalism, which it feared would spread throughout Southeast Asia, the Eisenhower administration refused to allow for elections to reunify the country, knowing that Ho Chi Minh, who led the liberation movement against France, would win. It instead attempted to consolidate the southern rule of Ngo Dinh Diem, a Catholic anti-communist who had limited popular backing and was referred by his own advisers as 'egotistical, neurotically suspicious, stubborn, self-righteous and a complete stranger to compromise'. According to the CIA, Diem was so dependent on American support that 'he would have fallen in a day without it'.[18]

The United States had always prized Southeast Asia as one of the richest and most strategic in the world, hoping to convert it into what General Douglas MacArthur characterized as an 'Anglo-Saxon lake'. In a March 1955 *Foreign Affairs* article, William Henderson of the Council on American Foreign Relations (which Laurence Shoup and William Minter aptly termed the 'imperial brain trust') wrote:

> As one of the earth's great storehouses of natural resources, Southeast Asia is a prize worth fighting for. Five sixth of the world's rubber, and one half of its tin are produced here. It accounts for two thirds of the world output in coconut, one third of the palm oil, and significant proportions of tungsten and chromium. No less important than the natural wealth is Southeast Asia's key strategic position astride the main lines of communication between Europe and the Far East.[19]

To help fulfil US imperial ambitions, in May 1955, the State Department contracted the Michigan State University School of Police Administration at a budget of $25 million to provide technical assistance and training to the South Vietnamese police, stressing mass surveillance capable of monitoring subversion and dismantling the political opposition to Diem, including Binh Xuyen gangsters, the Hoa-Hao and Cao Dai religious sects. The police were controlled by Diem's brother, Ngo Dinh Nhu, an opium addict who according to the British ambassador attached 'every bit as much importance to the apparatus of a police state as the most enthusiastic advocate of the social order of "1984"'.[20]

The contract with MSU was unique and presented limitations from the vantage point of the State Department 'because of the sensitive security aspects of the program'. A precedent was established six years earlier when at the behest of Professor Arthur Brandstatter, a public safety consultant to US High Commissioner John J. McCloy, the MSU School of Police Administration brought German police, including ex-Nazi soldiers, and South Koreans onto campus for an eight-week course and arranged for them to observe local law enforcement. Vietnam became a logical next undertaking, in part because of the close relationship between political science professor Wesley Fishel and Diem dating from a 1950 meeting in Japan.[21]

The 1290-d planning group emphasized the necessity of bolstering police 'counter-subversion' capabilities and their proficiency against the nationalist Vietminh, who resettled in the South following the victory at Dienbienphu and established shadow governments in the villages, extending 'their influence to many who are not communist party members through a substantial network of front organizations covering all sectors of the population'. It further warned that 'internal security was at present poor', and there appears to be 'little capability of opposition to Vietminh efforts to further internal chaos and eventually complete takeover probably through democratic means of free elections … . The governments survival will be determined in large measure by the degree of protection foreign sources will provide in guaranteeing its future'.[22]

These comments provide a striking acknowledgement of the weakness of Diem and his reliance on foreigners, and of the strength of the Vietminh, which was targeted for liquidation. MSU advisers, including a number of CIA agents, built up the paramilitary civil guard in violation of the Geneva agreements, which limited the size of the armed forces to 150,000, and worked closely with the Vietnamese Bureau of Investigations (VBI or Cong An), commanded by General Nguyen Ngoc Le, a twenty-year French army veteran. Cultivating networks of informants, the VBI operated in plain clothes and functioned principally as a 'political police' and 'political repression organization'. Its mission was to 'correlate information regarding the security of the state, manage political information services' and 'discover plots and activities capable of compromising public order'.[23]

In 2005, Ngo Vinh Long, a professor of history at the University of Maine, testified that as a teenager he worked undercover for the VBI as a 'public health specialist' in malaria eradication to access people's homes and search for information on their political affiliations.[24] Once identified, those on the blacklist, who included relatives of opposition leaders, had their homes raided by plain-clothes officers, usually in the predawn hours, and in a precursor to Phoenix were sent to rat-infested jails to face torture and possible death by guillotine. Frank Walton, director of public safety in Vietnam from 1959–61 to 1969–71, acknowledged that the Diem regime frequently employed the police in 'Gestapo-like operation[s] with midnight arrests, holding without charge, brutality and detentions in secret locations'.[25]

To bolster police efficiency in the attempt to counter 'communist subversion', the MSUG provided handcuffs, revolvers, tear gas weapons and crystal microphones for wiretapping, established an information clearing house equipped with polygraph and microfilm and ran an espionage and jungle warfare course at an old French Army installation near Saigon. American advisers further improved record-keeping and communications (one adviser, Lyman Rundlett, was forced to resign when it was discovered that he had previously worked for Motorola, which received bidding contracts for radio equipment) and set up a forensics lab including fingerprint identification and an identity card system for social control purposes.[26]

Financing for clandestine police operations was derived in part from the drug trade, controlled by Nhu and the Corsican mafia as well as CIA-backed warlords in Thailand and Laos, who, according to a public safety report, organized the 'considerable traffic in smuggling' as a means of raising money for a 'wave of repression against political opponents', including 'mass jailing and executions'.[27] The CIA improved its purchasing power by buying South Vietnamese piasters on the black market, which was illegal under both South Vietnamese and US law. Like its colonial predecessors, the 'agency' long relied on ethnic minorities and criminal elements in counter-insurgency operations. General Paul F. Gorman, head of the US Southern Command, commented that 'if you want to go into the subversion business, collect intelligence and move arms, you deal with the drug movers'.[28]

For all the outrage over 'Vietcong terrorism', MSUG's reports show that for every VBI or province chief assassinated, at least six suspected 'VC' were killed by state security forces and hundreds more arrested 'for breeches of security' and 'purely political violations' (later the kill discrepancy was far higher).[29] With no apparent objection, one MSU professor interviewed a local police chief in his headquarters where a twenty-year-old peasant was 'curled up, his feet in manacles, the left side of his face swollen and his eye and cheek badly bruised'.[30]

In 1959, Diem passed a law allowing for the execution of opponents within a period of three days, leading to the formation of the National Liberation Front (NLF), an amalgamation of opposition groups bent on overthrowing his regime and expelling American advisers. Led by a Saigon lawyer, Nguyen Huu Tho, a former prisoner in Diem's gulag, the NLF was supported by Hanoi, and it derived pronounced support as a result of wide-scale grievances and its promotion of land reform and literacy campaigns. According to journalist Joseph Buttinger, a one-time Diem supporter, the organization enlisted people 'willing to serve their country in the tens of thousands and extracted from them superhuman efforts and sacrifices in the struggle for independence'. The government meanwhile attracted 'officials with the lowest possible motivation for public service, the only ones fit to serve in a corrupt, inefficient and despised police-state'.[31]

By providing modern weapons and technical support to police and promoting political operations, the MSUG was pivotal in contributing to the climate of repression that gave rise to the NLF. Art Brandstatter wrote to colleague Ralph Turner in 1961 that he 'supported Diem's position regarding the role of the civil guard in "neutralizing VC activity"' and never agreed with the position that 'we should try to help develop a "democratic police force" under conditions of instability and insurgency ... . The responsibility for internal security belongs to the police.'[32] These comments epitomize how commitment to civil liberties and humane principles was subordinated to the goal of fighting communism and securing what were perceived as American strategic interests. The Vietnamese people suffered grievously as a result.

'The numbers just don't add up': Phoenix and state terrorism in the shadow war

As the war expanded, police training became even more central to American pacification efforts and contributed to the torture and killing of thousands of revolutionary fighters and civilians. The US received guidance from the British who sent ten ex-colonial police officers and secretly trained hundreds of South Vietnamese (along with Lao and Thai) police in riot control, jungle warfare and special branch intelligence in Malaysia.[33] Following a failed 1960 coup, Diem's brother Ngo Dinh Can formed a secret police organization at loggerheads with Security Director Tran Kim Tuyen, which extorted, tortured and murdered regime opponents, including five Hoa-Hao members, whose bodies were dumped in a canal in Saigon. Chief of Police Nguyen Van Hieu and two associates who had taken over the torture facility beneath the Saigon zoo were sentenced to life in prison following a sensational criminal trial.[34]

After the Ngo brothers were assassinated in a CIA-backed coup, the OPS worked to rebuild the police–intelligence–drugs apparatus under Saigon police chief Nguyen Ngoc Loan, who gained notoriety after being photographed shooting an NLF prisoner in the head. Trained at the French St. Cyr military academy, Loan was the power broker of Vice Premier Nguyen Cao Ky, a Hitler admirer previously removed from a CIA mission into Laos for smuggling heroin. An OPS report pointed to Loan's 'contempt for individual legal rights' after he had a member of the constituent assembly assassinated to break a legislative logjam. Four-star general William Corson wrote in *The Betrayal* that 'Loan's National police methods to enforce the "laws" make Himmler's Gestapo look like the board of overseers in a Quaker church'.[35]

Loan epitomized the danger of the police programmes in empowering warlords of an unsavoury character. After the 1968 Tet offensive (in which he was wounded), he lost his favoured status with the CIA because of his lukewarm backing for Phoenix, whose aim was to eliminate the 'Vietcong' infrastructure (VCI) through use of sophisticated computer technology and intelligence gathering and improved coordination between military and police intelligence agencies. The United States in turn elevated Loan's successor, Tran Thien Khiem, the power broker of Nguyen Van Thieu, who ousted Ky in a power struggle centred in part on control of the $88 million heroin trade.[36]

Focused initially in the revolutionary stronghold of Kien Hoa as part of Operation Speedy Express, which claimed over 10,000 Vietnamese lives, Phoenix (Phung Hoang in Vietnamese) was implemented after Tet as an extension of the police programmes. Run by the OPS and CIA at a cost of between $7 million and $15 million a year, it adopted wanted posters, blacklists, disguises and other psychological warfare techniques such as the playing off superstitions, spreading disinformation and stringing corpses on hooks for intimidation. One adviser, David Donovan, likened himself to a warrior-king, who at twenty-three had unprecedented power in his ability to imprison people in his district, direct development funds, and even order executions.

He and his colleagues were equipped with James Bond type gadgetry developed by the CIAs technical services division such as radio transmission devices designed to look like household utensils and camouflaged rocks that came apart inside and could contain messages.[37] Navy Seals were mobilized alongside the PRU to 'neutralize' high-value targets, including civilian officials running local administrations under NLF jurisdiction. Operations extended into Laos and Cambodia and 'rogue' Americans may have also been targeted.[38]

America's clandestine warriors believed the 'Vietcong' were monstrous yet effective in their 'application of torture and murder to achieve psychological advantage'. They in turn sought to emulate their tactics, which included selective assassination, inducing defections and winning over the population through civic action and political education. Third-country nationals were used for the dirtiest tasks, including South Korean, Chinese and Filipino mercenaries willing, in the words of one CIA officer, to 'slit their grandmother's throat for a dollar eighty-five'.[39]

Most of the Filipinos had served in Nenita hunter-killer teams developed by legendary CIA operative Edward Lansdale in the early 1950s to seek out and destroy leaders of the Huk revolutionary movement, which led the anti-Japanese struggle in the Second World War and promoted land reform. Headed by Napoleon ('Poling') Valeriano, a Lansdale protégé and PRU adviser, the Nenita, named after their skull and cross-bone emblem, practised the water cure, broke bones, cordoned off areas and stacked Huk corpses along the highways beneath warning placards to strike fear in the population. An internal study concluded that that they 'inflicted terror and oppression on the people of Central Luzon'.[40]

The PRU and their American counterparts wrought similar havoc across the Mekong Delta. A lot of the violence was indiscriminate, eroding support for the GVN. Political scientists Stathis N. Kalyvas and Matthew A. Kocher estimated that Phoenix victimized thirty-eight innocents for every one actual Vietcong agent. NLF fighters had access to things like safe houses that enabled them to evade capture, giving young men the incentive to join the NLF, which had a well-developed political infrastructure and skilful political organizers that, according to one Phoenix veteran, no political organization in the United States could remotely match.[41]

Thieu and various district chiefs at times used Phoenix to eliminate political rivals, including the non-communists opposition. Targets were also at times selected by the NLF, which widely penetrated the state security apparatus. One of Thieu's top intelligence advisers, Vu Ngoc Nha, who neutralized people that had nothing to do with official Phoenix goals, was found guilty of espionage and became a general in North Vietnam's secret service. He may have at one time been paid by the CIA to bring down Thieu's government.[42]

Theodore Shackley, CIA station chief in the late 1960s, wrote in his memoir that CIA officers generally found Phoenix 'repugnant. They felt that the dossiers were based on dubious information … . All too frequently, arrest efforts turned into firefights and more so-called VCI were killed than detained for processing.'[43] Declassified field reports point to the wide-scale corruption of PRU cadres who used their positions for revenge and extortion, threatening to kill people and count them as VCI if they did not pay them huge sums. When CIA officer John Stockwell reported that his police liaison was torturing and murdering suspects who could not pay ransom, he was threatened with reassignment.[44]

Many of the atrocities were committed by 'VC avenger units' prone to rape, pillage and body mutilation.[45] While the quantity of 'neutralizations' was reported to be high in many districts, the quality was 'poor'. Adviser Charles N. Philips lamented that there was a large number of 'phantom kills' which hampered good Phung Hoang statistics. There were also 'flagrant' cases of report padding, most egregiously in Long An province where CIA operative Evan Parker Jr. noted 'the numbers just don't add up'. Dead bodies were being identified as VCI, rightly or wrongly, in the attempt to at least approach an unrealistic quota. The catalogue of agents listed as killed included an inordinate number of 'nurses', a convenient way to account for women killed in raids on suspected VC hideouts.[46]

An artillery adviser to South Vietnamese army units in Long An stated in an interview that several women were killed in his district (of Tan An) because they spat at the PRU lieutenant after being tied to a tree. The women's bodies were then carried to the market place as a warning. As part of black operations, PRUs disguised as 'Vietcong' engaged in search operations in which air support and defoliation were ordered to wipe out villages. They also assassinated people in their sleep using silencers. A CIA agent commented that when he arrived in his district, he was given a list of 200 people who were to be killed; six months later 260 had been killed – but none of those on the list.[47]

A 1971 Pentagon study found that only 3 per cent of 'Vietcong' killed, captured or rallied were full or probationary party members above the district level. Ralph McGehee, CIA chief in the Gia Dinh province, who nearly committed suicide from guilt, stated in his memoirs that 'never in the history of our work in Vietnam did we get one clear-cut, high-ranking Vietcong agent'.[48] The reasons stem from faulty intelligence, lack of language skills by Americans and extraordinary NLF/NVA counter-intelligence as well as organizational protection afforded to top cadre by NLF shadow governments.[49]

Some PRU's were recruited from criminal gangs, giving them skills conducive to the clandestine arts. A Phoenix operative noted that they were 'a combination of ARVN deserters, VC turncoats and bad motherfucker criminals the South Vietnamese couldn't deal with in prison, so they turned them over to us. Some actually had an incentive plan: If they killed x number of Commies, they got x number of years off their prison term'.[50] In certain provinces, PRUs were recruited from among disaffected Catholics and Cao Dai and other religious sects with real grievances against the VCI who had killed members of their family. While some were well disciplined, the PRU were often hated by the population and even, according to an anonymous veteran, by the ARVN, which in his district fired machine guns into the PRU compound. One PRU cadre would cut the liver out of those killed and take it home in a plastic bag, an example of the dehumanized brutality bred by war.[51]

The CIA instructed the PRU in sophisticated psychological interrogation techniques designed to emphasize the prisoner's helplessness and dependence on his captor.

These methods led to systematic abuse, including an incident where officers planted electrodes in a prisoners' brain, and another where a detainee was kept in an air-conditioned room for four years to exploit his fear of the cold.[52] Military intelligence specialist K. Barton Osborn told Congress that he witnessed the starving of prisoners, their being thrown off helicopters and the prodding of a woman's brain with a six inch dowel through her ear until she died. In his year and a half with Phoenix, he did not see 'a single suspect survive interrogation'.[53]

Despite later attempts by conservatives to discredit Osborn's character, CIA Director William Colby conceded that much of what Osborn said was likely to be true. In testimony before Congress, Colby stated that Phoenix (which he defined as an 'attempt to identify the structure of the communist party and go out and capture or shoot them') led to 'unjustifiable abuses' and the death of over 20,000 people. The GVN placed the total at over 40,000, which many historians believe to be an underestimation. A Phoenix operative who served in Czechoslovakia during the Second World War commented, 'The reports I sent in from my province on the number of communists that were neutralized reminded me of the reports Hitler's concentration camp commanders sent in on how many inmates they had exterminated, each commander lying that he had killed more than the others to please Himmler.'[54] These comments epitomize the deadly ramifications of Phoenix, which unleashed violent social forces that took on a momentum of their own. War crimes were clearly committed, for which ultimate responsibility lay with the programme's architects.

'You ask me where is hell …' Prison overcrowding and the 'Tiger Cages' of Con Son

Phoenix's catastrophic impact was compounded by the atrocious conditions in the GVN's prisons, where overcrowding was rampant and many died from malnutrition, disease or torture. The total number of political prisoners was estimated at 200,000 at its peak, the highest in the world. Under the army's small wars doctrine, effective prison management was seen as crucial to counter-insurgency, as it provided a symbol of government authority and means of winning political converts through re-education. The State Department spent $6.5 million between 1967 and 1972 for the maintenance and renovation of the forty-two major prisons run by the GVN and built three additional facilities and a juvenile reformatory. It provided generators and handcuffs, built special isolation cells for hard-core 'Vietcong' and oversaw the construction of over thirty state-of-the-art detention centres (PICs – Provincial Interrogation Centers).[55]

Many of the supplies, however, were resold on the black market by local authorities, usually cronies of Ky or Thieu, or kept until wardens paid a bribe. William Colby wrote to the director of CORDS, the agency responsible for pacification, that commodities and money destined for correctional centres were 'held in Saigon until local authorities were presented with gifts or proper wining and dining'. Nguyen Van Thuc, deputy chief jailer of Kien Phong Correctional Center, reported that he had to take 'the right people' out to a 20,000 piaster meal ($250) and provide them with whisky and cash gifts to secure access to a generator. Other wardens paid 2,000 piasters for the use of a forklift and 3,000 for a dump truck.[56] No wonder most of the renovations were never completed.

Poor facilities and overcrowding were compounded by a lack of judicial process and access to fair trial or counsel. In Chau Doc in November 1968, Don Bordenkircher, a correctional officer at San Quentin in California who joined the Foreign Service to avoid sending his kids to school with 'flower children', noted to his boss Randolph Berkeley that only 27 of 457 prisoners had been sentenced and eleven children under the age of eighteen were currently detained. In Phan Ding the total was 2,550 prisoners out of 2,903 in a facility intended for only 440. To make up for the discrepancy, inmates had to begin cooking supper at 4.00 am.[57] In other facilities, inspector reports reveal that inmates withstood rodents the size of cats, ate in kitchens that doubled as garbage dumps and had to bathe in raw sewage. In Bac Lieu, Bordenkircher wrote irately to his superiors that 'political reeducation cannot occur until you enable a man to sleep away from his own urine and feces, give him wholesome food and the opportunity for rehabilitation'.[58]

Some of the worst abuses took place at the infamous Con Son prison, located on an archipelago 180 kilometres off the southern Vietnamese coast, where inmates reported being worked nearly to death in the fields, severely beaten by trusties and left on the verge of starvation.[59] Prisoner Thep Xanh wrote of his experience, 'Deep in my heart I remember nights at Con Son, the echo of the creaking door, the beatings, the crying out at midnight, the shouting of guards, you ask me where is hell; where on earth people cannot live as human beings, where people with heart and soul live like beasts.'[60]

In 1970, after veering from the itinerary during a congressional tour, International Voluntary Service (IVS) employee Don Luce found detainees crammed into six-foot windowless pits or 'Tiger Cages', where they were forced to subsist on three handfuls of milled white rice and three swallows of water per day and had lime thrown in their faces, causing lung disease and tuberculosis. OPS Director Frank Walton, a former LAPD deputy chief who also served in Libya, Philippines and Iran, sanctioned a report stating that non-cooperative prisoners, whom he referred to as 'reds who keep preaching the commie line', were 'isolated in their cells for months' and 'bolted to the floor or handcuffed to leg-irons'.[61] This resulted in wide-scale paralysis, which Dr John Champlin of the Air Force testified before Congress, resulted from 'severe nutritional deficiencies coupled with prolonged immobilization unique in the history of modern warfare … . A computer review of 1200 medical journals and a personal search through medical literature on the health of POW's produced no similar descriptions.'[62]

Phoenix and its antecedents can ultimately be seen to embody the repressive parastatal structures underlying American global hegemony. Financed in part through illicit channels, the Phoenix concept grew out of a larger web of clandestine policing operations, which aimed to root out leftist and revolutionary movements threatening US interests. Under the small wars doctrine, it was felt that costly military engagement could be avoided through carefully calibrated political policing operations designed to liquidate the revolutionary opposition. In Vietnam, however, these goals provide to be untenable, owing in part to deep-rooted support for the revolutionary movement and the absence of institutional correctives for false identification and inflated statistics. The Thieu government and US war effort was in turn undermined, with the NVA-NLF forces liberating the country by 1975.[63]

'You have to not mind killing innocents':
Phoenix's long staying power

Despite being publicly repudiated after its exposure in the United States, Phoenix served as a templar for future CIA operations, first in Central America during the 1980s and most recently in the War on Terror. With a large sector of the population opposed to large-scale military commitments and a revival of the draft, neoconservative policymakers and traditional elites bent on restoring US hegemony after Vietnam, relied on the subcontracting of counter-insurgency, largely to ensure deniability. Following the 9/11 attacks, Vice President Dick Cheney undertook research in the CIA archive and embraced Phoenix as a model for extrajudicial rendition and assassination programmes designed to obliterate the leadership of Al-Qaeda and insurgent movements opposing the US occupations of Afghanistan and Iraq.[64]

The Bush administration invested billions of dollars in police training under the premise that local 'police are often the best force for countering small insurgent bands supported by the local population. In COIN operations, special police strike units may move to different AOs [Areas of Operation] while patrol police remain in the local area on a daily basis and build a detailed intelligence picture of the insurgent strength, organization and support.'[65] This is a prescription for Phoenix-style policing operations little different from Vietnam, apart from in the use of private security corporations such as Blackwater and DynCorp and predator drone machines. And once again, the consequences have been deadly, with night-time snatch and grab raids, civilian killings, overcrowded prisons and systematic torture generating pronounced resistance to US policies.[66]

Reflecting the continuity in personnel, a number of OPS personnel served with police training operations in Afghanistan and Iraq. One was 75-year-old Adolph Saenz, a Korean and Vietnam War veteran who had hunted down Ché Guevara in Bolivia. The Bush administration's 2006 appointment to head the Abu Ghraib prison, Don Bordenkircher, oversaw the 'Tiger Cages' in Con Son as part of Operation Phoenix.[67] Another shadow operative in the War on Terror, Billy Waugh, was a Special Forces officer in Korea and Vietnam who led Hmong units in Laos and clandestine missions in Libya alongside disgraced CIA agent Edwin Wilson. After 9/11, the 72-year-old was asked to head a CIA-paramilitary unit in Afghanistan, which was authorized to assassinate enemy combatants by calling in air strikes using smart bombs and hellfire missiles controlled by remote control joystick. Waugh told a reporter that the way to win the war is to 'let them kill each other. Send up a satellite and take pictures. Keep the Special Operations teams in the hills, fifty miles out of the towns. Then go in at night and do your work. Kill them. Kill like we did in

Germany. Flatten the place. You have to not mind killing innocents. Even the women and children'.[68]

These comments epitomize the ends justifies the means philosophy of America's clandestine warriors operating beyond the pale of public accountability. The Phoenix Program was clearly an important watershed, contributing to the institutionalization of COIN strategies employing sophisticated social control technologies and sanctioning systematic torture and assassination, largely by proxy to ensure plausible deniability. The study of Phoenix and American police training programmes generally casts important light on the hidden, extra-legal methods that have been adopted to advance American global hegemony. The long staying power reflects in part the dictates of the national security bureaucracy and military-industrial complex which requires a constant stream of foreign enemies, both real and imagined, for its sustainability. The tactics adopted in Phoenix, it should be noted, are similar to those of previous colonial powers, including Britain, which also relied on clandestine policing operations to root out opposition movements.[69] Their eradication can only come through sweeping repudiation of the ideas underlying their implementation and demand for a peaceful resolution of international conflicts.

Notes

1 Frank Armbruster, *A Military and Police Security Program for South Vietnam* (Hudson, NY: Hudson Institute, 10 August 1967), HI-881-RR, DOD.

2 See Michael McClintock, *Instruments of Statecraft: U.S. Guerilla Warfare, Counterinsurgency and Counter-Terrorism, 1940-1990* (New York: Pantheon Books, 1992); Andrew R. Finlayson, *Marine Advisors With the Vietnamese Provincial Reconnaissance Units, 1966-1970* (Quantico, VA: United States Marine Corps, 2009). On the massacres in Indonesia, see John Roosa, *Pretext for Mass Murder: The September 30th Movement and Suharto's Coup d'état in Indonesia* (Madison: University of Wisconsin Press, 2006).

3 Robert Cribb, 'Introduction: Parapolitics, Shadow Governance and Criminal Sovereignty' in *Government of the Shadows: Parapolitics and Criminal Sovereignty*, ed. Eric Wilson (London: Pluto Press, 2009), 1. See also Peter Dale Scott, *The War Conspiracy: The Secret Road to the Second Indochina War* (Indianapolis: The Bobbs Merrill Co., 1972); Peter Dale Scott, *Deep Politics and the Death of JFK* (Berkeley: University of California Press, 1993).

4 Col. Virgil Ney, 'Guerrilla Warfare and Modern Strategy', in *Modern Guerrilla Warfare: Fighting Communist Guerrilla Movements, 1941-1961*, ed. F. M. Osanka, introduction by Samuel Huntington (New York: The Free Press, 1962), 25–38.

5 Walter Hixson, *American Settler Colonialism: A History* (New York: Palgrave McMillan, 2013). Scott, *Deep Politics and the Death of JFK*, 8. Scott writes about the psychological denial related to his thesis that the badly mismanaged investigation of the Kennedy assassination reflected deep structural defects and corruption in US governance. There are of course exceptions to the general pattern of neglect for the police programmes, including Douglas Valentine's *The Phoenix Program* (New York: William & Morrow, 1991) and Alfred W. McCoy's *A Question of Torture: CIA Interrogation From the Cold War to the War on Terror* (New York: Metropolitan, 2006).

6   See William Appleman Williams, *The Tragedy of American Diplomacy*, rev ed. (Cleveland: World Publishing, 1972); Noam Chomsky, *For Reasons of State* (New York: Pantheon, 1973); *Deterring Democracy* (New York: Pantheon, 1991).

7   See Martha K. Huggins, *Political Policing: The United States and Latin America* (Durham, NC: Duke University Press, 1998); A. J. Langguth, *Hidden Terrors: The Truth about U.S. Police Operations in Latin America* (New York: Pantheon Books, 1978).

8   See my *Modernizing Repression: Police Training and Nation Building in the American Century* (Amherst, MA: University of Massachusetts Press, 2012), ch. 3. Byron Engle to Chief PSD, 'Report on Communist Demonstrations', 3 June 1950, National Archives (NA), College Park MD, GHQ-SCAP, G-2, PSD, police branch 1945–52, box 332. On the Willoughby-Yakuza connection, see David E. Kaplan and Alec Dubro, *Yakuza: Japan's Criminal Underworld* (Berkeley: University of California Press, 2003), 45, 48.

9   Orrin DeForest with David Chanoff, *Slow Burn: The Rise and Bitter Fall of American Intelligence in Vietnam* (New York: Simon & Schuster, 1990), 76.

10 Daniel Fineman, *A Special Relationship: The United States and Military Government in Thailand, 1947-1958* (Honolulu: University of Hawai'i Press, 1997), 143; Garland Williams to American embassy Tehran, 'Narcotics Situation in Southeast Asia and the Far-East', August 4, 1959, RG 286, USAID, OPS, Africa and Near East, NA, box 62, folder Narcotics; Richard M. Gibson with Wenhua Chen, *The Secret Army: Chiang Kai-Shek and the Drug Warlords of the Golden Triangle* (Singapore: John Wiley & Sons, 2011), 258; For police training in South Korea and its connection to Phoenix, see Jeremy Kuzmarov, 'Police Training, "Nation-Building," and Political Repression in Postcolonial South Korea.' *The Asia Pacific Journal*, 1 July 2012, online: http://apjjf.org/2012/10/27/Jeremy-Kuzmarov/3785/article.html.

11 Minutes of Meeting OCB Working Group on NSC-Action 1290-d, 18 January 1955, OCB, NSC Staff Papers, Eisenhower library, Box 16, folder internal security; Eric Pace, 'Douglas MacArthur II, 88, Former Ambassador to Japan', *New York Times*, 17 November 1997; Wolfgang Saxon, 'Henry Villard, 95, Diplomat Who Wrote Books in Retirement', *New York Times*, 25 January 1996.

12 Albert R. Haney, 'Observations and Suggestions Concerning OISP', 30 January 1957, OCB, NSC, Eisenhower library, Box 18, folder internal security.

13 See Ola Tunander, 'Democratic State Versus Deep State: Approaching the Dual State of the West', in *Government of the Shadows: Parapolitics and Criminal Sovereignty*, ed. Eric Wilson (London: Pluto Press, 2009) and Scott, *The War Conspiracy*.

14 Robert W. Komer, 'Memo for Members of Study Groups on Deterrence of Guerrilla Warfare, Revised Draft Outline', 8 March 1961, John F. Kennedy presidential library (JFKL), Boston, MA, Robert W. Komer Papers (RWK), box 414, folder 1-Special Group; McClintock, 'The Kennedy Crusade', In *Instruments of Statecraft*.

15 'Policy Research Study – Internal Warfare and the Security of the Underdeveloped States', Department of State, 20 November 1961, JFK, Presidential Office File (POF), box 98; David G. Epstein, 'The Police Role in Counterinsurgency Efforts', *The Journal of Criminal Law, Criminology and Police Science* 58 (March 1968): 148–51; Nancy Stein, 'Policing the Empire', in *The Iron Fist and the Velvet Glove: An Analysis of the US Police*, 2nd edn (Berkeley: Center for Research on Criminal Justice, 1977), 42.

16 Robert W. Komer to McGeorge Bundy, Maxwell Taylor 'Cutbacks in Police Programs Overseas' 5 May 1962, JFKL, RWK, Box 414, folder-Counter-Insurgency Police Programs.

17   Charles Maechling Jr., 'Camelot, Robert Kennedy, and Counter-Insurgency: A
     Memoir', *The Virginia Quarterly Review* (Summer 1999). Also available online
     at http://www.vqronline.org/articles/1999/summer/maechling-camelot-robert-
     kennedy; Charles Maechling, Jr., 'Counterinsurgency: The First Ordeal by Fire', In
     *Low Intensity Warfare: Counterinsurgency, Pro insurgency, and Antiterrorism in the
     Eighties*, ed. Michael T. Klare and Peter Kornbluh (New York: Pantheon Books, 1987),
     33. On Maechling's earlier role in support of the programmes, Charles Maechling Jr.,
     'Proposed Plan of Operations for Interdepartmental Police Committee (NSAM 146)',
     27 April 1962, JFKL, RWK, box 413, folder Counter-Insurgency – Police Program,
     1961–3. Churchill quoted in Georgina Sinclair, *At the End of the Line: Colonial
     Policing and the Imperial Endgame 1945-1980* (Manchester: Manchester University
     Press, 2006), 189.
18   Seth Jacobs, *Cold War Mandarin: Ngo Dinh Diem and the Origins of America's War
     in Vietnam, 1950-1963* (New York: Rowman & Littlefield, 2006), 7, 17, 21; Causes,
     Origins and Lessons of the Vietnam War: Hearings Before the Committee on Foreign
     Relations, U.S. Senate, 92nd Congress, 2nd Session, 9, 10 May 1972 (Washington,
     DC: G.P.O., 1972), 198.
19   Quoted in Laurence H. Shoup and William Minter, *Imperial Brain Trust: The Council
     on Foreign Relations and United States Foreign Policy* (New York: Authors Choice
     Press, 1977), 228; MacArthur quoted in John Dower, 'The U.S.-Japan Military
     Relationship', in *Postwar Japan 1945 to the Present*, ed. Jon Livingston, Joe Moore and
     Felicia Oldfather (New York: Pantheon, 1973), 236.
20   British ambassador quoted in Marc Curtis, *Unpeople: Britain's Secret Human Rights
     Abuses* (London: Vintage, 2004), 203.
21   See John Ernst, *Forging a Fateful Alliance: Michigan State University and the Vietnam
     War* (East Lansing: Michigan State University Press, 1998), 13, 14; ICA Annual
     Status Report on Operations Pursuant to NSC-Action 1290-d to Operations
     Coordinating Board for the National Security Council, December 1955 to November
     1956, Eisenhower Presidential Library, OCB, NSC, box 18, folder Internal Security;
     Howard Hoyt, Chief of Police Kalamazoo Michigan and Coordinator German police
     training programme to Albert Scheiern, Grand Rapids, Michigan, Ralph Turner
     Papers, Michigan State University Archives, Vietnam Project, box 1684.
22   'Report of NSC 1290-D Working Group, Summary of Status of Internal Security
     Forces Prepared by the Pentagon, Appendix B Survey of the Vulnerability of Various
     Countries to Communist Subversion', 16 February 1955, Eisenhower library, OCB,
     NSC, box 16, folder Internal Security; Albert Haney, OCB Report Pursuant to NSC-
     Action 1290-D, 5 August 1955, OCB, NSC, box 17, folder Internal Security.
23   Jack E. Ryan, *Brief History of the Sureté in Indochina*, MSUG, 19 January 1956, 7;
     Arthur Brandstatter et al. 'Field Trip Report – Police and Security Services', 9–11
     May 1960; Field Trip Report VBI (Cong An), Long An, Kien Hoa and Binh Duong
     Provinces, 10–11 December 1959, MSU, Vietnam Project, Box 684; 'Report on
     the Police of Vietnam, by members of the police team and Ralph H. Smuckler',
     MSUG, Technical Assistance Project, December 1, 1955; 'Public Safety Assistance –
     Vietnam, Historical Background', CORDS, PSD, Public Safety Program, Information
     Handbook; Maxwell Taylor, 'Memo for Members of the Special Group: U.S. Support
     of Foreign Paramilitary Forces', RG 286, Records of the USAID, OPS, Program
     Surveys and Evaluations, NA, box 5, folder 1.
24   Noam Chomsky and Ngo Vinh Long, '30 Year Retrospective on the Fall of Saigon',
     Public Forum (Boston: Massachusetts Institute of Technology, 30 April 2005); 'John

McCabe to Martin L. Gross, Monthly Activity Report', December 1961, USAID, OPS, NA, RG 278, Operations Division, East Asia, Branch Vietnam, Police Operations, folder 1.

25 Thomas L. Ahern Jr., *The CIA and the House of Ngo: Covert Action in South Vietnam, 1954-1963* (Washington, DC: CIA, Center for the Study of Intelligence, 1999), 100, online at http://www.foia.cia.gov/vietnam.asp; Marilyn B. Young, *The Vietnam Wars, 1945-1990* (New York: Harperperennial, 1991), 339; Jack Ryan to Ralph Turner, 8 February 1961, Ralph Turner Papers, MSU archive, box 1694; Joseph Starr, 'Civil Police Administration Program', 18 October 1956, RG 469, Records of the U.S. Foreign Assistance Agencies, 1948–61, Office of Public Services, NA, box 1; William Rosenau, *US Internal Security Assistance to South Vietnam: Insurgency, Subversion and Public Order* (London: Routledge, 2005), 125.

26 Margaret Lauterbach, 'MSU-Trained Vietnamese Praised by U.S. Adviser', *East Lansing Town Courier*, 30 June 1965; MSUG September Monthly Reports, 8 October 1957; 'Jack E. Ryan to Howard Hoyt, General Information Regarding the VBI and Its General Headquarters', 17 April 1956; 'Ryan Interview with Mr. Phan Van Son, Study of the VBI in the Field, Tanan Province', 23 April 1956; E. C. Updike, Field Trip to Binh-Dinh, Phu-Yen, Khanh Hoa, Ninh Tuan Province with Director General of the Civil Guard, 19–22 March 1958, MSU, Vietnam Project, box 681.

27 Frank Walton, Paul Skuse and Wendell Motter, *A Survey of the Laos National Police*, Vientiane, USAID, OPS, 1965, vi, 1; Alfred W. McCoy, *The Politics of Heroin: CIA Complicity in the Global Drug Trade*, rev edn (New York: Lawrence Hill, 2005).

28 McCoy, *The Politics of Heroin*; Randall B. Woods, *Shadow Warrior: William Egan Colby and the CIA* (New York: Basic Books, 2013), 311; Jonathan Marshall, *Drug Wars: Corruption, Counterinsurgency and Covert Operations in the Third World* (San Francisco: Cohen and Cohen, 1991), 54.

29 September Monthly Report MSUG, 8 October 1957; August Monthly Report, 8 September 1958; November Monthly Report on Civil Police Administration Program for Republic of Vietnam, 3 December 1957; February Monthly Report, 12 March 1958, MSU, Vietnam Project, Box 679; Shields, Wiener, Siemek, Field Trip Report, VBI, Long An, KienHoa, Binh Duong, 10–11 December 1959, MSU Vietnam Project, Box 681; Field Trip Report, VBI (Cong An), Darlac, Pleiku, Kontum, 12–17 October 1959; Vinh Long, 17–20 November 1959, MSU Vietnam Project, box 684.

30 'Ryan Interview with Mr. Phan Van Son, Study of the VBI in the Field, Tanan Province', 23 April 1956, 'Ryan Interview with Mr. Hyunh Quang Phuoc, Can Tho Province', 19 April 1956, Texas Tech Virtual Vietnam Archive; Ahern, Jr., *The CIA and the House of Ngo*, 88, online at http://www.foia.cia.gov/vietnam.asp; Nguyen Thi Dinh, *No Other Road to Take*, trans. Mai V. Elliot (Ithaca: Cornell Southeast Asia Program, 1976), 56–8; Martin A. Nicolaus, *The Professors, the Policemen and the Peasants: The Sociology of the Michigan State University Group Vietnam Project, 1955-1962* (British Columbia, Canada: Simon Fraser University, 1966), 1.

31 Joseph Buttinger, *Vietnam: A Dragon Embattled*, vol. 2 (New York: Frederick A. Praeger, 1967), 952–3; Jeffrey Race, *War Comes to Long An: Revolutionary Conflict in a Vietnamese Province* (Berkeley: University of California Press, 1972), 197; David Hunt, *Vietnam's Southern Revolution: From Peasant Insurrection to Total War, 1959-1968* (Amherst: University of Massachusetts Press, 2009); Truong Nhu Tang, *A Vietcong Memoir: An Inside Account of the Vietnam War and Its Aftermath* (New York: Harcourt Brace Jovanovich, 1985); *Fascist Terror in South Vietnam: Law 10/59*, ed. Pham Van Bach (Hanoi: The Gioi, 1961).

32   Art Brandstatter to Ralph Turner, 'Paper Titled Analysis of Role of Security Services', 3 February 1961, Ralph Turner Papers, MSU Archives, Vietnam Project, box 1694.

33   Mr Ford to Mr Murray, 'Selection of Special Branch Advisors for Employment by the Americans in Vietnam', 1 March 1966; A. C. Buxton to R. A. Fyjis-Walker, 'Evidence That Training Courses in Malaysia for Vietnamese Police Are Proving Useful', 8 August 1966, Foreign Office Files 371; British National Archives, Kew Gardens, Police Training; L. P. R. Browning, 'Visit by Police Adviser to South Vietnam', 36–30 June 1964, Foreign Office Files 371, 175534, Police Training, Vietnam; 'S.A. Lockhart, "Police Training Committee, Annual Report for 1968,"' Counter-Subversion Committee, Riverwalk House, 13 February 1969.

34   R. I. T. Simons to Cromartie, 1 July 1964, Foreign Office File 371, 175534, British National Archives, Kew Gardens, England, Vietnam Police Training.

35   William Corson, *The Betrayal* (New York: W. W. Norton, 1968), 92; Thomas L. Ahern, Jr., *CIA and the Generals: Covert Support for Military Government in South Vietnam* (Washington, DC: CIA, Center for the Study of Intelligence, 2006), 46, online at http://www.foia.cia.gov/vietnam.asp; 'Leigh Brilliant to John Manopoli, Monthly Report', April 1968, RAFSEA, MACV, RG 472, CORDS, Public Safety Directorate General Records, NA, box 9 (hereafter CORDS, Public Safety); Tom Buckley, 'Portrait of an Aging Despot', *Harper's Magazine* (April 1972): 68–72.

36   Valentine, *The Phoenix Program*; 262; McCoy, *The Politics of Heroin*, 279.

37   Valentine, *The Phoenix Program*; author interview with anonymous Phoenix veteran; David Donovan, *Once a Warrior-King: Memories of an Officer in Vietnam* (New York: McGraw Hill, 1985).

38   See Monika Jensen-Stevenson, *Spite House: The Last Secret of the War in Vietnam* (New York: Norton, 1997); Daniel Marvin, *Expendable Elite: One Soldier's Journey into Covert Warfare* (Walterville, OR: Trine Day, 2003); Jerry L. Lembcke, *CNN's Tailwind Tale: Inside the Vietnam War's Last Great Myth* (New York: Rowman & Littlefield, 2004) questions whether Americans were ever targeted.

39   Virgil Ney, Col., 'Guerrilla Warfare and Modern Strategy', in *Modern Guerrilla Warfare*, 25–38; Valentine, *The Phoenix Program*, 25; Thomas L. Ahern Jr. *The CIA and Rural Pacification in South Vietnam* (Washington, DC: CIA, Center for the Study of Intelligence, 2006), 58; Peer De Silva, *Sub Rosa: The CIA and the Uses of Intelligence* (New York: Times Books, 1978).

40   Napoleon D. Valeriano and Charles T. R. Bohannan, *Counter-Guerilla Operations: The Philippine Experience* (New York: Praeger, 1962), 97; 'Edward Lansdale to Walt W. Rostow', 10 August 1961, JFKL, National Security File (NSF), Meetings and Memorandum, box 327A; Alfred W. McCoy, *Policing America's Empire: The U.S., the Philippines and the Rise of the Surveillance State* (Madison, WI: University of Wisconsin Press, 2009), 375; Benedict J. Kerkvliet, *The Huk Rebellion: A Study of Peasant Revolt in the Philippines* (Berkeley: University of California Press, 1977), 196; 'Role and Mission of Rural Police in South Vietnam, Roger Hilsman, report to John F. Kennedy', 55, JFKL, Hilsman Papers, box 332; 'Policy Research Study – Internal Warfare and the Security of the Underdeveloped States, Department of State', 20 November 1961, JFKL, POF, box 98.

41   Stathis N. Kalyves and Matthew Adam Kocher, 'How "Free" is Free Riding in Civil Wars? Violence, Insurgency, and the Collective Action Problem', *World Politics* 59, no. 2 (January 2007): 201. Interview with anonymous Phoenix operative. See also *A Vietcong Memoir* and Douglas Pike, *Vietcong* (Cambridge, MA: MIT Press, 1969).

42   Jensen-Stevenson, *Spite House*, 113; Michael T. Klare, 'Operation Phoenix and the Failure of Pacification in South Vietnam', *Liberation* 17 (May 1973): 21–7; Michael

Uhl, *Vietnam Awakening: My Journey from Combat to the Citizens' Commission of Inquiry on U.S. War Crimes in Vietnam* (Jefferson, NC: McFarland & Co, 2007).

43   Theodore Shackley with Richard A. Finney, *Spymaster: My Life in the CIA* (Dulles, VI: Potomac Books, 2005), 233; Douglas Blaufarb, *The Counterinsurgency Era: U.S. Doctrine and Performance, 1950 to the Present* (New York: Free Press, 1977), 247. CIA agent Frank Snepp said after the war that 'I was in charge of lists of targets. A lot of people who shouldn't have been, were hit … and it was a sin'.

44   'Phung Hoang, Monthly Report', 29 April 1971, CORDS, Public Safety, box 1; Tang, *A Vietcong Memoir*, 210; Al Santoli, *Everything We Had: An Oral History of the Vietnam War by Thirty-Three Americans Soldiers Who Fought It* (New York: Random House, 1981), 204–5; John Stockwell, *The Praetorian Guard: The U.S. Role in the New World Order* (Boston: South End Press, 1991), 47.

45   Alfred W. McCoy has suggested in a History News Network review of Nick Turse's, *Kill Anything that Moves: The Real American War in Vietnam* (New York: Metropolitan Books, 2013) that some of the atrocities may have been staged by NLF double agents who penetrated Phoenix as part of psychological warfare operations designed to discredit the ARVN and US invaders. The converse was also no doubt true.

46   'Monthly Report', 30 December 1970 and 'Monthly Report', 29 April 1971, CORDS Public Safety, box 13, folder Monthly Consolidated Reports; 'Martin E. Pierce, Consolidated VCI Infrastructure Neutralization Report', 1–30 April 1969, CORDS Public Safety, box 4; Evan Parker Jr. to Tucker Gougleman, 'VCI Neutralizations', 18 January 1969, CORDS Public Safety, Phung Hoang, box 1; 'Quality Neutralizations', 24 October 1971, CORDS, Public Safety, box 14, folder Quality Neutralizations; Iver Peterson, 'Vietnam: This Phoenix Is a Bird of Death', *New York Times,* 25 July 1971, E2; Robert Komer, 'The Phung Hoang Fiasco', CORDS, Public Safety, Phung Hoang, box 21.

47   'Minutes of Phung Hoang Advisor's Monthly Confirmation', 10 December 1971, RAFSEA, HQ MACV, RG 472, CORDS, Public Safety Directorate, Field Operations, General Records, NA, box 10; 'Phung Hoang Herbicide Operation', 17 June 1972, RAFSEA, HQ MACV, RG 472, CORDS, NA, box 6. Email correspondence, artillery adviser to South Vietnamese army (June 1966 to May 1967), 25 June 2011; Chomsky, *For Reasons of State.* Lt. Vincent Okamoto of the 25th Infantry Division, who later became a judge, referred to Phoenix as a programme of 'wholesale killing'. Once a target was identified, a Phoenix team often arrived at the suspects' house in the middle of the night. 'Whoever answered the door would get wasted. As far as they were concerned whoever answered was a Communist, including family members. Sometimes they'd come back to camp with ears to prove they killed people.' Christian G. Appy, *American Reckoning: The Vietnam War and Our National Identity* (New York: Viking, 2015), 179.

48   Ralph W. McGehee, *Deadly Deceits: My 25 Years in the CIA* (New York: Sheridan Square Publications, 1983), 156; Alfred W. McCoy, 'Torture in the Crucible of Counterinsurgency', in *Iraq and the Lessons of Vietnam: Or, How Not to Learn from the Past,* ed. Marilyn B. Young and Lloyd C. Gardner (New York: New Press, 2007), 241.

49   Valentine, *The Phoenix Program*; Uhl, *Vietnam Awakening.* On NLF/NVA spying and penetration of the GVN, see Larry Berman, *Perfect Spy: The Incredible Double Life of Pham Xuan Time Magazine Reporter and Vietnamese Communist Agent* (Washington: Smithsonian Books, 2007).

50   Valentine, *The Phoenix Program*, 61. See also Tang, *A Vietcong Memoir;* Woods, *Shadow Warrior, 288.*

51   Turse, *Kill Anything That Moves*; Interview artillery adviser to South Vietnamese army. During post-war people's trials, one Phoenix operative was accused of exposing

corpses, with their ears and nose cut off, of NLF fighters he had killed as a means of terrorizing the population. In Tiziano Terzani, *Giai Phong! The Fall and Liberation of Saigon* (New York: St. Martin's Press, 1976), 267–8.

52 Frank Snepp, *Decent Interval: An Insider's Account of Saigon's Indecent End Told by the CIA's Chief Strategy Analyst in Vietnam*, rev edn (Lawrence: University Press of Kansas, 2002), 31, 38; U.S. Congress. House. Subcommittee on Asian and Pacific Affairs. Hearings. *Testimony of David and Jane Barton, The Treatment of Political Prisoners in South Vietnam by the Government of the Republic of South Vietnam*, Hearings. 93rd cong., 1st sess., 13 September 1973 (Washington, DC: G.P.O., 1973), 50–1; Amnesty International, *Political Prisoners in South Vietnam* (London: Amnesty International Publications, 1973), 36; Holmes Brown and Don Luce, *Hostages of War: Saigon's Political Prisoners* (Washington, DC: Indochina Mobile Education Project, 1973), 71; Noam Chomsky and Edward S. Herman, *The Political Economy of Human Rights: The Washington Connection and Third World Fascism* (Boston: South End Press, 1979), 333; McCoy, *A Question of Torture*.

53 U.S. Congress. House Committee on Armed Services. 2, 20, 25 July 1973, U.S. Assistance Programs in Vietnam, 93rd cong., 1st sess. (Washington, DC:G.P.O., 1973), 319–21; *The Wasted Nations: Report of the International Commission of the Enquiry into United States Crimes in Indochina*, ed. Frank Browning and Dorothy Forman (New York: Harper, 1972), 203.

54 Valentine, *The Phoenix Program*, 192; Bernd Greiner, *War Without Fronts: The USA in Vietnam* (New Haven: Yale University Press, 2009), 62.

55 'The Rehabilitation System of Vietnam', PSD, USOM to Vietnam, foreword by Frank Walton, January 1961, 29, PSD, OPS East Asia, box 287, folder 1 Penology; Don Bordenkircher, *Tiger Cage: An Untold Story*, as told to Shirley Bordenkircher (West Virginia: Abbey Publishing, 1998). On the large volume of political prisoners, see Ngo Vinh Long, 'Legacies Foretold: Excavating the Roots of Postwar Vietnam', *in Four Decades On: Vietnam, The United States, and the Legacies of the Second Indochina War*, ed. Scott Laderman and Edwin Martini III (Durham, NC: Duke University Press, 2013), 16–44. Author conversation with the late Fred Branfman who snuck into South Vietnam to investigate the horrific conditions in South Vietnam's prisons working for Project Air War.

56 William Colby to CORDS, 'Allegations of Extortion', 24 April 1970, CORDS, Public Safety box 21.

57 'D. E. Bordenkircher to Randolph Berkeley, Survey of Chau Doc Prison', 25 November 1968, RAFSEA, HQ MACV, RG 472, CORDS, Public Safety, box 2, folder Correctional Centers.

58 'Memo for Mr. Randolph Berkeley, Public Safety Division', 25 November 1968, CORDS, Public Safety, box 2, folder Correctional Centers; 'D. E. Bordenkircher to Randolph Berkeley, An Xuyen Prison', 11 November 1968, CORDS, Public Safety Directorate, box 2, folder Correctional Centers. See my *Modernizing Repression*, chapter 7 for more details and sources.

59 Bordenkircher, *Tiger Cage*, 199; *Release Us From Bondage: Six Days in a Vietnamese Prison* ed. Doris Longacre and Max Ediger (Akron, PA: Mennonite Central Committee Peace Section, July 1974), 7; Fred Branfman, 'Vietnam: The POWs We Left Behind', *Ramparts* (December 1973), 14.

60 Longacre and Ediger, *Release Us from Bondage*, 9–10.

61 'The Rehabilitation System of Vietnam', PSD, USOM to Vietnam, Foreword by Frank Walton, January 1961, 29, PSD, OPS East Asia, NA, box 287, folder 1 Penology; Brown

and Luce, *Hostages of War*; Sylvan Fox, '4 South Vietnamese Describe Torture in Prison "tiger cages"', *New York Times*, 3 March 1973, 7; Bordenkircher, *Tiger Cage*, 180.

62 U.S. Congress, House, Committee on Foreign Affairs, Subcommittee on Asian and Pacific Affairs, *The Treatment of Political Prisoners in South Vietnam by the Government of the Republic of South Vietnam*, 93rd cong., 1st sess., 13 September 1973 (Washington, DC: G.P.O., 1973), 20; Lars Schoultz, *Human Rights and United States Policy Toward Latin America* (Princeton, NJ: Princeton University Press, 1981), 181.

63 'Summary of Problems of Phung Hoang Program-Recommendation for Turning it Over to the National Police', Secretary of State to American Embassy, PSD, OPS East Asia, (1971–3), NA, box 280; McLintock, *Instruments of Statecraft*, 190–2; Kalyvas and Kocher, 'How "Free" is Free Riding in Civil Wars?'

64 Robert Dreyfuss, 'Phoenix Rising', *The American Prospect*, 1 January 2004; Jane Mayer, *The Dark Side: The Inside Story of How the War on Terror Turned Into a War on American Ideals* (New York: Doubleday, 2008), 144; Peter Maas, 'The Salvadorization of Iraq: The Way of the Commandos', *The New York Times Magazine*, 1 May 2005, 1; Douglas Valentine, 'The CIA's Phoenix Program in Vietnam: A Template for Systemic Domination', in *The CIA as Organized Crime: How Illegal Operations Corrupt America and the World* (Atlanta: Clarity Press, 2017).

65 *The U.S. Army-Marine Corps Counter-Insurgency Field Manual: U.S. Army Field Manual No. 3-24, Marine Corps War Fighting Publication No. 3-33.5*, foreword by General David H. Petraeus and James F. Amos, foreword to the University of Chicago Press edition by Lt. Col. John A. Nagl with a new introduction by Sarah Sewall (Chicago: The University of Chicago Press, 2007), 231.

66 Jeremy Scahill, *Blackwater: The Rise of the World's Most Powerful Mercenary Army* (New York: Nation Books, 2007); Pratap Chatterjee, *Iraq Inc. A Profitable Occupation* (New York: Seven Stories Press, 2004); Jane Mayer, 'The Predator War', *The New Yorker*, 26 October 2009; McCoy, 'Torture in the Crucible of Counterinsurgency' and *A Question of Torture*.

67 Don Bordenkircher, *Tiger Cage*, 96; Ryan Mauro, 'U.S. Official: Iraqis told me WMDs sent to Syria', *World Net Daily*, 30 July 2008, available at http://www.wnd.com/index.php?fa=PAGE.view&pageId=71076; Author interview with Adolph Saenz, February 2011.

68 Robert Young Pelton, *Licensed to Kill: Hired Guns in the War on Terror* (New York: Crown Publishers, 2006), 17–35. See also Billy Waugh, with Tim Keown, *Hunting the Jackal: A Special Forces and CIA Ground Soldier's Fifty Year Career Hunting America's Enemies* (New York: William & Morrow, 2004).

69 See for example Caroline Elkins, *Imperial Reckoning: The Untold Story of Britain's Gulag in Kenya* (New York: Henry Holt, 2005).

Index

Lightning Source UK Ltd.
Milton Keynes UK
UKHW020818111120
373186UK00004B/180